THE
PERCEPTION
OF
STRUCTURE

THE

PERCEPTION

OF

STRUCTURE

Essays in Honor of Wendell R. Garner

Edited by
Gregory R. Lockhead
James R. Pomerantz

American Psychological Association
Washington, DC

Published by
American Psychological Association
1200 Seventeenth Street, NW
Washington, DC 20036

Copies may be ordered from
APA Order Department
P.O. Box 2710
Hyattsville, MD 20784

Book designed by Paul M. Levy. Cover designed by Grafik Communications Ltd.
Typeset by Harper Graphics, Waldorf, MD
Printed by Braun-Brumfield, Inc., Ann Arbor, MI
Technical editing and production coordinated by Olin J. Nettles
Copyediting by Naomi Thiers

Library of Congress Cataloging-in-Publication Data

The Perception of structure / edited by Gregory Lockhead and James R. Pomerantz.
    p.   cm.
    Papers presented at the Conference on the Perception of Structure, held at Yale University on May 22–23, 1989, sponsored by the American Psychological Association.
    Includes index.
    ISBN 1-55798-125-6 (acid-free paper): $40.00
    1. Whole and parts (Psychology)—Congresses. 2. Perception—Congresses. I. Lockhead, Gregory. II. Pomerantz, James R. III. Conference on the Perception of Structure (1989: Yale University) IV. American Psychological Association.
BF202.P47   1991
153.7'5—dc20
                          91-16071
                            CIP

Printed in the United States of America
First edition

CONTENTS

CONTRIBUTORS

Irving Biederman, *University of Minnesota*
Donald S. Blough, *Brown University*
Donald Broadbent, *Oxford University, England*
Michael F. Brown, *Villanova University*
Herbert H. Clark, *Stanford University*
Robert G. Crowder, *Yale University*
James E. Cutting, *Cornell University*
Howard E. Egeth, *Johns Hopkins University*
Charles W. Eriksen, *University of Illinois at Urbana-Champaign*
Wendell R. Garner, *Yale University*
David Gilden, *Vanderbilt University*
H. John Hilton, *University of Minnesota*
John E. Hummel, *University of Minnesota*
Mark Johnson, *MRC Cognitive Development Unit, London*
Michael Kubovy, *University of Virginia*
Sarah Hollingsworth Lisanby, *Duke University*
Gregory R. Lockhead, *Duke University*
George A. Miller, *Princeton University*
J. Toby Mordkoff, *Johns Hopkins University*
John Morton, *MRC Cognitive Development Unit, London*
James H. Neely, *State University of New York at Albany*
Stephen E. Palmer, *University of California, Berkeley*
James R. Pomerantz, *Rice University*
Donald A. Riley, *University of California, Berkeley*
Roger N. Shepard, *Stanford University*
Bryan E. Shepp, *Brown University*
Linda B. Smith, *Indiana University*
James D. St. James, *Millikin University*

Participants in the conference on the Perception of Structure.

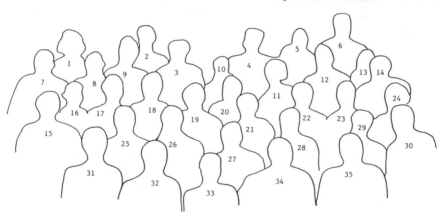

1. Soledad Ballesteros, UNID, Madrid
2. Herbert Clark, Stanford U.
3. Emanuel Leeuwenberg, U. of Nijmegen
4. Robert D. Melara, Purdue U.
5. John Flowers, U. of Nebraska-Lincoln
6. Gregory Lockhead, Duke U.
7. Sam Glucksberg, Princeton U.
8. James Neely, State U. of New York at Albany
9. Robert Crowder, Yale U.
10. Daniel Kahnemann, U. of California Berkeley
11. Anne Treisman, U. of California Berkeley
12. Michael Brown, Villanova U.
13. Susan Chipman, Office of Naval Research
14. Warren Torgerson, The Johns Hopkins U.
15. John Morton, MRC, London
16. Stephen E. Palmer, U. of California Berkeley
17. James Pomerantz, Rice U.
18. Anthony Cecala, Texas Instruments
19. Michael Kubovy, U. of Virginia
20. Brian Shepp, Brown U.
21. Ray Hyman, U. of Oregon

22. Donald Blough, Brown U.
23. Anthony Wright, U. of Texas
24. Linda Smith, Indiana U.
25. Charles Eriksen, U. of Illinois
26. Donald Broadbent, U. of Oxford
27. Donald Riley, U. of California Berkeley
28. Roger Shepard, Stanford U.
29. Deborah Kemler-Nelson, Swarthmore College
30. Larry Marks, Pierce Foundation
31. James Cutting, Cornell U.
32. Howard Egeth, The Johns Hopkins U.
33. Carolyn Paul, Yale U.
34. Wendell Garner, Yale U.
35. Irving Biederman, U. of Minnesota

Missing:
George Miller, Princeton U.
Toby Mordkoff, The Johns Hopkins U.
David Gilden, U. of Virginia
Sarah Lisanby, Duke U.
James St. James, U. of Illinois
Mark Johnson, MRC, London

FOREWORD

Wendell R. Garner, a pioneering scientist in the psychology of perception, has been a builder of ties among cognitive and behavior scientists and has had the sort of influence on students and colleagues that leads them to think about their research in a broad context. This volume is based in part on a May 1989 conference titled "The Perception of Structure," which honored Garner.

This tribute to Wendell Garner includes contributions from psychology's leading authorities in perceptual and cognitive psychology on various aspects of structure—ranging from structure in language to infant perception of facial structure. Topics among these exceptional chapters include the perception of color, the selection and structure, visual configurations, the structure of language, developmental processes, infants' perception of facial structure, and perception of musical timbre. The American Psychological Association (APA) is pleased to have sponsored this conference and now to make these original research presentations available in book form.

Federal research agencies stopped most support of investigator-initiated state-of-the-art research conferences in scientific psychology over a decade ago. During this period, however, scientific psychology has continued to grow, and scientific psychologists have adapted their talents to diverse areas. Yet, there have been few opportunities for investigators in new and promising research areas to convene in special settings to discuss their findings. As part of its continuing effort to enhance the dissemination of scientific knowledge in psychology, the APA established in 1988, in its Science Directorate, the Scientific Conferences program. An annual call for proposals is issued by the APA Science Directorate to solicit conference ideas. Proposals from all areas of psychological research are welcome. From the inception of this program in 1988 through mid-1991, 19 conferences have been funded, with a total outlay of more than $250,000.

The conferences funded thus far through the APA Science Directorate program include the following:

Research Community Psychology: Integrating Theories and Methodologies, September 1988

The Psychological Well-Being of Captive Primates, September 1988

Psychological Research on Organ Donation, October 1988

Arizona Conference on Sleep and Cognition, January 1989

Socially Shared Cognition, February 1989

Taste, Experience, and Feeding, April 1989

Perception of Structure, May 1989

Suggestibility of Children's Recollections, June 1989

Best Methods for Analysis of Change, October 1989

Conceptualization and Measurement of Organism-Environment Interactions, November 1989

Cognitive Bases of Musical Communication, April 1990

Conference on Hostility, Coping/Support, and Health, November 1990

Psychological Testing of Hispanics, February 1991

Study of Cognition: Conceptual and Methodological Issues, February 1991

Cardiovascular Reactivity to Psychological and Cardiovascular Disease: The Evidence, April 1991

Developmental Psychoacoustics, August 1991

Maintaining and Promoting Integrity in Behavioral Science Research, October 1991

The Contributions of Psychology to Mathematics and Science Education, October 1991

Lives Through Time: Assessement and Theory in Personality Psychology from a Longitudinal Perspective, November 1991

Lewis P. Lipsitt, PhD
Executive Director for Science

Virginia E. Holt
Manager, Scientific Conferences Program

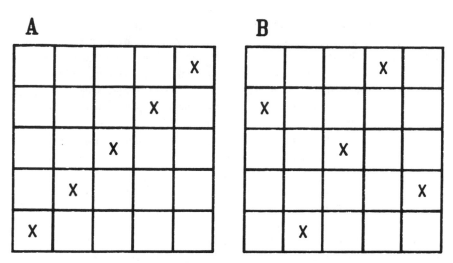

Figure 4.   An abstract representation of a stimulus space consisting of circles varying in the dimensions of size and lightness, with five steps shown on each dimension. A: A linearly correlated subset of five circles from a full set of 25 resulting from combining five different sizes with five different lightnesses. B: In this subset, size and lightness are related in a "sawtooth" fashion but are still perfectly correlated in the sense that each size is paired with a single, unique lightness. Size and lightness are used here only for illustrative purposes; many other pairs of dimensions would work equally well.

In judgment tasks, stimuli from this redundant set are identified better (i.e., with fewer errors and shorter response times) than are circles that vary only in size or lightness. This performance improvement resulting from correlated attributes, which is call a *redundancy gain*, demonstrates that the introduced structure (or some emergent property associated with this structure) is detected and capitalized on by subjects.

Structure and Amount of Information

Note that the critical factor distinguishing the above sets is not the amount of information they contain in the formal sense. The 1×5 arrays (where only size or only lightness varies) have the same amounts of information as do the redundant subsets of five stimuli selected from the 5×5 arrays: They both contain exactly five alternatives and thus have the same amount of uncertainty, namely $\log_2 5 = 2.32$ bits. This demonstrates that the amount of uncertainty or information in the stimulus domain is not what determines performance in this instance. Rather, as we show later in this chapter, the *form* in which the uncertainty exists is the critical factor.

Not all structure can be used equally well by subjects. How structure is used depends, for example, on whether the stimulus dimensions used are *integral* or *separable*. Briefly, dimensions are integral if they cannot be attended to individually, one at a time; otherwise, they are separable. Much of the evidence concerning this distinction was documented by Garner (1974). A history of the distinction and extensions from it are provided by Roger Shepard in the present volume.

A redundancy gain shows that the introduction of structure can improve performance, at least under some conditions. The amount of improvement depends, among other factors, on the amount of structure added. This can be demonstrated by continuing to add structure while holding constant the amount of information in the stimulus array. This has been done in identification studies by increasing the number of correlated dimensions along which the stimuli vary. For example, in Figure 4A we might add hue as a third dimension while continuing to limit to five members the subset of stimuli that subjects must identify. If hue were perfectly correlated with size and lightness, then performance might be even better than when only two dimensions (size and lightness) vary, even though hue alone is not identified especially well.

Although an experiment adding hue to size and lightness has not yet been reported, an analogous study adding hue to lightness and position has been conducted. In that experiment, these three-dimensional redundant stimuli were better identified than were two-dimensional-redundant stimuli, which in turn were better identified than were univariate stimuli (Lockhead, 1970). In summary, identification performance is usually better when there is more structure in the stimulus set.

Form of Structure

One can manipulate the form of structure as well as the amount of structure in a stimulus set. It is important to note that the form of structure can be varied while holding constant both the amount of information and the amount of structure present. Figure 4B shows a different subset of the original 25 stimuli that is equal in redundancy to the subset shown in Figure 4A. Again, each possible value of both attributes occurs equally often. In addition, the attributes remain perfectly correlated in the sense that the value on one dimension perfectly predicts the value on the other. There are $\log_2 5 = 2.32$ bits of uncertainty in both sets. Thus, the two sets are identical both in amount of information and in amount of structure, but they differ in the form of that structure.

If this form matters, then people's ability to identify stimuli might be different with the "sawtooth"-paired subset shown in Figure 4B than with the linearly paired subset in Figure 4A. This turns out to be the case: The stimuli in Figure 4B are better identified (with fewer errors and considerably shorter response times) than are those in Figure 4A. Thus, form of structure does affect performance.

In the discussions ahead about the importance of inferred subsets in memory representations, we interpret such results to indicate that, on any experimental trial, the stimulus presented is compared against known, plausible alternatives in memory. This comparison is easier for the stimuli in Figure 4B than for those in 4A, which in turn is easier than for stimuli that vary on only a single dimension.

This effect of the form of redundancy has some generality, as was shown in an identification experiment where 20 stimuli varied along four dimensions (Lockhead, 1970, Study 3). When all four dimensions were correlated linearly (as in Figure 4A, except with four rather than only two dimensions varying and with 20 rather than only 5 levels on each dimension), identification accuracy averaged 37% correct (compared with chance performance of 5%). This was trivially but reliably better than performance on the univariate sets, which was about 33% correct. But when the dimensions were sawtooth correlated, as in Figure 4B, performance reached 100% correct.

No outcome approaching this level of performance has ever been reported with univariate stimuli. For univariate stimuli, the well-known capacity limitation of about seven stimuli was firmly established some time ago (Miller, 1956). The reason for this performance difference (100% correct vs. 37% correct) lies neither with the amount of information available, nor with the amount of redundancy, nor with the amount of structure: These are all identical in the linearly and sawtooth-correlated conditions. Only the *form* of the redundancy differs. Form of redundancy, or perhaps something as yet undetected that is correlated with form, determines performance (Lockhead, 1970).

Context

The form of redundancy matters for performance. This is true not simply because there are different individual stimuli in the different subsets, but also because the precise alternatives to a stimulus determine how well that item will be identified. The form of redundancy that exists determines the particular subset of alternative possibilities. This is critical because individual stimuli are judged in terms of this context; they are not judged in and of themselves.

To demonstrate further this claim that stimuli are not identified directly but only by way of alternative possibilities, consider the middle stimuli (the central cell in Figures 4A and 4B in each grid). This stimulus is identical in both sets: It has the same lightness, same size, and same shape in the linearly correlated as in the sawtooth-correlated set. Also, the identical lightnesses and sizes are used equally often in both sets, and no other features are used. But performance is different. The identical, middle stimulus is identified well in subset 4B but poorly in subset 4A. The only possible reason for the difference lies in the form of structure in the two sets, that is, in the relations between the middle stimulus and the alternative stimuli that form the context of alternative possibilities in the two sets.

With this interpretation in mind, consider Sandra one last time. Just as with the simpler stimuli in Figures 4A and 4B, we would expect Sandra to be identified with differing levels of accuracy when she is seen in different situations or contexts. Just as with the circle of size 3 and lightness 3, Sandra too is (or at least could be) identical in different situations, but still she is identified in terms of her alternative possibilities and not just in terms of herself. Introspections notwithstanding, we appear to have no evidence that Sandra, or any other stimulus, is identified directly.

The only plausible hypothesis is that stimuli are compared against their alternatives in memory. Viewed in this fashion, object identification is clearly a cognitive act. This view is consistent with three facts summarized above. How well one identifies a stimulus that is a member of a set (and all stimuli are members of sets) depends on (a) the amount of information; (b) the amount of structure; and (c) the form of that structure in the set. Consistent with Garner's writings in 1962, we conclude that stimuli are identified by comparison with known or supposed possibilities, or in other words, with inferred subsets. Over the years since 1962, this view of perception has become thoroughly ingrained in the thinking of researchers in the field.

THE SIGNIFICANCE OF STRUCTURE

Structure is not limited to sets of stimuli. Structure can be part of any system, including the human perceptual or cognitive system. For example, a neural network in which only selected connections exist contains structure in the same sense in which we use the term here. This is of critical importance if one role of the mind is to model the structure that exists in the world.

The importance of structure is not limited to humans. As Blough and also Riley and Brown demonstrate in their chapters later in this volume, structure is also important to the performance of pigeons. Nor is the structure within a biological system fixed. The chapters by Morton and Johnson and by Smith reveal ways in which structure changes during human development.

The significance of structure for understanding perception resides in three tenets: first, that structure abounds in the physical world; second, that a perceptual system that knew about and capitalized on such structure would enjoy advantages in the speed and accuracy of perception; and third, that biological perceptual systems do exploit structure. We consider these points in turn.

Structure Abounds in the World

There is redundancy even in a temporally frozen scene from the ordinary world. This is apparent when we consider that any one point is generally quite predictable from the stimuli surrounding it. Just as the weather today is a good (albeit far from perfect) predictor of similar weather tomorrow, it is likely that adjacent points in visual space will be similar to one another. Even where discontinuities exist in a scene, such as the sharp luminance differences at an edge, they are usually smooth and thus internally predictable to some degree. In a world without structure, by contrast, neighboring points are no more alike than are distant points. An example is the situation in a video screen displaying pure noise: Energy values are unorganized among pixels within a frozen frame.

Advantages Accrue from Capitalizing Upon Such Structure

The perceptual world contains so much information that biological systems would be hard-pressed to keep up with it all if organisms perceived only separate pixels, for example. Any system that can internalize the various structures of the sensory environment could exploit these redundancies to reduce the time required for such perceptual operations as discrimination, recognition, and identification, or to increase the accuracy of these operations.

Perceptual Systems Do in Fact Exploit Structure

The literature documenting this is extensive, and much of it is cited throughout this volume. Perceivers detect and process edges and other discontinuities in displays, they infer detailed world structures by extrapolating from partial views, they are often better able to discriminate stimuli in sets with more structure, and they discriminate some forms of structure better than others. We suspect that perceivers have evolved or developed mechanisms and processes that capitalize on structures common to the natural environment.

Organisms use both those structures that are immediately available and those that are potentially available. People process stimuli with reference to both alternatives that are in the scene and alternatives that might have appeared but did not. To understand perceptual processes and to predict behavior, it is important to learn what those alternatives are.

There are at least three sources of information that can suggest these alternative stimuli. The most common of them is context. The stimuli to which we are exposed are surrounded in both space and time by other stimuli. In reading, for example, context suggests alternative letters, words, phrases, and other linguistic structures that are likely to follow and that allow us to interpret words or phrases (see Figure 2). The chapters in the present volume by Clark, by Miller, and by Neely elaborate extensively on this theme.

World knowledge is a second and related source of alternatives. Such knowledge ties the present to other contexts more distant in space and time. For example, when we walk into a kitchen, the context suggests alternative objects we are likely to encounter in that setting (Biederman, 1981; Palmer, 1975). Yet a third source is the stimulus itself: Its internal structure may suggest alternatives. A visual configuration such as an asymmetric dot pattern may suggest alternative patterns in which the elements are configured differently (see the chapters in the present volume by Biederman, Hilton, and Hummel; by Palmer; and by Pomerantz).

THE LOCUS OF STRUCTURE

A dominant theme of this book is that our perceptual systems are adept at processing structure. As one result, our perceptions of the world are structured. Within this overarching framework, however, a lively debate simmers concerning the origin of this structure: Does structure exist in the external world merely to be selected or "picked up" by the perceptual system, or is it created or actively imposed on perception by the organism? Or, to present the view we advocate here, is some combination of these two processes at work? For this last eventuality, we need to ask how the two processes would be coordinated such that the structure in our perceptions maps onto that of the world with sufficient veridicality for us to function as well as we do.

A framework for localizing structure, which is depicted in Figure 5, comes from ideas originating with numerous authors. Four domains are shown: a distal stimulus world, its corresponding proximal stimulus world, the short-term internal representations activated in part by the proximal stimulus (working memory), and the world of long-term memory.

Distal Stimuli

These are the objects of the external world. The external world consists of objects, places, and events that are constrained. This world is structured; it is not mush. We indicate this fact by portraying the distal world as a dimensional stimulus space with many empty locations. That is, of all the combinations of features and dimensions that might exist (or of all the physical structures, including objects and surfaces, that might exist), only some do in fact exist.

Proximal Stimuli

These are the energy distributions (which themselves originated at the distal stimuli) as they strike the receptor surface of the perceiver. Proximal stimuli are the sole source of external information that drives perception. For vision, the structure in the proximal stimuli resides in the organization of the image at the receptor, as described by Gibson (1950). Because the proximal stimulus provides only limited information about the distal stimulus, proximal stimuli constitute a subset of the distal stimuli. This is depicted in Figure 5 by a smaller space of potential alternatives for the proximal stimulus than for the distal. For vision, the proximal stimulus is a viewpoint-specific,

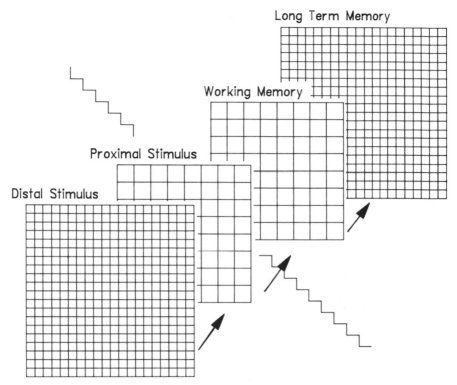

Figure 5. A framework in which to localize structure. Included here are the domains of the distal stimulus, the proximal stimulus, working memory, and long-term memory. The jagged line indicates the locus of sensory transduction, where external stimulus events are converted into internal mental representation.

two-dimensional projection drawn from an infinite number of potential projections of the distal, three-dimensional stimulus. The proximal stimulus often contains distortions of its own, introduced by the atmosphere, misshapen lenses, and so forth. For simplicity, we will ignore these nuisance factors here.

Sensory transductions constitute the boundary between the proximal stimulus and its mental representation. These transductions, which are provided by our sensory systems, further process and alter the stimulus. Sensory processes are represented in Figure 5 as a jagged line, to remind us of their presence and their importance.

Mental Representations

Figure 5 also shows two levels of mental representation. The smaller might be regarded as working or short-term memory. The larger might be regarded as long-term memory, a relatively permanent and abstract store. Just as the proximal stimulus is depicted as a subset of distal stimuli, so too is working memory depicted as a subset of long-term memory. The reasoning is analogous: Only a small subset of knowledge can be activated at any time.

The structure in long-term memory resides in the fact that not all representations that might exist actually do exist. Long-term memory is no more a buzzing confusion than the distal stimulus is a random array. The structures of long-term memory are of at least three types. First, there are the historical patterns and needs rooted in the evolution and development of the organism; essentially, these are the structures with which we are endowed at birth. Second, there are structures that represent specific distal stimuli, albeit through complex mappings. And third, structures exist that are essentially "invented" representations (that is, those that correspond to no genuine distal stimuli, as with the often-used example of a unicorn).

The organism's major challenge in perception is to ensure that the structure of its internal representations is more tightly linked to the distal stimulus than to the proximal stimulus. The proximal stimulus necessarily contains less information than the distal, and what information it does contain is often distorted. As a result, the proximal stimulus is sometimes inadequate for performing tasks required of the perceiver. Nonetheless, the proximal stimulus is all that is available to the perceiver about the distal world. This is one reason why internal representation involves more complex processes than a simple mapping of transductions provided on the proximal stimulus by sensory mechanisms. For this reason, the internal representation incorporates assumptions (e.g., inferred subsets), expectancies (e.g., sources of attention), and surely much more.

We must also keep in mind that internal representations are dynamic, not static. As documented throughout this book, as well as in the literature, internal representations change from moment to moment with changes in attention and with residual effects of prior experiences. Too, these fluctuations are not only momentary. There are important changes in internal representations over long time segments as the perceiver develops, matures, and learns.

THE STRUCTURE OF THIS VOLUME

The 20 chapters constituting this volume may be grouped in various ways. Below, we categorize them into six sections and indicate briefly for each section the underlying concept and the basic thrust of each chapter contained within the section.

Stimulus Structure

The six chapters in this section address general principles concerning the perception of structure.

Stephen Palmer extends and modifies Wendell Garner's seminal work relating goodness, inferred subsets, and pattern symmetry. Palmer shows how, with visual configurations, their axes of symmetry in space and time predict subjects' judgments of pattern goodness. His work suggests the powerful psychophysical statement that local symmetry subgroups will provide an understanding of figural goodness.

James Cutting demonstrates that specific structural relations among elements in complex arrays determine what will be perceived. Accordingly, to understand ordinary perception it is important to study complex scenes containing multiple sources of information that might be used by the perceiver in various combinations. This calls for understanding how elements of the environment combine perceptually. Unfortunately, there is no single rule that works in all instances, because the perception of combinations of some dimensions is qualitatively different from that of other combinations.

Roger Shepard summarizes one particularly critical aspect of this fact by giving a history of the development of the terms *integral* and *separable*. Shepard offers a theoretical account of the differences between these two stimulus classes, an account that advances the notion of a *consequential region*. The essential idea is that certain correlated aspects of the environment have been crucial during evolution. Stimuli possessing these historically correlated attributes are those we call integral, and they tend to be classified on the basis of their proximities to one another within important regions of the underlying dimensions of a stimulus space. Separable stimuli, on the other hand, are composed of dimensions that have not been so correlated historically. These tend to be classified on the basis of one or another dimension at a time. Shepard's theory holds out the possibility that a distinction between integral and separable stimuli might be made in terms of the development of the species.

Irving Biederman, John Hilton, and John Hummel consider how visual patterns are perceived out of elements. They focus on features that allow parsing of complex objects into components called *geons*, of which there are some 24. These geons remain invariant under changes in viewpoint. This approach treats goodness and related psychological aspects of forms as byproducts of perceptual mechanisms that infer three-dimensional objects from parts that are segmented from two-dimensional images.

Sarah Hollingsworth Lisanby and Gregory Lockhead examine perceptual structure in the absence of stimulus structure. Using no stimuli, they show that what appears to be random is also aesthetically pleasing and nearly symmetric. Their work suggests that performance in psychological studies should be evaluated against what people *perceive* as nonstructured rather than against an objective, statistical definition of nonstructured or random.

Finally, Michael Kubovy and David Gilden examine relations between apparent disorder and statistical disorder. They conclude that people pay attention to certain structures (e.g., numerical runs and symmetry) but not to others (e.g., figural redundancies) when they attempt to generate random patterns.

Attributes and Attention

The attributes of some stimuli are processed separately, whereas those of other stimuli are processed in some integrated fashion. This is one basis for the integrality-versus-separability distinction noted above. This leads to the possibility that instructions to direct attention toward attributes might have different effects on perception depending on the stimuli used. People might be able to ignore irrelevant aspects of separable stimuli but not of integral ones; they might process aspects simultaneously for some stimuli but not for others; and the particular task assigned to them might determine whether attributes are processed, or the manner or order in which they are processed. The six chapters included in this section consider the processing of stimuli and stimulus attributes in a variety of different tasks.

Howard Egeth and Toby Mordkoff, using color and form as dimensions in a search task, show that people may process the color and form of two objects simultaneously. In contrast to claims from feature integration theory (Treisman & Gelade, 1980), Egeth and Mordkoff suggest that people accomplish some form of spatially parallel processing when they search for a target that is defined by a conjunction of separable dimensions.

Robert Crowder, using pitch and timbre as stimulus dimensions, shows that people are better at reporting the sameness or difference in pitch of successive tones when the two tones happen to have the same timbre than when their timbres differ. Crowder shows that this is the case even when the first tone is imagined rather than actually heard. Thus, auditory attributes can have similar effects when they are imagined as they do when they actually occur.

James St. James and Charles Eriksen use a novel procedure to show that the fast same effect (FSE) may be due to response competition. In this chapter, which relates to one of Garner's most recent articles, they suggest that "same" and "different" responses are primed differentially by relevant and irrelevant information. Essentially, they argue that stimulus pairs that are different possess many similar features that tend to prime "same" responses or to inhibit "different" responses. But the reverse is not true: Stimulus pairs that are the same do not have many different features that inhibit same responses. To demonstrate that this phenomenon causes the FSE, researchers need a direct measure of response competition. To provide this measure, the position of a joystick was monitored (following a procedure introduced by St. James) to see if subjects start to move it slightly one way before beginning to move it the other (correct) way, a result that would indicate effects of both inhibition and excitation. The results indicate that this does indeed happen.

Donald Broadbent examines how one attribute affects the processing of another attribute. In work directly relevant to St. James and Eriksen, Broadbent shows how performance depends on the timing of instructions for attention and also on the structure of the stimulus set. Almost as an aside, he reports an important discovery: Time of day and liability to cognitive failure interact with effects of nontargets but not with other attentional phenomena (see Broadbent, Broadbent, & Jones, 1989). Instructions have different effects at different times of day for some subjects. Historically, neither time of day nor cognitive ability have been recorded systematically for cognitive studies. Clearly, that oversight should be corrected immediately!

Bryan Shepp reports that the perception of color stimuli is organized by color categories rather than by the dimensions of hue, saturation, and brightness. On the basis of the notion that color stimuli are first processed wholistically and then by dimensions (Lockhead, 1972), Shepp suggests that the hue category is processed first. The results support his idea that when two stimuli in a restricted classification task belong to the same hue category, processing is different than when the stimuli belong to different hue categories.

Finally, James Pomerantz asks if the notion of a visual configuration is better regarded as a stimulus concept or as an organismic concept. To answer this question, he examines the degree of control people demonstrate in selecting the stimulus parts to which they attend. Pomerantz shows several instances in which subjects apparently are free to choose these parts or features. Such results suggest reinterpreting previous reports of failures of selective attention, reports that have been interpreted to mean that a configuration is a stimulus concept (i.e., is determined by properties of the stimulus itself and is thus beyond the subject's control). For this research to progress further, it will be necessary to discriminate between situations where perceivers cannot attend to specific features and situations where they simply choose not to do so.

Animal Behavior

The two chapters in this section compare the perception of structure across species. Some of this work indicates differences between pigeons and people in how they process stimuli. Other work shows that some principles that have usually been considered only in terms of human behavior have relevance for animal behavior as well.

Donald Blough presents four lines of research indicating the prevalence of perceptual analysis, as opposed to wholistic perception, of visual patterns by pigeons. Pigeons, as well as humans, perceive letters of the alphabet that share more features (curves, lines, etc.) as more similar than letters sharing fewer features. Blough also shows that some forms can be discriminated equally well by pigeons whether or not an irrelevant dimension is varied. This indicates separability, or analytic perception. Blough additionally demonstrates search asymmetries in pigeon data that are similar to those in data from people (cf. Treisman & Gormican, 1988). Finally, he presents evidence in support of the notion that pigeons both analyze separate features and shift their attention between these features.

Donald Riley and Michael Brown conclude, on the basis of data collected in matching-to-sample procedures, that pigeons sometimes attend selectively but sometimes, instead, perceive compounds as unitary wholes. Riley and Brown conclude that which process occurs depends on the pigeon's past training and on the spatial separation of the elements of the compound stimulus. They consistently find that elements lead to better performance than do compound samples. Riley and Brown call this the *element superiority effect*. This supports their idea that pigeons can attend to only one dimension or one element at a time. Their general conclusion is that elements of stimulus compounds are processed independently and are summed linearly in their contributions to perception. This conclusion is generally supported here, with the further suggestion that independent processing of elements of a compound stimulus can result from a history of processing the elements outside of the compound.

Language

Just as questions pertaining to structure can be extended to other species, they can be extended within the study of humans to other cognitive domains beyond perception. In the three chapters in this section, the authors examine the importance of the same structural principles to an understanding of language.

George Miller shows ways in which the lexicon and perception are deeply related. Perceptual forms have parts, and their parts also have parts. The lexicon reflects this structure: One part of a hand is a finger, whereas the hand itself is part of an arm, and the arm is part of the body. In an elegant analysis, Miller shows how the folk psychology of both perception and lexical organization reflect such complexities in language.

Herbert Clark, in a related approach to our understanding of words, demonstrates how the meaning of a word in the mental lexicon is both different from and richer than the dictionary definition of that same word. Expanding Wendell Garner's concept of inferred subsets (which Clark calls *possibilities*), Clark shows that the meaning of a word depends, first, on the environment in which that word is embedded and, second, on what the speaker assumes about the audience.

James Neely describes how subjects select what information to use when making lexical decisions (i.e., when determining if a letter string constitutes a word in the language). In another demonstration of the importance of inferred subsets, Neely shows that people's decision-making performance depends on what alternatives are available to them, on the context in which events are presented, and on the procedures available to them to achieve optimum performance.

Development

The two chapters in this section examine the difficult but critical question of how the perception of structure develops over time. Perceptual structures are not frozen for individual perceivers; they develop and change over time with the maturation and experience of the perceiving organism. Although the structure in the world might not always change rapidly over time, it does take time for this structure to be internalized in a veridical fashion. In some cases, the learning process may involve false starts, with the child adopting structures that are subsequently abandoned.

Linda Smith's chapter takes issue with a position advanced by Garner (1974) that structure is a stimulus concept rather than a psychological one and that the perceiver's main job is to select a viable structure rather than to create structure. Smith examines cross-dimensional correspondences that, for example, lead adults to link *big* with *loud* (rather than with *soft*), but not to link *big* with *dark* (rather than with *light*). The experimental results that she presents here show that, by contrast, young children do not link *big* with *loud* (or with *soft*, for that matter). However, children aged two years or so link *big* with *dark*, only to lose that linkage as they grow. Smith concludes that structure is better thought of as a dynamic process than as static and that structures are actively created by the developing organism. Specifically, she argues that Stevens's distinction between prothetic and metathetic dimensions, which was based on investigations with adult observers, does not apply to young children, and thus this distinction is not "in the stimulus."

John Morton and Mark Johnson examine a particular form of structure in which infants may have a special interest: the configuration of the human face. In contrast with some recent studies interpreted as showing that infants respond only to the energy patterns (the amplitude spectrum) of schematic drawings of faces, Morton and Johnson argue that infants are also sensitive to the particular arrangement (phase spectrum) of the faces. They also show that infants progress significantly between the ages of 3 and 5 months in the manner in which they respond to motion that is introduced to animate the faces in a life-like manner.

Final Comment

It is fitting that the final words in this volume be reserved for the person responsible for generating or advancing so many of the concepts that fill these pages, Wendell R. Garner. In commenting on *The Perception of Structure*, Garner focuses on the subtleties and difficulties of establishing methods for studying perceptual structure.

The subtleties involve capturing sometimes elusive phenomenological states into tractable quantitative measurements. The difficulties involve persuading the discipline to accept, indeed to welcome, diverse measures of perceptual structure, diversity that is inherent in the use of converging operations. Garner illustrates this point with a few examples drawn from the large set of innovative methodologies he and his students have introduced into the literature.

In the chapters that follow, we will see many more examples of innovations in the perception of structure, innovations that are both conceptual and methodological. It is apparent to us, as coeditors of this volume, that many of the concepts and methods we need are at our disposal but that others will continue to emerge. It is our hope that this volume propels us all forward.

References

Biederman, I. (1981). On the semantics of a glance at a scene. In M. Kubovy & J. R. Pomerantz (Eds.), *Perceptual organization* (pp. 213–253). Hillsdale, NJ: Erlbaum.

Broadbent, D. E., Broadbent, M. H. P., & Jones, J. L. (1989). Time of day as an instrument for the analysis of attention. *European Journal of Cognitive Psychology, 1*, 69–94.

Garner, W. R. (1962). *Uncertainty and structure as psychological concepts*. New York: Wiley.

Garner, W. R. (1974). *The processing of information and structure*. Hillsdale, NJ: Erlbaum.

Gibson, J. J. (1950). *The perception of the visual world*. Boston: Houghton Mifflin.

Lockhead, G. R. (1970). Identification and the form of multidimensional discrimination space. *Journal of Experimental Psychology, 85*, 1–10.

Lockhead, G. R. (1972). Processing dimensional stimuli: A note. *Psychological Review, 79*, 410–419.

Miller, G. A. (1956). The magical number seven, plus or minus two: Some limits on our capacity for processing information. *Psychological Review, 63*, 81–97.

Palmer, S. E. (1975). Visual perception and world knowledge:Notes on a model of sensory–cognitive interaction. In D. A. Norman & D. E. Rumelhart (Eds.), *Explorations in cognition* (pp. 279–307). San Francisco: Freeman.

Stevens, S. S. (1975). *Psychophysics: Introduction to its perceptual, neural and social prospects* (G. Stevens, Ed.). New York: Wiley.

Treisman, A., & Gelade, G. (1980). A feature-integration theory of attention. *Cognitive Psychology, 12*, 97–136.

Treisman, A., & Gormican, S. (1988). Feature analysis in early vision: Evidence from search asymmetries. *Psychological Review, 95*, 15–48.

PART ONE

STIMULUS STRUCTURE

CHAPTER 2

GOODNESS, GESTALT, GROUPS, AND GARNER:
LOCAL SYMMETRY SUBGROUPS AS A THEORY OF FIGURAL GOODNESS

STEPHEN E. PALMER

In this chapter, I will describe a theory of the Gestalt notion of "goodness" on the basis of the mathematical construct of symmetry subgroups. There is a close relation between this theory and Garner's theory of rotation and reflection (R & R) subsets, and goodness rating data for spatial patterns favor the symmetry subgroup formulation. The theory can be extended to cover the judged goodness of events in space–time. I argue that the perceptual structure of space–time includes only reflectional symmetries about the spatial and temporal axes, and present preliminary data supporting this conjecture. Finally, the theory is elaborated to include local symmetries as well as global ones, and this augmented theory is formalized and tested against data on the rated goodness of the relation between a probe dot and a surrounding figure.

One important segment of my research over the past decade has been aimed at understanding the nature and function of "figural goodness." This topic has a long history dating back to the Gestalt movement, and many eminent psychologists have made important contributions to our knowledge of it, including Wertheimer,

This research was supported in part by Grant 1-RO1-MH33103-03 from the National Institute of Mental Health and by Grants BNS 83-19630 and 87-19934 from the National Science Foundation to Stephen E. Palmer. I would like to thank the many students who have helped with various phases of this research, including Paul Chase, Jack Gallant, John Kruschke, and Johanna Weber. The first and last portions of this chapter were presented at the Annual Meeting of the Psychonomic Society, San Diego, California, November 19, 1983.

Koffka, Attneave, Hochberg, and Leeuwenberg. But the person who has influenced my own work on this subject more than any other is the man we honor in this volume, Wendell R. Garner. I will describe some modifications, elaborations, and extensions I have made on the solid foundation his work has laid. Before I describe my own ideas, however, I want to present some history to place both the problem and Garner's contribution to it in a meaningful context.

TOWARD AN OBJECTIVE THEORY OF FIGURAL GOODNESS

The construct of "good Gestalt" was invented by Gestalt psychologists early in this century to identify what they believed to be an important perceptual fact: Some figures produce experiences of greater simplicity, order, and regularity than others, even if they contain the same number of obvious physical components. Gestalt theorists felt that this property of "goodness" was central to understanding the way in which the visual system organized and stored percepts. Since then, strong support for this view has come from Garner's extensive and careful experiments demonstrating some of the processing consequences of figural goodness: He and his collaborators have shown that human performance on several tasks covaries with people's ratings of the subjective "goodness" of stimulus figures. For example, relative to "poor" or "bad" figures, people can remember "good" figures better, match them more quickly for physical identity, describe them in fewer words, and learn them more quickly (Garner, 1974).

In their notion of "good Gestalt," the Gestaltists had identified a dimension of perceptual experience that corresponds to *subjective* simplicity–complexity, broadly construed, but they failed to relate this psychological dimension to physical measures of *objective* simplicity–complexity. For them, "goodness" was an undefined, primitive perceptual quality of whole figures, fundamentally irreducible to piecewise properties like the number of components or their physical qualities. If figural goodness was to be analyzed at all, they felt that it should be in terms of global properties of whole figures, such as bilateral symmetry. They did not believe that symmetry was sufficient to account for all of figural goodness, of course, but to them it had the right "holistic" flavor. No further progress was made by Gestalt theorists themselves, but I will argue that Garner's analysis follows in their footsteps, as does my own.

The first significant advance in objective theories of figural goodness came from applying basic concepts from mathematical information theory. The key idea was that good figures contained less information because they were internally more redundant (Attneave, 1954; Hochberg & McAlister, 1953). For instance, a bilaterally symmetric figure is redundant in the sense that the half on one side of the symmetry axis can be completely predicted from the half on the other side. Thus, if the perceptual system were coding figures optimally by eliminating all redundancies, then "good" figures would be coded and stored more efficiently than "bad" ones. This analysis fit nicely with the idea of goodness as perceived simplicity: Good figures were shown to be objectively simpler than bad ones in a well-defined informational sense.

As stated by theorists like Attneave and Hochberg, the informational analysis of figural goodness seems to imply that patterns are broken down into local components that are compared for identity. Although such theories seek to explain the Gestalt construct of figural goodness, they do not fit well into the Gestalt style of explanation, which staunchly opposed piecewise theories of perception (Wertheimer, 1924/1938). A formulation more in keeping with Gestalt lines of thought (at least to my own way of thinking) was provided by Garner (1974). He proposed that figures are redundant (i.e., "good") to the extent that they are the same as transformed versions of themselves. He formalized this notion in his now-famous theory of *rotation and reflection (R & R) subsets*.

Rotation and Reflection Subsets

When a particular set of spatial transformations are applied to a figure, they produce a set of transformational variants of that figure. The key observation for Garner's theory of figural goodness was that "better" figures produced fewer transformational variants than "poorer" figures. In the original application of the theory, Garner and Clement (1963) used simple patterns consisting of five dots within a 3 × 3 matrix and applied a set of eight possible transformations: four central rotations (through angles of 0°, 90°, 180°, and 270°) and four central reflections (around axes aligned with vertical, horizontal, left diagonal, and right diagonal). These transformations define the *R & R set*, some examples of which are illustrated in Figure 1. Within this set, there is a subset of distinguishably different figures called the *R & R subset* (which are enumerated in Figure 1 by the numbers below the transformational variants). Garner and Clement (1963) found that patterns rated as "good" (such as the top one in Figure 1) had few transformational variants, whereas those rated as "bad" (such as the bottom one) had many transformational variants. Thus, they proposed that goodness of a figure was an inverse function of the measure (size) of its R & R subset.

This analysis is particularly appealing from the Gestalt perspective because it works on whole figures. There is no sense in which patterns need to be broken down into piecewise components to apply the analysis. In fact, patterns that do not change after central reflections, such as those used by Garner, are just those patterns that have bilateral symmetry, which was a Gestalt prototype for good figures. Even so, Garner did not couch his theory in terms of "symmetry" because he and Clement found that rotational invariance was also important, and this did not seem to fit with the idea of symmetry, at least in its everyday, commonsense form. However, rotational invariance actually conforms precisely to the mathe-

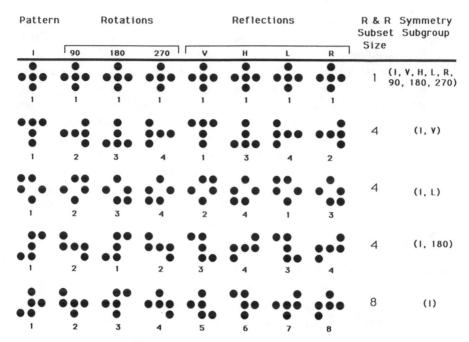

Figure 1.   Transformational analyses of figural goodness for dot patterns in terms of R & R subset size (Garner, 1974) and symmetry subgroups. (I = identity; 90 = 90° rotation; 180 = 180° rotation; 270 = 270° rotation; V = vertical reflection; H = horizontal reflection; L = left diagonal reflection; R = right diagonal reflection. From Palmer, 1983. Reprinted by permission.)

matical definition of symmetry, and this fact forms the cornerstone of the present proposal.

Symmetry Subgroups

In modern mathematics, the standard analysis of symmetry is in terms of *transformational invariance* (Weyl, 1952). Intuitively, a figure is symmetrical with respect to a given transformation if applying that transformation leaves the figure unchanged. For the standard example of bilateral (or "mirror image") symmetry, the underlying transformation is a reflection of the figure around the axis of symmetry. Thus, vertically symmetric patterns (e.g., an upright A or T) remain the same after being reflected around a central vertical line, and horizontally symmetric patterns (e.g., an upright C or B) remain the same after being reflected around a central horizontal line. Within this general framework of symmetry as transformational invariance, rotational symmetry is exactly analogous, except that the transformation involved is a central rotation through an angle of some specified size. Thus, a pattern that has 180-degree rotational symmetry (e.g., an S or a Z) remains the same after being rotated 180° around a point at its center.

It is easy to see, then, that one can characterize the symmetries of a given figure as the subset of spatial transformations that leave it invariant or unchanged. One would simply apply every candidate transformation to the figure and include in its "symmetry subset" only the ones that leave it unchanged. Some examples of such symmetry subsets are given in the rightmost column of Figure 1 for the same patterns that were used to illustrate R & R subsets.

It turns out that the subsets so constructed have some special structural properties that qualify them as instances of mathematical groups and subgroups rather than as sets and subsets. (Technical descriptions of these properties of groups and subgroups can be found in Weyl [1952] or almost any textbook on abstract algebra.) The effect of this additional structure is that not all logically possible subsets of transformations exist as symmetry subgroups. For instance, a pattern cannot have both vertical and horizontal reflectional symmetry (e.g., an H or an X) without also having 180-degree rotational symmetry. Similarly, a pattern cannot have 90-degree rotational symmetry (e.g., a swastika) without also having 180- and 270-degree rotational symmetry. For present purposes, however, it will suffice to think of what are technically symmetry subgroups simply as symmetry subsets.

Given that "better" figures have more symmetries (i.e., more transformations in their symmetry subgroups) than "poorer" figures (see Figure 1), the obvious hypothesis to be explored is whether the goodness of a figure is some relatively simple function of its symmetry subgroup. The first possibility to consider is that it is a function of the order (or size) of its symmetry subgroup (i.e., the number of transformations that belong to its symmetry subgroup). In fact, this version of the symmetry subgroup theory is isomorphic to Garner's R & R subset theory because these two subset sizes are inversely related to each other: $R \cdot S = T$, where R is the size of the R & R subset, S is the size of the symmetry subgroup, and T is the size of the total group of transformations used to generate both of these subsets (see also Royer, 1981). Because they are formally equivalent, there is no reason to prefer one theory over the other, and given that Garner proposed his theory first, it should not be supplanted. That they are isomorphic should not be too surprising given that the two theories are conceptually so closely related to each other. In fact, they only differ by something akin to a theoretical figure–ground reversal: Garner's theory focuses on the *patterns* generated by the group of transformations, whereas the present theory focuses on the *transformations* over which the patterns are invariant.

Despite the close relation between the theories, I will argue that there are potential advantages to analysis in terms of symmetry subgroups. The most important of these advantages, one which I call *cross-figural comparability*, arises precisely because the symmetry subgroup formulation focuses on transformations rather than on patterns. The key feature is that the elements in symmetry subgroups are the same for all possible figures: namely, the *transformations* over which the given figure is invariant. As a result, symmetry subgroups can be compared directly across figures for possible effects of the *identity* of transformations in the subgroup in addition to their *number*. This is not possible with R & R subsets because the elements of the subsets are *figures*, which cannot be meaningfully compared for identity across different figures. To illustrate the difference, consider the three middle patterns in Figure 1. All have exactly four different figures in their R & R subsets (given Garner's particular group of eight rotations and reflections) and exactly two transformations in their symmetry subgroups. But comparing the symmetry subgroups yields the potentially important information that the figures differ in the transformations over which they are symmetrical. No such conclusion can be reached by comparing the figures in the corresponding R & R subsets. As a result, the analysis in terms of symmetry subgroups is potentially more powerful because it allows further distinctions that might turn out to be important.

Evidence for Symmetry Subgroups

The empirical question is now clear: Does the *identity* of the transformations in the symmetry subgroup matter for figural goodness, or only their *number* (i.e., R & R subset size)? Garner and Clement (1963) found no significant differences due to the identity of the transformations in symmetry subgroups, thus supporting their analysis in terms of R & R subsets. Since 1963, however, several results have been reported in the literature on perception of goodness and detection of symmetry that suggest that identity does indeed matter.

Perhaps the most direct and relevant evidence was reported by Chipman (1977), who collected complexity ratings for patterns with several different kinds of symmetry. In Experiment 5, Chipman found that figures with a single vertical symmetry of reflection were rated as significantly simpler (less complex) than those with a single horizontal symmetry, and that figures with horizontal symmetry were rated as significantly simpler than those with a single diagonal symmetry of reflection. Although this stimulus set also contained figures whose parts were related by rotation, they were not rotationally symmetric figures and so cannot be used in the present context to determine whether rotational symmetries differ systematically from reflectional ones in perceived complexity. In Experiment 7, Chipman replicated the difference between single vertical and horizontal symmetries of reflection and included figures with true rotational symmetry. Unfortunately, the latter set contained more than one rotation in their symmetry subgroups (four, in fact) and so cannot be compared to the single reflectional symmetries.

There are also results suggestive of differences in perceptibility between different types of symmetry in the literature on explicit symmetry detection. Although it is not logically necessary that symmetry detection be related to perceived goodness, it makes intuitive sense that easily detected symmetries might affect perceived goodness more strongly. Indeed, this seems to be the case. Palmer and Hemenway (1978) found that when subjects were required to detect reflectional symmetry in simple closed polygons in a reaction-time task, vertical symmetry was detected some 400 ms faster than horizontal symmetry, which was detected some 200 ms faster than diagonal symmetry. Error rates followed essentially the same pattern, with fewest errors being made on vertical symmetries and most on diagonal ones. Similar results were obtained by Royer (1981) in a symmetry-detection task, but using a larger set of symmetries. Royer found that 180-degree rotational symmetries were detected even more slowly than reflectional ones. Thus, these results seem to converge with Chipman's (1977) findings for complexity ratings in the sense that they all produce the same salience ordering over symmetry types.

Despite this somewhat indirect evidence supporting the analysis in terms of symmetry subgroups, it would be preferable to test its predictions directly. Paul Chase and I therefore collected more complete evidence about the effects of different symmetries by having subjects rate the perceived goodness of dot patterns much like the ones Garner and Clement (1963) used in their seminal experiment. We chose slightly more complex patterns that contained 9 or 10 dots from a 5 × 5 matrix to produce more patterns and more symmetry conditions than are possible with Garner's original 3 × 3 matrix. There were four examples from each of the 10 symmetry subgroup conditions. Subjects rated each of the 40 patterns on a scale from 1 to 7, with 1 indicating very "bad" patterns and 7 indicating very "good" ones.

The results are shown in Figure 2 as graphs of the partial orderings defined by significant differences between conditions. The left–right position of each node (as projected onto the scale below) indicates its mean rating. All nodes that are strictly ordered in these graphs (i.e., connected by links that can be traversed in a single direction) were significantly different from each other. The results make it clear that there are several significant differences among classes of figures whose subset sizes are the same but whose symmetry subgroups contain different trans-formations. In the case of an R & R subset size of four, for example, figures with vertical (V) symmetry were judged "better" than figures with horizontal (H) symmetry, and these, in turn, were judged "better" than figures either with either left-diagonal (L) or right-diagonal (R) symmetry or with 180-degree (180) rota-tional symmetry. The latter condition did not differ significantly from either of the diagonal conditions, however. In the case of an R & R subset size of two, patterns with H-V-180 symmetry were judged significantly better than patterns

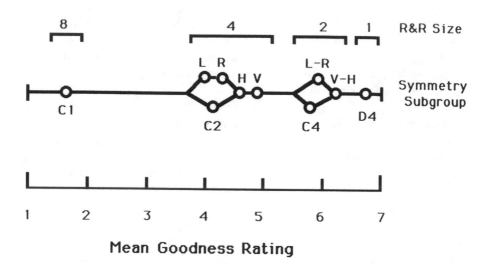

D4 = (I, V, H, L, R, 90, 180, 270)

V-H = (I, V, H, 180)

L-R = (I, L, R, 180)

C4 = (I, 90, 180, 270)

V = (I, V)

H = (I, H)

L = (I, L)

R = (I, R)

C2 = (I, 180)

C1 = (I)

Figure 2. Mean goodness ratings of dot patterns for various symmetry subgroups as depicted in a graph indicating the partial ordering determined by significant differences between conditions. (I = identity; 90 = 90° rotation; 180 = 180° rotation; 270 = 270° rotation; V = vertical reflection; H = horizontal reflection; L = left diagonal reflection; R = right diagonal reflection.)

with either L-R-180 symmetry or those with 90-180-270 symmetry, the latter pair
of which did not differ from each other.

Together with the prior evidence cited above, these data provide convincing
evidence that there are indeed differences over transformations within symmetry
subgroups. The analysis in terms of symmetry subgroups is therefore preferable
to that in terms of R & R subsets because the former is able to account for these
differences, whereas the latter cannot.

GOODNESS OF PATTERNS IN SPACE-TIME

I now want to consider a case in which the differences due to different transformations in the potential symmetry subgroup are far more profound: perceived
goodness of patterns that vary in time as well as space. I will argue that in this
case, there are certain kinds of symmetry in the geometry of space–time that do
not influence perceived goodness at all. If this is true, it is an extreme example
of the need for a theory of perceived goodness that allows for differential contributions from different symmetries, because some symmetries simply may not
be represented within the perceptual system.

The research project began with the empirical question of whether the perceived goodness of purely spatial patterns would differ systematically from the
goodness of space–time patterns, and if so, how. Because the goodness of space-
time patterns has seldom been investigated, there were almost no empirical findings
to constrain my thinking about the problem. My intuition led me to suspect that
the perceived goodness of the ''events'' we constructed in two-dimensional space-
time (one spatial and one temporal dimension) would indeed differ from that of
corresponding ''patterns'' in normal two-dimensional space–space, because the
temporal dimension of space–time might not be fully integrated with the spatial
dimension in the same sense that two spatial dimensions seem to be. The most
important implication of this idea is that perception of two-dimensional space–
time events would not support the full set of two-dimensional symmetries that are
available for perception of purely spatial patterns. Although I expected that perceived goodness would be affected by reflections about the purely spatial axis and
about the purely temporal axis, it seemed quite possible that it would not be
affected by reflections about ''mixed'' axes that involved both space and time:
that is, reflections about space-time axes that were oblique with respect to the
axes of an event's space–time diagram. For similar reasons, I doubted that the
perceptual system could appreciate symmetries of rotation in space–time patterns,
because these transformations likewise seem to require dealing with simultaneous
changes in both spatial and temporal dimensions. In other words, I suspected that
the temporal dimension of space–time did not combine with the spatial dimensions
of perception to produce the full dimensional structure implied by the usual representation of time as an ''extra'' spatial dimension in space–time geometry.

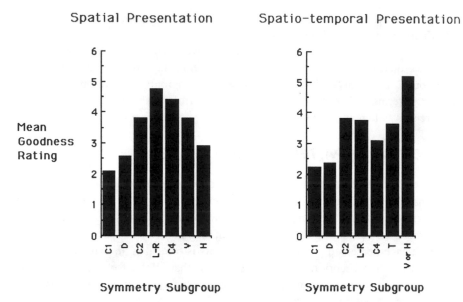

Figure 3.   Mean goodness ratings of patterns for various symmetry subgroups under purely spatial or spatio-temporal presentation conditions. (I = identity; C1 = (I); D = (L) or (R); C2 = (I, 180); L–R = (I, L, R, 180); C4 = (I, 90, 180, 270); V = vertical reflection; H = horizontal reflection.)

Johanna Weber and I have completed some pilot studies on these issues by comparing goodness ratings of the same two-dimensional patterns when they were presented in two different ways. The patterns consisted of 8, 9, or 10 filled-in squares within a 5 × 5 matrix. In the purely spatial condition, these patterns were presented all at once in two spatial dimensions, and subjects had up to 32 s to rate their goodness as spatial patterns on a 6-point scale. In the space–time conditions, the same patterns were used to generate space–time events simply by displaying each column of the matrix in sequence at a rate of two columns per second (each column was on for 450 ms and off for 50 ms). After all five columns had been presented, there was a 3-s pause before the pattern was repeated again. The event repeated until either the subject made a goodness rating or 32 s had elapsed. Three different groups of subjects rated the patterns in the three different conditions: as purely spatial patterns, as space–time events in vertically displayed columns, and as space–time events in horizontally displayed rows.

The results of main interest are shown in Figure 3, averaged over the row and column space–time conditions. Let us first consider the question of whether "diagonal" space–time symmetries of reflection—those not parallel to either the spatial or temporal axis of space–time—contribute to the perceived goodness of space–time patterns. One piece of evidence consistent with the conclusion that they do not is that the rated goodness of space–time patterns with "diagonal" space–time symmetries (D) are not rated significantly better than patterns with no space–time symmetry at all (C1). This is in contrast with the results for the purely spatial patterns, in which diagonal symmetries are rated significantly higher than the asymmetrical controls. The second piece of evidence is that the L-R-180 (L-R) events are not rated as significantly better than the 180 events (C2) in the space–time conditions despite their extra symmetries around mixed space–time axes. In the purely spatial condition, however, the L-R-180 patterns are rated as significantly better than the 180 patterns.

Thus, it seems that there is fairly strong evidence that symmetries of reflection around "mixed" space–time axes do not contribute to ratings of perceived goodness in events. However, the lack of such effects might also be due simply to forgetting over the duration of the event. This is certainly a possibility, but if forgetting were the whole story, then one would expect that purely temporal symmetry would also fail to have an effect on goodness ratings. As the data in Figure 3 show, however, there are clear and robust effects due to purely temporal symmetry in the space–time conditions as compared with the asymmetrical controls. Although the ratings in the temporal symmetry condition are not as large as the effects of purely spatial (V or H) symmetries in space–time events (which do not require memory to process), they are roughly comparable to vertical and horizontal symmetries in the purely spatial condition. Thus, it seems that there must be factors beyond simple forgetting at work to account for the observed lack of effects due to diagonal symmetries in the space–time conditions.

Let us next consider the question of whether symmetries of rotation would contribute to the perceived goodness of space–time events. At first glance, the evidence seems to show that they do, contrary to the expectation stated earlier. Patterns with 180-degree rotational symmetry (C2) are rated better than those with no symmetry (C1) in both spatial and space–time presentation conditions. Moreover, the same is true for patterns with L-R-180 symmetry (L-R) and 90-180-270 symmetry (C4). It turns out that there is a catch here, however. What we have been calling "180-degree rotational symmetry" is not necessarily a symmetry of rotation at all: This same transformation can be brought about in several different ways, one of which is simply a sequence of two reflections around axes parallel to the dimensional axes of the space. To achieve this sequence, one would first reflect the pattern around one dimensional axis, and then around the other. Thus, 180 symmetry can equally well be construed as H + V symmetry (or V + H symmetry), and this combination of transformations does not require simultaneous manipulations of the spatial and temporal dimensions at all.

The important implication is that comparing 180 conditions to asymmetrical conditions is an invalid test of the hypothesis under consideration. The appropriate comparison is between 180 (C2) and 90-180-270 (C4) symmetry conditions, because 90- and 270-degree rotations cannot be reduced to a sequence of reflections around the axes of space–time. Thus, the C4 patterns should be rated no higher than the C2 patterns in the space–time conditions, in contrast with their higher ratings in the purely spatial conditions. In fact, C4 patterns are rated significantly lower than C2 patterns in the space–time conditions. Exactly why this might be true is somewhat mysterious because it is unclear how this sort of structure could have a negative effect on perceived goodness without having been somehow detected. The effect might be due to the particular set of patterns used in this study. In any case, further experiments will be required to clarify the status of this unexpected effect.

In summary, however, perceived goodness of space–time events does seem to differ systematically from that of corresponding spatial patterns. Moreover, the differences seem to be precisely the sort that would be expected if only reflections around the axes of space–time were available to the perceptual system. Regardless of how one accounts for these findings in detail theoretically, the radical differences in the salience of corresponding transformations in the two cases strongly imply that an analysis in terms of symmetry subgroups is required.

LOCAL SYMMETRY

In the final section of this chapter, I would like to extend the symmetry subgroup analysis of figural goodness in a different direction by considering the possibility that local as well as global symmetry structure may be important. Geometrically speaking, the transformations we have used in constructing symmetry subgroups thus far have been global in the sense that the entire space, rather than a restricted subregion of it, is subjected to the transformation. Although this assumption makes perfect sense from an idealized mathematical standpoint, it seems perceptually unrealistic for at least two reasons. First, there are compelling physiological reasons to think about symmetry in local rather than global terms: The visual field itself covers only a restricted region of space, and the visual system seems to analyze it through cells with relatively small receptive fields. Second, the visual field is almost always cluttered with extraneous structure surrounding the figure of interest, and this would prevent global transformations from doing the job for which the symmetry subgroup analysis was intended. Thus, it seems appropriate to think about perception of symmetry as being spatially restricted, that is, as a *local symmetry* that results from applying a given transformation just to a restricted region of space. This certainly must be true for the subregion of space that currently falls within the visual field, because we cannot actually see anything outside of this region. It is probably also true for the smaller subregion that surrounds the attended figure, because it is not hard for us to perceive symmetry in a figure as long as other figures do not overlap it.

I now ask whether it might be useful to think about perceptual structure in terms of restricted local symmetries within subregions of a single figure. Work along these lines has appeared in the computer vision literature (e.g., Blum, 1973; Brady, 1983) but has received only scant attention in psychological studies of figural goodness (Alexander & Carey, 1968; Chipman, 1977; Psotka, 1978). It should be noted that this move of analyzing local symmetries runs counter to Gestalt ideas of holism, although it is intended to supplement rather than replace the holistic analysis of global symmetries.

Let us begin by considering local transformations that act only on a subregion of a figure, such as reflecting it around a specified axis or rotating it through a specified angle. If the figure turns out to be the same following the local transformation as it was before, then it has local symmetry of the specified sort in exactly the same sense as for global symmetries. Because there are more local than global transformations, correspondingly more parameters are needed to describe them. The extra parameters are needed to define the subregion of space to which the local transformation is applied. For instance, if one makes the assumption that the regions of interest are circular, then one extra parameter is required for local rotations (to define the radius) and two extra parameters for local reflections (one to define the center point along the axis of reflection and one to define the radius). A circle is perhaps the most logical choice for the shape of local regions, not only because it requires the fewest extra parameters, but because it will support the maximal set of local transformations, including all central reflections and rotations.

The idea that perception of figural goodness might be based on local symmetries may not seem intuitive, but it makes a certain amount of sense considering the fact that low-level vision seems to occur within many small receptive fields that cover only local portions of the retina. If the visual system compares the outputs of such receptive fields for identity (i.e., redundancy) and makes use of the results, then it is effectively computing local symmetries (see Palmer, 1982, 1983, for a more detailed presentation of this idea). The rationale is thus not unlike that of the so-called "aperture problem" in motion perception (Marr, 1982).

We now have an empirical question before us: Do local symmetries actually affect ratings of perceived goodness? The difficulty is in figuring out how to test this question. Unfortunately, a fairly detailed theory would be required to answer the question using goodness ratings of whole figures. However, it is rather easy to answer it in a different way that depends on finding positions within figures where only local symmetries exist. I have taken this approach by having subjects rate the goodness of the relationship between a small probe circle and a larger figure that surrounds it to see whether evidence for local symmetry structure would emerge.

As an example, consider the rectangle shown in Figure 4A. It has two axes of global symmetry (shown by the long-dashed lines) plus four prominent axes of local symmetry along the bisectors of its angles (shown by the short-dashed lines). In one experiment, I studied the 35 positions shown in Figure 4B by

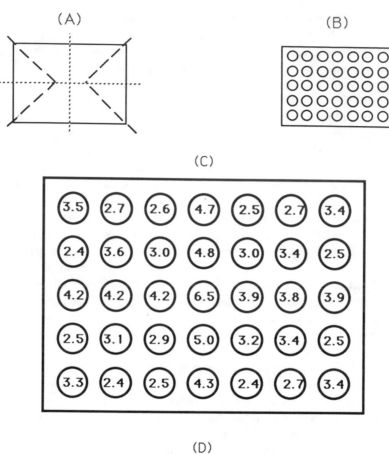

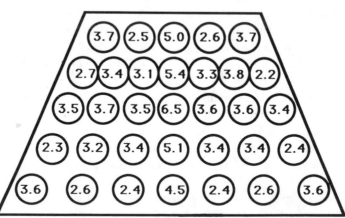

Figure 4.   A: Local (short-dashed) and global (long-dashed) symmetry axes of a rectangle. B: Thirty-five stimuli in a goodness rating experiment using single dots inside the rectangular frame. C and D: The mean goodness ratings for each dot position inside a rectangle (C) and trapezoid (D).

constructing 35 stimuli, each of which contained a single circle (at one of the 35 probe positions) inside the rectangle. Subjects were asked to rate each stimulus for the "goodness" of the relation between the circle and the rectangle on a scale from 1 ("bad") to 7 ("good")—that is, to rate how well the circle "fit" into the context provided by the outer figure. (This technique is analogous in many ways to Krumhansl's [1979] "probe tone" technique for measuring the perceived structural relations of a given pitch to a preceding musical context, but in a spatial rather than a tonal medium.)

The results (shown in Figure 4C) were encouraging from a symmetry analytic point of view. The highest rating was at the center, where the global symmetries coincide. The next highest ratings were along the vertical axis of global symmetry, followed by the horizontal axis of global symmetry. The result of particular interest for the present discussion, however, is that the ratings were also elevated along the local symmetries on the angle bisectors. (Although certain aspects of these results are reminiscent of Blum's [1973] "grassfire transformation" (see also Lockhead's chapter of this volume), they differ in the prominence of the short global axis of symmetry and of the ends of the long global axis of symmetry.) Qualitatively similar effects were also present for other figures, like the trapezoid shown in Figure 4D. Goodness ratings were again elevated for local symmetries along the angle bisectors.

Given that such local symmetry effects seem to exist, I will now consider how a theory based on local symmetry subgroups might be formalized. In this theory, we want local and global symmetries to be treated uniformily so that global symmetries are just a limiting case of local ones. We begin with the idea of groups of *local transformations* that operate within a specified circular subregion, including local reflections around a given axis and local rotations through a given angle. Global transformations are then just local transformations with an infinite radius. Then, we can define the *local symmetry subgroups* for any given figure as the subset of these local transformations that leaves the figure unchanged. Obviously, there will be many such subgroups for a single figure—besides just the one composed of global symmetries—because each local symmetry subgroup is specific to a particular position and radius. The representation can be simplified by considering for each transformation type only the largest circular region around a specified point that can be transformed without changing the figure. No useful information is lost because the figure necessarily has local symmetries for all smaller regions and for no larger ones.

This model says that ratings of subjective goodness, S, can be predicted by the following equation,

$$S = k + \sum_{o=1}^{n} w_o \cdot r_o$$

where k is a scaling constant, o is the set of orientations, w is the weight (or salience) for each orientation, and r is the maximal radius of local symmetry at each orientation, where the value of r can vary from 0 to G, the "effective radius" of global symmetry.

This model was fit to goodness ratings from another experiment in which a small circular probe was positioned at various places within a larger rectangle, square, and circle. Best-fitting values of the parameters were estimated using a program called STEPIT. The model was fit to the data from all three figures simultaneously, using six parameters in the standard model: the additive constant, k, the weights for the four orientations, w, and the value of G. Two further multiplicative parameters were added to scale the values of the maximal radii, r, for the rectangle and the square relative to the circle, because there was no reason to suppose that the units of distance would be exactly equal across the three figures. The model's fit was good, accounting for 88% of the variance in 77 data points with eight parameters. Moreover, the estimated values of the parameters were quite sensible. The salience weighting was highest for vertical symmetries (1.6), next highest for horizontal ones (1.1), and lowest (and about equal) for diagonal ones (0.6 and 0.5 for the left and right diagonals, respectively). The scaling parameters were close to unity (1.12 for the square and 1.21 for the rectangle), indicating that the distance units were nearly the same for the three figures. The value of the effective radius of global symmetry was about twice the largest dimension of the surrounding figure, indicating that symmetry beyond this circular region has no further effect. Naturally, I plan to get rating data from other figures to test the model further, but its initial performance is promising.

My conclusion from this work is that local symmetry subgroups—in the general mathematical sense defined by invariance over locally as well as globally defined transformations—provide an important tool for constructing theories of figural goodness. They are consistent with what we already know from Garner's pioneering work on R & R subsets, and they are rich enough to have made some interesting new predictions that seem to be correct. I am not sure that local symmetry subgroups will explain all there is to know about figural goodness, but it will be informative just to find out how far they will take us toward achieving what both the Gestaltists and Garner were after: an adequate understanding of the structure of visually perceived shapes.

References

Alexander, C., & Carey, S. (1968). Subsymmetries. *Perception and Psychophysics, 4,* 73–77.

Attneave, F. (1954). Some informational aspects of visual perception. *Psychological Review, 61,* 183–193.

Blum, H. (1973). Biological shape and visual science, Part 1. *Journal of Theoretical Biology, 38,* 205–287.

Brady, M. (1983). Criteria for representation of shape. In J. Beck, B. Hope, & A. Rosenfeld (Eds.), *Human and machine vision* (pp. 39–84). San Diego: Academic Press.

Chipman, S. (1977). Complexity and structure in visual patterns. *Journal of Experimental Psychology: General, 106,* 269–301.

Garner, W. R. (1974). *The processing of information and structure.* Potomac, MD: Erlbaum.

Garner, W. R., & Clement, D. E. (1963). Goodness of pattern and pattern uncertainty. *Journal of Verbal Learning and Verbal Behavior, 2,* 446–452.

Hochberg, J., & McAlister, E. (1953). A quantitative approach to figural "goodness." *Journal of Experimental Psychology, 46,* 361–364.

Krumhansl, C. (1979). The psychological representation of musical pitch in a tonal context. *Cognitive Psychology, 11,* 346–374.

Marr, D. (1982). *Vision.* San Francisco: Freeman.

Palmer, S. E. (1982). Symmetry, transformation, and the structure of perceptual systems. In J. Beck (Ed.), *Representation and organization in perception* (pp. 95–144). Hillsdale, NJ: Erlbaum.

Palmer, S. E. (1983). The psychology of perceptual organization: A transformational approach. In J. Beck, B. Hope, & A. Rosenfeld (Eds.), *Human and machine vision* (pp. 269–339). San Diego, CA: Academic Press.

Palmer, S. E., & Hemenway, K. (1978). Orientation and symmetry: Effects of multiple, near, and rotational symmetries. *Journal of Experimental Psychology: Human Perception and Performance, 4,* 691–702.

Psotka, J. (1978). Perceptual processes that may create stick figures and balance. *Journal of Experimental Psychology: Perception and Performance, 4,* 101–111.

Royer, F. (1981). Detection of symmetry. *Journal of Experimental Psychology: Human Perception and Performance, 7,* 1186–1210.

Wertheimer, M. (1938). Gestalt theory. In W. D. Ellis (Ed. and Trans.), *A sourcebook of Gestalt psychology* (pp. 1–11). New York: Harcourt, Brace. (Original work published 1924)

Weyl, H. (1952). *Symmetry.* Princeton, NJ: Princeton University Press.

CHAPTER 3

WHY OUR STIMULI LOOK AS THEY DO

JAMES E. CUTTING

Perception is sometimes thought to be an inferential process and sometimes thought not to be. In fact, inferences are broad enough to encompass all theories of perception. I will explore this breadth in three kinds of perceptual inference, one inductive and two deductive. The inductive view, consistent with Garner's ideas of critical realism, demands a role for cognition in perception because information underspecifies what is perceived. This view may at times be true, but only, I claim, because researchers use reduced, or relatively impoverished, stimuli. The first deductive view, consistent with Garner's and Gibson's ideas on direct realism, claims that information in natural environments specifies (i.e., is exactly matched to) percepts. Researchers of this persuasion appeal to enriched stimuli but typically satisfice in their search for information. A second deductive view, which is mine, claims that potentially useful information overspecifies what is to be perceived; the perceiver selects or combines sources of available information according to needs and contexts.

Twenty years ago, I completed a graduate psychology course at Yale University under Wendell Garner. In the course, we compared and contrasted the views of many 20th-century perceptual theorists. The final exam was a series of take-home essays on theory, epistemology, and their relation to perceptual research. As students, we worried over the essays, handed them in with great trepidation, and had them returned with even more anxiety. Garner's comments on my essays were

This research was supported by National Institutes of Mental Health Grant MH37467 and National Science Foundation Grant BNS-8818971.

kind, if not overly enthusiastic. They included the terse note, "A well worked-out set of answers, but not really strong re critical realism." My comments here should be taken as a second draft.

In his writings, Garner (1966, 1974, 1986; Garner, Hake, & Eriksen, 1956) has long shown an interest in the relations among perception, science, and ep-istemology. His starting point has often been a contrast between direct (or naive) realism and critical realism. The difference is that the direct realist believes in a one-to-one mapping between perceived qualities and physical attributes, whereas the critical realist does not. Going beyond Garner, I claim that there is a third member of the set. I also claim that these three positions dictate why we conduct our perceptual experiments the way we do and why participants' data dictate the form of perceptual theory that can be supported. Before I expand on these ideas, let me discuss a concept that has caused extraordinary mischief in our understand-ing of perceptual theory.

INFERENCE: A LOGICAL DIGRESSION

Helmholtz (1925) and Mill (1843) thought perception was an inferential process. James (1890), Gibson (1979), and many others, however, have railed against this characterization. I claim that this debate is based on misunderstanding (see also Bennett, Hoffman, & Prakash, 1989). The concept of inference does not constrain theories of perception. What follows is an explanation of why.

Hidden Premises

In logic, inference divides two ways: There are deductions, which are sure, and inductions, which are not.[1] Each is made up of premises and a conclusion. De-ductions are well understood in logic; inductions are hardly understood at all. There have been attempts to understand inductions as deductions, rewriting them and shoring them up with what I call *hidden premises*. These attempts have been incompletely successful in logic, in part because the issue of surety can no longer play a role. Nonetheless, such rewrites set an interesting stage for discussions of perception.

Consider Syllogism 1 in Figure 1. If this syllogism is written with only Premise 1 and the Conclusion (and without the bracketed Premise 2), it is an induction. That is, logically and perceptually speaking, the conclusion of trian-

---

[1]In logic, if the premises dictate only one true conclusion, the conclusion is *deductively valid*; if, on the other hand, the premises allow for several possible conclusions, one of which is more likely than the others, the conclusion is *inductively strong* (e.g., Skyrms, 1975). Thus, technically speaking, deduction and induction differ in probability: Deductions are 100% sure, inductions less so. I will not use this manner of dividing inferences, however. Instead, because I will rewrite inductions as deduc-tions, I will preserve the distinction in another way: Inductions have mental (nonperceptual) premises; deductions do not.

Syllogism 1

Premise 1:   Image data:

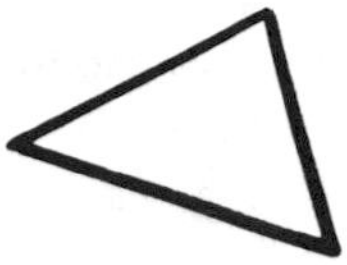

Premise 2:   Conceptual data: All closed 3
                                                sided figures
                                                are triangles.

Conclusion.   Percept: The image is
                                                a triangle

Figure 1.   A representation of the perception of a triangle as an induction. By rules
outlined in the text, this scheme is inductive because Premise 2 must come
from stored knowledge. Thus, the labeling and categorization of this stimulus goes beyond the information given in the stimulus and beyond the
capacities of a bottom-up process.

gleness is underspecified by an image of a closed figure with three sides. If,
instead, the syllogism is rewritten with Premise 2, offering definitive information
and knowledge about triangleness, then it becomes a logical deduction.

Although completely trivial, this syllogism and its rewrite procedure serve
as an important entrée. Mill and Helmholtz thought that perception is inductive
because many premises, like Premise 2, "go beyond the information given" in
the stimulus (e.g., Bruner, 1957). Such premises, therefore, must be experience-
based, part of knowledge, and irreconcilably mental.

In a similar way, Garner has separated direct realism from critical realism.
For the direct realist, there are no premises hidden in the mind; stimulus information is sufficient to drive perceptual conclusions. For the critical realist, like
Garner, stimulus information is important, but "there may be other characteristics,
or modified characteristics, that are not independently properties of the physical
objects" before us (Garner, 1986, p. 200). These are hidden premises.

Where Perceptual Premises Hide

In any discussion of perceptual inference, then, we must be clear about where
premises can hide. Garner (1986) wants to hide them in either of two places: "the
basic concern of our research is to differentiate the concept of critical realism into
its two parts: 'realism' as a reflection of the contributions of the real world to

perception . . . and 'critical' as the contribution of the organism that is doing the perceiving'' (p. 200).

It seems to me that Garner's analysis is insufficiently fine-grained. I think that premises can hide in at least three places. First, they can hide as knowledge in the mental repertory of the perceiver, as Garner would claim. If they hide in the mind, then a given act of perception must be inductive, as Mill and Helmholtz declared. Garner (1986) has regarded perception that is based on premises not in the stimulus as manipulable and optional (but see Mill, 1842/1978, for an anticipatory counterargument).

Second, premises may actually "hide" in the object or event, which means they really are not hidden at all. Perceivers may not actually go beyond the information given in a perceptual situation; instead, we, as perceptual scientists, have not been clever enough to discern what the critical information is. Notice that if premises "hide" in information about the physical object or event, perception is deductive, at least by rules elaborated from Mill and Helmholtz.[2]

Third, and new to the set, some premises hide in what I will call the biological endowment of the organism and its perceptual system. This is the trickiest place for them to hide, but as a beginning it might be useful to think of this hiding place as entailing everything in Marr's (1981) conception of vision up to the $2\frac{1}{2}$-D sketch, and more. Conclusions using these premises are generally mandatory, as Garner (1986) might require.

Notice that, for purposes of historical and theoretical continuity in psychology, I am defining perceptual deductions and inductions differently than they are defined in modern logic. I define them according to the hiding place of needed premises. If they hide in the stimulus or biological endowment of the organism, perception is deductive; if they are in the mind, perception in inductive. Thus, despite my rewrite procedure, Syllogism 1 is a perceptual induction by these rules, with or without Premise 2.

THREE KINDS OF INFERENCE IN PERCEPTION

Given this digression, the stage is now set for discussion of three types of perceptual inference. By convention, I will call the first type *indirect perception*. This type of perception is typified in the writings of many contemporary theorists who can be called "critical realists," including Garner. It entails at least two ideas: (a) Stimulus information underspecifies what is perceived, and thus, (b) the perceiver must make mental contributions to the act of perception. Thus, stimulus information is

---

[2] At this point, one should quibble about the relation between perceptual inference and perceptual error. That is, if perception does not always reflect truth about the real world, how can it be deductive? The short form of my retort is that percepts, as deductive conclusions, are 100% sure, but not necessarily 100% correct. Deductions can proceed from invalid premises and be wrong, but they are still deductions with inescapable conclusions.

necessary for perception, but is insufficient. Garner's idea of inferred subsets—stimuli implying their alternatives—is perhaps his most relevant example here. Garner (1974, pp. 183–186) regards these subsets as built around a given stimulus, and it is difficult not to consider these as elaborations by a sentient perceiver.

The second type of inference is the logical counter of the first: *direct perception*. It is best known through the writings of Gibson (e.g., 1979) and involves two ideas: (a) Stimulus information specifies what is perceived, and (b) the perceiver, although physically (and even mentally) active, need not actively "figure out" what the stimulus must be; he or she simply processes (or picks up) information. Thus, stimulus information is both necessary and sufficient for perception.

The third inference type is new, and I call it *directed perception* (Cutting, 1986). Perhaps those who espouse this position would be *directed realists*. This position outdistances Gibson in some regards and is my own invention by dint of data. Its hallmarks are that (a) stimulus information overspecifies what is perceived and that (b) perceivers must select or combine sources of information suitable to a perceptual situation (see also Massaro, 1987) but do not need to do so by recourse to knowledge or learned rules. Thus, reversing the tenet of critical realism, particular stimulus information may be sufficient for perception but not necessary.

WHY DIRECTED PERCEPTION IS NECESSARY

Let me discuss two sets of data on the perception of surfaces. The first set explored the perceptual use and nonuse of invariants (Cutting, 1986); the second, the use and nonuse of gradients (Cutting & Millard, 1984). To do justice to the idea of inference, I will continue to consider perception as the conclusion from premises in a syllogism.

Multiple Deductions and Moving Surfaces

Syllogism 2 in Figure 2 concerns the use of the cross ratio, an invariant from projective geometry. Premise 1 of the syllogism, as before, corresponds to the image of the object, but here it is a moving image of four parallel lines on a rotating plane. The perceptual conclusion is that the lines are rigidly affixed to that rotating flat plane.

Premise 2 is the computational workhorse. The cross ratio, for our purposes, is measured on combinations of three angles, each of which has its vertex at the observer's eye and has its legs on the figure. The ends of the legs are marked by lines A and B, B and C, and C and D, and these angles are designated α, β, and γ, respectively. It is then mathematically determined that, as long as the lines remain in rigid configuration,

$$[\sin(\alpha + \beta) \cdot \sin(\beta + \gamma)]/[\sin(\beta) \cdot \sin(\alpha + \beta + \gamma)] = k,$$

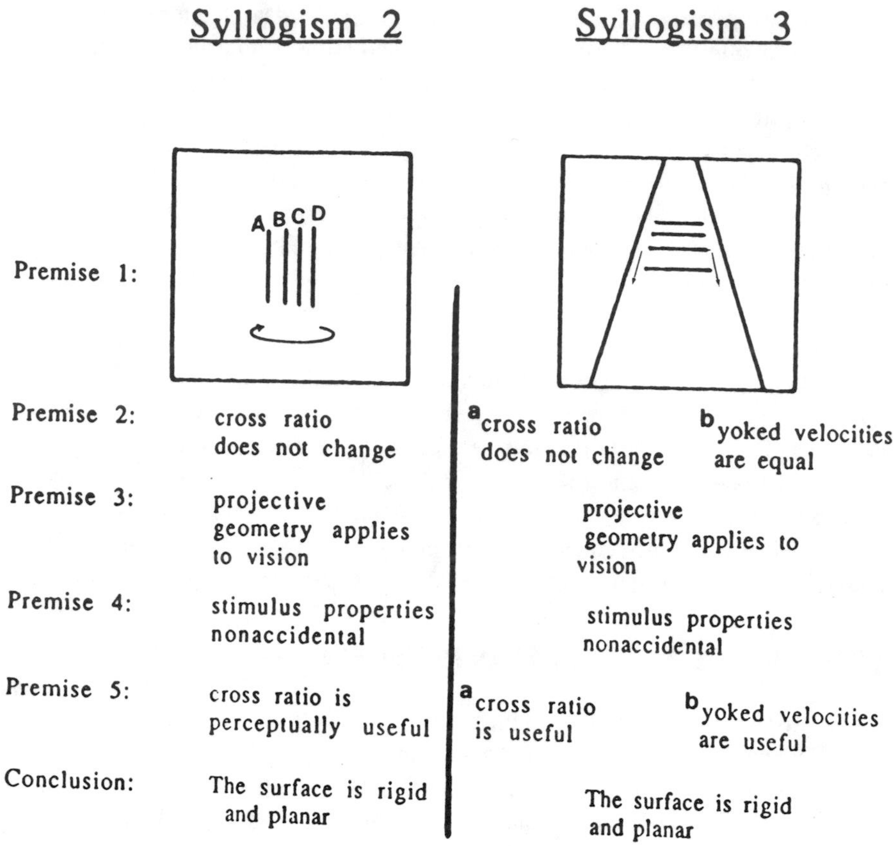

Syllogism 2   Syllogism 3

	Syllogism 2	Syllogism 3
Premise 1:		
Premise 2:	cross ratio does not change	[a]cross ratio does not change [b]yoked velocities are equal
Premise 3:	projective geometry applies to vision	projective geometry applies to vision
Premise 4:	stimulus properties nonaccidental	stimulus properties nonaccidental
Premise 5:	cross ratio is perceptually useful	[a]cross ratio is useful [b]yoked velocities are useful
Conclusion:	The surface is rigid and planar	The surface is rigid and planar

Figure 2.   Two representations of the perception of a moving surface as a deductive process with stimulus information overspecifying what is perceived. By rules outlined in the text, these are deductions because no premises are mental. The existence of multiple deductions supports directed perception, against both direct and indirect perception.

or a constant, regardless of the motion of the plane on which the lines are fixed or the movement of the observer (see Cutting, 1986, for proof). Thus, Premise 2 "hides" in the stimulus.

Premise 3 states that the rules of projective geometry, like the cross ratio, are applicable to vision. This is an idea that has been promoted most recently and systematically by Johansson (1978) but that has been vigorously opposed at least since the writings of Berkeley in 1709 (Berkeley, 1709/1871). With Johansson, I claim that this premise hides in our biological endowment; vision simply works by projections, and projective geometry is their formal systematization.

Premise 4 states that a constant cross ratio is a *nonaccidental property* (Witkin & Tenenbaum, 1983) in this moving stimulus. Although possible, it is extremely unlikely that cross ratio invariance would be obtained through nonrigid means. Again, I claim that this assumption is part of our biology. Although it is quite close to Helmholtz's principle of maximum likelihood (Hochberg, 1981), I claim that this heuristic need not be learned; it is hardwired within human beings.

Finally, Premise 5 concerns the perceptual utility of the cross ratio. There is reasonable evidence that human observers, within threshold limits, can use changes in the cross ratio to make judgments of nonrigidity for rotating planes (Cutting, 1986, 1987; but see Niall, 1987). The ability to determine nonrigidity by cross-ratio change implies an ability to determine rigidity by cross-ratio invariance. Given that the arrangement of parallel lines must then be rigid and planar, all motion in the stimulus must be rotation; hence, the perception of a rotating rigid plane. This last premise, I claim, also hides in human biology; our visual system simply picks it up, or computes it.

Given Premises 1 through 5, the conclusion is deductively specified; there are no mental premises. Because the experimenter knows the conclusion to be true, Premise 3 is validated, at least in this domain; Premise 2 is subject to a bit of measurement error, noted in the full form of Premise 5; and Premise 4, as long as it is true, renders the conclusion deductively valid. So far, Gibson might be pleased, and direct perception could reign.

But consider next Syllogism 3, also in Figure 2. Again, Premise 1 is the moving image of four coplanar parallel lines, but this time they move as if on an unseen conveyor belt toward the observer, or, alternatively, as if a moving observer approached them in a hallway. Premises 2a through 5a are the same as in Syllogism 2, but alternate premises come to the fore.

Premise 2b is a new computation; it is the instantaneous velocity of the four lines as they move through any and all particular points anchored in the optic array. If the lines move with the same (yoked) optical velocity at any and all optic angles (measured from the horizon to one's eye to a specific angle below the horizon), they must be on the same plane (Cutting, 1986). Again, as with Premise 2a, this premise is in the stimulus.

Premises 3 and 4 remain unchanged, but Premise 5b states that the visual system, within threshold limits, can compute these yoked optical velocities suggested in Premise 2b. Indeed, there is evidence for such computations (Cutting, 1986). Again, I claim that Premise 5b hides in the biological makeup of humans' visual system.

Note there are now two subsyllogisms. Both include Premises 1, 3, and 4, but one uses Premises 2a and 5a, and other Premises 2b and 5b. Both lead to the same perceptual conclusion and both are deductions. Data suggest, however, that only Subsyllogism 3b is used.

Syllogism 4   ## Syllogism 5

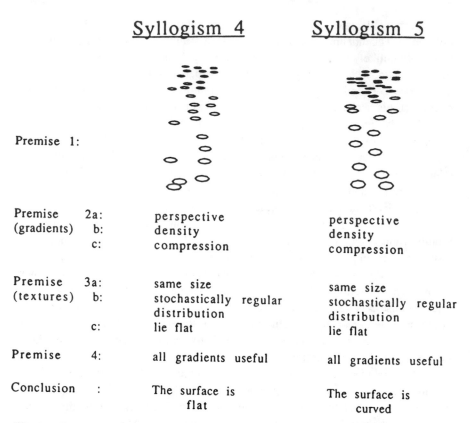

		Syllogism 4	Syllogism 5
Premise 1:			
Premise (gradients)	2a:	perspective	perspective
	b:	density	density
	c:	compression	compression
Premise (textures)	3a:	same size	same size
	b:	stochastically regular distribution	stochastically regular distribution
	c:	lie flat	lie flat
Premise	4:	all gradients useful	all gradients useful
Conclusion	:	The surface is flat	The surface is curved

Figure 3.   Two representations of the perception of static surfaces as a deduction process, again supporting directed perception.

This fact is embarrassing for advocates of both direct perception and direct realism; information overspecifies what is perceived, and the visual system appears to select one source of information (the yoked optical velocities of elements) over another source (the cross ratio) even though it can perfectly well compute the other, as shown in Syllogism 2. Before discussing broader implications, let me replicate this conundrum in another experimental situation concerning the perception of surfaces.

Multiple Deductions and Stationary Surfaces

Syllogism 4 in Figure 3 concerns texture gradients. Again, Premise 1 is an image, a cross section of the optic array. This time, it corresponds to a textured surface beneath the feet of the observer. The perceptual conclusion is of a flat surface receding in depth.

There are two triplets of hidden premises for the conclusion—this is a flat surface—to be granted. There are three gradients of information in the stimulus: (2a) a perspective gradient, in this case the change in projected width of each texture element as one moves up the image plane; (2b) a density gradient, the change in spacing of elements as one moves up the image plane; and (2c) a compression gradient, the change in ratio of the projected height–width of elements as one moves up the plane.

The second triplet of premises hide, I claim, in the biology of the visual system. These are more specific examples of the assumed efficacy of projective geometry to vision and the assumed nonaccidental quality of stimulus properties. These premises are (3a) a particular surface's textures are roughly the same size; (3b) they are spread out in a stochastically regular manner; and (3c) they lie flat on (are part of) the surface.

Finally, Premise 4 is that our visual system can measure and use these gradients when perceiving surfaces. Indeed, data indicates that this is true (Cutting & Millard, 1984). Note that each matched pair of premises in these triplets specifies flatness, yielding three deductive subsyllogisms.

The question, of course, is not what is needed logically to conclude flatness, but what is needed psychologically to perceive it. The answer proves interesting: Data suggest that 65% of this judgment is made on the basis of the perspective gradient (Premises 2a and 3a), 30% on the basis of density (Premises 2b and 3b), and almost none on compression (Cutting & Millard, 1984). Thus, observers seem to combine two sources of information and ignore another.

But now consider Syllogism 5, also shown in Figure 3. It has a new Premise 1, an image corresponding to textures laid on a curved surface. Premises 3a, 3b, and 3c are identical to those in the previous syllogism; Premises 2a, 2b, and 2c have the same names, but would have different graphical representations. Moreover, and most important, the conclusion is different: This surface is curved, sloping up and then away from the viewer.

Again, there are three subsyllogisms, all logical deductions about a curved surface. And again, one can empirically determine which ones carry perceptual weight. Interestingly, about 95% of the information is carried by compression (Premises 2c and 3c) and virtually none by the other two (Cutting & Millard, 1984). Thus, perceivers appear to select one source of information and ignore two others.

These syllogisms about the perception of moving and stationary surfaces demonstrate the necessity for directed perception in certain perceptual situations. With this background, I will now consider our craft.

ARE WE SUFFICIENTLY CRITICAL ABOUT OUR STIMULI?

Let me pervert Koffka's (1935) famous question: "Why do things look as they do?" (p. 75) by asking, "Why do our stimuli look as they do?" My answer, not all that different from Garner's (1974, p. 191) or Kanizsa's (1979, pp. 1–24), is the following: We conduct our experiments and, more particularly, we design and select our stimuli under the aegis of a particular realist position. Why do we take a particular position? My answer centers on pragmatics and control.

The essence of experimentation is control; the essence of visual research is image control. Traditionally, this control has been achieved by using reduced, or (to use a more negative tone) impoverished, stimuli. Since the advent of relatively inexpensive computer graphic techniques, reduced stimuli are no longer necessary. Indeed, one might ask, "Were the study of visual perception to start independently and anew today, would our stimuli look different?" The answer can only be yes. Indeed, the field of machine vision within computer science is new, and stimuli there are usually very rich, even though the essential research effort is the same as that in perceptual psychology.

Given the technical nonnecessity of reduced stimuli, perceptual psychologists who are critical realists must be clear about why they continue to use them. What rationale is there for studying the perception of such things? How does their study inform us about perception generally? Once these reduced stimuli are studied, to what extent can we generalize our findings?

Obviously, there are many good answers to these questions, and some center on the nature of tasks. Let me ignore task factors and consider the following chain of responses and queries. Starting pragmatically, (a) we have found out many interesting psychological principles using reduced stimuli, and we want to find out more. Fine, but what kind of principles are these? Theoretically, following Shepard (1984), (b) we force cognition to complete the perceptual act by using reduced stimuli. Any principles of completion are inherently interesting and important because they tell us about the structure of the mind. Garner's inferred subsets are an example. Again, fine, but why study completion principles? Again following Shepard (1984), (c) we study completions because perception does not always occur in optimal circumstances—occlusions, darkness, quick glances taken in times of stress and cognitive overload, and perhaps other factors reduce useful information in everyday environments. Thus, one might argue, normal perception often involves acts of completion in which the mind must elaborate on stimulus information.

At this point, I disagree. First, most experimental stimulus reductions bear no systematic relation to naturalistic reductions. For example, are quick glimpses of parts of interconnected, complex, natural, three-dimensional scenes really like quick glimpses of a few black lines on an isolated two-dimensional white background? We do not really know, and we have no theory connecting the two situations. Second, directed perception dictates a plethora of relevant information even in reduced situations. If one source is degraded by some factor, it may be unlikely that another source will be equally affected, a benefit of modular design

(Marr, 1981). Thus, directed perception and many-to-one mappings between information and percept are robust against degradation of a single information source.

In other words, information is truly redundant, and its redundancy can serve many purposes (Garner, 1974). When there are process limitations on one source of information, perhaps degraded in some way, there may be no such limitations on another source, and performance may not suffer; and when there are state limitations on the perceiver, when he or she may have inadequate representation of one information source, there may be no such limitations for another, and again performance may not suffer. Here, directed perception finds its best rationale.

CONCLUSION

Perceptual theorists' heritage has constrained much of our research to odd corners of perceptual study. The use of reduced stimuli reduces the available stimulus information in ways typically irrelevant to everyday perception; this reduction necessitates "going beyond" stimulus information. Thus, any demonstration of perceptual success on the part of the perceiver (and the experimenter) must be taken as support of indirect perception and critical realism. It simply could be no other way.

Gibson (1950) paved the way for the study of perception in richer situations and for new theories of perception. When one enriches stimuli, one enriches information about objects and events, reduces the necessity of perceivers to engage cognitive resources, and, I would claim, reduces the relevance (and even the possibility) of inferred subsets. This allows direct perception to occur and fosters the position of direct realism. But direct perception does not go far enough; it assumes a one-to-one mapping between information and percepts (Cutting, 1986). Pragmatically, then, the research procedure is to satisfice; if one finds any adequate information, by definition it must be necessary and sufficient.

Clearly, this procedure is wrong. I hope my syllogisms demonstrate that perception is often a choice among, or a combination of, multiple sources of information (see also Massaro, 1986). Particular information may be sufficient to drive a logical deduction but unnecessary for a perceptual deduction. My experiments demonstrate, even with my crude computer-graphic stimuli (in their own way quite impoverished), that one can easily find a superfluity of information. Imagine what the situation must really be like in a fully natural environment.

References

Bennett, B. M., Hoffman, D. D., & Prakash, C. (1989). *Observer mechanics: A formal theory of perception*. San Diego, CA: Academic Press.

Berkeley, G. (1871). An essay towards a new theory of vision. In *The works of George Berkeley* (pp. 369–400). Oxford, England: Clarendon Press. (Original work published 1709)

Bruner, J. S. (1957). On perceptual readiness. *Psychological Review, 64*, 123–152.

Cutting, J. E. (1986). *Perception with an eye for motion.* Cambridge, MA: Bradford Books/MIT Press.

Cutting, J. E. (1987). On cross ratios and motion perception: A reply to Niall. *Journal of Mathematical Psychology, 31*, 439–440.

Cutting, J. E., & Millard, R. T. (1984). Three gradients and the perception of flat and curved surfaces. *Journal of Experimental Psychology: General, 113*, 198–216.

Garner, W. R. (1966). To perceive is to know. *American Psychologist, 21*, 11–19.

Garner, W. R. (1974). *The processing of information and structure.* Potomac, MD: Erlbaum.

Garner, W. R. (1986). Interactions of stimulus and organism in perception. In S. H. Hulse & B. F. Green (Eds.), *One hundred years of psychology in America: G. Stanley Hall and the Johns Hopkins tradition* (pp. 199–240). Baltimore: Johns Hopkins University Press.

Garner, W. R., Hake, H. W., & Eriksen, C. W. (1956). Operationism and the concept of perception. *Psychological Review, 63*, 149–159.

Gibson, J. J. (1950). *Perception of the visual world.* Boston: Houghton Mifflin.

Gibson, J. J. (1979). *The ecological approach to visual perception.* Boston: Houghton Mifflin.

Helmholtz, H. von (1925). *Treatise on physiological optics* (Vol. 3, 3rd ed., J. Southall, Trans.). Menasha, WI: Optical Society of America.

Hochberg, J. (1981). Levels of perceptual organization. In M. Kubovy & J. R. Pomerantz (Eds.), *Perceptual organization* (pp. 255–278). Hillsdale, NJ: Erlbaum.

James, W. (1890). *The principles of psychology* (Vol. 2). New York: Holt.

Johansson, G. (1978). About the geometry underlying spontaneous visual decoding of the optical message. In E. Leeuwenberg & H. Buffart (Eds.), *Formal theories of visual perception* (pp. 265–276). New York: Wiley.

Kanizsa, G. (1979). *Organization in vision.* New York: Praeger.

Koffka, K. (1935). *Principles of Gestalt psychology.* New York: Harcourt.

Marr, D. (1981). *Vision.* San Francisco: Freeman.

Massaro, D. (1986). *Speech perception by ear and eye: A paradigm for psychological inquiry.* Hillsdale, NJ: Erlbaum.

Mill, J. S. (1978). Bailey on Berkeley's theory of vision. In J. M. Robson and F. E. Sparshott (Eds.), *Essays on philosophy and the classics by John Stuart Mill* (pp. 245–270). Toronto: University of Toronto Press. (Original work published 1842)

Mill, J. S. (1843). *System of logic.* London: Longmans.

Niall, K. K. (1987). Perspectives yet unseen. *Journal of Mathematical Psychology, 31*, 429–438.

Shepard, R. N. (1984). Ecological constraints on internal representation: Resonant kinematics of perceiving, imagining, thinking, and dreaming. *Psychological Review, 91*, 417–447.

Skyrms, B. (1975). *Choice and chance* (2nd ed.). Belmont, CA: Wadsworth.

Witkin, A. P., & Tenenbaum, J. M. (1983). On the role of structure in vision. In J. Beck, B. Hope, & A. Rosenfeld (Eds.), *Human and machine vision* (pp. 481–543). New York: Academic Press.

CHAPTER 4

INTEGRALITY VERSUS SEPARABILITY OF STIMULUS DIMENSIONS:
FROM AN EARLY CONVERGENCE OF EVIDENCE TO A PROPOSED THEORETICAL BASIS

ROGER N. SHEPARD

Noting the importance that W. R. Garner has long attached to the concepts of integrality and separability of stimulus dimensions and to the use of converging operations for establishing such psychological concepts, this chapter first reviews two types of converging evidence that originally pointed toward the integral–separable distinction: (a) evidence that stimulus similarities implicate the Euclidean metric for stimuli that differ along psychologically integral dimensions (such as lightness and saturation of colors) and something closer to the city-block metric for stimuli that differ along psychologically separable dimensions (such as size and orientation of shapes); and (b) evidence that classification learning and performance are determined more by overall similarities for stimuli differing along integral dimensions and by dimensional structure for stimuli differing along separable dimensions. Drawing on a recently proposed theory of generalization, the integral or separable character of the relation between dimensions is considered as a possible accommodation

Preparation of this chapter was supported by National Science Foundation Grant BNS 85-11685. The final version of this chapter has benefited from a number of helpful suggestions made by Gregory Lockhead.

to the correlational structure of natural kinds in the world in which we have evolved.

Among Wendell Garner's contributions to psychological science, two must surely be counted among his most influential: (a) his advocacy of *converging operations* to establish general psychological concepts (Garner, 1954, p. 223; Garner, Hake, & Eriksen, 1956), and (b) his central role in sharpening and consolidating the distinction between *integrality* and *separability* of stimulus dimensions (Garner, 1970, 1974; Garner & Felfoldy, 1970). Indeed, the establishment of the integrality–separability distinction has, according to Garner, been his "best example of the formal use of converging operations" (Garner, 1974, p. 187). In this chapter, I propose, first, to review some of the early convergence of evidence that initially directed my own thinking toward a distinction of this kind and, then, to outline how a recent cognitive theory of generalization (Shepard, 1987) may offer a theoretical basis for such a distinction.

The converging operations that Garner has taken to establish the distinction between integrality and separability can be grouped into those concerning the metric of the stimulus space and those concerning performance in various classification tasks. To quote Garner's (1974) succinct summary, "In direct similarity scaling, integral dimensions produce interstimulus relations with a Euclidean metric; separable dimensions produce interstimulus relations with a city-block metric. In perceptual classification, stimulus sets defined by integral dimensions are classified primarily in relation to similarities; sets defined by separable dimensions are classified in relation to dimensional structure" (p. 120).

EARLY CONVERGENCE OF EVIDENCE CONCERNING THE METRIC OF THE STIMULUS SPACE

Richardson (1938) provided an early indication of how a Euclidean color space might be constructed from judgments of similarities between presented colors. A neural mechanism that Householder and Landahl (1945) later proposed for stimulus comparison implicated, however, a different kind of stimulus space in which the psychological distance between two stimuli is given simply by the sum of the differences between them on the underlying dimensions of the space rather than by the square root of the sum of the squares of those differences (as in a Euclidean space). The first empirical evidence to force serious consideration of these two different psychological metrics, Euclidean and "city-block," then emerged from four doctoral dissertations completed between 1950 and 1955.

The first was Fred Attneave's 1950 dissertation at Stanford (see Attneave, 1950). It was, in fact, this path-breaking work that inspired me, as a Stanford undergraduate, to pursue a career in psychological science and, in particular, to explore the possibility of representing stimuli as points in a "psychological space"

(Shepard, 1989). Using converging operations of subjective judgments of similarity and objective measures of generalization (namely, the frequencies with which the response associated with each stimulus was made to each other stimulus during identification learning), Attneave obtained evidence favoring the city-block over the Euclidean metric (Attneave, 1950). Significantly, Attneave's stimuli were not colors but shapes differing along what are now termed separable dimensions, such as size and lightness.

By the following year, however, Warren Torgerson, in his own 1951 dissertation (which developed the first satisfactory numerical method of multidimensional scaling; see Torgerson, 1952), had obtained good fits with the Euclidean metric (Torgerson, 1951, 1958 [Chapter 11]). Torgerson's similarity data were, however, for nine shades of red varying along what we now call (following Lockhead, 1966, 1972) "integral" dimensions of lightness and saturation. Similarly Messick, in a 1954 dissertation (see Messick, 1956), obtained good Euclidean fits to two further sets of similarity data, collected and analyzed in different ways for those same colors.

Then, in a 1955 Yale dissertation, also using Torgerson's nine shades of red, I showed that objective measures of generalization during identification learning were, to a good approximation, exponential decay functions of the Euclidean distances between those colors in a stimulus space constructed (by multidimensional scaling) from those same generalization data (Shepard, 1955, 1958). The striking agreement among the four spatial configurations (reproduced in Shepard, 1958) obtained for these same colors by different researchers using different methods attests to the power of converging operations.

It was Attneave, however, who first set us on the path toward the integrality–separability distinction when he noted, concerning the Euclidean and city-block hypotheses, that "the former assumes one frame of reference to be as good as any other, whereas the latter implies a unique set of psychological axes" (Attneave, 1950, p. 555). The unique psychological axes, he suggested, correspond to the dimensions of the stimuli that the perceiver finds "obvious" (Attneave, 1950, p. 554).

Torgerson (1958), while agreeing that Attneave's city-block model "might be appropriate in those situations where the different dimensions are obvious and compelling" (p. 292), argued that if, as in the case of colors, "separate dimensions are not obvious, the subject might be more likely to judge the over-all difference directly" and that "in this event, we would expect the Euclidean model to show more promise" (p. 254).

Torgerson (1958) then raised the possibility that "in many situations, the subject's judgment falls somewhere in between" the Euclidean and city-block metrics (pp. 292–293). For such intermediate cases, Torgerson proposed a more general metric (or "spatial model") of the form

$$d_{ij} = \left[\sum_k | x_{ik} - x_{jk} |^r \right]^{1/r}. \tag{1}$$

This model specifies how the distance between two stimuli, i and j, depends on the absolute differences, $|x_{ik} - x_{jk}|$, between those two stimuli on each dimension k (Torgerson, 1958). This more general metric, already then known to mathematicians as the *Minkowski r-metric*, reduces to the Euclidean metric when $r = 2$ and to the city-block metric when $r = 1$, and yields intermediate metrics when $1 < r < 2$ (as well as other metrics when $r > 2$). In the 1950s, however, there was no method for fitting non-Euclidean models to data or for determining what the most appropriate metric might be for a set of data.

Direct Tests of the Implications of the Euclidean and City-Block Metrics

One approach taken to the problem of determining the form of the metric was to seek direct evidence about the locus of stimuli having equal perceived similarity to (or distance from) a given stimulus in the parameter space of the stimuli. Equation 1 (together with the assumption that the psychophysical mapping is suitably continuous and differentiable) implies that such a contour should approximate an ellipse if the psychological metric is Euclidean, a diamond if it is city-block, and an intermediate, rounded diamond if $1 < r < 2$ (see Figure 1 in Shepard, 1964a).

For stimuli chosen to vary along dimensions that seemed especially "obvious," "compelling," "analyzable," or (as we now say) "separable"—namely, circles, each of a specified size with a single radial line drawn at a specified angle—both subjective judgments of relative similarity and objective measures of generalization during identification learning proved to be more consistent with the diamond-shaped equal-similarity contours of the city-block metric than with the elliptical contours of the Euclidean metric (Shepard, 1964a). Figure 1 presents the results for a small illustrative subset of these relative similarity data. Among stimuli that differed along only one of the two dimensions (size or angle) people uniformly selected a stimulus that closely matched a standard stimulus, S, on that variable dimension (Figure 1A). Among stimuli that differed along both dimensions (size and angle) in a perfectly correlated manner, however, people variously selected the stimulus matching S in size, the stimulus matching S in angle, or any stimulus falling between these two (Figure 1B). As Attneave (1950) had discovered using different methods and different stimulus dimensions, judgments of the similarities among these highly analyzable stimuli were based more on the psychologically unique dimensions (size and angle, here) than on direct Euclidean distances between the stimuli.

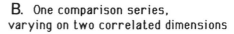

A. Two comparison series,
each varying on one dimension

B. One comparison series,
varying on two correlated dimensions

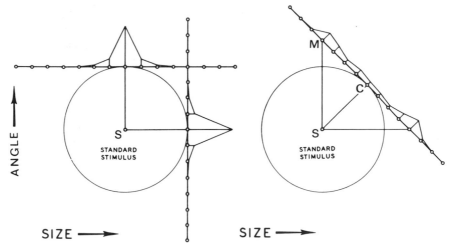

Figure 1.   Distributions of choices of stimuli, as most similar to a standard stimulus
S, from a linear comparison series differing only in size or in angle (A) and
from a linear comparison series differing along both dimensions together
(B). (From Shepard, 1964b, p. 272. Adapted by permission.)

If the psychological metric had been Euclidean—as might be expected, say,
for colors—the metric would have been invariant under rotation. A similar, uni-
modal distribution of choices would then be expected for all such linear test series,
regardless of their orientations around the standard stimulus, S (Shepard, 1964a,
p. 80). Correspondingly, Shepard and Chang (1963, p. 101) noted that people
"immediately say of two triangles—one large and black, the other small and
white—that they differ in two respects (namely, size and color). But, when . . .
shown two colors . . . they typically report simply that the two colors are 'different
shades of red,' or that one looks like 'tomato soup' while the other is more 'rose
colored'."

Many experiments have since distinguished between integral and separable
dimensions on the basis of whether a stimulus (S) is more readily classified with
a stimulus (like C in Figure 1B) that is *close* to it in the Euclidean metric or with
one (like M in Figure 1B) that *matches* it on some dimension. Such experiments
have contributed considerable support for Garner's conclusion that "stimulus sets
defined by integral dimensions are classified primarily in relation to similarities;
sets defined by separable dimensions are classified in relation to dimensional
structure" (Garner, 1974, p. 120).

The first direct comparison between the highly analyzable circle-with-radius
stimuli used by Shepard (1964a) and the more unitary shades of red that Torgerson,

Messick, and Shepard each used was carried out by Hyman and Well (1967). They collected ratings of dissimilarity in a manner designed to minimize the fluctuations of attention between separable dimensions suggested by the data reported by Shepard (1964a) and by Shepard, Hovland, and Jenkins (1961). Hyman and Well's (1967) results still favored the city-block metric for the shapes differing along separable dimensions of size and angle and favored the Euclidean metric for the colors differing along integral dimensions of lightness and saturation (also see Hyman & Well, 1968).

Estimations of Minkowski r-Values Through Multidimensional Scaling

A second approach taken to the problem of determining the appropriate metric was to seek a method of multidimensional scaling that did not presuppose either a particular form for the relation between the similarity data and distances in psychological space or a Euclidean metric for that space. The result was the ''nonmetric'' type of multidimensional scaling developed and refined at the Bell Telephone Laboratories by Shepard (1962) and Kruskal (1964). This approach used iterative methods to adjust the coordinates of the points to attain a best fit between the similarity data and distances computed in accordance with whatever metric was specified—essentially ''by appropriately altering the subroutine that computes the distances from the coordinates during each iteration'' (Shepard, 1962, p. 244). The metric yielding the smallest departure from a perfect fit might then be taken as the psychological metric of the stimulus space.

Kruskal (1964) first illustrated this possibility in a reanalysis of Ekman's (1954) data on the perceived similarities among 14 colors differing in hue—data for which an excellent fit in a two-dimensional Euclidean space had already been obtained by Shepard (1962, p. 236). As might be expected, on the assumption that the dimensions of color are integral, Kruskal obtained the smallest departure from good fit (''stress'') when the parameter, r, of the Minkowski r-metric was set at a value (viz., 2.5) that was closer to the Euclidean value of 2 than to the city-block value of 1.

In anticipation of this presentation in honor of Wendell Garner, and of a preceding presentation in honor of Fred Attneave (Shepard, 1989), I recently attempted to estimate, in this way, the goodnesses of fit of different Minkowski r-metrics to the data originally collected by several early researchers, including Attneave, Torgerson, and myself. These reanalyses use the multidimensional scaling program KYST (an acronym for Kruskal, Young, Shepard, and Torgerson). To avoid ''degeneracies'' (Shepard, 1974), a quasi-metric option was selected that seeks to minimize deviations simultaneously from a merely monotonic and from a quadratic function. (As a consequence of the additional, quasi-metric constraint, the residual stress values are higher than they would have been with a purely nonmetric analysis.)

For the non-Euclidean cases of interest here, the gradient method used to minimize stress proved to be more seriously limited than I had previously recognized (compare Shepard, 1974). For $r \neq 2$, the method generally failed to rotate the configuration into the orientation yielding minimum stress. Worse, Hubert and Arabie (1988) have recently shown that when $r \sim 1$, merely local minima become so prevalent that the globally optimum configuration is unlikely to be achieved unless special procedures are used to construct each starting configuration. Accordingly, for $r \sim 1$, I had to try many starting configurations that I had reason to believe were close, in intrinsic structure, to the optimum configuration and, for each of these, to try many different starting orientations, separately, for values of $r < 2$ and values of $r > 2$. The final results, although not guaranteed to achieve the exact optimum for every value of r and set of data, are sufficient, I believe, to support some useful conclusions.

The plots relating the residual stress values to the various Minkowski r-values tried are displayed in Figure 2. In the special case of two dimensions, the city-block metric ($r = 1$) is necessarily identical, except for a 45° rotation and uniform size scaling, to the "dominance" or "supremum" metric ($r = \infty$). Therefore, the curve relating stress to r value is expected to approach exactly the same value of stress as $r \to \infty$ as it attains for $r = 1$ (see Shepard, 1974). Indeed, the plots for the two-dimensional case should exhibit a (skewed) symmetry in which a minimum stress attained for any finite value of r greater than 2 is approximated by a corresponding minimum stress for some value of r between 2 and 1.

The results for stimuli differing along *separable* dimensions of size and lightness (Attneave, 1950) or of size and angle (Shepard, 1964a) supported the conclusions that the original investigators had reached on the basis of quite different analyses. For each such set of data, whether based on subjective judgments of similarity (Panel A in Figure 2) or on objective measures of generalization during identification learning (Panels B and C), minimum stress was attained with $r = 1$. Indeed, the Euclidean value of $r = 2$ uniformly yielded maximum stress. Moreover, as expected, for the non-Euclidean metrics ($r \neq 1$), minimum stress was achieved only when the configuration was oriented so that the psychologically salient dimensions—of size and lightness or of size and angle—were aligned with the coordinate axes. The marked drop in stress as r approached 1 in each case cannot, of course, be attributed to a failure (of the sort discussed by Hubert & Arabie, 1988) to obtain lowest stress configurations for $r = 1$. This drop thus favors the city-block metric over any metric with $r > 1$.

Nearly opposite results were obtained for stimuli differing with respect to the more *integral* dimensions of color, including those of hue (Ekman, 1954) and of lightness and saturation (Shepard, 1955, 1958; Torgerson, 1951, 1958). As

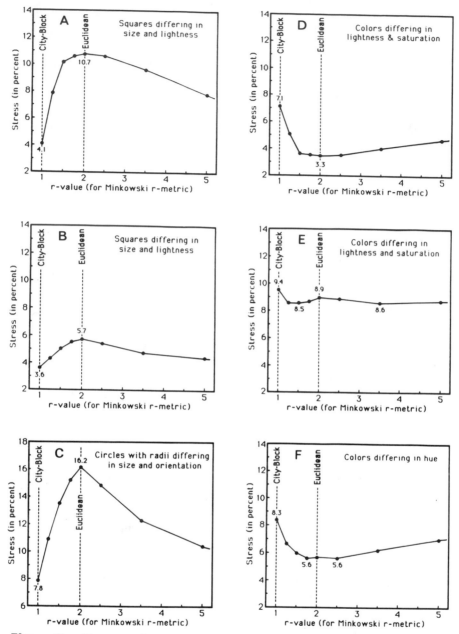

Figure 2. Departure of multidimensional scaling solutions from perfect fit ("stress"), plotted as a function of the Minkowski r values tried for six sets of data—obtained for stimuli differing along dimensions presumed to be separable (A, B, and C) or integral (D, E, and F), and based on subjective judgments of similarity (A, D, and F) or objective frequencies of generalization errors during identification learning (B, C, and E). (Based on the author's reanalyses of data from experiments described in Attneave, 1950; Ekman, 1954; Shepard, 1958, 1964a; Torgerson, 1958.)

expected for such relatively integral dimensions, the city-block metric ($r = 1$) did not lead to minimum stress but, in every case, to maximum stress. And, although minimum stress was not always attained at exactly $r = 2$, it was generally attained at r values close to (and on either side of) that Euclidean value.

Here, though, we confront the possibility, raised by Hubert and Arabie (1988), that higher stresses obtained as r approaches 1 may be artifactual, arising from entrapment in one of the many suboptimal stationary configurations when $r = 1$. Alternative methods of the sort proposed by Hubert and Arabie (1988) may soon permit a check on this possibility. In the meantime, two considerations suggest that the results obtained here are not far from the truth. First, the present reanalyses, although applied in the same way to all the sets of data, led to results for the colors that differed markedly from the results for the more analyzable stimuli. Furthermore, in unpublished applications of this kind of analysis to the data reported by Hyman and Well (1967), Hyman has obtained results for the shades of red and for the circle-with-radius stimuli essentially like those shown in the present Figure 2 (personal communication, May 22, 1989). Also suggestive was a relatively smaller dependence of obtained stress on the orientation of the configuration (for $r = 2$) in the case of color stimuli.

Provisionally, then, these reanalyses indicate that pure integrality is more or less approximated, if perhaps never strictly achieved. Some directions through the stimulus space (such as those of lightness and saturation—see Attneave, 1950, p. 521; Shepard & Chang, 1963, p. 102), although not fully separable, may always be somewhat more psychologically salient or preferred. Such a possibility is consistent with the conjectures of Torgerson (1958, p. 292), Shepard (1964a, p. 80), Lockhead (1972), Garner (1970, p. 354; 1974, p. 27), Foard and Kemler Nelson (1984), and Grau and Kemler Nelson (1988, p. 369) that integrality and separability may define a continuum rather than a dichotomy.

Cheng and Pachella (1984) have argued that results previously taken to support a Euclidean metric may be an artifact arising because investigators made incorrect assumptions about which directions through a stimulus space correspond to the true psychological dimensions (see also Pachella, Somers, & Hardzinski, 1981). The present reanalyses, however, have not depended on any assumption about which are the psychologically significant directions through the space. Yet the obtained patterns of results were consistently different for stimuli taken to exemplify integrality than for stimuli taken to exemplify separability.

Tversky and Gati (1982) have claimed that for highly separable dimensions, the attainment of a best fit can require r values even smaller than 1 (entailing a violation of the triangle inequality). Such a possibility is also consistent with the earlier evidence for concave equal similarity contours—at least when the data are averaged from individuals in different states of attention—reported in Shepard (1964a). This possibility is not further pursued here; the KYST program tended to "blow up," yielding numerous infinities, when solutions were attempted with $r < 1$.

Finally, Nosofsky (1985, 1989) has reported that with stimuli having high mutual similarities, asymptotic discrimination performance is better fit by the Euclidean than by the city-block metric, even when the stimuli differ along separable dimensions. Asymptotic discrimination may thus be determined by a Gaussian process, which does implicate the Euclidean metric. A different cognitive process seems to underlie generalization and similarity assessment between discriminable stimuli, however. This latter process appears to implicate a non-Euclidean metric for separable dimensions (Shepard, 1986, 1987).

EARLY CONVERGENCE OF EVIDENCE CONCERNING CLASSIFICATION PERFORMANCE

The evidence that Garner himself amassed in support of the distinction between integrality and separability has primarily come from classification experiments (Garner, 1974). These experiments have yielded data of two principal kinds: (a) the times people take to complete various constrained classification tasks (as exemplified by Garner & Felfoldy, 1970; Gottwald & Garner, 1975) and (b) the stimulus groupings produced by people in free classification (as exemplified by Handel & Imai, 1972; Imai & Garner, 1968).

Through such data, Garner and his co-workers established the following facts (as summarized by Garner, 1974, p. 118; Garner & Felfoldy, 1970, p. 238): (a) Speed of classification with respect to one dimension is markedly increased or decreased by, respectively, correlated or uncorrelated variation on an irrelevant dimension if the two dimensions are integral, but speed is largely unaffected if the two dimensions are separable; (b) free classifications tend to be based on the overall similarities of stimuli differing along integral dimensions, but on single dimensions of stimuli differing along separable dimensions; (c) individuals manifest stronger dimensional preferences for separable than for integral dimensions; and (d) such preferences are more affected by manipulations of discriminability for integral than for separable dimensions. All of these facts can be understood as consequences of the single, already quoted principle that "stimulus sets defined by integral dimensions are classified primarily in relation to similarities; sets defined by separable dimensions are classified in relation to dimensional structure" (Garner, 1974, p. 120).

The evidence first explicitly interpreted in this way was, I believe, the evidence from the classification learning experiments of Shepard, Hovland, and Jenkins (1961) and Shepard and Chang (1963). For what we then referred to as "unitary" or "unanalyzable" stimuli—specifically, eight of the already mentioned nine red colors differing along integral dimensions of lightness and saturation—Shepard and Chang (1963) obtained the following result: The different

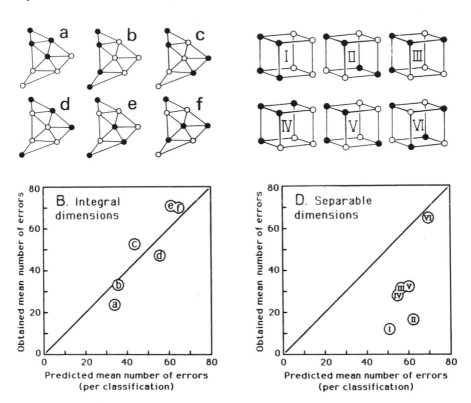

A. Six classifications of eight stimuli differing in two integral dimensions: lightness (vert.) & saturation (horiz.)

C. Six classifications of eight stimuli differing in three separable dimensions (represented by the axes of the cube)

Figure 3.   Predictions of errors during classification learning from pairwise errors during identification learning. Plots A and B are for stimuli differing on two integral dimensions, and Plots C and D are for stimuli differing on three separable dimensions. The six learned classifications are indicated (in A and C) by the (black vs. white) coloring of the points corresponding, in the stimulus space, to the stimuli assigned to the two responses. (Plots A and B are adapted from Shepard & Chang, 1963, pp. 97, 99; Plots C and D are adapted from Shepard, Hovland, & Jenkins, 1961, pp. 4, 27. Copyright 1963 and 1961 by the American Psychological Association. Adapted by permission.)

frequencies of errors made during the learning of different classifications of these eight stimuli into two subsets (Figure 3A) could be largely predicted from the pairwise identification error frequencies previously found for these same colors by Shepard (1955, 1958; see Figure 3B, where 78% of the variance is accounted for). For eight analyzable stimuli taking on one of two values on each of three highly separable dimensions (Figure 3C), however, Shepard, Hovland, and Jenkins

(1961; also Chang & Shepard, 1964) found that such a prediction breaks down in just the way to be expected if individuals attended only to those dimensions that were relevant for the given classification (see Figure 3D, where only 41% of the variance is accounted for).

The Shepard, Hovland, and Jenkins study also yielded other kinds of evidence converging toward an integral–separable distinction. Only for analyzable stimuli did individuals adopt recoding strategies that markedly affected the patterns of their errors in both identification and classification learning (Shepard et al., 1961, pp. 35–38; see also Torgerson, 1965, p. 383). Recoding strategies also enabled individuals to realize powerful positive transfer of learning to subsequent classification problems of the same abstract structural type, even when the concrete dimensions of the stimuli were entirely changed (Shepard et al., 1961, pp. 24, 33–35).

Lockhead and his associates then added significant evidence that stimuli differing along integral dimensions tend not to be analyzed or recoded, but to be processed as unitary wholes. They did this, moreover, for tasks both of identification (Lockhead, 1966, 1970, 1972; Monahan & Lockhead, 1977) and of classification (Lockhead & King, 1977).

Since 1985, the modeling of identification and classification data, begun 30 years earlier (by Shepard, 1955, 1958; Shepard & Chang, 1963; Shepard et al., 1961), has been carried to unprecedented heights of generality and quantitative precision by Robert Nosofsky (e.g., 1985, 1986, 1987, 1989). Nosofsky's success has been achieved by collecting extensive data under asymptotic conditions of learning and by extending the type of model originally explored by Shepard (1955, 1957) and by Shepard and Chang (1963) to take quantitative account of selective attention (of the sort that emerged in the studies by Shepard, 1964a, and Shepard et al., 1961). By means of his "general context model," Nosofsky obtained fits to data that are appreciably tighter (e.g., 98% of the variance accounted for) than those obtained in the earlier studies (exemplified here by Figure 3B), and he did so even for stimuli differing along separable dimensions (in contrast with the breakdown of such prediction illustrated in Figure 3D).

TOWARD A THEORETICAL BASIS FOR THE INTEGRAL–SEPARABLE DISTINCTION

Garner has suggested that the source of psychological principles is ultimately to be found in the "stimulus world" (Garner, 1970, 1974):

> The fact that we are psychologists and thus use people in our experiments does not mean that we can only learn about people and nothing at all about the stimulus world to which people react. I think that dimensional integrality is a stimulus concept . . . If, however, it is a stimulus concept, then sooner or later shouldn't we be able to specify whether a pair of dimen-

sions is integral or separable without having to run through the set of converging operations? My answer is, yes, sooner or later, even though not now. (Garner, 1974, p. 187)

The remainder of the present chapter considers how the convergence of evidence between the psychological metric and classificatory performance might reflect an enduring fact about the world that humans and other animals may have internalized through natural selection.

A recently proposed cognitive theory of generalization (Shepard, 1987) is based on the following simple idea: Generalization is the result not of a failure of sensory discrimination among stimuli, but of a cognitive process of integration over all hypotheses about the disposition, in psychological space, of the set of stimuli having the same consequence as some particular stimulus. Such a set constitutes a *consequential region* in the individual's psychological space. Given that an individual discovers a novel stimulus to have an important consequence, the problem of generalization then reduces to one of probabilistic geometry: If a point in stimulus space is discovered to fall within a consequential region (which is of otherwise unknown location, size, and shape in that space), what is the conditional probability that any other specified point of the space also falls within that consequential region?

According to this theory of generalization, the precise way in which the conditional probability should fall off with distance from a training stimulus (in psychological space) depends on the particular assumption an individual makes about the probability distribution for size of a consequential region in psychological space—that is, for the range of stimulus variation within the unknown consequential region. Clearly, generalization will extend less widely for an individual who assumes a priori that the relevant consequential region is likely to be very small (that is, to include only stimuli that are highly similar to the original training stimulus).

The shape of the fall-off of conditional probability (and hence of generalization) with distance turns out, however, to be relatively independent of the probability density function, $p(s)$, assumed for size, s, of the consequential region. Figure 4 displays the derived generalization functions for the one-dimensional case. The small shaded insets show six quite different assumed probability density functions for $p(s)$—including functions that are constant or rectangular (Panel A), decreasing (Panels B and C), increasing (Panel D), and increasing and then decreasing (Panels E and F). Yet, when the integration over all possible sizes of consequential region is carried out, the theory yields generalization functions (the dotted curves) that are all monotonically decreasing, concave upward, and quite close to a simple exponential decay function (the smooth curve in each panel).

But how does the conditional probability that a test stimulus falls in the same consequential region as the training stimulus decay in a psychological space of two or more dimensions? Two cases must be distinguished. The first case is

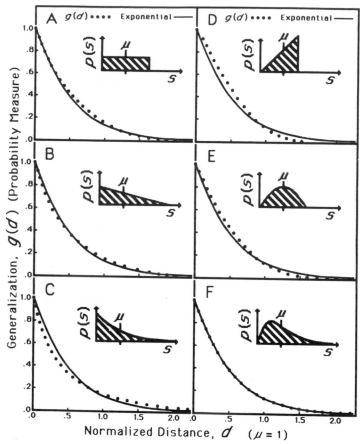

Figure 4.   Six theoretical functions, *g(d)*, relating probability of generalization to distance in psychological space. The dotted curves were derived by substituting the different probability density functions, *p(s)*, shown in the shaded insets, and integrating over all possible sizes *s*. The smooth curves are all the same simple exponential decay function. (From Shepard, 1987, p. 1320. Copyright 1987 by the AAAS. Adapted by permission.)

that in which an individual assumes that the possible extensions of the consequential region, along orthogonal dimensions of the stimulus space, are perfectly correlated. In this case, an individual who assumed the consequential region to be square (or circular) would still assume that the region might be of any overall size and that it might be centered anywhere in the space, but the individual would assume that the consequential region is not a flattened or elongated rectangle (or ellipse). In short, only the sizes and shapes indicated in heavier lines along the diagonal in the appropriate array in Figure 5 would be considered possible for the consequential region. The second case is that in which an individual assumes that

A   B

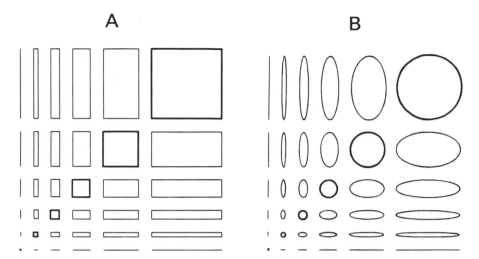

Figure 5. Illustration of the possible extensions of a consequential region along the underlying dimensions of a stimulus space for a consequential region whose shape is assumed to be rectangular (A) or elliptical (B).

the possible extensions of the consequential region along the orthogonal dimensions of the stimulus space are uncorrelated. That is, the individual assumes that the consequential region could have (in addition to any location in the space) any of the sizes and shapes depicted in the appropriate array in Figure 5. Under a wide variety of assumptions that an individual might still make about the distributions of possible shapes and extensions of the unknown region, integration over all such possibilities leads to the following remarkably uniform results.

First, just as in the one-dimensional case (Figure 4), the conditional probability taken to underlie generalization falls off with distance between stimuli in the stimulus space in accordance with a monotonically decreasing concave upward function. Moreover, the function more and more closely approximates the simple exponential decay function as the "maximum entropy" condition is approached in which an individual has no prior knowledge about the possible location, size, and shape of the consequential region—and in which $p(s)$ accordingly approaches the Erlang probability density function, as in Panel F of Figure 4. In support of this deduction, measures of generalization do fall off approximately exponentially with distance in the space recovered, by multidimensional scaling, from the generalization data themselves (see Figure 1 in Shepard, 1987).

Second, contours of equal conditional probability are approximately elliptical regardless of the individual's assumption about the shape of the consequential region, provided that the individual assumes a perfect positive correlation between the possible extensions of the consequential region along the underlying dimensions of the space. Moreover, the approximation becomes exact under the condition in which the individual has no prior knowledge about the orientation of the consequential region in the space (see Figures 3a and 3b in Shepard, 1987). Elliptical contours are the signature of the Euclidean metric.

Third, equal-probability contours are approximately diamond-shaped regardless of the individual's assumption about the shape of the consequential region, provided that the individual assumes a zero correlation between the possible extensions of the consequential region along the underlying dimensions of the space. Moreover, the approximation becomes exact under the condition in which the individual otherwise has no prior knowledge about the distribution of possible extensions of the consequential region (see Figures 3c and 3d in Shepard, 1987). Diamond-shaped contours are the signature of the city-block metric.

Fourth, equal-probability contours take on a concave, star-like shape if the individual assumes a negative correlation between the orthogonal extensions of the consequential region. Some data have pointed toward such a possibility (Shepard, 1964a; Tversky & Gati, 1982). In this case, dimensions might be not just separable but, to some degree, psychologically competitive.

Finally, an assumption of an intermediate correlation between the orthogonal extensions of the consequential region entails an intermediate metric (for example, with $1 < r < 2$). The theory thus provides for a graded series of cases between perfect integrality and perfect separability.

Possibly, then, the degree of integrality of any two dimensions arises as an accommodation of the perceiver to an enduring property of the world. Integral dimensions may be those in which there has been a positive correlation between the ranges of variation of stimuli associated with important consequences. Separable dimensions may be those in which there has been little or no such correlation—in which, say, knowledge of the range of sizes of objects of a natural kind has provided no information about the range of lightnesses or orientations of objects of that kind.

The proposed theory of generalization points to a deep, nonarbitrary source for the empirically established convergences (a) between the Euclidean metric and similarity-based classification performances and (b) between the city-block metric and dimension-based classification performances. To the degree that the extensions of consequential regions along underlying dimensions of psychological space have been positively correlated in the world, candidate regions varying in size but not in elongation will have become most heavily weighted. Individuals will then tend to classify objects on the basis of their proximities in psychological space. Moreover, integration over all such nonelongated "hypotheses" will necessarily yield an approximately Euclidean metric. But, to the degree that the extensions of consequential regions along dimensions have been uncorrelated, candidate regions varying in their relative elongations along those dimensions will become heavily weighted. Individuals will then tend to classify objects on the basis of one dimension or another, separately. Moreover, integration over all of these variously elongated "hypotheses" will necessarily yield an approximately city-block metric. In conclusion, then, we may be approaching the day when, in Garner's (1974) words, we will yet "be able to specify whether a pair of dimensions is integral or separable without having to run through the set of converging operations" (p. 187).

References

Attneave, F. (1950). Dimensions of similarity. *American Journal of Psychology, 63*, 546–554.

Chang, J.-J., & Shepard, R. N. (1964). Meaningfulness in classification learning with pronounceable trigrams. *Journal of Verbal Learning and Verbal Behavior, 3*, 85–90.

Cheng, P. W., & Pachella, R. G. (1984). A psychophysical approach to dimensional separability. *Cognitive Psychology, 16*, 279–304.

Ekman, G. (1954). Dimensions of color vision. *Journal of Psychology, 38*, 467–474.

Foard, D. F., & Kemler Nelson, D. G. (1984). Holistic and analytic modes of processing: The multiple determinants of perceptual analysis. *Journal of Experimental Psychology: General, 113*, 94–111.

Garner, W. R. (1954). Context effects and the validity of loudness scales. *Journal of Experimental Psychology, 48*, 218–224.

Garner, W. R. (1970). The stimulus in information processing. *American Psychologist, 25*, 350–358.

Garner, W. R. (1974). *The processing of information and structure*. Potomac, MD: Erlbaum.

Garner, W. R., & Felfoldy, G. L. (1970). Integrality of stimulus dimensions in various types of information processing. *Cognitive Psychology, 1*, 225–229.

Garner, W. R., Hake, H. W., & Eriksen, C. W. (1956). Operationism and the concept of perception. *Psychological Review, 63*, 149–159.

Gottwald, R. L., & Garner, W. R. (1975). Filtering and condensation tasks with integral and separable dimensions. *Perception and Psychophysics, 18*, 26–28.

Grau, J. W., & Kemler Nelson, D. G. (1988). The distinction between integral and separable dimensions: Evidence for the integrality of pitch and loudness. *Journal of Experimental Psychology: General, 117*, 347–370.

Handel, S., & Imai, S. (1972). The free classification of analyzable and unanalyzable stimuli. *Perception and Psychophysics, 12*, 109–116.

Householder, A. S., & Landahl, H. D. (1945). *Mathematical biophysics of the central nervous system*. Bloomington, IN: Principia Press.

Hubert, L., & Arabie, P. (1988). Relying on necessary conditions for optimization: Unidimensional scaling and some extensions. In H.-H. Bock (Ed.), *Classification and related methods of data analysis* (pp. 463–472). Amsterdam: North-Holland.

Hyman, R., & Well, A. (1967). Judgments of similarity and spatial models. *Perception and Psychophysics, 2*, 233–248.

Hyman, R., & Well, A. (1968). Perceptual separability and spatial models. *Perception and Psychophysics, 3*, 161–165.

Imai, S., & Garner, W. R. (1968). Structure in perceptual classification. *Psychonomic Monograph Supplements, 2*(9, Whole No. 25), 153–172.

Kruskal, J. B. (1964). Multidimensional scaling by optimizing goodness of fit to a nometric hypothesis. *Psychometrika, 29*, 1–27.

Lockhead, G. R. (1966). Effects of dimensional redundancy on visual discrimination. *Journal of Experimental Psychology, 72,* 95–104.

Lockhead, G. R. (1970). Identification and the form of multidimensional discrimination space. *Journal of Experimental Psychology, 85,* 1–10.

Lockhead, G. R. (1972). Processing dimensional stimuli: A note. *Psychological Review, 79,* 410–419.

Lockhead, G. R., & King, M. C. (1977). Classifying integral stimuli. *Journal of Experimental Psychology: Human Perception and Performance, 3,* 436–443.

Messick, S. J. (1956). An empirical evaluation of multidimensional successive intervals. *Psychometrika, 21,* 367–375.

Monahan, J. S., & Lockhead, G. R. (1977). Identification of integral stimuli. *Journal of Experimental Psychology: General, 106,* 94–110.

Nosofsky, R. M. (1985). Overall similarity and the identification of separable-dimension stimuli: A choice model analysis. *Perception and Psychophysics, 38,* 415–432.

Nosofsky, R. M. (1986). Attention, similarity, and the identification–categorization relationship. *Journal of Experimental Psychology: General, 114,* 39–37.

Nosofsky, R. M. (1987). Attention and learning processes in the identification and categorization of integral stimuli. *Journal of Experimental Psychology: Learning, Memory, and Cognition, 13,* 87–108.

Nosofsky, R. M. (1989). Further tests of an exemplar-similarity approach to relating identification and categorization. *Perception and Psychophysics, 45,* 279–290.

Pachella, R. G., Somers, P., & Hardzinski, M. (1981). A psychophysical approach to dimensional integrality. In D. J. Getty & J. H. Howard, Jr. (Eds.), *Auditory and visual pattern recognition* (pp. 107–126). Hillsdale, NJ: Erlbaum.

Richardson, M. W. (1938). Multi-dimensional psychophysics [Abstract]. *Psychological Bulletin, 35,* 659.

Shepard, R. N. (1955). *Stimulus and response generalization during paired-associates learning.* Unpublished doctoral dissertation, Yale University.

Shepard, R. N. (1957). Stimulus and response generalization: A stochastic model relating generalization to distance in psychological space. *Psychometrika, 22,* 325–345.

Shepard, R. N. (1958). Stimulus and response generalization: Tests of a model relating generalization to distance in psychological space. *Journal of Experimental Psychology, 55,* 509–523.

Shepard, R. N. (1962). Analysis of proximities: Multidimensional scaling with an unknown distance function (Parts I & II). *Psychometrika, 27,* 125–140, 219–246.

Shepard, R. N. (1964a). Attention and the metric structure of the stimulus space. *Journal of Mathematical Psychology, 1,* 54–87.

Shepard, R. N. (1964b). On subjectively optimum selection among multiattribute alternatives. In M. Shelley & G. L. Bryan (Eds.), *Human judgment and optimality* (pp. 257–281). New York: Wiley.

Shepard, R. N. (1974). Representation of structure in similarity data: Problems and prospects. *Psychometrika, 39,* 373–421.

Shepard, R. N. (1986). Discrimination and generalization in identification and classification: Comment on Nosofsky. *Journal of Experimental Psychology: General, 115,* 58–61.

Shepard, R.N. (1987). Toward a universal law of generalization for psychological science. *Science, 237,* 1317–1323.

Shepard, R. N. (1989, May). *Two fundamental contributions to cognitive psychology: Dimensions of similarity and morphophoric media.* The Inaugural Fred Attneave Lecture, University of Oregon, Eugene.

Shepard, R. N., & Chang, J.-J. (1963). Stimulus generalization in the learning of classifications. *Journal of Experimental Psychology, 65,* 94–102.

Shepard, R. N., Hovland, H. I., & Jenkins, H. M. (1961). Learning and memorization of classifications. *Psychological Monographs, 75*(13, Whole Number 517).

Torgerson, W. S. (1951). *A theoretical and empirical investigation of multidimensional scaling.* Unpublished doctoral dissertation, Princeton University [Educational Testing Service Research Bulletin, 1951].

Torgerson, W. S. (1952). Multidimensional scaling: I. Theory and method. *Psychometrika, 17*, 401–420.

Torgerson, W. S. (1958). *Theory and methods of scaling.* New York: Wiley.

Torgerson, W. S. (1965). Multidimensional scaling of similarity. *Psychometrika, 30*, 379–393.

Tversky, A., & Gati, I. (1982). Similarity, separability, and the triangle inequality. *Psychological Review, 89*, 123–154.

CHAPTER 5

PATTERN GOODNESS AND PATTERN RECOGNITION

IRVING BIEDERMAN, H. JOHN HILTON,
AND JOHN E. HUMMEL

Pattern goodness, or pragnanz, *has been a subject of study and theorizing for over half a century, but its role in vision remains uncertain. The traditional theoretical dispute as to whether goodness reflects a tendency for perception to derive the simplest interpretation of the stimulus versus the most frequently occurring pattern in the environment is probably unresolvable in the absence of a theory that defines what a stimulus is (particularly one projected from a three-dimensional object) so that its likelihood can be determined, and the manner in which constraints toward simplicity can or cannot be regarded as something extractable from the regularities of images. We argue that goodness effects may be epiphenomenal, reflecting the operation of perceptual mechanisms designed to infer a three-dimensional world from parts segmented from a two-dimensional image and to provide descriptions of objects that can be recognized from a novel viewpoint or that are partially occluded. These perceptual mechanisms are scale sensitive and include processes for viewpoint-invariant edge characterization, segmentation, and the activation of shape representations. In terms of a neural net model of object recognition (Hummel & Biederman, in press), goodness ratings may reflect the stability of the pattern of activation over the brief time slices required to achieve binding through temporal firing of activated units.*

This research was supported by Grant 88-0231 from the Air Force Office of Scientific Research to Irving Biederman, a National Sciences and Engineering Research Council of Canada Graduate Fellowship to H. John Hilton, and a National Science Foundation Graduate Fellowship to John E. Hummel.

73

About a quarter of a century ago, W. R. Garner addressed a hallowed but neglected problem in perceptual psychology: pattern goodness. Given an ambiguous pattern, observers tended to interpret it in a way that maximized its simplicity and symmetry. The Gestaltists termed pattern goodness *pragnanz*. Their demonstrations were appreciated for decades by perceptual psychologists, but little acceptable theorizing was developed to account for them. Garner and his students devised a methodology that appeared to hold some promise for the rigorous experimental investigation of pattern goodness.

This chapter is an admittedly speculative and nonexhaustive examination of pragnanz, its study, and its interpretation from the standpoint of the visual system's task of object recognition.

GARNER'S PARADIGM FOR THE STUDY OF PATTERN GOODNESS

In a series of experiments, Garner and Clement (1963) and Handel and Garner (1966) collected goodness ratings ("good" was not defined as part of the instructions to the raters) of a set of patterns produced by placing a dot in the center of five of the nine cells of a 3 × 3 matrix of cells, subject to the constraint that at least one dot occupy every row and column. Highest goodness ratings were obtained from patterns that were invariant over 90° rotations and reflections (R & Rs) of the original. The lowest goodness ratings were obtained from patterns that yielded eight distinguishable alternatives from each of the eight 90° R & Rs. Patterns that had an intermediate number of rotation–reflection (R & R) cohorts produced intermediate goodness ratings. Garner and his collaborators demonstrated that patterns would be spontaneously grouped with their cohorts in R & R subsets. The inverse relation between goodness and the size of the inferred subset of patterns confirmed a speculation of Garner's (1962) that good patterns have few alternatives.

Garner's paradigm led to several studies exploring the effects of pattern goodness on classification reaction times (RTs). Checkosky and Whitlock (1973), Garner and Sutliff (1974), and Pomerantz (1977) found that shorter RTs were associated with the good patterns. The general conclusion that emerged from this effort, with additive factors logic, was that the benefit of good patterns was not at the earliest stages of perception, but rather at a later memory stage.

Questions still remain as to what it was that was measured in Garner's procedure. Garner (1974) sought to exclude global symmetry as a single factor accounting for the goodness ratings, but there can be little doubt that much of the variance of Garner's dot patterns can be captured by symmetry (Palmer, 1977, 1989). Actually, Garner's attempt to discount symmetry is somewhat puzzling, because it provides some basis for understanding a possible underlying mechanism for some of the variance in the goodness ratings. Even then, the equivalence set of 90° planar R & Rs would appear to be much too limited a basis for characterizing shapes in general. To the extent that goodness ratings are worth obtaining at all, it would be preferable to have a measure that would reflect differences in goodness ratings among the infinity of patterns that have no global symmetry. Minimally, a principled basis would be needed to handle the goodness effects of symmetrical three-dimensional objects that may be projecting an asymmetrical image.

WHAT PATTERN GOODNESS IS NOT GOOD FOR

In his 1974 monograph, *The Processing of Information and Structure,* Garner asked (with some jest but with some concern that pattern goodness might be epiphenomenal), "What good is goodness?" (p. 23). We approach this problem by posing the negative form of an answer to that question in this section heading. It is difficult to imagine that the process underlying such a well-behaved phenomenon as goodness ratings evolved solely to serve as a curiosity for psychological experiments. The functional implications of pragnanz have been generally described as providing the basis for pattern grouping or organization and figure–ground segregation, presumably for purposes of pattern recognition. But why should patterns be grouped or segregated according to what was simplest? What role does pragnanz play in object recognition?

Are Simpler Objects More Quickly Identified Than More Complex Objects?

Does the previously mentioned advantage of good patterns on classification RTs (Checkosky & Whitlock, 1974; Garner & Sutliff, 1974; Pomerantz, 1977) generalize directly to the identification of familiar objects? We would assume that, other things being equal, more complex objects would be rated as lower in goodness than objects that cannot be readily parsed into parts. For example, a cylinder joined to a cube might receive lower goodness ratings than the cylinder alone or the cube alone.

Consider the time required to identify an object made up of many parts, such as an airplane. A given view of a commercial jetliner might consist of eight parts: a body, two wings, two parts to the tail, two engines, and a nose. As a shape, the airplane is highly irregular, complex, and would appear to qualify as a bad object. A relatively simple (good) object, such as a knife, might be composed of only two parts, a blade and a handle. One might think that the apparent simplicity (goodness) of the knife relative to the airplane would render it more quickly recognizable than the airplane. But in an experiment on the speed and accuracy of naming briefly presented object pictures, Ginny Ju, John Clapper, and I (reported in Biederman, 1987) found that complex objects, defined as those requiring more than six parts to appear complete, were not more difficult to recognize than simple objects. In fact, they enjoyed a slight advantage.

In an extreme form of this study, two of us (Hilton and Biederman) recently examined the recognition of the simplest objects—those made up of only one part, such as a barrel, sneaker, banana, or cap—as shown in the left column of Figure 1. Whereas line drawings showing only the orientation or depth discontinuities of objects composed objects of two or more parts can generally be named with near perfect accuracy in about 700 ms, recognition was extraordinarily difficult for these single-component objects, with an error rate of 47% and naming RTs of 983 ms (at least 500 ms are required for selecting and producing the name itself, so the 283 ms increase over the multipart control objects more than doubles the perceptual processing time required for the controls). Such single-part objects often require specification of color, texture, or fine surface detail to be identified with reasonable accuracy. Indeed, adding the surface detail or texture, as shown in the right column of Figure 1, reduced error rates to 23% and RTs to 859 ms, but both values were still markedly higher than those for complex objects. So these "good" objects were not readily identifiable.

The resolution of these paradoxical results about the relation of goodness to object recognition is, we believe, straightforward and amounts to an application of Garner's (1974) insight that pattern complexity, while increasing the difficulty of recall, can furnish additional information to aid discrimination. Specifically, the additional parts allow a complex object to be discriminated from other objects in an object space generated by combinations of geons and their relations (Biederman, 1987). If the parts are identified in parallel with modest demands on processing resources, then the complexity could produce a redundancy gain. Put another way, simple objects will tend to have many neighbors; complex objects, few. It is possible, of course, that in our studies of object recognition, a beneficial distinctiveness effect of complexity masked an effect of goodness operating in the other direction. A direct, albeit difficult, test of this conjecture might be conducted by comparing the identification of objects varying in complexity where the similarity of the closest neighbor(s) is somehow equated. But on a first pass, we have no evidence that simpler objects are easier to identify than more complex objects.

WHAT IS PATTERN GOODNESS GOOD FOR?

We have just considered what pattern goodness is not good for. But what is it good for? In 1974, Garner did not really have an answer to this question. He argued that goodness affected performance in a broad range of tasks. But such observations do not directly speak to the issue of the functional significance of goodness.

Figure 1.   Examples of some of the single-geon stimuli. Left column: objects with only their bounding contours. Right column: objects as in the left column, but with texture and surface detail added.

Simplicity, Likelihood, or Veridical Perception?

Much of the discussion of pragnanz in the psychological literature has focused on whether stimuli are interpreted the way they are because they are simpler or because a given interpretation of the pattern occurs more frequently than another interpretation (see Pomerantz & Kubovy, 1986, for an extensive review of this issue). So, for example, Pomerantz and Kubovy's (1986) discussion of pragnanz considered whether the trapezoidal window is perceived as a rectangle because it is simpler or because rectangles are more common than trapezoids. (Actually, it might have been more appropriate to consider whether any given rectangle is more common than any particular trapezoid.)

  Can organizational competence be distinguished from organizational performance? Pomerantz and Kubovy (1986) argued that the issue of pragnanz versus likelihood could be evaluated independently of issues of how a system, using either principle, is instantiated. They thus adopted a Marrian (1982) assumption that perceptual theories can be regarded at the level of a general theory of the goals of the computation, independent of the details of the algorithm or its implementation. Although such analyses can be enlightening in some cases (and in the abstract), in fact, ambiguity as to just what is entailed by a statement at the most abstract level often means that the clean sectioning of levels suggested by the Marrian ideal may not be achieved in practice. Often it is the details of the algorithm or its implementation that render the statement of the general goal of the computation unambiguous. But one cannot appeal to such details in evaluating classical statements of the pragnanz versus likelihood issue, because the theory needed to supply the details does not exist. (An exception to this is the Leeuwenberg Structural Information Theory [e.g., Buffart & Leeuwenberg, 1983], which seeks to provide a measure of pragnanz through a syntax of symbols that provide a measure of the repetition, symmetry, and alternation regularities in lines and angles of two-dimensional patterns. These symbols are discussed later in this chapter.) Consider the issue of whether likelihood affects organization. The first question to be raised is, Likelihood of what? Is it likelihood of the complete stimulus (a trapezoidal window, for example), or of specific features, or of certain "regularities" (Attneave, 1982)? These details are not specified in the traditional discussions of pragnanz.

  But there is another reason why the Marrian categories may not be appropriate for evaluating pragnanz versus likelihood: The criteria for evaluating perceptual organization are psychological. Indeed, the most common method is to appeal to observer judgments as to which of several possible alternatives would be the preferred mode of organization. That is, the claims about pragnanz are *implementational*. But if organizational effects are to be interpreted as reflecting an early process by which shape is determined, then it is possible that the *judgments* of organization might be influenced by other factors, possibly having effects later in the sequence of processing operations. Multistage theories, such as Selfridge's (1959) Pandemonium model, McClelland and Rumelhart's (1981) model of word recognition, or Biederman's (1987) Recognition-by-components (RBC) theory of object recognition could accommodate likelihood effects at a number of stages of processing.

Another point, noted by Pomerantz and Kubovy (1986), is whether likelihood is to be determined ontologically, through individual learning and development, or phylogenetically, on an evolutionary scale. Once we allow for "certain regularities" operating on an evolutionary scale, we have a likelihood theory that would be virtually indistinguishable from the standard statements of pragnanz.

The better question to explore, it seems to us, is not whether to perceive according to the simplest or most frequent interpretation, but how to achieve veridical perception, in general, and object recognition, in particular. Of course, both likelihood and pragnanz theorists argued that their constraints were in the service of veridical perception. They noted that patterns will be perceived in as good a fashion "as the prevailing conditions will allow" (Koffka, 1935/1963). "Likely" could be substituted for "good" in the preceding sentence to derive the corresponding statement for the likelihood theorists. But, by relegating a potentially major determinant of veridicality (viz., "prevailing conditions") to an undefined and secondary status, the classical theories provided little insight into just what the problems of veridicality might be and how a general theory might be developed to address those problems.

VERIDICALITY AND DEPTH INVARIANCE

Central to the veridical perception of shape is the problem of how to interpret a three-dimensional (3D) world from the two-dimensional (2D) image. The solution to the 2D→3D perception requires coming to grips with two problems. One is the underconstraint of the familiar "inverse optics problem." That is, there are an infinity of 3D worlds that could project any given 2D image. To solve the inverse optics problem, the visual system must make some assumptions to select one of the infinity of possible 3D interpretations. We shall argue, as have others (Lowe, 1984), that projective geometry provides a more principled basis for understanding the organizational effects than does pragnanz or likelihood.

There is a second problem, often neglected in discussions of perception, that is important when considering object recognition: Any single 3D object (other than a sphere) can project an infinity of 2D images. We will call this the *inverse object problem*. Assumptions are also needed to allow activation of an object when it is viewed at an arbitrary orientation, perhaps one never experienced previously, without positing an infinity of representations for each possible viewpoint of each object. In our opinion, the Gestalt organizational principles, including pragnanz, are consequences of these assumptions.

Pragnanz effects may thus be epiphenomenonal, reflecting not a system seeking simplicity or likelihood, but a consequence of constraints designed to allow veridical 3D object perception.

VIEWPOINT-INVARIANT PROPERTIES AND OBJECT DECOMPOSITION: DETERMINANTS OF PRAGNANZ

We will now examine some of the presumed subprocesses of object recognition and how these may lead to the phenomena associated with pragnanz.

Object Recognition

One way to achieve real-time 3D object recognition from a 2D image is to posit an intermediate representation consisting of viewpoint-invariant volumetric primitives. In Biederman's (1987) RBC account of object recognition, the image of a complex object is segmented, typically at regions of matched concavities, into regions that tend to be convex or singly concave. The contours in the parsed region are coded according to categorical contrasts of *viewpoint-invariant properties* (VIPs) of image edges (described below), such as whether an edge is straight or curved, whether pairs of edges are parallel or not, and the vertices formed at the cotermination of edges. These VIP-coded features activate the closest-fitting primitive.

There are 24 geons in the current version of this theory. The set of geons is composed of common volumes such as bricks, cylinders, wedges, cones, and their curved-axis counterparts. The geons are generated by a partition of the set of convex or singly concave generalized cones with convex cross sections. Marr (1977) showed that any (well-behaved) shape can be modeled as a generalized cone with a convex cross section. Objects are modeled as an arrangement of geons, with the relations (such as ''top-of,'' ''side-connected'') specified as part of the object model.

The geons are *good volumes* in that they tend to be regular and simple and to have redundant features. Like most good figures, they are robust to noise in that they can be identified even when portions of their edges and vertices are occluded or deleted. Most important for the present purposes, they are invariant under rotation in depth. It is this function of the geon, and the associated theoretical implications, that we will consider later in this chapter.

There are two early processes specified by RBC. One is the characterization of contours according to VIPs. The other is segmentation (or grouping) of a complex image into components. Both processes appear to have an ample presence in demonstrations of pragnanz effects; these will be considered in turn.

Viewpoint Invariant Properties

What are the constraints that allow inference of a 3D world from a 2D image and the selection of a particular orientation of an object from its image? In a seminal dissertation on perceptual organization, Lowe (1984) argued that 2D→3D indeterminacy is solved by reference to a set of *nonaccidental* properties (NAPs). We prefer to call them VIPs. VIPs (or NAPs) are properties of an image that are invariant with modest changes in viewpoint. For example, if the 2D retinal image of an edge is straight, it is highly likely that the 3D world projecting that image is also straight. The same is true for curved edges. If two or more edges coterminate at a common point in the 2D image, it is highly likely that they coterminate in the real world.

Recent progress in the mathematics of projective geometry has provided a general foundation for how the discontinuities in an image of a complex scene can be organized into an appropriate 3D representation that correctly labels convex, concave, occlusion, and shadow edges, even for curved surfaces and objects with holes (Malik, 1987; Nalwa, 1988). These developments in projective geometry provide a general theoretical derivation of the VIPs. Included in this work is the derivation of constraints from vertexes. For example, barring accidents of cotermination, the three segments of a Y vertex (i.e., a three-pronged vertex with none of the angles greater than 180°) must be all convex, all concave, or have one concave and two occluding segments. As another example, none of the surfaces on either side of an X vertex (two segments crossing without a change of direction at the junction) can be occluding.

With respect to the classical likelihood characterization of pragnanz, it should be recognized that VIPs specify not the probability of the world being straight, curved, coterminating, symmetrical, or parallel, but a *conditional* probability: If the image has a particular VIP (e.g., a straight contour), then that same property (viz., a straight contour) is perceived as an attribute of the 3D world. The VIPs thus become the assumptions by which a 3D world can be inferred from a 2D image. Of course, a form of likelihood theory must be correct, perhaps on an evolutionary scale, for the conditional itself. That is, straight contours in the real world project straight contours in a 2D image and have been doing so for the whole time that visual systems have been evolving. What matters, though, is not the probability of a straight contour in the world but the *consistency* that a straight contour in the image can be taken as evidence that there is a straight contour in the world.

Some of the classic Gestalt organizational principles, such as good continuation, are fundamental to the VIPs. But others, such as the constraints from vertexes, were not considered. Indeed, a number of the demonstrations of ambiguous figures are derivable from the constraints from vertexes. For example, the X vertexes in the Necker cube provide local evidence that neither surface can be occluding. Thus, the central Y vertex can be interpreted as being convex or concave, two of its possible interpretations, as noted previously.

Regularization Biases

The notion that perceptual organization might be driven by a system attempting to infer a 3D shape from a projected 2D image offers a number of insights into effects that hitherto have been considered as a tendency toward goodness. We will here concern ourselves with "regularization biases." Consider, for example, the biases toward assuming that a trapezoidal shape is rectangular, as in the trapezoidal window illusion or the Ames room. What value would there be for a system to manifest such a bias? One possibility is that the mechanisms for interpreting parallelism (and symmetry) of edges in three-dimensional space might be broadly tuned, so that edges that are approximately parallel when extended in depth (or when depicted as extended in depth) can be interpreted as parallel. That is, because it is unlikely that approximately parallel or symmetrical edges are a consequence of an "accident" of viewpoint of eye and object, the visual system interprets such 2D image features as parallel or symmetrical edges in the 3D world. One value of this bias is that it helps to correct for perspective effects— the 2D convergence of parallel edges extending in depth. Indeed, these biasing effects are primarily manifested when there is evidence in the image array that the edges do extend in depth (King, Meyer, Tangney, & Biederman, 1976). King et al. argued that "approximately" as in "approximately parallel" can be understood in terms of the uncertainty of the shape's slant in depth. The uncertainty defined a range of slant values such that if a symmetrical shape *could* be oriented within those values to produce the aspect ratio of the projected image, the shape would be perceived (not just judged) as symmetrical.

Segmentation of Complex Shapes

There is another process that is critically important in understanding pragnanz: shape decomposition. Complex shapes or objects often lend themselves to a decomposition into parts. Marr (1982) noted that segmentation at matched deep concavities provides a natural way to perceive the part structure of complex objects. Hoffman & Richards (1985) proposed that a result from topology, the transversality regularity, had strong relevance to shape decomposition. The transversality regularity, which is a VIP, holds that whenever two shapes are interpenetrated, a pair of matched cusps (discontinuities of curvature at minima of negative curvature) will be produced with probability measure one (Figure 2, top).

The important point about the transversality regularity with respect to pragnanz is that it provides a principled basis for the tendency toward organizing shapes into good figures: A cusp that is formed by the combination or interpe-

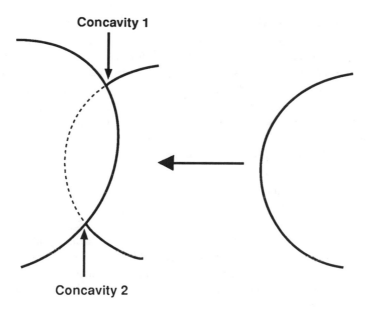

Concavity 1

Concavity 2

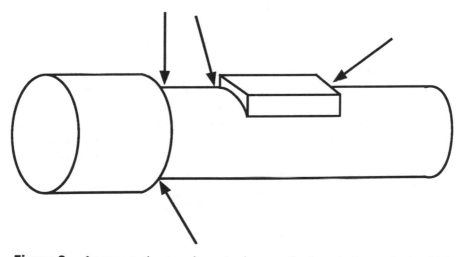

Figure 2. Interpenetrating two shapes produces a pair of matched cusps (top), which provide an illustration of the transversality regularity (Hoffman & Richards, 1985), which is useful for decomposing an object into its components, as illustrated with the object shown in the bottom. (From "Higher Level Vision" by I. Biederman, 1990, in D. N. Osherson, S. M. Kosslyn, & J. M. Hollerbach, Eds., *An Invitation to Cognitive Science: Visual Cognition and Action.* Copyright 1990 by MIT Press. Reprinted by permission.)

netration of shapes—and which would make a figure complex—is interpreted as
a property of the join, not of the component parts of a figure.

The transversality regularity provides a strong basis for decomposing complex shapes when matched cusps can be found, as illustrated in the lower portion
of Figure 2. Recent work by Vaina and Zlateva (1990) may provide a basis for
generalizing transversality to regions of smooth or single minima under variations
in scale. Their algorithm, which decomposes shapes into the largest convex surface
patches and the smallest nonconvex surface patches, holds promise as a general
solution to shape decomposition in that it provides an ordered segmentation of a
complex shape that is sensitive to variations scale.

Scale

Scale is a factor that is often absent in discussions of pragnanz. Generally, constraints operating at a coarse scale will dominate constraints at a finer scale.
Ginsburg (1986) showed that a number of pattern organizational effects were
produced by the output of low spatial-frequency channels. But there is still much
consciousness raising to be done on this account among students of pragnanz.
Consider, for example, the upper panel of Figure 3, which is modified from a
figure of Kanizsa (1979). One notices the black, convex asymmetrical shapes,
and it is only with scrutiny that the symmetry of the intervening concave white
figures is recognized. Kanizsa's figure has been interpreted as a demonstration
that symmetry has less of an effect of perceptual organization than does convexity.
This may well be true, but it is not entirely clear how well Figure 3 establishes
that fact. One problem with the figure is that the colliniarity of the top and bottom
edges of the white figures integrates them into one long, horizontal, white strip
that bridges the local asymmetrical sections. To detect the symmetry, one has to
decompose the single strip into separate white shapes. The components of the
black figures are much smaller, and their occluded portions are not collinear, so
they are not integrated. The lower panel shows a modification of the upper panel,
with the white patterns varied in size so as to disrupt, modestly, the collinearity
of their edges. Here, the symmetry of the white figures is more apparent, particularly of the larger figures (which may be another scale effect). We note that this
critique does not hold for all of Kanizsa's demonstrations of convexity dominating
symmetry.

A THEORY, NOT A SHOPPING LIST

Space does not permit a more extended discussion of how a wide range of phenomena, such as shape constancy and illusions, associated with the simplicity
principle or pragnanz can be understood as applications of VIPs based on projective
geometry. The more general issue raised by considerations of scale is that serious

Figure 3.   Top: In this figure, convexity dominates over symmetry in that the symmetry of the white regions is not readily perceived. Bottom: A modification of the upper figure in which the collinearity of the top and bottom contours of the white shapes has been reduced by varying the size of the white shapes and omitting the asymmetrical shape at the left. The symmetry of the white shapes is more apparent. (From Kanizsa, 1979, Fig. 5.21a, p. 112. Reprinted by permission of Greenwood Publishing Group, Inc., Westport CT.)

discussions of pattern organization must be placed in a context of a theory of shape and object processing.

Although a complete theory of object perception is not yet on hand, we can start to sketch the outlines of one possible neural net (NN) version (Hummel & Biederman, in press) that is consistent with what is known about the neurophysiology of the cortical system for object recognition extending from V1 (the primary visual projection area of the cortex) to the inferior temporal cortex (Mishkin & Appenzeller, 1987). Figure 4 shows the overall architecture of the model.

The Hummel & Biederman (in press) model takes as input the contours corresponding to the occlusional and orientation discontinuities in an image. As output, the model activates a unit that is selective for a specified arrangement of simple volumes (or geons), and thus achieves a basic level (or entry level) classification according to Biederman's (1987) RBC theory of object recognition. The model solves four fundamental problems in object recognition: (a) translational, size, and general viewpoint invariance; the same output unit(s), corresponding to the object, are activated no matter where the image falls in the visual field, the

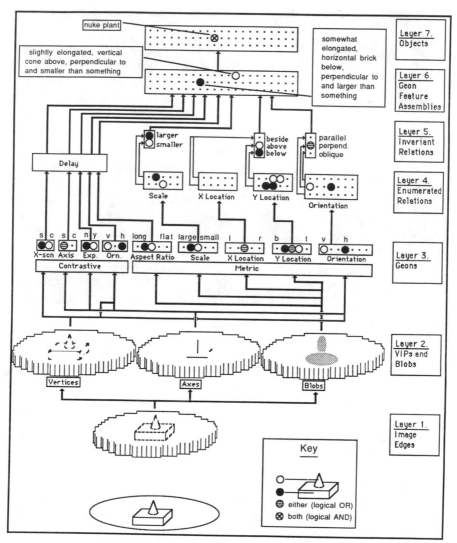

Figure 4. The architecture of the Hummel–Biederman neural net implementation of RBC. Black- and white-filled cells each fire simultaneously but out of synchrony with each other, representing the activation of the brick and cone, respectively. (Modified from Hummel & Biederman, in press. Adapted by permission.)

size of the image, or the orientation in depth (up to parts occlusion); (b) grouping (or organization) of image elements into appropriate parts; (c) a basis of determining invariant object-centered relations (such as TOP-OF or SIDE-CONNECTED); and (d) a basis for computing the similarity (or equivalence) of object images.

These problems all require a solution to the "binding problem"—determining what groups with what. In the present case, for example, this problem included the grouping of the various segments and vertices to a given geon and the grouping of a given geon to an orientation (such as vertical) and a relation. Most NN models have used enumeration, assigning a unit to each attribute combination. Such enumerative schemes are unsatisfactory because they require a prohibitively large number of units to represent even modest input domains. Moreover, they do not express the equivalence of inputs. By using different units to represent the different locations of an object, for example, the information that it is the same object in the different locations is not represented.

The Hummel and Biederman (in press) model achieves binding through phase locking of the oscillatory activity of cells that are tuned to oriented image edges. The phase locking (or synchrony) is established by "fast enabling links" (FELs) between pairs of collinear, coterminating, and parallel adjacent edge cells. Activation from an FEL causes an active unit to fire independently of where that unit is in its refractory period. The particular set of FELs can emerge from a learning experience (on an individual or evolutionary scale) such that the strength of an FEL between two units is a function of the probability that both units are active when random images are presented to the model's retina.

The phase-locked activation of these units is transmitted to units for invariant representations of geons and relations in intermediate layers. For example, an object consisting of a vertical cylinder on top of a horizontal brick would activate units representing cylinder, "top-of," and vertical in one time slice, and brick, "below," and horizontal in another.

In addition to providing a model of shape recognition, the model also provides some insight into the relation between attention and the perceptual organization of shape. Attention would be required to overcome accidental synchrony. Therefore, it must be inhibitory. Neural evidence for attentional inhibition has been documented by Moran and Desimone (1985).

Goodness and Binding

The general theme of this chapter is that pattern organizational effects should be derived from a general system of shape processing designed to solve the inverse optics problem. In the context of the neural net model, we offer the following speculation as to the underlying basis of pragnanz: Goodness is the extent to which a pattern manifests a stable phase set.

That is, given a set of contours in a display, a good pattern will bind together into a single, stable phase set through the action of the FELs activated by its contours. A bad pattern, on the other hand, will have contours that either do not group together or else group one way or the other through accidental synchrony.

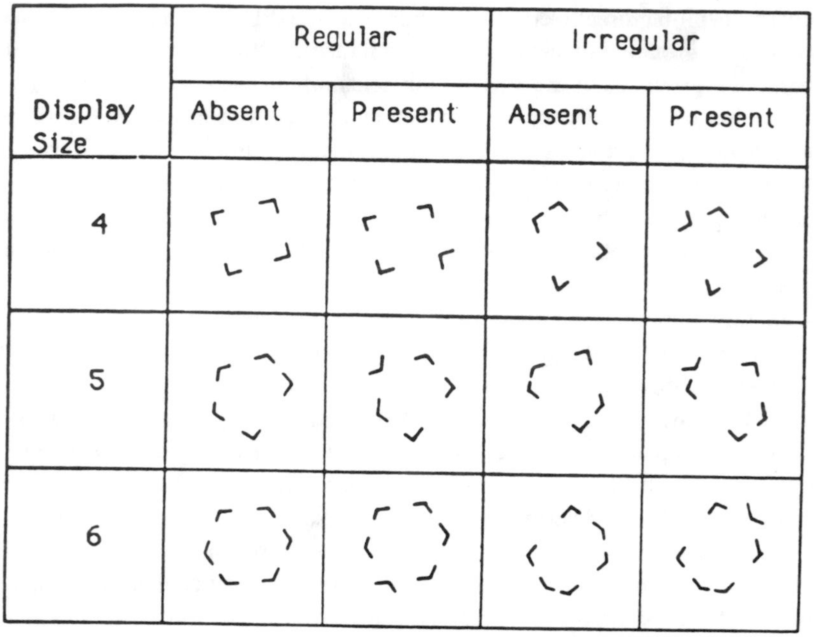

Display Size	Regular		Irregular	
	Absent	Present	Absent	Present
4				
5				
6				

Figure 5.   Stimuli from Experiment 1 of Donnelly, Humphreys, and Riddoch (1991). Note that the distractor vertices are collinear through their endpoints. The target was an outward pointing vertex. (From Donnelly, Humphreys, & Riddoch, 1991, Figure 1, p. 563. Copyright 1991 by the American Psychological Association. Reprinted by permission.)

Accidental synchrony will tend to be unstable. Temporal stability has the advantage that bindings produced by the FELs do not require attention for their grouping.

This definition, in fact, captures the original notion of pragnanz as a stable, unambiguous pattern. In specifying a *mechanism* for pattern grouping, it has the advantage of producing testable predictions for various shapes.

A recent experiment by Donnelly, Humphreys, and Riddoch (1991) serves well to illustrate the potential fruitfulness of this analysis. These investigators varied the number of L vertices in a display. In one experiment, the segments were aligned through their terminators so that they appeared to group into a single polygon (a quadrilateral, pentagon, or hexagon) in the target absent condition, as shown in Figure 5. Subjects searched for a misoriented vertex, one with the corner (cotermination point) pointing in, as shown in the Target Present column of Figure 5. With the terminators collinear (or approximately collinear), the FELs would cause the units representing the vertices to fire in synchrony. In the target absent condition, these vertices would then activate a single entity in the object layer, independent of the number of vertices making up the polygon. In the neural net model, a collinear signal from an endstopped FEL is inhibited when other endstopped cells coterminating with that endstopped cell are also activated. This occurs when two or three activated, coterminating endstopped cells form an activated vertex. The inhibition from the vertex cells prevents the FEL grouping signals from extending through the endstopped point (through the vertex). The target vertex would then form part of a different phase set. Independent of the number of vertices in the display, in the target absent condition, only one phase set would be formed; in the target present condition, only two phase sets would be formed. Consistent with the preceding analysis, the data revealed no effect on search RTs of the number of vertices and that absent RTs were shorter than present RTs. These results held for both regular (left panel, Figure 5) and irregular (right panel) stimuli. With the latter displays, the vertex-to-vertex lengths were not equal.

The inhibition of collinear FELs through a vertex was not an ad hoc "cludge" to handle the Donnelly et al. results, but an important constraint in the model needed, as noted previously, to prevent grouping beyond the surface of an object. Blickle (1989) showed that this constraint provides an interpretation of why the imposition of an occluding surface in Bregman's (1981) demonstration of un-identifiable fragments of Bs renders the fragments identifiable. The occluder converts L vertices that inhibit the appropriate grouping to T vertices, which allow grouping. Blickle also showed that it was the presence of inappropriate L vertices that was responsible for the difficulties in identifying Leeper's (1935) pictures of objects.

The model yields a very different set of predictions when the segments of the distractors are collinear through their vertices, as shown in Figure 6. These vertices would not group into a single polygon, but, instead, each vertex would each form its own phase set, so there would be an increase in the number of phase sets with the number of vertices. (Illusory surfaces are formed at the regions within the vertices of these stimuli, but these surfaces do not bind the vertices into single figures.) Indeed, RTs increased linearly with the number of vertices (with the present RTs shorter than the absent RTs). Most important, these RTs were all longer than those in the previous experiment, in which the vertices grouped through their endpoints. As with the grouped vertices, these results held for both regular and irregular stimuli.

It is interesting to note that these effects of whether segments were collinear through their endpoints or vertices, a distinction not made by students of pragnanz, were substantially greater than the effects of regularity, a distinction heavily stressed by students of pragnanz (e.g., L).

Repetition Regularities

There is no doubt that people readily encode regularities in the repetition of elements or combinations of elements, as in simple repetitions, alternations, and reversals, as described by Buffart and Leeuwenberg (1983) and van der Helm (1988). To take a simple example, a display of four cylinders in the visual field

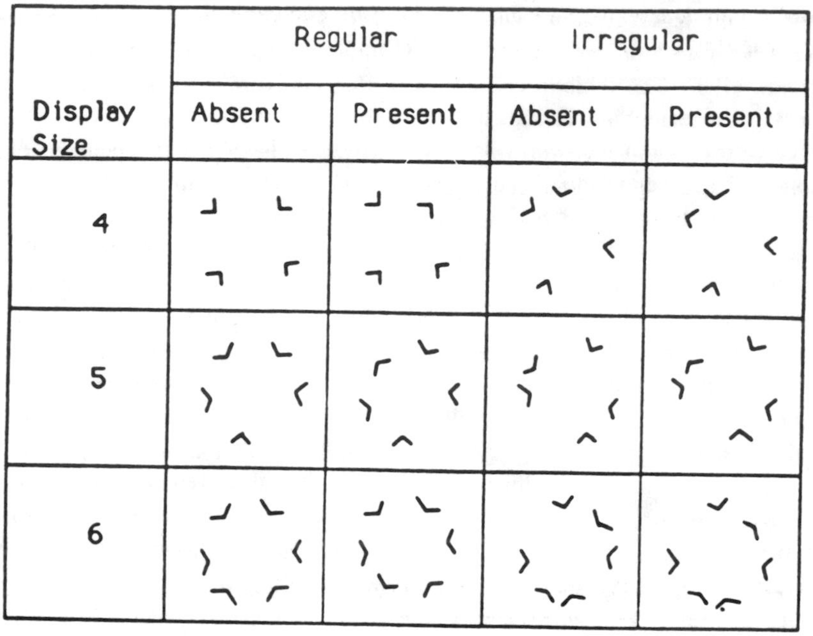

Display Size	Regular		Irregular	
	Absent	Present	Absent	Present
4				
5				
6				

Figure 6. Stimuli from Experiment 2 of Donnelly, Humphreys, and Riddoch (1991). Note that the distractor vertices are collinear through their vertices. The target was an inward-pointing vertex. (Copyright 1991 by the American Psychological Association. Reprinted by permission.)

would probably be judged to be a better pattern than a cylinder, a brick, a cone, and a wedge. Would the stability of binding in the Hummel–Biederman model also hold for this case?

With repeated shapes (e.g., four cylinders), the three pairs of cells representing contrastive geon attributes in the third layer of the model for cross-section (straight vs. curved), axis (straight vs. curved), and expansion (parallel [no] vs. nonparallel [yes] sides) would fire in synchrony with each of four different blob cells, each blob cell indicating the location of each of the volumes. With the cylinder, the curved cross-section, straight axis, and parallel (no) cells would fire. Over the four time slices representing the four geons, the pattern of activation of these cells would be constant. (The pattern would vary, however, over the location cells activated by the blob units.) With four different volumes, however, the pattern of activation over the contrastive geon cells would vary over the time slices.

An increase in the number of elements in the visual field causes an increase in the probability of accidental synchrony. Accidental synchrony would have no effect when the geons were all the same. If the axis cell activated by one geon accidentally synchronized with the cross-section cell of another geon, they would

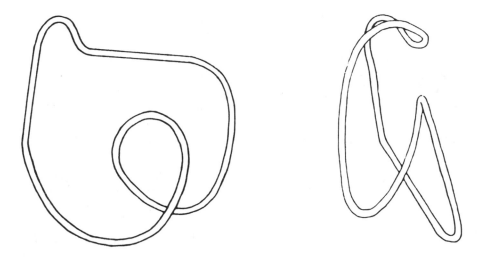

Figure 7.   Left: An example of Rock and DiVita's (1987) novel three-dimensional wire
objects. Right: A view of the same object with a diagonal translation. (From
Rock & DiVita, 1987, Figure 1, p. 282. Reprinted by permission.)

still yield the same pattern of activation as when the attributes of the same geon
were in synchrony. However, with varied geons, accidental synchrony would
yield conjunctions of attributes not necessarily in the input, which would further
increase the variability of the pattern of activation of the contrastive cells.

With a constant pattern of activation, attentional inhibition would not be
required to know what volumes were present in the visual field. With the varied
patterns, attentional inhibition might be required to ensure that the current pattern
was not accidental.

PART GOODNESS AND ROTATIONAL INVARIANCE

What is it that allows an object to be identified when viewed at a new rotation
in depth? A number of theorists have argued that a 3D model can be built up out
of smooth variations in the luminance gradient (e.g., Marr, 1982), although Todd
and Reichle (1989) have challenged whether people can actually use this information to determine depth relations. Other authors have argued for a central role
of familiarity, in which separate models are created for each experienced viewpoint
to mediate recognition (e.g., Tarr, 1989).

An experiment by Rock and DiVita (1987) offers, at first examination,
evidence against 3D model construction and for the role of familiarity. Rock and
DiVita's subjects studied a series of smoothly curved wire-frame objects, such as
the one shown in Figure 7, for 4 s at a given orientation. Rock and DiVita then
tested subjects' recognition of the object when it was viewed at a diagonal rotation

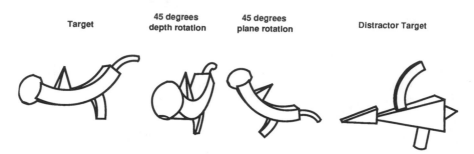

Figure 8. Example of the nonsense objects used in the experiment by Biederman and Gerhardstein. Same–different shape matching RTs for such stimuli are only slightly affected by differences in orientation.

in depth. (The actual procedure was that the subjects viewed the object in one quadrant of the visual field, such as upper left. They would then be tested for recognition of the object when it was presented in the lower right quadrant.) The remarkable result was that Rock and DiVita's subjects could recognize the original object only 39% of the time against similar smoothly curved wire-frame objects, when viewed at the new orientation. (Objects in their original positions could be recognized 75% of the time.) Indeed, Rock, Wheeler, and Tudor (1989) showed that people cannot even imagine how smoothly curved wire-frame objects look when rotated. The inability to recognize objects from a different viewpoint was not limited to wire-frame objects. Rock and DiVita presented a demonstration of two views of a blobby clay construction and crumpled paper, in which it was subjectively clear that it would be extremely difficult to determine that the same object was projecting each image.

For all of Rock and DiVita's objects, the relative depth of each point on the object can be perceived. Rock's demonstrations are important because they show that, even with depth information present in the image, a viewpoint-invariant representation will not necessarily be derived for an object. Rock and DiVita's objects were unfamiliar. But are there limitations on their results other than familiarity?

Gerhardstein and Biederman (1991) have recently been investigating the recognition of objects such as those shown in Figure 8. In contrast with Rock and DiVita's stimuli, depth-rotated versions of these stimuli could readily be recognized. These stimuli, like Rock's, were unfamiliar, but they differed from Rock's in a fundamental way: They readily allowed a geon description that remained invariant over rotations in depth. The information in Rock's wire frame objects— X vertexes and variations in the degree of curvature of particular portions of wire—were all viewpoint-dependent. Under even slight rotations in depth, vertexes would appear and disappear and image curvature would change. None of

Rock's objects—the wire-frame constructions, the clay blobs, or the crumpled newspapers—had structures that were easily decomposable into parts.

It is hard to know whether the objects in Figure 7 or either of the objects in Figure 8 would receive the highest goodness rating. From a Garnerian perspective, it might be argued that the inability to discriminate the object in Figure 4 from other smoothly curved wire-frame objects might imply a larger rotational subset than that for Figure 5 and that, consequently, Rock's object should be designated as worse than the Biederman and Gerhardstein objects. But a rotation of one of Rock's objects does not even include itself. From that perspective, Rock's objects have very small subsets. For this fundamental rotational property of object representation—invariance under rotation in depth—the best conclusion is that goodness is irrelevant.

SUMMARY AND CONCLUSION

Measures of pattern goodness may essentially be irrelevant to the representation of objects. Instead, effects attributable to pragnanz may reflect the workings of a general system for three-dimensional object recognition in which complex images are segmented into parts whose representations are viewpoint-invariant and robust to noise. In particular, good patterns may yield more stable patterns of activation for hidden shape units than patterns judged to be bad.

References

Attneave, F. (1982). Pragnanz and soap bubble systems: A theoretical explanation. In J. Beck (Ed.), *Organization and representation in perception* (pp. 11–29). Hillsdale, NJ: Erlbaum.

Biederman, I. (1987). Recognition-by-components: A theory of human image understanding. *Psychological Review, 94*, 115–147.

Blickle, T. W. (1989). *Recognition of contour-deleted images*. Unpublished doctoral dissertation, State University of New York at Buffalo.

Bregman, A. S. (1981). Asking the "What for" question in auditory perception. In M. Kubovy & J. R. Pomerantz (Eds.), *Perceptual organization* (pp. 99–118). Hillsdale, NJ: Erlbaum.

Buffart, H. E., & Leeuwenberg, E. L. J. (1983). Structural information theory. In H. G. Geisler, J. F. J. M. Buffart, E. L. J. Leeuwenberg, & V. Sarris (Eds.), *Modern issues in perception* (pp. 48–71). Berlin: VEB Deutscher Verlag der Wissenschaften.

Checkosky, S. F., & Whitlock, D. (1973). Effects of pattern goodness on recognition time in a memory search task. *Journal of Experimental Psychology, 100*, 341–348.

Donnelly, N., Humphreys, G. W., & Riddoch, M. J. (1991). Parallel computation of primitive shape descriptors. *Journal of Experimental Psychology: Human Perception and Performance, 17*, 561–570.

Garner, W. R. (1962). *Uncertainty and structure as psychological concepts*. New York: Wiley.

Garner, W. R. (1974). *The processing of information and structure.* Potomac, MD: Erlbaum.

Garner, W. R., & Clement, D. E. (1963). Goodness of pattern and pattern uncertainty. *Journal of Verbal Learning and Verbal Behavior, 2,* 446–452.

Garner, W. R., & Sutliff, D. (1974). The effect of goodness on encoding time in visual pattern discrimination. *Perception & Psychophysics, 16,* 426–430.

Gerhardstein, P. C., & Biederman, I. (1991, May). *3D orientation invariance in visual object recognition.* Paper presented at the annual meeting of the Association for Research in Vision and Ophthalmology, Sarasota, FL.

Ginsburg, A. P. (1986). Spatial filtering and visual form perception. In K. R. Boff, L. Kaufman, & J. P. Thomas (Eds.), *Handbook of perception and human performance* (Vol. 2, pp. 36-1–36-41). New York: Wiley.

Handel, S., & Garner, W. R. (1966). The structure of visual pattern associates and pattern goodness. *Perception & Psychophysics, 1,* 33–38.

Hoffman, D. D., & Richards, W. (1985). Parts of recognition. *Cognition, 18,* 65–96.

Hummel, J. E., & Biederman, I. (in press). Dynamic binding in a neural network for shape recognition. *Psychological Review.*

Kanizsa, G. (1979). *Organization in vision: Essays on gestalt perception.* New York: Praeger.

King, M., Meyer, G. E., Tangney, J., & Biederman, I. (1976). Shape constancy and a perceptual bias towards symmetry. *Perception & Psychophysics, 19,* 129–136.

Koffka, K. (1963). *Principles of Gestalt psychology.* New York: Harcourt, Brace & World. (Original work published 1935)

Leeper, R. (1935). A study of a neglected portion of the field of learning: The development of sensory organization. *Journal of Genetic Psychology, 46,* 41–75.

Lowe, D. (1984). *Perceptual organization and visual recognition.* Unpublished doctoral dissertation, Department of Computer Science, Stanford University.

Malik, J. (1987). Interpreting line drawings of curved objects. *International Journal of Computer Vision, 1,* 73–103.

Marr, D. (1977). Analysis of occluding contour. *Proceedings of the Royal Society of London B., 197,* 441–475.

Marr, D. (1982). *Vision.* San Francisco: Freeman.

McClelland, J. L., & Rumelhart, D. E. (1981). An interactive activation model of context effects in letter perception, Part 1: An account of basic findings. *Psychological Review, 88,* 375–407.

Mishkin, M., & Appenzeller, T. (1987). The anatomy of memory. *Scientific American, 256,* 80–89.

Moran, J., & Desimone, R. (1985). Selective attention gates visual processing in the extrastriate cortex. *Science, 229,* 782–784.

Nalwa, V. S. (1988). Line-drawing interpretation: A mathematical perspective. *International Journal of Computer Vision, 2,* 103–124.

Palmer, S. E. (1977). Hierarchical structure in perceptual representation. *Cognitive Psychology, 9,* 441–474.

Palmer, S. E. (1989, May). Goodness, Gestalts, groups, and Garner: Symmetry subgroups as a theory of figural goodness. Paper presented at a conference on "The Perception of Structure," Yale University.

Pomerantz, J. R. (1977). Pattern and speed of encoding. *Memory & Cognition, 5,* 235–241.

Pomerantz, J. R., & Kubovy, M. (1986). Theoretical approaches to perceptual organization. In K. R. Boff, L. Kaufman, & J. P. Thomas (Eds.), *Handbook of perception and human performance* (Vol. 2., pp. 36-1–36-46). New York: Wiley.

Rock, I., & DiVita, J. (1987). A case of viewer-centered object perception. *Cognitive Psychology, 19,* 280–293.

Rock, I., DiVita, J., & Barbeito, R. (1981). The effect of form perception of change in the orientation in the third dimension. *Journal of Experimental Psychology: Human Perception and Performance, 7,* 719–732.

Rock, I., Wheeler, D., & Tudor, L. (1989). *Can* we imagine how objects look from other viewpoints? *Cognitive Psychology, 21,* 185–210.

Selfridge, O. G. (1959). PANDEMONIUM: A paradigm for learning. In *Proceedings of the Symposium on Mechanization of Thought Processes,* National Physics Laboratory.

Tarr, M. J. (1989). Orientation dependence in three-dimensional object recognition. Unpublished doctoral dissertation, Department of Brain and Cognitive Sciences, Massachusetts Institute of Technology.

Todd, J. T., & Reichle, F. D. (1989). Ordinal structure in the visual perception and cognition of smoothly curved surfaces. *Psychological Review, 96,* 643–657.

Vaina, L. M., & Zlateva, S. D. (1990). The largest convex patches: A boundary-based method for obtaining object parts. *Biological Cybernetics, 62,* 225–236.

van der Helm, P. (1988). *Accessibility and simplicity of visual structures.* Unpublished doctoral dissertation, The Catholic University of Nijmegen, The Netherlands.

CHAPTER 6

SUBJECTIVE RANDOMNESS, AESTHETICS, AND STRUCTURE

SARAH HOLLINGSWORTH LISANBY AND
GREGORY R. LOCKHEAD

Subjective randomness is related to what people expect to encounter; it is different from stochastic randomness. To examine what determines whether an event will be judged as random or as not random, we asked people to generate strings of random digits, to judge if digit strings were random, to place random or not-random dots in geometric figures, and to place dots in aesthetically pleasing locations. The results show that subjectively random events are structured. Compared to chance expectations, in numerical strings that only appear random, successive numerals repeat too infrequently but otherwise are overly similar, and nonsuccessive numerals are too different from one another. Also, human-generated numerals appear more random than do stochastically independent numerals. When dots within a square, rectangle, or diamond appear to be randomly located, they tend to be in a figural balance with features of the stimulus. This structure is highly similar to that of aesthetically pleasing locations. We suggest that some art forms that have been considered to be random may, instead, be structured according to the same principles involved in subjective randomness. We conclude that when people attempt to produce a random event, they do so by beginning with an aesthetically pleasing response, which they then modify slightly so

---

This research was supported in part by the Air Force Office of Scientific Research, the American Psychological Association, the Office of Naval Research, and the National Institutes of Mental Health. We thank Ulysses Balis, Ron Collis, Herb Crovitz, Mike Hunseder, Gregory Lawler, Christine Pratt, and Douglas Ricard for their help with this project, and we thank the many students who participated as subjects.

that it appears random; and that when people judge whether an event is random, they compare it to an aesthetically pleasing event.

There is no chance;
And what seems hazard in our eyes
Arises from the deepest source.
      –Schiller

In defining meaning, Garner (1962) distinguished between meaning as signification (e.g., *Hund* in German signifies *dog* in English) and meaning as structure, which he defined as "the totality of the relations between events. When we say that a picture composed of randomly located dots is meaningless, we imply that we see no relations between the dots and that, therefore, the picture has no structure" (Garner, 1962, p. 141; see also Clark, this volume). This second definition equates the absence of perceived structure with randomness and is the focus of this chapter.

Absence of perceived structure does not always correlate with absence of statistical structure. Some statistically random events are perceived as structured, whereas some structured events are perceived as random. This chapter examines certain situations in which randomness and the perception of randomness are not correlated. Our goal is to better understand how subjective and statistical randomness differ.

For this purpose, it is necessary to define or describe the terms *random* and *subjectively random*. Randomness can be described with probabilistic statements that reveal the distribution of outcomes of a system that cannot be described deterministically or explicitly. Such events are stochastically independent.

Subjective probability was described by von Mises (1957) as dependent on the degree of knowledge one has about the system. Lack of knowledge results in equal subjective probability of all known possible outcomes. This is the Principle of Indifference espoused by Czuber, which applies when we have "not the slightest knowledge of the conditions" (von Mises, 1957, p. 75). Laplace's assertion that "chance is but the expression of man's ignorance" (Cohen & Hansel, 1956, p. 1) seems consistent with the inference.

Subjective randomness concerns how one relates to structure or its absence in the environment. Perfectly determined events can appear random, as in the case of irrational decimal expansions known as chaos equations (May, 1976). It is also true that random events can appear determined, as is often demonstrated by the behavior of people in games of chance and in studies such as those reported or referenced in this chapter.

Another aspect of this issue is seen in the fields of inference and statistical design, where many models are based on assumptions of stochastic independence. However, because elements in the real world are not generally independent of one another, one might look for deviations between the modeled and existing structures in order to characterize this structure more exactly.

When considering an organism, this same argument may again be applied. That organism's baselines might not be characterized as well by stochastic independence as by subjective independence. If so, then perceptual structure would be different from stochastic structure, and perceptual models and stochastic models ought to be examined from different baselines. In other words, the discovery of a statistically nonrandom outcome in data is not necessarily a demonstration that the performance producing those data was other than chance from the subjects' point of view.

IDENTIFYING SEQUENCES OF RANDOM DIGITS

Sequences in the stock market, runs at the gambling table, and "hot streaks" in sports are used by many people in attempts to predict future events. This is true in spite of the facts that reliable stock-market trends are elusive, that there are probably no statistically reliable trends at the dice table, and that successive trials that have been examined in sports are largely independent (Gilovich, Vallone, & Tversky, 1985). That is, strings of numerals or other events that are random are often judged as structured.

On the other hand, strings of numerals that people produce as being random are structured (Wiesgersma, 1986). To learn if such strings are indeed perceived as random, we gave 23 college students 23 pairs of strings each containing 25 numerals between 1 and 5.[1] In each pair, one string was taken from a table of random numbers and the other string was generated by other subjects under the instruction to produce random numerals. The students judged which string in each pair was random.

The human-generated strings were judged to be random more often than were the computer-generated strings, p (binomial) < 0.02. Consistent with other reports (Budescu, 1987; Neuringer, 1986; Wiesgersma, 1986), this implies that the human-generated strings were not random. This is the case. Compared with what is expected for stochastic independence (all $ps < 0.01$), the human-generated "random"-digit strings had fewer stimulus repetitions, smaller differences in magnitude between successive numbers (assimilation), and more occasions of two adjacent numbers alternating with two other adjacent numbers, (e.g., 2145; contrast). This result further implies that the reason why human generated strings are structured is not because of any motor or other generation difficulties; these structured events also appear random to other people.

An apparently related observation is that these patterns are like those found in data from other judgment tasks. Examples are absolute identifications, in which people attempt to identify the stimulus on each of many trials, and magnitude estimations, in which people judge the amount of some attribute (e.g., loudness,

---

[1] This study was conducted by John Monahan.

brightness, or weight) on each of many trials. In every such data set examined, the differences between successive stimuli were underestimated (assimilation), often by large amounts. Also, in all such studies in which subjects received feedback, as well as in many studies in which feedback was not given, the differences between the current stimulus and stimuli on earlier trials were over-estimated (contrast).

These same patterns were also found in guessing tasks in which people predicted events that were never presented (Lockhead, 1983). This sequential structure, assimilation followed by contrast, might be a general characteristic of behavior.

SELECTING RANDOM DOT LOCATIONS

The study mentioned above shows some ways that subjective randomness is different from statistical randomness when numerals are used. We conducted a study to examine subjective randomness for spatial locations.

Procedure

We tested 195 Duke University undergraduate volunteers in groups. The testing material was simply an outline square drawn on paper. The instruction given was, "We are interested in what people do when asked to behave randomly. Please place a single point, a dot, inside the square below." Responses were made with pen or pencil.

Results

Each subject produced one dot. These 195 responses were plotted onto a single square and are shown in Figure 1. These cumulated responses appear structured. There are more dots in the upper than the lower half of the square, and there appears to be a tendency for the dots to cluster near the diagonals of the square in an X-like arrangement.

To test for this apparent convergence toward the diagonals, we reflected the responses around the imaginary vertical and horizontal axes that bisect the square so that all responses were placed into one quadrant. That result is shown in Figure 2. The Pearson product–moment correlation between these resulting X and Y values is $r = 0.77$ ($p < 0.001$).

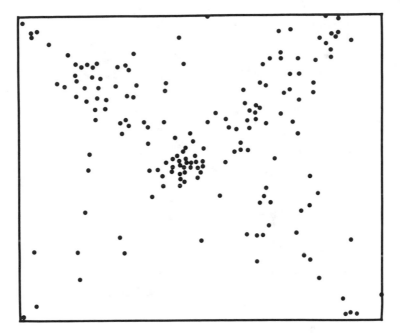

Figure 1. Cumulated responses when each of 195 students were asked to place a single random dot in a square.

Discussion

Collectively, people do not have a perception of randomness as being a uniform distribution when they place a single dot in a square. Rather, they have a tendency to place the dot along the imaginary diagonals and near the center of the figure.

These results are essentially identical to data reported by Psotka (1978), who had people place a dot on a figure "in the first place that comes to mind" (p. 103). Using a variety of figures as stimuli, including a square, Psotka concluded that the responses tend to reflect a symmetry axis of each figure. He further noted that this symmetry axis appears to be described by a model based on Blum's (1973) point and disc geometry and called a *stick figure*. A grassfire metaphor describes this aspect of Blum's model of organic shapes: If the entire perimeter of an outline figure is ignited simultaneously and the fire burns at a steady rate away from each ignited point, then where the fire from different aspects of the figure meets and is thus quenched defines the stick figure for that shape. For a square, this stick figure is the diagonals.

Although psychological randomness was not a concern for Psotka's work, his "first-place-that-comes-to-mind" instruction might have been interpreted by subjects in the same way as the "place-a-dot-at-a-random-location" instruction

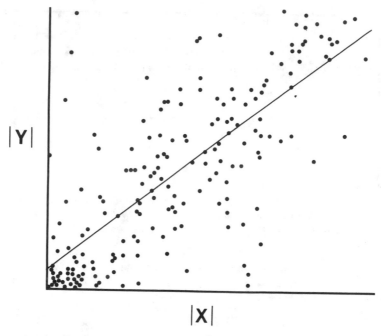

Figure 2. The result when the data in Figure 1 are reflected around the horizontal and vertical axes of the square.

used here, but this was not known. The following experiments help identify which features of a figure affect the locations of perceptually random dots; further examine Blum's model; and examine the proposal that performance in all of these tasks is related to aesthetics.

RAINDROPS AND NOT-RANDOM LOCATIONS

The instructions to place a "random" dot and to put a dot in "the first place that comes to mind" produce similar results. To examine if this is because instructions do not matter, the study by Psotka discussed above was repeated, except with changed instructions and using a rectangle rather than a square as the stimulus.

Procedure

We tested 161 undergraduate volunteers in classrooms. The simple stimuli were outline rectangles (6.8 cm × 10 cm) drawn in the center of sheets of paper (21.6 cm × 27.9 cm; 8½ in. × 11 in.). Responses were made with pen or pencil. There was no time limit.

There were two tasks, called *raindrops* and *not-random*. Each subject first performed the raindrop task with the following instruction: "Imagine that a rain-

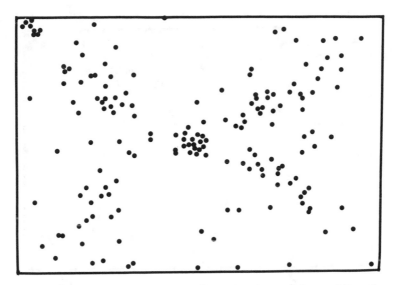

Figure 3.   Where a raindrop might fall in a rectangle, according to 161 students.

drop fluttered to earth and landed in the field outlined below. Using a pen or pencil, please place a single dot, a point, to indicate a *random* location at which the raindrop might have landed.''

Each subject then performed the not-random task with the following instruction: ''Please place a single dot, a point, in the figure below at a position that does *not* appear to be a random location.''

Finally, each subject was instructed as follows: ''In just a few words or phrases, please indicate what determines that a point appears to be at a random location or at a nonrandom location.''

Results

The 161 responses in the raindrop and not-random conditions were cumulated onto separate rectangles. Visual inspection of the raindrops (Figure 3) indicates a structure consistent with Psotka's (1978) earlier data. The dots tend to form a Muller–Lyer figure with wings that project to the corners of the rectangle and a bar across the center.

The not-random dots (Figure 4) show a very different pattern: Seventy percent of the subjects placed these dots quite precisely in the center of the rectangle, and 15% placed them directly on a corner. Most of the remaining 15% of the dots were also logically placed (e.g., on a side or near a corner).

The subjects' written descriptions of what determines that a point appears to be at a random or a nonrandom location were consistent and easy to interpret. More than 75% of the descriptions of a not-random spot included such comments

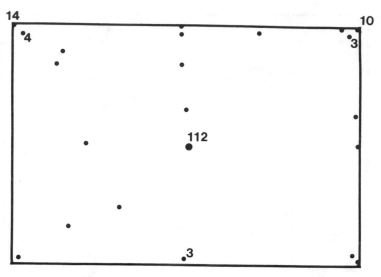

Figure 4.   Not-random locations in a rectangle, according to 161 students. When more than one dot occurred at the same place, numerals indicate the number of responses there.

as "symmetry," "equal distances from reference sides," "the center dot suggests a reason, therefore nonrandom," "orderly," "logical," and "have to think about it."

The descriptions of a random spot included statements such as "without thinking about it," "divorced of reason," "automatic," and "where the eye focuses first."

In addition to these consistent statements, there were seven statements to the effect that "some type of symmetry denotes a random dot" and six atypical statements like "imbalance or asymmetry denotes a random dot."

Discussion

Requests for a random location, for the "first place you think of," and for a raindrop all produce similar data. This is not because instructions do not matter; the results are very different when a nonrandom location is requested.

The subjects' verbal descriptions suggest that features or landmarks are important in these tasks. For the rectangle, the most important landmarks are the center and corners. These are perceived as not-random locations. Subjectively random locations are distant from these landmarks, and the subjectively most-random locations might be those with the greatest overall distance from all landmarks.

REFERENCE LOCATIONS

A dot on a plane defines a simple yet fundamental visual context. The dot defines a point or a region in the plane, and the plane sets the location and scale of the dot. Thus, the addition of a dot to a figure might affect the symmetry of the display, and this effect might be related to the role of reference points or landmarks in the figures. The following experiment examined dot placements in figures containing landmarks in various places.

Procedure

The subjects were 33 volunteers from the Duke University community. Each was given 10 pages of outline squares (15 subjects) or diamonds (18 subjects). The pages were 8.5 in. wide × 11 in. tall; each centered figure was 5 in. long on each side. The first figure was empty. Each successive figure had a dot at one of nine locations: center (one stimulus), halfway between the center and each side (four stimuli), and halfway between the center and each corner (four stimuli). The subjects were asked to place a random dot in each figure.

Results

No dot. Responses to the empty square and diamond were cumulated separately. Both data sets show an X or partial X. The correlations calculated as described earlier are $r = 0.55$ and 0.56 ($ps < 0.05$).

Center dot. There was little apparent structure when a landmark was in the center of either the square or the diamond, and neither correlation is significant. This may be because there were too few observations.

When 23 high school students did these same tasks, their responses tended to be on the diagonals of both figures. The correlation for their data combined over figures and stimuli was $r = 0.59$.

Corner dots. These landmarks were midway between a corner and the center of each figure. For analytical purposes, the four stimuli for each figure, one for each corner, were rotated so that each landmark was in the same quadrant. These data were cumulated across subjects and are shown in the left column of Figure 5.

Responses to the square show a preference for the quadrant diagonally opposite the landmark; there were 31 dots in that quadrant (not all are shown because two responses sometimes occurred at the same location), and there were 12, 11, and 6 dots in each of the other three quadrants. The correlation for these rotated and cumulated data (four responses from each of 15 subjects) was $r = 0.24$.

Responses to the diamond containing a corner dot show a preference for the axes relative to the subject (i.e., the diagonals relative to the square): forty-eight

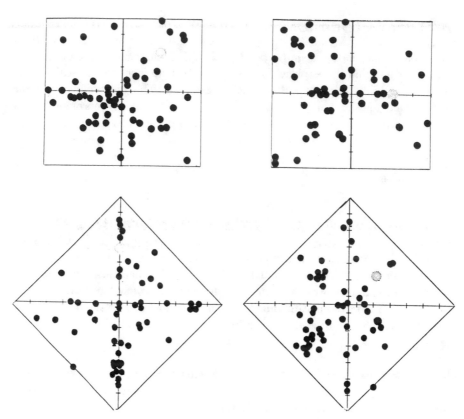

Figure 5.   Locations selected as random in a square (top row) and a diamond (bottom row) that already contained a dot, either near a corner (left column) or near a side (right column). The initial dot locations are indicated by a stippled disc.

of the 64 responses, or 75%, were within an area along the axes comprising 40% of the area of the card. The correlation was $r = 0.83$.

Side dots. These landmarks were on the axes and halfway between the side and center of the figure. The four patterns, one for each side, were superposed by rotation; these data were cumulated over subjects and are shown in the right column of Figure 5.

For the squares with a side dot, 77% of the responses were on the side of the figure opposite the landmark. The correlation was $r = 0.39$.

For the diamonds with a side dot, there is a strong preference for the diagonals of the card (the axes of the square) and some preference for the vertical. Also, 77% of the responses were on the side of the diamond opposite the landmark. The correlation was small ($r = 0.13$) because responses were both on the axes and on the diagonals, not because of no structure.

Discussion

For squares and diamonds, a landmark in the center results in relatively little observed structure, a corner dot results in some preference for the opposite corner, and a side dot results in some preference for the opposite side.

These tendencies for responses to be removed from landmarks might occur because people do not expect random events to occur close together. This would be consistent with several observations: People do not expect numbers to repeat in a random sequence (Wiesgersma, 1986), they tend not to repeat responses when guessing random sequences (Lockhead, 1983), and they do not place random marks adjacent to one another (Falk, 1981–1982). Note that this tendency to respond opposite the landmark produces symmetry. People create symmetry and thus order when they attempt to generate a random location.

THE GRASSFIRE MODEL AND SYMMETRY

People tend to place dots on the diagonals of a square. In Blum's (1973) geometric model, these diagonals are axes of symmetry. Any point on a diagonal is equally distant from adjacent sides of the square.

Blum's model and the aesthetic view to be suggested here both predict the same structure for empty figures. However, if a figure contains a landmark, there can be differences between the predictions. The difference examined here occurs when a square contains a landmark near a corner as compared with relatively far from a corner. We call these conditions *toward-the-corner* and *toward-the-center*. These conditions were generated by moving the corner dot for the above study closer to the corner of the square in one condition and closer to the center of the square in another condition.

Because aesthetics (*symmetry* might be a preferred term) predicts a tendency for balance, responses to a square containing the toward-the-corner landmark should be near the opposite corner of the square and thus far from that corner having the landmark; responses to the square having the toward-the-center landmark should be relatively more distant from the opposite corner. The grassfire model predicts the opposite ordering, that responses to the toward-the-corner stimulus should be closer to that corner than are responses to the toward-the-center condition. Figure 6 shows these grassfire predictions, calculated with the assumptions that all stimulus points (the outline square and the landmark) are ignited simultaneously and that the fire burns at a steady rate from each point until it meets the fire from some other point. The lines within Figure 6, which were not on the stimuli, show where the fires are quenched. The model predicts that responses tend to be on these quench lines.

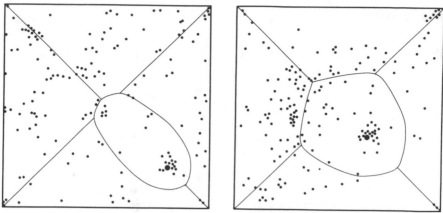

Figure 6.   The toward-the-corner (left panel) and toward-the-center (right panel) stimuli. The solid line within the square is the quench region according to the
grassfire model. The large dot in each figure is the landmark. Small dots
are the responses, a few of which are superposed.

Procedure

We tested 160 Duke University undergraduates individually. Each subject was
given an outline square on each of three pages. For half of the subjects, the first
page contained the toward-the-corner dot and the second page contained the toward-the-center dot. For the other subjects, this order was reversed. For all subjects, the last page had an empty square. The subjects were asked to place a
random dot on each page.

Results and Discussion

We cumulated responses across subjects and order for each condition. The empty-
square data show an X pattern, as before, and are not discussed further.

Responses to the landmark conditions are shown in Figure 6. These responses
are less structured than those in the landmark study discussed earlier. This may
be because each subject made only one response to each landmark, whereas they
made four responses previously. Also, the most obvious structure in these data is
independent of the contrast of concern. There is a cluster of responses near each
landmark.

Concerning symmetry, Figure 6 shows a cluster of responses symmetrically
opposite the toward-the-corner dot and several responses symmetrically opposite
the toward-the-center dot. Furthermore, the region of the cluster in the toward-
the-corner stimulus has few dots in the other stimulus, and the region with several
responses in the toward-the-center stimulus has few dots in the toward-the-corner
stimulus. This is consistent with a symmetry interpretation but not with the grassfire

model. Even more difficult for the grassfire model is the absence of any apparent relation between responses and the quench lines.

The grassfire analysis shown in Figure 6 assigned the landmark equal status with the square. This could be inappropriate. However, omitting the landmark from the analysis is also not effective. Grassfire then predicts the diagonals, and few responses occurred along those. Also, when subjects placed a dot in a circle that contained one or more dots (Psotka, 1978, Figures 6 and 8), those data again did not support the grassfire prediction. Rather, they tended to be in balance with the landmarks. Psotka suggested that "two distinct principles of balance are in operation with these stimuli. One is the grassfire process that produces the stick figure. . . . The other process would seem to be balance points in a structured space" (1978, p. 107).

Psotka's analysis might be correct. However, balance alone seems to be sufficient to describe all of the data. Balance and grassfire make the same predictions when the stimulus is empty, and balance, but not grassfire, is supported when the stimulus contains a dot. Blum's model does not aid predictions when people place dots in figures (Blum himself did not attempt to apply his model to dot-placement data). Rather, what appears to happen is that people tend to respond symmetrically to any stimulus when they are asked to place a random dot.

AESTHETICS

Placing a dot symmetrically suggests an aesthetic or artistic quality. To examine if "random" choices might be made in terms of pleasing or aesthetic locations, the following study examined which locations are pleasing.

Procedure

Three undergraduate volunteers were tested individually. Stimuli were presented within a square outline on a video display. Subjects responded by manipulating the cursor keys and the space bar of a standard keyboard.

Each subject produced 56 responses, with the following instruction: "Move the cursor to an aesthetic location inside the figure." On each trial, the cursor appeared on the screen at a computer randomized location. The subject moved the cursor by manipulating the cursor keys and pressed the space bar to indicate the response chosen. The screen then went blank and the next random cursor position was presented 1 s later.

Results and Discussion

There was a marked preference for the diagonals. This is reflected by high correlations in the data of two subjects, $r = 0.99$ and $r = 0.66$. Although the correlation for the third subject is low, $r = 0.10$, visual inspection shows a strong preference for both diagonals and for the vertical and horizontal axes. Combining these responses resulted in a low correlation, although the data are highly structured. Also, we replicated this study with 23 high school students as subjects. That correlation is $r = 0.98$.

We conclude that the structure of "aesthetic" judgments is similar to the structure of "random" judgments.

GENERAL DISCUSSION

Subjective randomness has a statistically nonuniform probability distribution for both sequential arrays and spatial arrays. Accordingly, von Mises's description of subjective randomness and the principle of indifference are rejected. In addition, Garner's (1962) definition of meaning as structure is interpreted to relate that structure to subjective randomness rather than to stochastic independence.

It has been known for a long time that stochastic and perceptual independence are different. The primary question here has been what determines whether an event will be judged as random or as not random. A partial answer is found in subjects' expectations concerning aesthetics or balance among relevant attributes.

Although no attempt is made here to predict what attributes and relations determine performance in all situations, some generalizations may be available. Concerning serial arrays, on those occasions on which structure is not perceived, successive items are overly similar and separated items are overly different. There is both assimilation and contrast. This occurs whether people attempt to generate random digits, identify strings of digits as random, identify stimulus intensities, judge stimulus magnitudes, or guess events.

Concerning spatial structure, people are not successful in selecting random locations. Rather, their choices are structured in relation to features of the stimulus. For an empty square or rectangle, the center, sides, and corners are referents for determining "random" responses.

Still, there is variability in the "random" responses. They do not all occur at the same place. This is because there are many referents and there is no unique solution to the problem of determining the subjectively most random location. For example, if the response is moved away from one referent, it necessarily becomes closer to another. Hence, some compromise is needed. Consider the square. If a subject attends to one corner, the optimum response is on the diagonal bisecting that angle. This is because this is the maximum distance possible from the attended two sides. Where to respond on the diagonal becomes the next problem. If the response is moved far from that corner, it becomes too close to the opposite corner, which is also a referent. The best choice in terms of corners and sides is the center, but that is also a referent. There is no good "random" location. The summary outcome is that responses tend to be near one or the other diagonal and tend to be near, but not at, the center.

The fact that "random" dots tend to be near, but not at, regions of balance is not because of careless responding or an inability to place a dot accurately. In the "aesthetic" and "not-random" tasks, many responses were placed quite precisely at the center. These observations, plus simply watching people perform the tasks (which is somehow even more compelling), suggests that two steps are involved when people attempt to make random responses. They first select a location within the figure; that selection is based on aesthetics. They then move their pencils just enough to respond at nonpredictable places (i.e., places not precisely defined by referents). In addition, it appears that some subjects, rather than wobble the pencil a bit at the aesthetic location, instead quickly move their pencils along the diagonal of the figure and respond directly opposite the "predicted" place, which of course is another aesthetic place.

Aesthetics

The aesthetic task was conducted to learn something about the bases for this proposed initial response, the one on which the "random" response would be based. The aesthetic data specify the same referents as the random data, except with greater precision. Aesthetic dots are placed in clear balance, and random dots are placed in noisy balance, with features of the stimulus.

Aesthetic responses and random responses are thus similar. We infer that aesthetic judgments reveal underlying tendencies that guide "random" judgments and that some elementary processes involved in aesthetic choice are also involved in judgments of randomness.

Art

Aesthetics have sometimes been associated with randomness or chance by both artists and viewers. Many artists have spoken of a tension between order and chaos or randomness. Others have spoken of producing chaos to offset order. Still others have reported using mechanical means to create artistic expressions that escape individual and societal biases. These artists report seeking freedom through chance.

Artist George Brecht (1966) defined *automatism* as a chance process of creating art under the guidance of the unconscious. Dadaists used what they considered meaningless babble in searching for images unbiased by society or artificial restriction (Brecht, 1966). Surrealists used chance constructions in searching for unconscious content.

Surrealist Gregory Gillespie has said that the subconscious provides the raw material upon which his conscious operates (personal communication, March 20,

1986). He combined doodles to produce symmetric patterns and make new order out of what he described as initially arbitrary elements. Mechanical processes have also been used to produce chance images. Duchamp dropped an inked thread onto a page three times, creating the three images he titled "3 stoppages etalon." He also used variations produced by wind and gravity to produce chance images. Arp and Ernst also explored chance effects: Arp shuffled scraps of paper to create chance collages, and Ernst developed the "decalcomania of chance" by spreading ink between papers that were then pulled apart, perhaps reminiscent of a Rorschach ink blot. Later, Jackson Pollock flung paint onto the canvas, creating what has been interpreted as an intricate web of variety and as demonstrating the unpredictability of vital energy. Concerning this, Brecht (1966) acclaimed that "Pollock has demonstrated that the ability of humans to appreciate complex chance images is almost unlimited" (p. 7) and that "chance in the arts provides a means for escaping the biases ingrained in our personality by our culture and personal past history, that is, it is a means of attaining greater generality" (p. 14). Concerning consumers of such art, it has been reported that "the random or arbitrary qualities of his [Jackson Pollock's] paintings have disturbed many viewers" (Rohn, 1987, p. 1).

Is this really the case? Do such presentations totally escape personal biases in the production of art? Suppose the artist chooses whether or not to accept a product of the mechanical process, or to sometimes try again. Then the artist would be judging which images were subjectively random or aesthetic. He or she would not be presenting truly random (stochastically independent) occurrences. We have no direct evidence of whether or not this occurred in works that have explicitly been claimed to be totally mechanical. But if it did, then, in much the same way that our subjects selected strings of numerals or locations as being random, these artists selected what only appears random but what is actually aesthetic and nonrandom.

The view of Irwin Kremen, who creates collages, is consistent with this suggestion. When he transforms bits of colored papers into a new synthesis, Kremen accepts that chance occurrences may happen. But he further explains that "I decide whether or not to use the chance effects, and I transform them into the integration I seek" (Kremen & Flint, 1978). It is also true, despite Arnheim's (1966) conclusion that Pollock and other abstract expressionists left too much to chance, that Pollock's work is not random. Rather, Pollock practiced his "spontaneous" strokes for years and "his paintings are filled with these accidental and random irregularities, which the artist has generally resolved by a counterbalancing element that lies off center" (Rohn, 1987, p. 108). Such control is nicely demonstrated by Rohn's analysis of Pollock's painting titled "November 11, 1949." This square-format abstract is clearly based on poles that are drawn in strict symmetry in each quadrant of the square. Rhythmic structure in the painting is achieved by the addition of strokes that are only superficially random but that actually provide the overall integrity of the work.

Possibly, the subjects in our experiments are fledgling Jackson Pollocks. They too tended to place "random" marks near the center of each quadrant and to make adjustments to these aesthetic locations to mask this underlying structure.

Conclusion

We infer a two-step process that takes place when people attempt to generate a random event. They first select an aesthetic event, which they then change sufficiently for that event to appear unpredictable. The results are that (a) perceived structure is measureably different from stochastic structure; (b) structure as meaning must be referenced to subjectively random events rather than to statistically independent events; and (c) art, aesthetics, and subjective randomness are intimately related.

References

Arnheim, R. (1966). *Toward a psychology of art*. Berkeley: University of California Press.

Blum, H. (1973). Biological shape and visual science (Pt. 1). *Journal of Theoretical Biology, 38*, 205–287.

Brecht, G. (1966). *Chance–Imagery*. New York: Great Bear.

Budescu, D. V. (1987). A markov model for generation of random binary sequences. *Journal of Experimental Psychology: Human Perception and Performance, 13*, 25–39.

Cohen, J., & Hansel, M. (1956). *Risk and gambling: The study of subjective probability*. New York: Philosophical Library.

Falk, R. (1981–1982). On coincidences. *The Skeptical Inquirer, 6*, 18–31.

Garner, W. R. (1962). *Uncertainty and structure as psychological concepts*. New York: Wiley.

Gilovich, T., Vallone, R., & Tversky, A. (1985). The hot hand in basketball: On the misperception of random sequences. *Cognitive Psychology, 17*, 295–314.

Kremen, I., & Flint, J. (1978). Why collage? An interview with the artist. In *Collages by Irwin Kremen*. Washington, DC: Smithsonian Institution Press.

Lockhead, G. R. (1983). Sequential predictors of choice in psychophysical tasks. In S. Kornblum and J. Requin (Eds.), *Preparatory states and processes* (pp. 27–47). New York: Erlbaum.

May, R. M. (1976). Simple mathematical models with very complicated dynamics. *Nature, 261*, 459–467.

Neuringer, A. (1986). Can people behave "randomly?": The role of feedback. *Journal of Experimental Psychology: General, 115*, 62–75.

Psotka, J. (1978). Perceptual processes that may create stick figures and balance. *Journal of Experimental Psychology: Human Perception and Performance, 4*, 101–111.

Rohn, M. L. (1987). *Visual dynamics in Jackson Pollock's abstractions*. Ann Arbor: University of Michigan Press.

von Mises, R. (1957). *Probability, statistics, and truth*. New York: Macmillan.

Wiesgersma, S. (1986). A control theory of sequential response production. *Psychological Research*, *44*, 175–188.

CHAPTER 7

APPARENT RANDOMNESS IS NOT ALWAYS THE COMPLEMENT OF APPARENT ORDER

MICHAEL KUBOVY
AND DAVID GILDEN

We asked 124 subjects to simulate a series of 240 tosses of a fair coin. Multiple regression analyses revealed that sequence generation is constrained by run length, the frequency of alternation, and the imbalance between heads and tails. Subjects did not avoid patterned or symmetric subsequences. These results are discussed in terms of the way subjects view the history of prior responses as they form future responses.

In *Uncertainty and Structure as Psychological Concepts* (1962), Garner introduced the idea of psychological redundancy as the size of an inferred subset by comparing two sequences, each of which consists of five Xs and five Os:

O X O X O X O X O X
X O O O X O X X O X

This research was supported by National Science Foundation Grant BNS-8796287 to the University of Virginia (Michael Kubovy, principal investigator). David Gilden was supported at the University of Virginia by National Institute of Child Health and Human Development Post-Doctoral Fellowship 5F32-HD07036.

We thank Ruma Falk, William P. Gardner, Daniel Kahneman, J. Jack McArdle, Dennis R. Proffitt, Eric Turkheimer, and Amos Tversky for their helpful comments at various stages of this project.

If these symbols represented tosses of a fair coin, with X standing for heads and O standing for tails, each of these sequences of events would be equally likely to occur at random, with a probability of 2^{-10}. So says the statistician, who assumes the coin to be fair and pays attention to the process generating the sequences. But, according to Garner, "any but the most perverse subject would say . . . that the first pattern was more regular, more meaningful, and even more redundant than the second" (1962, p. 202). This is because when people are asked to compare two such sequences, their attention is not drawn to the generating mechanism but to the surface characteristics, to the way they might dictate each sequence to a secretary. The first sequence could be described as "OX repeated five times." The second is much harder to describe: "an X followed by three Os, and X, an O, two Xs, an O, and an X."

When people say that the first sequence is more regular, meaningful, and redundant than the second, they are not thinking of the set of 1,024 equiprobable patterns envisaged by the statistician, but of the small subset of patterns that might be dictated in almost the same way. The first sequence has a siamese twin: "X O repeated five times." The second sequence is related to a vast tribe of equally unruly relatives: the sequence read back to front, the Xs and Os interchanged, the first half interchanged with the second, and so on. The smaller the subset people tend to infer from the description of a sequence, the greater the regularity, the meaningfulness, and the redundancy they ascribe to it.

Apparent disorder and randomness might be expected to be the converse of apparent regularity, meaningfulness, and redundancy. That is, one might think that the less regularity people find in a sequence, the more likely they are to consider it random. But Kahneman and Tversky (1972) showed that this hypothesis is only partly correct. It is true that subjects estimate the number of families in which the exact order of births of boys and girls was BBBGGG to be significantly lower than the number of families in which the order of births was GBBGBG. However, apparent disorder is not sufficient to get subjects to label a sequence random; the sequence must also reflect "salient features of the process by which it is generated" (Kahneman & Tversky, 1972, p. 430). Laymen insist that even a short random sequence must contain about the same number of Xs and Os; to ensure rough equality of frequency, they believe that there must be fewer long runs of Xs or Os, that is, more frequent alternations between Xs and Os, than expected in Bernoulli trials. This is the gambler's fallacy. But the logic behind this fallacy is not all that different from correct probabilistic reasoning, which also requires that the sequence reflect features of the generating process. The difference is in the choice of features. According to probability theory, all *sequences of events*, all sequences of Xs and Os, regardless of length, are equally probable in equiprobable Bernoulli trials. Laymen, to the contrary, view chance "as a self-correcting process in which a deviation in one direction induces a deviation in the opposite direction to restore the equilibrium. In fact, deviations are not 'corrected' as a chance process unfolds, they are merely diluted" (Tversky &

Kahneman, 1974, p. 1125). Thus, they believe that all *events* must be equally frequent in all sequences of Xs and Os, whatever their length. Because this belief is a better approximation to the truth for longer sequences (the Law of Large Numbers), and because laymen do not know that their belief is true only for infinitely long sequences, Tversky and Kahneman (1971) called this common fallacy the Law of Small Numbers (LSN).

Taken together, LSN and the requirement that sequences avoid conspicuous patterns instantiate Kahneman and Tversky's (1972) representativeness heuristic as applied to random sequences. All random sequences must be representative of the two fundamental properties of the generating process (as laymen understand it): equiprobability and disorder.

It has been argued that the representativeness heuristic has "little predictive value" (Wallsten, 1980, p. 219), or that it "is but a redescription of the phenomenon" being explained (Gigerenzer & Murray, 1987, p. 155). Indeed, one has to think through the implications of the representativeness heuristic afresh for each new probabilistic judgment, inference, or production task it explains. For instance, the representativeness heuristic as applied to understanding the gambler's fallacy takes on a different form when it is applied to the phenomenon of base-rate neglect (Kahneman & Tversky, 1973; Tversky & Kahneman, 1971, 1974, 1982). These different forms depend strongly on analyses of the subject's understanding of the task and on an analysis of subtle effects of verbal framing that may affect the subject's interpretation of the situation.

Whatever the level of generality of the concept of representativeness, in the case of binary random sequences, which concern us here, the representativeness heuristic has been made satisfactorily specific. Indeed, the representativeness heuristic has testable implications: If we ask subjects to simulate Bernoulli trials, we expect them to equalize the frequencies of the two event types in short subsequences, and to avoid conspicuous patterns in short subsequences of responses.

THE EXPERIMENT

We handed out test answer sheets designed for multiple-choice and true–false tests to students in a large Introduction to Psychology class. There were 240 items on the sheet, organized in six columns of 40 items (see Figure 1). The students were asked to fill in circles A or B according to whether they had imagined the coin to have come up heads or tails. After the participants had all produced 240 responses, they were asked to write on their answer sheet whether they had filled in their responses in order or haphazardly. The following analysis is based on the 126 subjects whose responses were entered in order and who had produced 240 computer-readable responses.

Our subjects produced $240 = u + v$ binary symbols $e_1, \ldots, e_{240}$, where u stands for the number of 0s and v stands for the number of 1s.

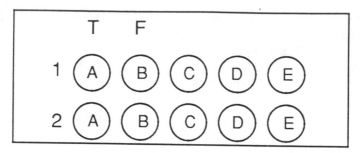

Figure 1.   The first two items on the Test Answer Sheet.

Preliminary Analyses

Before proceeding with the main analysis, we performed two preliminary analyses:

Equiprobability

First, $u = v$? Not quite. The 95% confidence interval for the proportions had a lower limit of .490 and an upper limit of .498.

Stationarity

Second, are the time series generated by the subjects stationary? To answer this question, we tested two hypotheses regarding stationarity.

Hypothesis 1 was that the proportion of runs of length 1 did not differ in the first and second halves of the runs. These proportions of runs of length 1 were 53.60% and 55.04% for the first and second halves, respectively. Two parametric tests did not reject the hypothesis. The difference was not significant either by t tests for paired samples on the proportions ($t_{127} = 1.82$, ns) or on their folded logs (Tukey, 1977, p. 670; $t_{127} = 1.52$, ns). One re-expression of the data did yield a significant difference: the folded root (Tukey, 1977, p. 670; $t_{127} = 1.99$, $p \le .0477$). This is, however, a small effect: It explains 14% of the variance. Because the histograms of the differences between proportions and their re-expressions showed notable deviations from normality, we performed two distribution-free tests, and both rejected the hypothesis: Wilcoxon's signed rank test (large sample approximation), $T^* = 2.31$, $p \le .0104$, and Fisher's sign test (large sample approximation), $B^* = 2.21$, $p \le .0136$.

Hypothesis 2 was that the distribution of runs longer than 1 did not differ between the first and second half of each subject's data. We calculated two sets of observations: the lengths of runs in the first half of the data and the lengths of runs for the second half of the data of each subject. We performed a Kolmogorov–Smirnov test on the data of our 128 subjects to determine whether both samples were drawn from the same population. We rejected the hypothesis ($\alpha = .05$) for

The sequence:

0 1 1 0 1 1 1 0 1 0 1 0 1 1 . . .

1:	0
	1
	1
	0

2:	0 1
	1 1
	1 0
	0 1

3:	0 1 1
	1 1 0
	1 0 1
	0 1 1

4:	0 1 1 0
	1 1 0 1
	1 0 1 1
	0 1 1 1

. . . .

11:	0 1 1 0 1 1 1 0 1 0 1
	1 1 0 1 1 1 0 1 0 1 0
	1 0 1 1 1 0 1 0 1 0 1
	0 1 1 1 0 1 0 1 0 1 1

Figure 2. Generating the *k*-tuple frequency tables. At the top of the table is a hypothetical subject's sequence. In each box are the length of the *k*-tuple (on the left in bold numbers) and successive *k*-tuple tokens, drawn from the sequence at the top, whose frequency is to be tallied (on the right, in staggered rows).

only one of our subjects, whereas we had expected to observe significant outcomes (5% of 128) for 6 or 7 subjects by chance.

Although the tests of the first hypothesis present a mixed picture, our analyses are favorable overall to the conclusion that the first and the second halves of the data are equivalent and that the time series is therefore stationary.

Type Counts

We arbitrarily divided the 124 subjects into two groups of 62. We then considered each subject's data as a series of overlapping *k*-tuple tokens (see Figure 2). In the case of 4-tuples, responses $e_i e_{i+1} e_{i+2} e_{i+3}$ form the *i*th token, and responses $e_{i+1} e_{i+2} e_{i+3} e_{i+4}$ form the $(i + 1)$th token. Each 4-tuple represents one of $2^4 = 16$ types (e.g., 0000, 0001, 0010, 0011, . . . , 1111). We formed

Table 1.

A k-TUPLE TYPE COUNT FOR $k = 6$

Type		Count		Features				
				Law Small Numbers			Pattern	
Decimal	Binary	Ob-served	Ex-pected	Im-balance	Longest Run	Alter-nations	Palin-drome	Period-icity
0	000000	85	227.656	3.0	6	0	1	0
1	000001	129	227.656	2.0	5	1	0	0
2	000010	191	227.656	2.0	4	2	0	0
3	000011	214	227.656	1.0	4	1	0	0
4	000100	184	227.656	2.0	3	2	0	0
5	000101	527	227.656	1.0	3	3	0	0
6	000110	486	227.656	1.0	3	2	0	0
7	000111	245	227.656	0.0	3	1	0	0
8	001000	232	227.656	2.0	3	2	0	0
9	001001	376	227.656	1.0	2	3	0	2
64	111111	96	227.656	3.0	6	0	1	0

a table of the counts of each k-tuple type (see Table 1) and obtained k-tuple type counts for subject groups $g = 1, 2$, for k-tuple lengths $k = 4, \ldots, 11$, and k-tuple types $t = 0, \ldots, 2^k - 1$. The data for each subject give us 240 $- k + 1$ k-tuples, for a total of $62 \times (240 - k + 1)$ k-tuples per group. If the process generating the data were Bernoulli, we would expect $62 \times (240 - k + 1)/2^k$ tokens for each type. For the amount of data we collected, the practical upper bound on the value of k is 11 because when $k = 11$, the expected count of tokens per type of 11-tuple is only 6.96. We did not use $k = 2$ or 3 because we know from analyses not presented here that such short sequences do not determine subjects' responses.

From this point on, our dependent variables will be 16 (2 groups $\times$ 8 types) type-count tables (each 2^k long). Each group of subjects gives us tables for $k = 4, \ldots, 11$ (see a graphic representation for the two groups, with $k = 10$, in Figure 3). Each such table allows us to obtain a count of basic counts (Tukey, 1977, p. 550) or a discrete frequency distribution (Hoaglin & Tukey, 1985): We count how many types were generated with a basic count of one, two, $\ldots$, up to the basic count of the most often chosen type(s). We observed that all of these discrete frequency distributions are skewed downward (shown on the left side of Figure 4). Because the square root approximately stabilizes the variance of a Poisson random variable (Emerson, 1983, Section 8G) or of a binomial random variable when n is large and np is small (as may happen in a frequency distribution), we transform our distribution by using the square roots of the type counts instead of just type counts. As expected, the discrete frequency distribution of the square roots of the type counts for $k = 11$ is symmetric (right side of Figure 4); it is

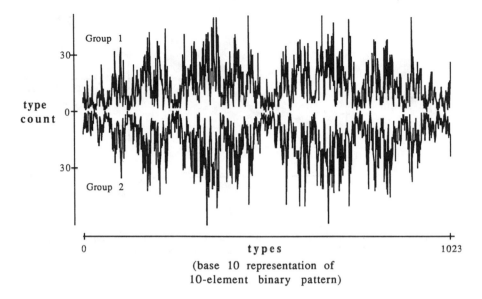

Figure 3. A graphic representation of a *k*-tuple type count for *k* = 10, comparing the type counts for the two groups of subjects. Each type is interpreted as a binary number and plotted in ascending order. (The numbers on the abscissa are the decimal equivalents of the binary numbers.)

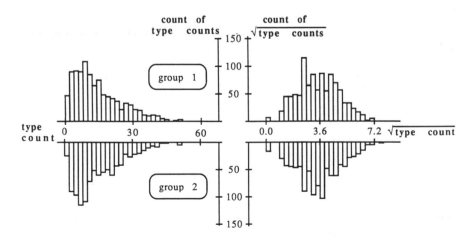

Figure 4. Left: frequency (count) of type counts for the two groups of subjects. Right: count of the square roots of the type counts for the two groups of subjects.

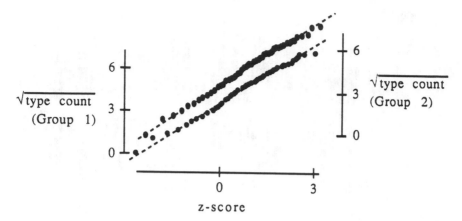

Figure 5. Normal probability plots of the square roots of the type counts for the two groups of subjects, showing that we have succeeded in re-expressing the data into a Gaussian distribution.

also well approximated by a Gaussian distribution (Figure 5). Therefore all analyses were done on the square root of type counts.

Main Analysis

We have one goal: to determine how the representativeness heuristic manifests itself in the subjects' patterns of responding.

Type Features: Their Two Classes

Each of the 2^k k-tuple types for $k = 4, \ldots, 11$ can be characterized by five features:

1. *Imbalance:* $|(k/2) - u|$, where k is the length of the k-tuple, and u is the number of 0s (e.g., for 0001000, imbalance = 2.5).
2. *Longest run* (e.g., for 0010001, longest run = 3).
3. *Alternations* (e.g., for 0010001, alternations = 3).
4. *Palindrome* (e.g., for 001100 and 0010100, palindrome = 1).
5. *Periodicity* (e.g., for 011011011, the subpattern 011 is repeated three times, so periodicity = 3).

We grouped these features into two classes. The first three features are *LSN features*: A subject who uses the LSN part of the representativeness heuristic will avoid generating patterns with a high imbalance, a long run, or too many alternations. The two remaining features are *pattern features*: A subject who avoids conspicuous patterns will avoid generating palindromes or periodic patterns.

The Heart of the Analysis

To establish the relative importance of the two classes, for each k we regressed the square roots of the type counts separately on the LSN features and the pattern features to determine which explains a greater percentage of the variability of the square roots of the type counts.

Because the two classes of independent variables are not of equal size, we used cross-validation to make a parameter-free comparison. In other words, we tried to circumvent the problem that would arise if the three LSN independent variables were to predict the dependent variable better than the two pattern independent variables had: Did the LSN variables predict better because they are more numerous? For each value of k, we performed the regression for each group and obtained the predicted square roots of the type counts. Then, as a parameter-free comparison of the effectiveness of the two classes of features, we regressed the observed square roots of the type counts for one group on the predicted square roots of the type counts derived from the other. The percentage variability explained by these two regressions for each k must be adjusted for the following reason: The cross-validated values of R^2 in question are bounded by the reliability of the data being explained—the percentage variability in the observed square roots of the type counts in one group explained by their variation in the other (see Figure 6), which we call the *percentage of explainable variability*. That is why it is relative to this upper bound that we calculate the "percentage explainable variability explained" shown in Figure 7.

From Figure 7, it is clear that the pattern features explain essentially none of the variability beyond 4-tuples, whereas the LSN features do well throughout the range of k-tuples. In an analysis too extensive to be presented in this chapter, we showed that subjects are probably not considering k-tuples shorter than 5 or longer than 7. Hence, LSN features are essentially in complete control of the subjects' behavior, accounting for 80–90% of the available variance.

Discussion

In the generation of random sequences, people evidently pay little attention to the figural redundancies of the patterns they are generating. Sequences that were redundant by virtue of containing the repetition of a subsequence or by containing a mirror symmetry were not avoided. On the other hand, people attend to the numerical properties of sequence counts: length of longest run, number of alternations, and imbalance between head and tail count. These results are in apparent conflict with the notion that figural symmetries are not perceived to be the output of a random process. The exclusive control exercised over the numerical properties of the sequence counts may stem from the task imposed on the subject: the generation of a random sequence.

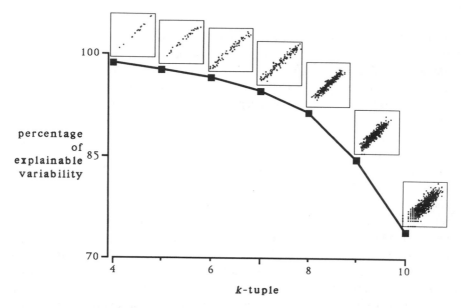

Figure 6.   Intergroup reliability for seven *k*-tuple lengths: percentage variation explained when regressing the square roots of the type counts of one group
on the other. The inset scatter diagrams show the data to which the graph
applies.

Consider subjects who weigh the responses they have generated when they
choose their current response (i.e., they open a window on their recent responses).
Analyses that we have performed suggest that this window comprises between
four and nine responses. The subjects' ability to control patterning of the responses
depends on how they use this window. If subjects look at a range of windows
rather than a window of a fixed size, they will find it difficult to remove patterning
from all window sizes simultaneously. In numerical studies, we found that palindromes of length 4 to 11 could not be removed simultaneously from a sequence
of Bernoulli trials. Repeating subsequences could be expunged from Bernoulli
trials, but all algorithms explored required several passes through the sequence.
Thus, pattern symmetries are not controlled because they cannot be removed in
the range of window sizes subjects use to determine future responses.

The constraints imposed by simultaneous window sizes do not pertain to
the numerical (LSN) properties of sequences. Sequences that alternate often on
small scales will also alternate often on large scales. Similarly, if the imbalance
between heads and tails is moderated in small windows, it will also be moderated
in large windows (although the converse is not true). But subjects do not always
use small windows to control the numerical properties of sequences. For example,
runs of length 4 are common. We do not have a theory of how subjects generate

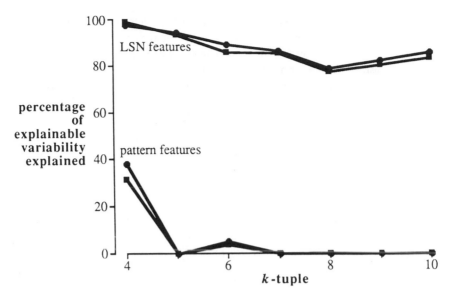

Figure 7.   Percentage variation explained by the two classes of features—law of small
numbers (LSN) features and pattern features—for seven k = tuple lengths.

sequences, but it appears that they use windows of fluctuating size as they generate
new responses.

The issue of window size and the problems associated with the simultaneous
satisfaction of a given criterion on a range of scales does not exist in the stimuli
used by Garner or by Kahneman and Tversky discussed at the beginning of this
chapter. The stimuli they used were fixed in length, and their length was small.
Given a string representing birth order, BBBGGG, subjects cannot analyze its
symmetries on a range of scales. The natural scale of the stimulus is compelling,
and an analysis of the pattern's symmetries is readily achieved.

It is not hard to understand why subjects generating sequences such as ours
do not avoid subsequence repetition and symmetry. Consider the following sequence:

BBBGGGBBGBGGGBBBGGGGBBBBBB . . .

Although this sequence contains many symmetric subsequences, they are not
salient. Here are some of them, indicated in boldface:

BB**BGGGB**BGBGGGBBBGGGGBBBBBB,
BBBGGGBBG**BGGGB**BBGGGGBBBBBB,
BBBGGGBBGBGG**GBBBG**GGGBBBBBB,
BBBGGGBBGBGGGBB**BGGGGB**BBBBB.

We believe that subjects do not avoid symmetries in the generation of random sequences because they are not salient. The symmetry of a five-element string embedded in a long sequence can be perceived only if two conditions are met: (a) Segmentation forms a partition of the sequence (i.e., subdivides the sequence into subsequences, called *cells*, that are disjoint and whose union is the sequence), and (b) the five-element string is one of the cells of the segmentation.

For guidance on how to think about the segmentation of long sequences, we turn to Garner's (1974, Lecture 3) work on periodic sequences of auditory events. Consider the following sequence, which has a period of nine elements:

... XXOXOOOOOXXOXOOOOOXXOXOOOOO ...

Garner has shown that in such sequences, the preferred segmentation is one bracketed by the longest runs. In the example above, a repeating pattern is heard: It starts with "**X X**" and ends with "**O O O O O**."

We do not know how people would segment the *aperiodic* sequences that were generated in the present experiment. It is unlikely that the cells of the partition would be of fixed size. To the extent that subjects segmented the sequence at all, we expect that they used a rule akin to the one Garner proposed for periodic sequences: They segment the sequence into short (<10 elements) patterns that begin and end in relatively long runs. Thus, for instance, in the example given earlier, the sequence . . . GG**GBBBG**GGG . . . could be a cell of the segmentation, but the symmetric pattern printed in bold characters would not be. It would not be noticed, and therefore would not be avoided.

Furthermore, it is not likely that the segmentation of a sequence that is growing could affect the growth of the sequence. If a pattern requires both a perceived beginning and a perceived end to become a cell, then its symmetry can be perceived only after the leading edge of the sequence has passed it by, that is, after it is complete. At that point, it cannot be undone.

Thus, if the sequence is long, people will not notice symmetries. Subjects can do no more than control the numerical properties of subsequences when they apply the representativeness heuristic.

We are left with doubts regarding the status of the representativeness heuristic as a theory of judgment and choice. We are not convinced that it constrained our thinking beyond what had already been said about the perception and generation of randomness (by Garner, for example). Although it is useful to have solid evidence on the relative importance of LSN features and pattern features, we should have known all along that pattern features would not play a major role. We may have taken the implications of the representativeness heuristic too seriously. There is no procedure for deducing just how representativeness will be implemented in a given context, such as the one studied here, and we perhaps should not have tried.

If we approach our subjects' behavior assuming that representativeness is the heuristic guiding their behavior, then we will say—as we have said above—that not all aspects of representativeness manifested themselves in this task because not all of the relevant information was perceptible to the subjects. But perhaps we ought to interpret the data reported in this chapter as undermining the theory, for otherwise we are placing the notion of representativeness in an empirically invulnerable position, because it is unlikely that we will ever observe more directly whether subjects use a tacit heuristic when they judge and choose courses of action. Kahneman and Tversky's notions of heuristics, such as availability and representativeness, are not theories; they are at best frames for theories, to be filled with an account of how and why people do what they do in particular situations. The epistemological role of such theory frames has yet to be explicated.

References

Emerson, J. D. (1983). Mathematical aspects of transformation. In D. C. Hoaglin, F. Mosteller, & J. W. Tukey (Eds.), *Understanding robust and exploratory data analysis* (pp. 247–282). New York: Wiley.

Garner, W. R. (1962). *Uncertainty and structure as psychological concepts*. New York: Wiley.

Garner, W. R. (1974). *The processing of information and structure*. Potomac, MD: Erlbaum.

Gigerenzer, G., & Murray, D. J. (1987). *Cognition as intuitive statistics*. Hillsdale, NJ: Erlbaum.

Hoaglin, D. C., & Tukey, J. W. (1985). Checking the shape of discrete distributions. In D. C. Hoaglin, F. Mosteller, & J. W. Tukey (Eds.), *Exploring data tables, trends, and shapes* (pp. 345–416). New York: Wiley.

Kahneman, D., & Tversky, A. (1972). Subjective probability: A judgment of representativeness. *Cognitive Psychology, 3*, 430–454.

Kahneman, D., & Tversky, A. (1973). On the psychology of prediction. *Psychological Review, 80*, 237–251. [Reprinted in Tversky & Kahneman, 1982]

Tukey, J. W. (1977). *Exploratory data analysis*. Reading, MA: Addison-Wesley.

Tversky, A., & Kahneman, D. (1971). Belief in the law of small numbers. *Psychological Bulletin, 2*, 105–110.

Tversky, A., & Kahneman, D. (1974). Judgment under uncertainty: Heuristics and biases. *Science, 185*, 1124–1131. [Reprinted in Tversky & Kahneman, 1982]

Tversky, A., & Kahneman, D. (1982). Evidential impact of base rates. In D. Kahneman, P. Slovic, & A. Tversky (Eds.), *Judgment under uncertainty: Heuristics and biases* (pp. 153–160). Cambridge, England: Cambridge University Press.

Wallsten, T. S. (1980). Processes and models to describe choice and inference behavior. In T. S. Wallsten (Ed.), *Cognitive processes in choice and decision behavior* (pp. 215–237). Hillsdale, NJ: Erlbaum.

PART TWO

ATTRIBUTES AND ATTENTION

CHAPTER 8

REDUNDANCY GAIN REVISITED:
EVIDENCE FOR PARALLEL PROCESSING OF SEPARABLE DIMENSIONS

HOWARD E. EGETH
AND J. TOBY MORDKOFF

According to feature-integration theory (e.g., Treisman & Gelade, 1980), when subjects search for a target defined in terms of a conjunction of several separable dimensions, such that each nontarget shares a feature with the target, each display element must be examined in turn until the target is found. The usual method for assessing whether search is serial and self-terminating is to measure reaction time as a function of display numerosity. However, serious problems with this methodology have been pointed out (e.g., Townsend, 1972). In the present experiments, subjects indicated whether a specific target element was present; on some trials, two targets were presented. Analysis of the reaction-time distributions using a method introduced by Miller (1982) indicated that the decrease in reaction time found on redundant-target trials was too great to be compatible with any sort of serial-decisions model (as well as certain varieties of parallel models). We conclude that at least two objects may simultaneously have their color and form conjoined into unified percepts.

The research reported in this chapter was supported in part by grants from the Air Force Office of Scientific Research (87-0180), the National Aeronautics and Space Administration (JRI NCA2-171), and the National Institute of Mental Health (R01-MH43924). We gratefully acknowledge the advice of Steven Yantis, Anne Treisman, William Bacon, Dale Dagenbach, Bruce Hamill, Douglas Johnson, and Richard Powell, as well as the aid of Katrina VanValen and Craig McDowell, in collecting the data. A preliminary report was made at the 60th Annual Meeting of the Eastern Psychological Association, Boston, Massachusetts, April 1989.

The issues that we address in this chapter relate to several of the topics to which Wendell Garner has made important contributions in the course of his career. These issues include the divisibility of attention, the use of the redundancy-gain paradigm, and the processing of separable dimensions.

One of the most interesting developments in the study of dimensional interaction is an extension of Garner's original characterization of separable and integral dimensions (e.g., Garner & Felfoldy, 1970). We refer to Treisman's work on feature-integration theory (e.g., Treisman & Gelade, 1980; Treisman & Gormican, 1988). This work suggests that separable dimensions can be characterized by two diagnostic criteria in addition to those proposed by Garner. First, discriminations involving a single dimension can be handled in a spatially parallel manner. Thus, when searching for a target that differs from nontargets in terms of a single conspicuous feature (such as color, orientation, motion, or shape), the total number of elements in the display matters little. Second, when the target of a search is defined in terms of the conjunction of several separable dimensions, such that each nontarget shares a feature with the target, then each display element must be examined in turn until the target is found. In other words, search is serial and self-terminating.

A central aspect of feature-integration theory is that conjunctions need to be processed one location at a time. We question whether this assumption is correct; several recent findings suggest that it may not be. For example, Egeth, Virzi, and Garbart (1984) showed that subjects do not have to search randomly through stimulus locations, but instead may be guided by one of the conjunction target's features. For example, when searching for a red O among red Ns and black Os, subjects were able to search only through the red items when so instructed. In one experiment, the total number of display elements was varied, but the number of red items was held constant at three. The response-time functions were flat, as would be the case if subjects were ignoring the varying number of black items and restricting their search to just the red items.

This finding does not by itself undermine the basic tenet of feature-integration theory that attention, and thus serial processing, is required to conjoin two features into a single representation, but it does indicate that not all items receive equal consideration. Some items may be excluded from further analysis by an early, parallel process and, thus, never reach the serial decision stage (Cave & Wolfe, 1990; Treisman & Sato, 1990). Similar problems for the theory have recently been reported by others, including Nakayama and Silverman (1986) and Wolfe, Cave, and Franzel (1989).

Problems of a rather different sort for the serial-processing account of feature-integration theory arise from a paper by Pashler (1987). In a series of experiments, he found that when one restricts analysis to display sizes of eight and under, the slope ratio of target-absent to target-present trials was closer to 1:1 than 2:1. This result was observed both when only these small displays were used and when such displays were analyzed separately in experiments that allowed display size to range as high as 32. These 1:1 slope ratios might suggest that search is serial and exhaustive for small displays. However, in a final experiment, Pashler added a second target on some trials and showed a redundancy gain—that is, mean response time was faster when there were two targets in the display than when there was just one.

Note that a redundancy gain is incompatible with a simple serial exhaustive model; if processing is exhaustive, then it shouldn't matter how many targets are found before the end of processing. Pashler suggested that the overall pattern of his data might best be interpreted as showing limited-capacity parallel processing for both small displays and small "clumps" within larger displays. However, although Pashler succeeded in providing evidence that is incompatible with both exhaustive and self-terminating varieties of serial models, he did not have a paradigm that could provide strong evidence of parallel processing.

The usual method for determining whether processing is serial or parallel is to examine the effect of display size on response time. However, in view of the problems with that method pointed out by Townsend (1971, 1972; see also, Townsend & Ashby, 1983), it is useful to have alternative methods such as the redundant-target paradigm as applied by Pashler. Unfortunately, even the redundant-target experiment has problems. It turns out that it is not sufficient simply to compare overall mean response times and to conclude in favor of parallel processing if the redundant-target condition is faster than the average of the single-target conditions. There are certain artifacts that can produce such a redundancy gain even if processing is not parallel. Suppose, for example, that for each subject there is a particular favored position in the display that is processed more quickly than the others, perhaps because it is inspected first in a serial scan. The greater the number of targets, the greater the probability that one of them will be in the favored position and, thus, the faster the mean response time. Some analyses have been proposed to deal with this problem (e.g., Biederman & Checkosky, 1970; Miller & Lopes, 1988), but there is another even more insidious problem lurking: There may be a favored position that is not fixed but varies randomly over trials. Van der Heijden, La Heij, and Boer (1983) have proposed an analysis to deal with this problem; however, it now appears that even this analysis is inadequate (for a more complete discussion, see Mullin, Egeth, & Mordkoff, 1988).

Is there any way to proceed in this somewhat disheartening situation? One approach that recommends itself has been described in some detail by Miller (1982). Miller's procedure uses the redundant-target paradigm but uses a more fine-grained method of data analysis (thus, in many ways, Miller's method is similar to that presented by Mulligan & Shaw, 1980).

The approaches considered so far have conceived of the stimuli in various locations as producing separate activations. On any particular trial, responding is controlled by the detection of a signal on one channel or another. In their parallel instantiations, these models are typically race models because the response to redundant signals is determined by the fastest among several simultaneous response-activating processes. For familiar statistical reasons, the winning time in a race is faster than the mean time for any of the competitors as long as the completion-time distributions overlap. Thus, the standard redundancy benefit is the result of what has been called *statistical facilitation* (Raab, 1962).

An alternative conception is that activation from separate channels may combine to satisfy a single criterion for response initiation. This is what Miller has referred to as *coactivation*. One way to conceptualize this model is to posit a single response logogen that receives input from both channels simultaneously. Naturally, activation builds more quickly when it is provided by several channels rather than just one. This provides an alternative explanation for the redundancy benefit.

Although both separate-activation and coactivation models can account for a redundancy gain, they do not do so in the same way. This can be seen most easily by considering the fastest responses times in a distribution. Statistical-facilitation and serial models hold that there should be more of these fastest times when there are more targets and that this is why we get a redundancy benefit. However, according to a coactivation model, the fastest times in a multiple-target condition may be faster than the fastest times in any of the corresponding single-target conditions because activation is summed across targets.

More formally and more generally, Miller has shown that the following relation must hold for all separate-activation models. Assume here that there are two possible target locations, labeled 1 and 2, so that S_1 indicates a target in location 1 and S_2 indicates a target in location 2:

$$P(RT < t | S_1 \text{ \& } S_2) = P(RT < t | S_1) + P(RT < t | S_2)$$
$$- P[(RT < t | S_1) \text{ and } (RT < t | S_2)] \tag{1}$$

The left side of Equation 1 corresponds to the cumulative distribution function (CDF) of response time on redundant-signal trials, and the first two terms on the right correspond to the CDFs for the two single-target conditions. The final term reflects the correlation between the two activations.

The correlation between two activations would be difficult to measure experimentally (cf. Van der Heijden, Schreuder, Maris, & Neerincx, 1984); however, from the preceding basic equation, a prediction can be derived for all separate-activation models:

$$P(RT < t | S_1 \text{ \& } S_2) \leq P(RT < t | S_1) + P(RT < t | S_2) \tag{2}$$

This is true because the right-most term in Equation 1 must be greater than or equal to zero.

Simulated Experiments

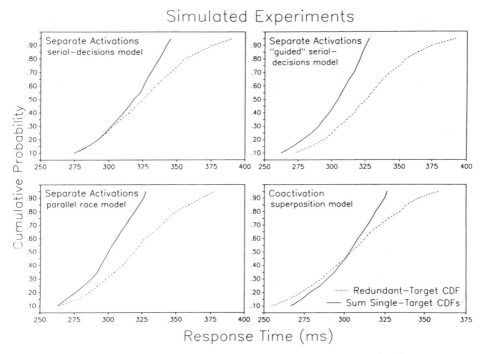

Figure 1. Cumulative distribution functions of the data from four simulated experiments. The first (upper left panel) assumed a self-terminating, serial-decisions model that works through displays in a random order. The second simulated model (upper right panel) was a guided serial model like that proposed by Cave and Wolfe (1990). The third (lower left panel) was a standard race model with independent, separate activations. Note that in each of these three panels the cumulative distribution functions (CDFs) do not cross. The fourth experiment (lower right panel) simulated a coactivation model very similar to that presented by Schwarz (1989); it assumed that activations are directly summed at the decision level. Under this model there is a crossover in the CDFs.

What Equation 2 says is that if separate-activation models hold, and we plot the CDF for redundant-target trials and compare it to the sum of the two single-target CDFs, then the curve for redundant trials should always be below and to the right of the curve representing the sum of the two individual stimuli (see the first three panels of Figure 1). However, if coactivation occurs, then the curves might well cross. That is, at the faster tail of the CDFs, the curve for the redundant-target trials might be above and to the left of the curve representing the sum of the two individual stimuli (see the lower right panel of Figure 1).

When coactivation is found, it implies parallel processing—how else could two activations be summed unless the two stimuli were processed simultaneously?

Put another way, no serial-decisions model is consistent with violations of the inequality. However, this is a very stringent test, and so the converse does not apply; failure to find a crossover in the CDFs does not necessarily mean that processing is not parallel.

To turn now to our first experiment, on each trial we presented subjects with two stimuli, one above the other. The assigned task required subjects to respond only on those trials that included at least one red X—that is, responding was "Go–No-Go" and the target was a conjunction of two separable dimensions, color and shape. The nontargets were red Os and green Xs. Eight subjects served in a single session of about 560 trials.

The stimuli used (and their frequencies of usage) are shown in Figure 2. Note, in particular, the examples in the fifth row. These trials do not contain a target but do contain a red item and an X. Such trials ensure that subjects search for the conjunction "red X" and not just the presence of both redness and an X. A substantial fraction (33%) of the trials were of this type.

Mean response time on redundant-target trials was 296 ms; on single-target trials, it was 322 ms. The observed redundancy gain of 26 ms was reliable, $t(7) = 15.77$, $p < .005$. However, for reasons mentioned earlier, this result does not constitute strong evidence of parallel processing.

The CDFs necessary for a coactivation analysis were formed by calculating the cumulative density of response time at 18 points corresponding to the 10th through 95th percentiles at 5% intervals (see Figure 3). From the 10th to the 35th percentile, the redundant-target CDF was displaced to the left of the curve representing the sum of the two single-target CDFs, violating the separate-activations inequality (Equation 2). Pairwise t tests revealed significant evidence for coactivation at the 10th and 25th percentiles ($ps < .05$). These violations seem to provide strong evidence of spatially parallel processing.

However, there is a possible loophole in the design adopted for Experiment 1: When the number of targets was one, there was a distractor element also present to keep display size fixed at two for all trials. It is therefore conceivable that what our data really show is not that redundant trials are fast, but that the processing of a single target is slowed down by the presence of a distractor. Indeed, this explanation, dubbed the *distraction decrement*, has already been proposed as an alternative account of cross-over in CDFs (Grice, Canham, & Boroughs, 1984; Van der Heijden et al., 1984).

To test the hypothesis that the observed evidence for coactivation was actually due to a distraction decrement, we conducted a second experiment (with a new group of 8 subjects) and included additional trial types in which a single stimulus was displayed. These were added to the set of stimuli used in Experiment 1. Half of these were target trials and half were distractor trials so that in all, there were now six types of trials (see Figure 2).

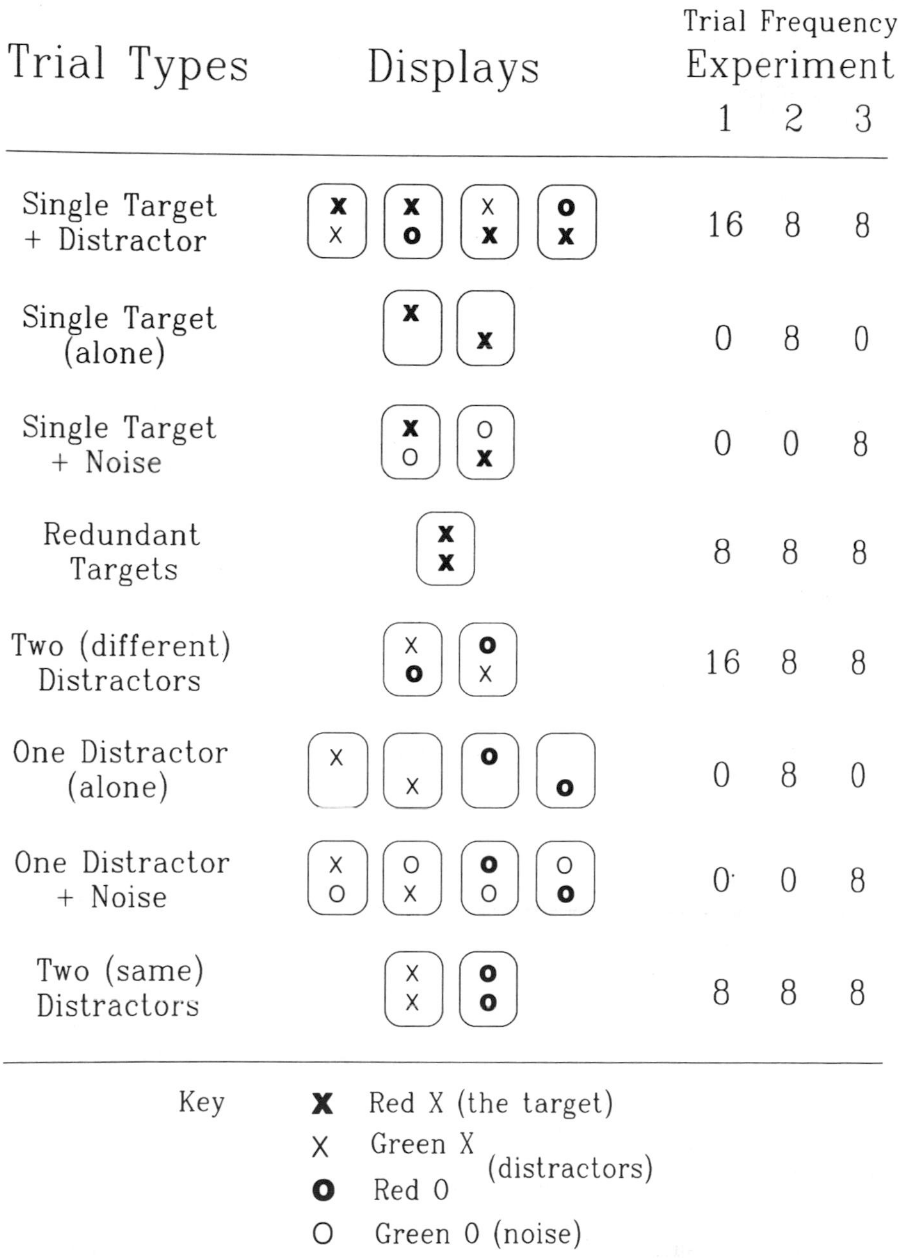

Trial Types — Displays — Trial Frequency Experiment

Trial Types	Displays	Experiment 1	2	3
Single Target + Distractor	**X**/**X** **X**/**O** X/**X** **O**/**X**	16	8	8
Single Target (alone)	**X** **X**	0	8	0
Single Target + Noise	**X**/O O/**X**	0	0	8
Redundant Targets	**X**/**X**	8	8	8
Two (different) Distractors	X/O **O**/X	16	8	8
One Distractor (alone)	X X **O** **O**	0	8	0
One Distractor + Noise	X/O O/X **O**/O O/**O**	0	0	8
Two (same) Distractors	X/X **O**/**O**	8	8	8

Key
X   Red X (the target)
X   Green X
O   Red O   (distractors)
O   Green O (noise)

Figure 2.   Trial types, example displays, and frequencies of occurrence from Experiments 1, 2, and 3. Display locations were 1.5° above and below fixation, and each letter subtended 1.4° × 0.9°. Note that the trial frequencies are given as the number of trials per block of 48, such that a frequency of zero implies that the given condition was not included in the associated experiment.

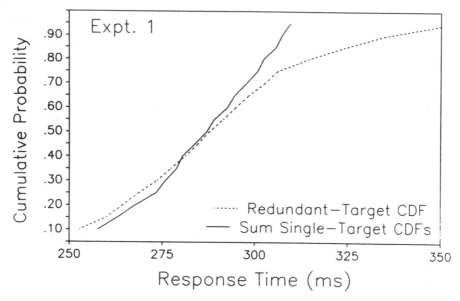

Figure 3.   Cumulative distribution functions (CDFs) from Experiment 1. The crossover in CDFs represents evidence of coactivation and support for spatially parallel processing.

Mean response time on redundant-target trials was 316 ms; on single-target trials with a distractor, it was 347 ms; on single-target trials without a distractor, 343 ms. The redundancy gain was significant in both cases: Comparing the redundant-target and single-target-with-distractor conditions, the redundancy gain was 31 ms, $t(7) = 7.88$, $p < .005$; for single-target trials without a distractor, 27 ms, $t(7) = 7.33$, $p < .005$. The magnitude of the two redundancy gains did not differ, $t(7) = 1.14$.

The relevant CDFs are shown in Figure 4. We once again found significant evidence of coactivation. There were crossovers in the CDFs both when we compared redundant-target trials against single-target-with-distractor trials, as in Experiment 1 (see Figure 4, upper panel), and when we compared redundant-target trials against the new single-target trials created for Experiment 2 (see Figure 4, lower panel). In the former case, the violations at the 10th and 15th percentiles were reliable ($ps < .05$). In the latter, the violations were significant from the 10th to the 35th percentile ($ps < .05$). Thus, the data indicate that a distraction decrement cannot account for the CDF cross-overs that we have found. Whether or not a distractor was included on single-target trials, redundant-target conditions yielded responses that were too fast to be explained by any separate-activations model. Thus, these findings rule out all serial-decision models, as well as certain

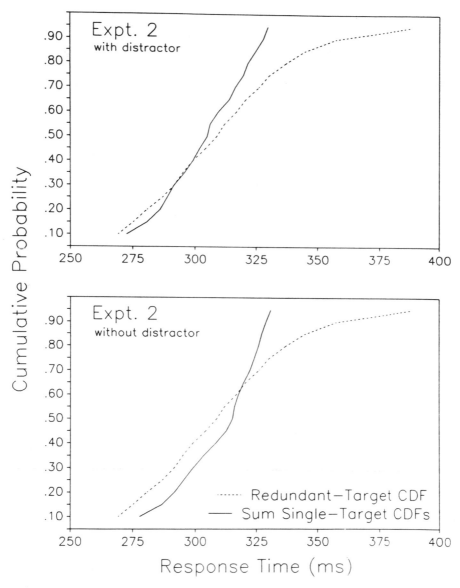

Figure 4. Cumulative distribution functions (CDFs) from Experiment 2. The upper panel compares the redundant-target CDF to the sum of two single-target CDFs calculated using the data from trials on which distractors were included. The lower panel displays the redundant-target CDF and the sum of the two single-target CDFs for those trials on which single targets were presented without a distractor. The CDF crossovers are evidence for parallel processing.

parallel models such as the independent-channels race model. What remains plausible is a model based on a rather strong form of parallel processing.

However, although Experiments 1 and 2 succeed in providing strong evidence favoring the parallel processing of separable dimensions, there is still another issue that needs to be addressed before we can safely conclude in favor of the spatially parallel processing of integrated objects. A close reading of feature-integration theory (Treisman, 1982, 1988) suggests that the task used in Experiments 1 and 2 might not have forced subjects to conjoin shape and color information at each location. That is, the task might have been solved by separately determining the activation level within various form and color "maps" (Treisman, 1985) without determining whether specific features were conjoined at particular locations.

For example, under our first two designs, the presence of three or more target features in a two-element display (e.g., one red object and two X-shaped objects) necessarily implied the presence of at least one target (a red X). More generally, when three or four target features are detected, then the correct response must be *target present*, and feature integration is not necessary to solve the task. Because all target-present trials in Experiment 1 always included at least three target features, it is not sufficiently demonstrated that the parallel processing of two complete objects is possible. Similarly, all target-present trials in Experiment 2 included twice as many target features as display elements; this also necessitates the presence of at least one target, and removes the need for features to be integrated.

How exactly does this alternative, feature-counting model work? Step 1 would be the following: Count the number of red objects and the number of X-shaped objects (i.e., calculate the number of target features present in the display). Step 2a: If the total number of target features is three or four, then respond "yes" immediately. Step 2b: If the total number of target features is two and display size is one, then stop and respond "yes." Step 2c: If the total number of target features is zero or one, then respond "no" (or terminate processing under "Go–No-Go") because no target is possible. Step 3 (which is only used when there are two target features in a two-element display): Check the display locations serially, integrating features across dimensions and testing the temporary object representation against the target template.

Note how the coactivation observed in Experiments 1 and 2 can be explained by this model: When two targets are present, then four target features are present, and the response criterion of *three* (used in Step 2a) may be reached more quickly than when there is only one target. Note also that feature integration (Step 3) is only necessary when there are two target features in a two-element display (i.e., when there is the possibility of an "illusory" target; Treisman & Schmidt, 1982). Neither Experiment 1 nor Experiment 2 included any two-element, target-present displays with exactly two target features, so we have not yet demonstrated true spatially parallel processing.

At the suggestion of Anne Treisman, we tested this feature-counting model by manipulating the number of target features on single-target trials while holding display size constant at two. This required that we introduce a third type of nontarget, one that has no features in common with the target (labeled *noise* in Figure 2). Thus, Experiment 3 involved two types of single-target trials: Half included three target features (see the top row in Figure 2) and by the feature-counting model would not require the integration of features into complete objects. The other half included only two target features (see the third row in Figure 2) and would require that subjects use serial attention because without feature integration the subject would not know if the two target features belonged to the same or different objects. This experiment was conducted using a new group of 8 naive subjects.

When either type of single-target condition was compared with the redundant-target condition, a substantial redundancy gain was observed (both *p*s < .001). It should be noted as well that both comparisons with the redundant-target condition yielded significant violations of the separate-activations inequality. In this experiment, however, what we were really interested in was the difference in mean response time between the two types of single-target trials: those that included one of the standard distractors (red O or green X) in the location opposite the target (mean RT = 306 ms), and those that included what we have called *noise* (green O; mean RT = 314 ms). The observed difference between these two conditions was an insignificant 8 ms, $t(7) = 1.62$. We interpret this result as contrary to the notion that full object integration only occurs (in these tasks) when there is the possibility of an illusory conjunction. This rules out the three-step, feature-counting explanation of Experiments 1 and 2.

Our conclusion from the results of these three studies taken together is that at least two objects may simultaneously have their color and form conjoined into unified percepts. This is inconsistent with serial-decision models such as those proposed by Treisman and Gelade (1980) and by Cave and Wolfe (1990), among others. Instead, the data suggest that some degree of spatially parallel processing is possible, although we cannot say yet how much. It is possible that as many as eight stimuli can be examined in a glance, as Pashler (1987) has suggested. We think, to cite yet another strand of Garner's work, that a definitive result awaits further research with a set of converging operations designed to overwhelm collectively the artifacts that plague individual research paradigms (e.g., Garner, Hake, & Eriksen, 1956).

References

Biederman, I., & Checkosky, S. F. (1970). Processing redundant information. *Journal of Experimental Psychology, 83*, 486–490.

Cave, K. R., & Wolfe, J. M. (1990). Modeling the role of parallel processing in visual search. *Cognitive Psychology, 22*, 225–271.

Egeth, H. E., Virzi, R., & Garbart, H. (1984). Searching for conjunctively defined targets. *Journal of Experimental Psychology: Human Perception and Performance, 10*, 32–39.

Garner, W. R., & Felfoldy, G. L. (1970). Integrality of stimulus dimensions in various types of information processing. *Cognitive Psychology, 1*, 225–241.

Garner, W. R., Hake, H. W., & Eriksen, C. W. (1956). Operationism and the concept of perception. *Psychological Review, 63*, 149–159.

Grice, G. R., Canham, L., & Boroughs, J. M. (1984). Combination rule for redundant information in reaction time tasks with divided attention. *Perception & Psychophysics, 35*, 451–463.

Miller, J. (1982). Divided attention: Evidence for coactivation with redundant signals. *Cognitive Psychology, 14*, 247–279.

Miller, J., & Lopes, A. (1988). Testing race models by estimating the smaller of two true means or true median reaction times: An analysis of estimation bias. *Perception & Psychophysics, 44*, 513–524.

Mulligan, R., & Shaw, M. (1980). Multimodal signal detection: Independent decisions vs. integration. *Perception & Psychophysics, 28*, 471–478.

Mullin, P. A., Egeth, H. E., & Mordkoff, J. T. (1988). Redundant-target detection and processing capacity: The problem of positional preferences. *Perception & Psychophysics, 43*, 607–610.

Nakayama, K., & Silverman, G. H. (1986). Serial and parallel processing of visual feature conjunctions. *Nature (London), 320*, 264–265.

Pashler, H. (1987). Detecting conjunctions of color and form: Reassessing the serial search hypothesis. *Perception & Psychophysics, 41*, 191–201.

Raab, D. (1962). Statistical facilitation of simple reaction time. *Transactions of the New York Academy of Sciences, 43*, 574–590.

Schwarz, W. (1989). A new model to explain the redundant-signals effect. *Perception & Psychophysics, 46*, 498–500.

Townsend, J. T. (1971). A note on the identifiability of parallel and serial processes. *Perception & Psychophysics, 10*, 161–163.

Townsend, J. T. (1972). Some results concerning the identifiability of parallel and serial processes. *British Journal of Statistical Psychology, 25*, 168–199.

Townsend, J. T., & Ashby, F. G. (1983). *Stochastic modeling of elementary psychological processes*. Cambridge, England: Cambridge University Press.

Treisman, A. (1982). Perceptual grouping and attention in visual search for features and for objects. *Journal of Experimental Psychology: Human Perception and Performance, 8*, 194–214.

Treisman, A. (1985). Preattentive processing in vision. *Computer Vision, Graphics, and Image Processing, 31*, 156–177.

Treisman, A. (1988). Features and objects: The Fourteenth Bartlett Memorial Lecture. *Quarterly Journal of Experimental Psychology, 40A*, 201–237.

Treisman, A., & Gelade, G. (1980). A feature integration theory of attention. *Cognitive Psychology, 12*, 97–136.

Treisman, A., & Gormican, S. (1988). Feature analysis in early vision. *Psychological Review, 95*, 15–48.

Treisman, A., & Sato, S. (1990). Conjunction search revisited. *Journal of Experimental Psychology: Human Perception and Performance, 16*, 459–478.

Treisman, A., & Schmidt, H. (1982). Illusory conjunctions in the perception of objects. *Cognitive Psychology, 14*, 107–141.

Van der Heijden, A. H. C., La Heij, W., & Boer, J. P. A. (1983). Parallel processing of redundant targets in simple search tasks. *Psychological Research, 45*, 235–254.

Van der Heijden, A. H. C., Schreuder, R., Maris, L., & Neerincx, M. (1984). Some evidence for correlated separate activations in a simple letter-detection task. *Perception & Psychophysics, 36*, 577–585.

Wolfe, J. M., Cave, K. R., & Franzel, S. L. (1989). Guided search: An alternative to the feature integration model for visual search. *Journal of Experimental Psychology: Human Perception and Performance, 15*, 419–433.

CHAPTER 9

IMAGERY AND THE PERCEPTION OF MUSICAL TIMBRE

ROBERT G. CROWDER

A pitch-discrimination method for the study of auditory imagery is described. Following the demonstration that people make same-pitch judgments more readily if two successive tones have the same timbre, I show that this matching effect occurs even when the first of the tones is imagined rather than actually heard. Synthesized tones were introduced in several new experiments to discover whether the capacity for forming mental images of timbre cues is based on their spectral properties or their dynamic (onset) properties. The results are clear in showing the former supposition, but not the latter. Large individual differences in the capacity to separate the qualities of pitch and timbre are discussed.

In the last chapter of the book that provides the theme for this conference, Garner (1962) discussed "the search for structure" as being inevitable. He said that

> subjects will find any cue at all to which they can relate their responses, and if a small artifactual cue exists which is, strictly speaking, irrelevant to the defined task, the subject will nevertheless relate his responses to that artifactual cue (Garner, 1962, page 341).

I will not dwell on artifacts in this chapter, but I will discuss individual differences in the ease with which people can disregard one salient cue in favor of another, perhaps less salient, cue that is more relevant to the defined task. Before returning to that problem, which evolved in Garner's later work (Garner, 1974) on integrality and separability, I will introduce a research program of mine related to two more of his enduring interests, auditory perception and the issue of imagery.

Table 1.

A TAXONOMY OF MENTALISTIC TERMS

	Top-down		Bottom-up	
Time	Original sensory code	Propositional	Original sensory code	Propositional
Now	Hallucination	Idea	Sensation, perception	Idea
Later	Generated image	Memory	Afterimage, eidetic image, memory image	Memory

TERMINOLOGY

The distinction between sensory perception and imagery is at least a two-dimensional one. Imagery is both top-down and removed in time relative to perception, which is correspondingly bottom-up and immediate (perhaps a *hallucination* would be an immediate top-down counterpart to perception). Images and memories share the time-delayed aspect, but here the format of the storage is what counts. Images must preserve the coding format of the original experience, whereas memories need not. Farah (1988) has made this criterion explicit in the case of visual imagery, following on suggestions by Hebb (1968).

Some of these distinctions are suggested by the layout of mentalistic taxonomy in Table 1. I have deliberately avoided two of the distinctions that Hebb (1968) found important over 20 years ago: the degree of sensory detail held by the representation and the role of spontaneous neural firing, which is of course neither top-down nor bottom-up. These and other considerations will be needed to carry this taxonomy further, but the present effort serves both to set the agenda for future analyses and to put in context the current work on imagery. In a nutshell, images and memories are similar in that both are delayed in time and both derive from both bottom-up and top-down sources. The main difference is that images remain formatted in the code of the original or generated experience, whereas memories are recoded, usually verbally.

AUDITORY MENTAL IMAGERY

Imagery for auditory events has definitely been a poor cousin to visual imagery, where grave issues for cognitive science have been debated for the last 20 years or so. One reason for this, besides the historical lag that seems to delay most work on audition relative to work on vision, may be that some demonstrations of auditory imagery cannot easily be separated from production of the imagined stimulus on one's own: Halpern (1988) demonstrated that people could engage in something like mental scanning for well-known songs, a feat that is indistinguishable from singing to one's self. Farah and Smith (1983) demonstrated that holding an image of a particular test tone increased psychophysical sensitivity for that very tone relative to an image of an unexpected frequency. (Use of the two-alternative forced-choice method precluded a criterion effect.) The two tones were well within normal singing, or humming, range. If subjects were very softly humming to themselves during this experimental test, we should perhaps not be so surprised that sensitivity was affected. The activity of singing to one's self in Halpern's (1987) study is likewise unsurprising. No corresponding ability, like drawing for one's self, is present for the visual imagery demonstrations.

IMAGERY FOR TIMBRE

My own experiments (Crowder, 1989) relied on musical timbre as the quality to be the target of imagery. Even given full freedom to articulate, people cannot ordinarily twang like a guitar or blast like a trumpet. Of course, some instrumental sounds could be crudely approximated by some subjects, in principle. However, later experiments in the series used synthetic timbres that could not possibly be approximated in this way. The carrier task in these experiments was same–different discrimination of two pitches. No differential response to timbre was ever man-dated by the instructions. Two tones were sounded, one after the other, and the task was to press one key if the two pitches were the same and the other key if they were different. In each experiment, three pitches could occur, corresponding to three adjacent diatonic scale steps (whole tones, F, G, and A above middle C). In the first part of each experiment, timbre varied unpredictably in both tones, whether or not they were the same pitch. This corresponds to Garner's *orthogonal* case in information processing (Garner, 1974). In the first report (Crowder, 1989), the same three notes were played on three real instruments—trumpet, guitar, and flute—forming a three-by-three vocabulary of digitized tones. Instructions were to respond only on the basis of pitch, as fast as possible. The results are given in Table 2.

In both speed and accuracy for the group as a whole, acknowledgment that two pitches were indeed the same was impaired by a mismatch between the tones in musical timbre. Unexpectedly, the effect on "different" responses was not reliable in this experiment, but the effect on same-pitch judgments was highly reliable and was true of 11 of the 12 subjects. Table 2 is constructed to isolate the performance of three "outliers" whose behavior was discontinuous with the other 9 people. These subjects each had error rates of 96% in the condition where the two pitches were the same but the timbres were different. Evidently, in their "search for structure" they could not disregard the cue of timbre, which was only a distraction in the experiment. Pitch and timbre were to some extent integral for all participants, but for these outliers no amount of extra processing time could compensate for this integrality.

The question concerning these three outliers is whether they were insensitive to pitch or rather simply overwhelmed by the more salient (for them) cue of

Table 2.

MEANS FROM CROWDER'S (1989) EXPERIMENT 1

Measure	Same pitch		Different pitch	
	Same instrument	Different instrument	Same instrument	Different instrument
Reaction time				
All subjects	737.4 (311)	940.7 (537)	789.8 (233)	777.3 (252)
Three outliers removed	708.6 (350)	924.6 (596)	746.0 (237)	777.4 (294)
Percent accuracy				
All subjects	95.5 (7.3)	66.3 (37.9)	77.2 (32.2)	94.0 (6.9)
Three outliers removed	95.1 (8.4)	86.3 (12.6)	94.3 (6.4)	94.3 (7.0)

Note. Standard deviations are in parentheses. Copyright 1989 by the American Psychological Association. Adapted by permission.

timbre. To decide which explanation was correct, we invited them back to the laboratory and administered a set of "pure" trials in which the timbres of the two tones were always the same, again asking subjects to respond "same" or "different" depending on the pitch match between them. This arrangement corresponds to Garner's (1974) "control" discrimination situation, in which variation on the second attribute does not occur. In such pure trials, none of the three subjects had any difficulty responding to pitch at far above chance levels, so insensitivity to pitch was not the cause of their disastrous performance in the orthogonal condition. Furthermore, one of the three, when replaced in the mixed (orthogonal) situation of the original experiment, could now cope with the processing interference that had plagued the outliers so much originally. Mark Pitt and I have since conducted a much more extensive study of such individual differences (Crowder & Pitt, in press; Pitt & Crowder, 1990), and I will therefore defer my summary comments until I discuss that new study.

So far, I have not discussed imagery for musical timbre because the results presented are only the first necessary part of a two-part demonstration of imagery. Following a lead from Posner's research (Posner, Boies, Eichelman, & Taylor, 1969) on visual codes in memory, I tried to determine whether subjects could produce an auditory image that had the same information-processing characteristics as the real thing. Thus, in the second part of the demonstration (Crowder, 1989), subjects were again presented with two tones, but the first tone was always a sine wave at one of the three pitches defined earlier. A sine wave is generally considered to have no timbre, or at least a neutral or unnaturally pure one. Simultaneously with the presentation of this sine wave, subjects were given a written instruction indicating what instrument they were to imagine playing that note—flute, guitar, or trumpet. When they indicated they "had" the image, a second tone was presented as in the first part of the experiment—a genuine flute, guitar, or trumpet

Table 3.

MEANS FROM CROWDER'S (1989) EXPERIMENT 2

	Same pitch		Different pitch	
Measure	Same instrument	Different instrument	Same instrument	Different instrument
Reaction time				
All subjects	1224 (366)	1366 (456)	1471 (464)	1299 (325)
Four outliers removed	1165 (366)	1274 (428)	1280 (373)	1257 (361)
Percent accuracy				
All subjects	93.4 (12.0)	75.5 (37.0)	74.9 (34.0)	88.7 (15.0)
Three outliers removed	96.5 (5.0)	95.2 (10.0)	92.8 (11.0)	90.4 (10.0)

Note. Standard deviations are in parentheses. Copyright 1989 by the American Psychological Association. Adapted by permission.

playing the scheduled pitch, either the same as or different from the sine-wave pitch. The results are shown in Table 3, which is organized in the same way as Table 2. The results shown in the two tables are similar as well: As before (although these were 15 new subjects), processing was impaired in both latency and accuracy in the mismatched pitch–timbre condition as compared with the matched condition. As would befit performance based on a mental image rather than on an explicit tone, reaction times were about half a second slower in Table 3 than in Table 2. Of the 15 subjects in this experiment, all but one showed a reaction-time difference when pitch was the same, favoring the same-instrument condition even though the first instrument was only an imagined tone. In this experiment, too, several subjects could not resist saying ''different'' when pitches were the same but timbres were mismatched. These four outliers had error rates in this condition of 98%, 89%, 92%, and 36%. With these four subjects removed, the remaining group had no reversals of the reaction-time pattern of an advantage for same-instrument over different-instrument conditions when pitch was the same in the tones, even though the first tone had been imagined with respect to timbre.

Together, these two demonstrations indicate that people can deliberately produce a mental representation for tonal experiences that preserves timbre in a way that is faithful to the properties of real timbres. This result establishes a new dimension in auditory imagery, and one that is not likely subject to corruption by some motoric component such as humming or singing to one's self. As such, the imagery is more nearly sensory than previously demonstrated.

TWO COMPONENTS OF INSTRUMENTAL TIMBRE

In collaboration with Mark Pitt, I have been trying to analyze the acoustic correlates of timbre with respect to imagery (Crowder & Pitt, in press; Pitt & Crowder, 1990). Two such correlates are the spectral (harmonic) and dynamic characteristics

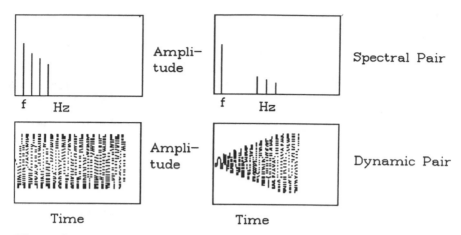

Figure 1.   Schematic illustration of differences between spectral and dynamic pairs of
tones used in the experiment on synthetic timbres. The top panels represent
the spectral pair in terms of Fourier spectra (f = fundamental pitch). The
lower pair of panels represent the dynamic pair in terms of (idealized) wave-
form envelopes. The spectral tones were equivalent in dynamic properties
and the dynamic tones were spectrally equivalent.

of the sound wave. The resonant properties of different instruments are characteristically different. As a result, they emphasize different harmonics. These spectral differences would be observed, for example, if one placed identical mouthpieces
in an oboe and a clarinet: They would still sound different. The clarinet would,
because of its cylindrical bore, produce mainly the odd-numbered harmonics,
whereas the oboe, with its conical bore, would produce both odd and even harmonics (Seashore, 1938). The dynamic aspect of natural timbres is easiest to
imagine with one single instrument, say a violoncello. If a cello string were
plucked, it would sound different than if it were bowed. The resonant properties
of the instrument are identical, yet the timbres sound different at least partly
because of markedly different onset characteristics of plucking and bowing. With
ordinary instrumental comparisons, say between a flute and a trumpet, both spectral
and dynamic differences are mixed together. In the first experiment using this
technique (Crowder, 1989), I willingly accepted this confounding in favor of
ecological validity. Pitt and I wanted to use synthetic timbres to take them apart
analytically. Using the same three pitches as before, we constructed a "spectral
pair" of instrumental sounds using only the presence and absence of harmonics
to effect the distinction. Essentially, one emphasized harmonics above the fourth
partial, and the other emphasized those below the fifth partial. The fundamental
pitches were, of course, prominent in each timbre, and we equalized their overall
intensities. Schematic diagrams of the two are shown in the top half of Figure 1
in the form of Fourier spectra. In the lower half of the figure are the two tones

Table 4.

MEANS FROM SPECTRAL TIMBRE EXPERIMENT

Measure	Same pitch		Different pitch	
	Same timbre	Different timbre	Same timbre	Different timbre
Reaction time	624.1 (142.6)	546.6 (429.9)	675.6 (186)	677.9 (182.8)
Percent correct	98.12 (5.32)	56.04 (46.02)	91.4 (19.51)	94.58 (15.53)

Note. Standard deviations are in parentheses. $N = 50$.

used in the "dynamic pair" of instrumental synthetic sounds, drawn as schematic wave forms. Their spectral components were identical, but one was highly ramped at the onset and the other was abrupt. We did not face the thorny issue of coming up with appropriate names for these synthetic instruments in the first part of the two-part experiment because, as before, the subjects' responses were to be based only on pitch. I will first describe the two parts of the "spectral" experiment, and then the two parts of the "dynamic" experiment.

For reasons that will soon become apparent, we decided to test a large number of student volunteers on both the spectral and the dynamic parts of this project, in counterbalanced order. At first, we tested unselected subjects, but soon found that many individuals were falling into the pattern observed for the outliers in the first experiment. That is, they were responding partly or entirely on the basis of timbre when told to attend only to pitch. Thereafter, we still accepted all volunteers for the experiment but posted our sign-up lists in the vicinity of Yale's music department. For all subjects, we administered a musical-background questionnaire, and we discovered that musical background made a difference.

In short, people were listening to two tones of either the same or different pitches played on synthetic "instruments" with either the same or different timbres. In counterbalanced order, some subjects completed the task with the spectral timbres first and others with the dynamic timbres first. Remember that the information presented here as either spectral or dynamic was always irrelevant. Table 4 presents the overall results of the half of the experimental protocol concerned with spectral timbre. The means are based on the performance of 50 subjects. A glance at the reaction times indicates that Pitt and I did not obtain the same pattern of latencies as before. In particular, times in the same-pitch/different-timbre trials were not slower than in the same-pitch/same-timbre trials. However, the accuracy rates indicate that the group as a whole was not appreciably better than chance in the troublesome condition with the same pitch and different timbres. The data for individual subjects indicate that this condition was nearly impossible for some subjects and easy for others, with no one scoring near the mean. For example, 15 people never made a correct response in this condition, and another 16 never made an error.

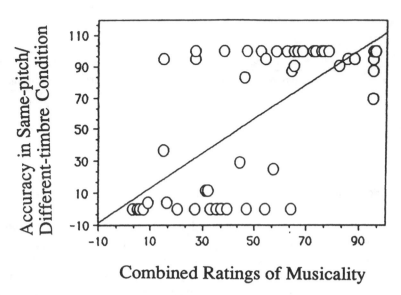

Figure 2. The relationship between ratings of general musical background, combined
across two independent judges, and percent accuracy in the condition with
two tones of the same pitch but different timbres.

We were amazed by the dramatic bimodality of individual differences in
this condition, which requires attending to the pitch aspect of a tone and filtering
out the timbre aspect. In most psychological measurements I have made, people
differ from one another according to well-understood principles of normal sampling
error. The data of Figure 2 give an indication both of the distribution of accuracy
scores in this condition and of who the people were in each group. The scatter
plot shows percent correct scores in this condition plotted against a rough index
of musical background, which we determined from the routine questionnaires
filled out before the experiment. The questionnaire asked questions such as (a)
how many years of formal instrumental or vocal training the student had, (b) how
recent this activity was, and (c) how many academic courses in subjects pertaining
to music the student had taken.

The first thing to notice about Figure 2 is the marginal distribution of obtained
accuracy in our target condition. Although the distribution of musical background
was reasonably normal, performance in the same-pitch/different-timbre condition
was not. No scores at all occurred between 37% and 70% correct. Second, the
overall linear correlation between musical ability and performance in the same-
pitch/different-timbre condition was .66. People with more musical experience
were better able than their less experienced classmates to ignore orthogonal variation in timbre and process pitch on its own. Of course, we cannot infer causality
from this correlation: Young people who cannot abstract variation in pitch from

Table 5.

MEANS FROM 28 "QUALIFIED" SUBJECTS IN SPECTRAL TIMBRE
EXPERIMENT

Measure	Same pitch		Different pitch	
	Same timbre	Different timbre	Same timbre	Different timbre
Reaction time	576.2 (117.8)	732.8 (176.5)	630.7 (133.3)	682.7 (190.4)
Percent correct	99.29 (1.78)	95.68 (6.98)	94.5 (17.29)	92.82 (19.56)

Note. Standard deviations are in parentheses.

timbre might well drop out of musical activities at an early age. Here, more dramatically than elsewhere, we see that terms such as *integral* and *separable* cannot be taken to refer inherently to stimulus dimensions but are a function of the individual doing the perceiving.

Among the 28 people in the higher-accuracy group for the same-pitch/ different-timbre condition, every individual had slower reaction times in this condition than in the same-pitch/same timbre condition, exactly the same result that was found in my earlier study. These results are shown in Table 5. Thus, even for subjects who could perform as if pitch were separable from timbre, this process cost them time. The probability of this outcome by chance alone is $\frac{1}{2}^{28}$.

For the second part of this project—the part that depends on imagery for timbre—Pitt and I decided to use only subjects from this first phase who "qualified" among the 28 high-scoring subjects when pitches were the same and timbres different. We were able to persuade 15 of these people to return to the laboratory for another session. In this second session, the assigned task was more complicated than in the first, although we had reason to believe that these subjects all had no difficulty understanding that pitch comparison was the basis for the same–different judgments. Subjects were taken through a protocol based on the one used for the imagery portion of the Crowder (1989) experiment: They first listened to the six tones that could occur for the second comparison tone (three pitches × two synthetic, spectrally defined timbres). During this demonstration phase, we suggested that the tones could be designated verbally as "organ" and "car horn," but subjects were free to substitute another terminology for the two "instruments" if they wished. In the next phase of training, subjects heard sine waves at various pitches, accompanied by a written indication of one of the two "instruments," and had as long as they wanted to form a mental image of how that pitch would sound as played in the designated timbre. Finally, as before, the next phase was the target task, in which when the subject pressed a button to indicate achievement of the image, the second tone of the pair was presented in either the imagined timbre or the other one.

Table 6.

MEANS FROM IMAGERY SESSION OF SPECTRAL TIMBRE EXPERIMENT

Measure	Same pitch		Different pitch	
	Same timbre	Different timbre	Same timbre	Different timbre
Reaction time	666.3 (259.1)	691.6 (261.2)	662.7 (237.2)	676.3 (253.5)
Percent correct	86.2 (1.60)	72.33 (3.06)	86.0 (2.96)	98.0 (4.45)

Note. Standard deviations are in parentheses.

The results are shown in Table 6, which is organized exactly as the previous tables. As in those tables, the timbre difference is enclosed in quotation marks because the match or mismatch depended on subjects' ability to form accurate mental images of the tones. The reaction times in the four crucial conditions were all within less than 30 ms of each other; however, the simple effect of timbre in the same-pitch condition was statistically reliable ($p < .036$); (no main effect or interaction was significant in the omnibus analysis of variance for these times). Turning to the accuracy data, we find stronger evidence that matching an imagined timbre to the second of two tones produced an advantage. All of the 15 subjects had higher accuracy in the match condition than in the mismatch condition, even though the mean in the poorer condition (72.33% correct) was comfortably better than chance. These individuals showed a corresponding effect of timbre on the different-pitch trials: All 15 of them were more accurate when both pitch and timbre were different than when the pitches were different and timbres the same. This effect on judgments of different pitch was not evident in the earlier study of natural timbres. For all of these reasons, then, we conclude that even for subjects who are minimally able to perceive pitch and timbre as separable dimensions, a residual integrality exists in the form of poorer performance when timbre and pitch do not match than when they do. Furthermore, this integrality is with respect to a mental image of the first comparison tone. Nothing in this experimental arrangement prevents subjects from just matching the sine wave against the presented second tone. To the extent that this had been a prevalent strategy, the differences obtained here would not have occurred.

Turning to the dynamic half of this experiment with 50 subjects, we find a different situation. The data are presented in Table 7 in the usual format. Inspection of both the reaction times and accuracy and their associated analyses of variance makes a single point: Dynamically defined timbres had no effect at all on performance. Nothing in these data denies the proposition that people were insensitive to our manipulation of this stimulus attribute. From this data, however, we may not conclude that, in principle, people are insensitive to dynamic, as opposed to spectral, cues to timbre. Pitt and I think it more likely that our variation of this cue was insufficient in this experiment. We are now performing an experiment

Table 7.

MEANS FROM DYNAMIC TIMBRE EXPERIMENT

Measure	Same pitch		Different pitch	
	Same timbre	Different timbre	Same timbre	Different timbre
Reaction time	621.3 (174)	641.4 (231.4)	616.5 (212.6)	603.5 (185.3)
Percent correct	96.6 (8.34)	93.7 (16.7)	92.7 (18.7)	92.6 (16.8)

Note. Standard deviations are in parentheses. $N = 50$.

with digitized natural timbres from one single instrument, a cello, played with either a bowed attack or a plucked attack. Although we understand that spectral source differences may exist for this distinction, they are minimized compared with the spectral variation in the original experiment (Crowder, 1989). We have already established that pitch judgments are affected by the pluck–bow timbre difference; now we want to verify that imagined timbres respect the same principles. Our next step will be to purify, either acoustically or synthetically, the dynamic timbre distinction.[1]

In any case, the research completed so far shows clearly that mental imagery can include distinctions among musical timbres that the motor system cannot match. To an attitude such as Hebb's (1968), of course, it is immaterial whether the motor system can produce the input; what counts is the top-down activation of brain patterns that would have been recruited by stimulation.

References

Crowder, R. G. (1989). Imagery for musical timbre. *Journal of Experimental Psychology: Human Perception and Performance, 15,* 472–478.

Crowder, R. G., & Pitt, M. A. (in press). Research on memory/imagery for musical timbre. In D. Reisberg (Ed.), *Auditory imagery.* Hillsdale, NJ: Erlbaum.

Farah, M. J. (1988). Is visual imagery really visual? Overlooked evidence from neuropsychology. *Psychological Review, 95,* 307–317.

Farah, M.J., & Smith, A. F. (1983). Perceptual interference and facilitation with auditory imagery. *Perception and Psychophysics, 33,* 475–478.

Garner, W. R. (1962). *Uncertainty and structure as psychological concepts.* New York: Wiley.

Garner, W. R. (1974). *The processing of information and structure.* Potomac, MD: Erlbaum.

---

[1]In subsequent experiments in this series, Pitt and I have found that the digitized, natural pluck-bow distinction in cello tones does produce the matching advantage both in comparing two successive tones and in comparing a real tone with an imagined tone. However, we have found that with two kinds of synthetic pairs of tones differing only on dynamic properties, people reliably showed the two-tone matching effect but not the imagery-based matching effect.

Halpern, A. R. (1988). Mental scanning in auditory imagery for songs. *Journal of Experimental Psychology: Learning, Memory, and Cognition, 14,* 434–443.

Hebb, D. O. (1968). Concerning imagery. *Psychological Review, 75,* 466–477.

Pitt, M. A., & Crowder, R. G. (1990). *The role of spectral and dynamic cues in imagery for musical timbre.* Manuscript submitted for publication.

Posner, M. I., Boies, S. J., Eichelman, W. H., & Taylor, R. L. (1969). Retention of visual and name codes of single letters. *Journal of Experimental Psychology: Monographs, 79* (1, Pt. 2).

Seashore, C. E. (1938). *Psychology of music.* New York: McGraw Hill.

CHAPTER 10

RESPONSE COMPETITION PRODUCES A "FAST SAME EFFECT" IN SAME– DIFFERENT JUDGMENTS

JAMES D. ST. JAMES
AND CHARLES W. ERIKSEN

Eriksen, O'Hara, and Eriksen (1982) have proposed that one basis of the "fast same effect" obtained on comparison tasks arises from response competition. Feature or dimensional similarities or overlap between the comparison targets prime a "same" judgment, which tends to inhibit the execution of the response signifying "different." Garner (1988) has recently extended this competition process to account for the inconsistency of results that are obtained for integral and separable dimensions between classification tasks and comparison tasks. In the present experiment, we used a recently developed direct measure of response competition (abortive responses; St. James, 1990) to assess the degree of response competition that occurred on same and different trials. Subjects judged letter pairs on a criterion of physical identity. In addition to "same" pairs, there were "slightly different" pairs and "very different" pairs. In accordance with the prediction of the Eriksen et al. (1982) model, the incidence of abortive double responses was appreciably and significantly greater for "slightly different" pairs. Pairs that were the same or "very different" did not differ significantly on either response time or the direct measure of response competition.

This research was supported by Public Health Service Research Career Program Award K06-MH22014 to Charles W. Eriksen, by Public Health Service Research Grant MH 01206, also to Charles W. Eriksen, and by a small grant from the University of Illinois Research Board.

The literature has shown varying results regarding the separability or integrality of dimensions, depending on whether classification or comparison tasks are used. For example, Santee and Egeth (1980) found that size and brightness operated as separable dimensions on a classification task but as integral dimensions when a same–different task was used. Garner (1988) has recently offered an explanation for this anomaly. He proposed that response compatibility is an inherent aspect of the comparison or same–different paradigm. The different dimensional values in the stimuli can activate either compatible or incompatible response tendencies. If incompatible response tendencies are activated, response competition occurs, with the resulting increase in response time (RT).

Eriksen, O'Hara, and Eriksen (1982) have previously advanced the response competition explanation for the "fast same effect" that is commonly found when the comparison or matching paradigm is used. A judgment that two stimuli are the same is typically made faster than a judgment that they are "different," provided the stimuli do not differ in gross characteristics. This "fast same effect" is intuitively surprising, as Nickerson (1972) has noted, because a judgment of "same" would seem to require an exhaustive comparison of the stimuli on all relevant features or dimensions, whereas a judgment of "different" could be made by the detection of a single disparity.

Eriksen et al. (1982) proposed that during the comparison process, the overt responses by which the subject signifies his or her judgment are differentially primed. They assumed continuous flow processing (Eriksen & Schultz, 1979) in which the percept of the stimulus pair develops over time. The less pronounced or discriminable the difference in a stimulus pair, the more fully developed the percept must be, on the average, for these differences to be detected. In keeping with the continuous flow concept, priming of relevant responses begins early in percept development. Even stimulus pairs that are different will appear similar on many gross features during these early stages of percept development. These similarities begin to prime the response signifying "same," with the result that when the percept reaches the stage of development sufficient to detect the difference, the "different" response is partially inhibited by the priming that is built up in the response for "same." Physically identical stimulus pairs, on the other hand, would not (except for random noise in the perceptual system) lead to a priming of the "different" response during percept development. As a consequence, the "same" response can be executed faster because its execution is not inhibited by a buildup of priming in the competing alternative response.

To prime the "different" response when same pairs were being judged, Eriksen et al. (1982) presented an extraneous letter in the display that varied in its similarity to the identical pair of letters being judged. The RTs for "same" judgments were found to increase as the similarity of the extraneous letter decreased. The amount of response competition for the "different" judgment was also manipulated. The RTs for judgments of "different" were significantly slower when the extraneous letter was identical to one of the letters in the different letter pair than when the extraneous letter was different from either of the target letters.

The response competition interpretation of the fast same effect has been dismissed by Farell (1985). Although the experiments that have introduced extraneous differences into the displays during "same" trials have uniformly found that "same" RT increases, Farell noted that the evidence is inconsistent or negative with respect to "different" RTs. But when seeming inconsistency occurs among experiments, one cannot simply dismiss one set of experiments. The logical approach is to look for other differences between the seemingly conflicting studies. In the negative experiments cited by Farell, there are important differences in method and conditions that would make these experiments quite insensitive to response competition effects on judgments of "different." These experiments were concerned with different issues, such as mental rotation (Bagnara, Simion, & Umiltà, 1984; Bundesen & Larsen, 1975; Bundesen, Larsen, & Farell, 1981; Kubovy & Podgorny, 1981), and competition effects were likely confounded with or masked by these other variables and the processes they activated. The experiment by Nickerson (1975) that Farell finds compelling used as stimuli letters incompletely made up of dots against a random dot background. The difficulty of the deciphering task for the subjects is indicated by mean RTs for the experimental conditions that range from 600 to 1200 ms, as contrasted with the RTs of about 400–600 ms usually obtained from matching tasks. Because response priming effects have been found to dissipate rather quickly over time (Flowers & Wilcox, 1982; Grice, Boroughs, & Canham, 1984), it is unlikely that these effects would be readily detected in Nickerson's experiment.

In contrast with the negative experiments cited by Farell, Garner's (1988) experiment was designed to examine response compatibility effects on different judgments. A matching procedure was used in which the subjects judged whether the presented pair was made up of the "same" or "different" letters. The stimuli were composed of pairs of the letters C, O, L, and T. This choice of stimuli permitted classifying different trials in terms of whether the discrimination required was "hard" (e.g., O–C) or "easy" (e.g., L–O). In the control condition, the letters were always black, but the experimental conditions added color (red or green) as an irrelevant dimension. In keeping with the prediction from response competition, the longest RTs were obtained for different pairs that were the same color. This was true for both the hard and easy letter discriminations. For the "hard" different pairs, the control condition (where both stimuli were again the same color, black) also resulted in longer RTs than when the pairs differed on the irrelevant color dimension.

What is needed to unequivocally establish a response compatibility or competition effect on different trials in the comparison task is an independent direct measure of response competition. All of the relevant experiments so far have inferred response competition from mean RT differences, which is the same variable they are invoked to explain. Several more direct and independent measures of response competition are available. Eriksen, Coles, Morris, and O'Hara (1985) used the Eriksen response competition paradigm in which discriminatory RT is determined both when the target letter is flanked by repetitions of itself (response compatible) and when it is flanked by the other target letter (response incompatible). Subjects responded to one of the target letters with one hand and to the other target letter with the opposite hand. In addition to RT, electromyographic recordings from forearm muscles were obtained on each trial. The results showed clearly that on response-incompatible trials, there was incipient activation of the response appropriate to the flanking noise letters even though the correct response was executed.

Coles, Gratton, Bashore, Eriksen, and Donchin (1985) confirmed these results and, in addition, showed that the incipient activation of the competing response was also measurable with sensitive strain gauges. They had subjects squeeze a dynamometer with the right and left hands to signify their judgments. Strain gauges attached to the dynamometers recorded the presence of squeeze activity in the incorrect hand that was significantly more frequent and at a higher level when the target was flanked by the opposite target letter than when the flanking letters were response-compatible.

Most recently, St. James (1990) has developed another measure of response competition. Researchers had noticed that in response-competition experiments in which the subjects moved a small lever to the right or left to signify their choices, there was a relatively high incidence of the subject initially starting to move the lever in the wrong direction on trials with incompatible noise. These abortive responses were of slight extent, with rapid correction to a movement in the direction appropriate to the target stimulus. St. James replaced the lever with a precision joystick and programmed the lab computer to sample the position of the joystick every 10 ms beginning with target presentation. In this manner, he was able to measure precisely the frequency and extent of these abortive or double responses, as well as the velocity and extent of the correct movement response.

St. James found not only that the double responses were much more frequent on incompatible than on compatible noise trials, but, in addition, that the extent of movement of the joystick on correct responses was significantly less when the target was flanked by incompatible noise. This latter finding suggests that the correct signifying response is modified by inhibition of the competing response. St. James, using the joystick procedure, then performed several experiments in which he manipulated variables that had previously been found to affect the amount of response competition, such as the spacing of the flanking letters (nearer or farther from the target). Double responses and the extent of movement on correct responses were found to reflect faithfully the effect of these variables.

In the present experiment, we used the joystick procedure as a measure of response competition. We used a letter-matching task in which the choice of letters as stimuli was such as to provide a group of very different pairs and a group of slightly different pairs for the different trials. If response competition underlies or at least materially contributes to the fast same effect, then we should find that the frequency of double responses is appreciably greater on the slightly different trials than on the same trials and the very different trials. If our choice of the very different trials is such as to yield RTs significantly greater than the RTs for same trials, the very different trials should also have a greater incidence of double responses than do the same trials. On the other hand, if the very different trials turn out to be so discriminable that a fast same effect is not obtained, then the double responses on same and very different trials should not differ. We have chosen to use the joystick measure of response competition rather than electromyography or the strain gauge method used by Coles et al. (1985) because the methodology is more readily available to other investigators who may wish to replicate or extend these findings.

METHOD

Subjects

Six women and two men served as paid volunteer subjects. All were students at the University of Illinois at Urbana–Champaign. Subjects were right-handed and, by self-report, had normal or corrected vision.

Apparatus and Procedures

Stimulus presentation and data collection were controlled by a DEC LSI-11 microcomputer, using a Hazeltine 1500 CRT terminal. Viewing of the stimuli was binocular at a viewing distance of 36 in. Subjects placed their faces against a viewing hood to control distance from the CRT screen. At the distance used, the characters presented as stimuli were 0.25° of visual angle in height. A fixation point was displayed 0.44° below the target position and remained on display between trials and during stimulus presentation. The subject initiated stimulus presentation by pressing a foot pedal. The stimulus was presented 200 ms later and remained on for 200 ms. Stimulus presentation was done in a darkened room. Stimuli were thus clearly visible and in a known location.

The subject indicated a response by pressing a joystick to the right or left. The joystick used was a fingertip-controlled Measurement Systems Model 521R with high-resolution potentiometers. Subjects were instructed to grip the joystick between the thumb and middle finger with the index finger resting on top. It was emphasized to them that they were to be gripping the joystick in that manner before initiating a trial, to ensure that the entire reaction was recorded. Return-to-center detent springs centered the joystick in both axes, with a breakout force of 85 g and a pull of 170 g at the maximum deflection of 27.5°. An analogue-to-digital converter permitted the collection of the position of the joystick in units of 0.16°. Sampling was done every 10 ms beginning with the subject's initiation of the trial and continuing for 1,200 ms.

Following the lever-press reaction, the CRT displayed both RT and whether the reaction was correct or incorrect. Reaction time was the time from stimulus onset to a criterion deflection (correct or error) to the left or right, with an error recorded if the deflection exceeded the criterion in the wrong direction. The criterion deflection was 19.13°. Subjects were instructed to react to the target as quickly as possible while keeping errors to a minimum, and were warned verbally by the experimenter if error rates were above 10%.

Subjects were tested in a single session of about 1½ hr. After a series of 56 practice trials, there were two blocks of 196 trials each, separated by a 10-min break. Same and different trials occurred equally often, in random order, with the different trials evenly divided between slightly different and very different. The direction of responses for "same" and "different" was counterbalanced across subjects. The stimulus letters appeared just above and to the left and the right of the central fixation point (+), with a center-to-center separation of 0.32° of visual angle. Stimulus letters were displayed for 200 ms, beginning 200 ms after the subject pressed a foot switch to initiate the trial.

The letter pairs used as stimuli were chosen on the basis of Gilmore, Hersh, Caramazza, and Griffin's (1979) confusion matrix for upper-case letters presented on a DEC VR14 CRT. Although the font used on the Hazeltime 1500 CRT used in this experiment differed slightly, the Gilmore et al. data provided a reasonable choice of letters for the various conditions. Note that their confusion matrix is asymmetrical, with confusion tending to be directional. Thus, a stimulus letter M had a probability of .391 of eliciting a response of "H," whereas the stimulus letter H had a probability of only .063 of eliciting a response of "M." Fourteen letters were chosen that permitted the formation of 7 slightly different pairs (MH, AR, PF, CG, XK, VY, and QO) and, by rearrangement, 7 very different pairs (MG, AY, PH, CR, XF, VO, and QK). This letter set also permitted 14 same pairs of each letter paired with itself. For the Gilmore et al. data, the average probability of a confusion (ignoring direction) of these slightly different pairs was .143, whereas the average probability of confusion for the very different pairs was .009. Average percent correct for their subjects was .51, with rapid presentation intended to produce fairly high error rates. Gilmore et al. also reported a Euclidean similarity measure derived from multidimensional scaling. Euclidean distances were 0.0 for same pairs (by definition), whereas the distance was 0.407 for the slightly different pairs and 1.017 for the very different pairs.

RESULTS

Data analyses are based on univariable repeated-measures analyses of variance, corrected by the Huyhn-Feldt procedure, with alpha equal to 0.05. Post hoc pairwise comparisons were performed with the Tukey honestly significant difference (HSD) procedure.

Although subjects were required to have the joystick positioned within close tolerances of vertical at the beginning of a trial, small constant errors could have occurred as a result of the subject "leaning" slightly on the joystick. To remove this constant error, we corrected individual trials in the following manner. The mean joystick position (for the x axis) was calculated for the time between the initiation of a trial and the stimulus onset. This constant error was then subtracted from the measure of each of the subsequent samples of joystick position. This procedure also served to correct any error in calibration of the joystick. With this correction, and on the basis of visual inspection of several hundred individual trials, a deflection of 1.59° (10 "units") was chosen as indicating a voluntary movement by the subject. This deflection was small enough to detect nearly all movements (such as the initial error deflection in double responses) but large enough to rule out small, random fluctuations in joystick position.

Trials on which no deflection occurred for 800 ms after stimulus onset were discarded from further analysis. Such trials are likely to reflect momentary inattention on the part of the subject or some other extraneous interference. The largest number of such trials for any subject in this experiment was five.

Mean correct RTs and their standard deviations are reported in Table 1, along with the means and standard deviations of the percentage of double responses and the percent errors. There was a significant effect of trial type, $F(2,14) = 7.81$. Tukey HSD post hoc pairwise comparisons indicated significantly slower RT for the slightly different pairs than for either the same or very different pairs, which did not differ significantly (HSD = 35 ms). Note that the trials on which double responses occurred, but where the initial error deflection did not exceed the criterion for a choice response, were omitted from this analysis. We performed a separate analysis including those trials, but that analysis yielded essentially the same results as when the trials were omitted.

The pattern of double responses was similar to that of RT, as indicated in Table 1. The percentage of double responses differed by trial type, $F(2,14) = 10.18$. Post hoc pairwise comparisons found a significantly greater number of double responses for the slightly different pairs than for the other trial types, which did not differ among themselves (HSD = 4.5%).

Errors were those trials on which an error movement occurred but was not corrected. The percentage of errors by trial type is also presented in Table 1. The omnibus comparison of means was significant, $F(2,14) = 16.82$. Post hoc comparison of pairs of means found that all pairs differed (HSD = 3.1%), with the

Table 1.

THE DEPENDENT VARIABLES BY TRIAL TYPE

Variable	Trial type		
	Same	Slightly different	Very different
RT (ms)			
M	499	551	512
SD	58	40	43
Percent double responses			
M	4.2	10.5	3.5
SD	3.8	8.1	3.5
Percent errors			
M	4.2	7.7	0.7
SD	2.1	3.5	0.9

Note. RT = reaction time.

greatest percentage of errors occurring for the slightly different pairs and the smallest percentage for the very different pairs.

DISCUSSION

The results are quite clear in showing that response competition, as indexed by double responses, occurs significantly and appreciably more often on "different" trials involving hard discriminations than on "same" trials or "different" trials where the discrimination is easy. The number of double responses on very different trials is actually less than on same trials, although not significantly so, which shows that the occurrence of double responses is not somehow associated with the making of the response "different." These very different trials also do not show a fast same effect, and therefore would not be expected to manifest much, if any, response competition in terms of the theory proposed by Eriksen et al. (1982).

Other research (Derks, 1972) has shown that if the difference between the paired stimuli on matching tasks is salient enough or extensive enough, the fast same effect disappears. The response competition explanation accounts for this finding by noting that the less discriminable differences in stimuli do not become resolvable until the percept is well developed. But until these differences become resolvable, the "same" response continues to receive priming. If the differences in the stimulus pair are salient or numerous, a difference between the pair will, on the average, be detected earlier in the percept development and the "different" response will be executed with less priming in the competing "same" response. In the present experiment, we could not be sure in advance that the differences on the very different trials would be sufficient to eliminate the fast same effect and therefore response competition, but we could predict that the incidence of double responses would be less when the magnitude of the fast same effect decreased.

Although double responses were observed in only 10.5% of the slightly different trials, it is reasonable to conclude that more sensitive measures of response competition would have revealed its presence on a much higher proportion of the trials.[1] Coles et al. (1985) found that electromyographic responses occurred more frequently in the presence of response-competitive stimuli than did abortive motor movements measured by strain gauges. Even the seemingly simple movement of a joystick involves complex motor adjustments of the neck and upper skeletal muscles, and lesser degrees of response competition would probably be manifest at these levels if we had the sophisticated equipment available with which to measure it.

Theories that have been advanced to describe the processing that underlies judgments of "same" and "different" (e.g., Krueger, 1978; Proctor, 1981; Ratcliff, 1981; Taylor, 1976) have taken as their point of departure the fast same effect. In fact, they have been oriented primarily to explaining this effect. Unlike the response competition theory, none of the above theories would predict that double responses would be more frequent on different trials, nor can they readily provide an *ex post facto* account for the finding. The present results, as well as those of Eriksen et al. (1982), strongly indicate that the fast same effect is a product of the response system. As a response system effect, it cannot be used to infer the cognitive processes that underlie "same" and "different" judgments. Instead, inferences about processing need to be addressed to how response competition is activated and involved in the comparison procedure. The theory of Eriksen et al. (1982) is one attempt. It is based on a continuous flow (Eriksen & Schultz, 1979) model of information processing in which sensory information accumulates over time with a concurrent priming of the response system. However, other models would appear possible that can account for the response competition without necessarily assuming continuous flow.

Because of the presence of response competition that slows the execution of the "different" response, we cannot infer that the cognitive comparison itself is slower in detecting differences than in detecting sameness. It may or may not be. The question can only be answered when the response-competitive effects can be eliminated from the responses signifying "same" and "different." Similarly, because of the presence of response competition, differences in response criteria for "same" and "different" judgments cannot be inferred from RTs and error rates (Ratcliff, 1981).

---

[1] The 10% incidence of double responses is about the same as the result that St. James (1990) obtained with incompatible flanking letters in the standard response competition paradigm. This suggests that the response competition obtained with hard discriminations in the present experiment is on the same order of magnitude as that obtained with the well-recognized response competition procedure.

Garner's (1988) experiment provided strong support for the role of response competition on difference trials. Garner, however, preferred to use the term *response compatibility* rather than *competition* because he has interpreted his data as showing that irrelevant dimensional differences between the paired stimuli can facilitate RT. But there are difficulties in determining if there is true facilitation rather than a greater or lesser amount of response competition. To determine facilitation, a neutral stimulus condition is necessary. In Garner's experiment, facilitation was concluded on the basis of performance under the control condition, where the hard-discrimination pairs O–C and L–T were the same color, black. Relative to this control, RT was greater when these stimulus pairs were red or green and less when one letter of the pair was red and the other green.

We would argue that the control condition was not a suitable neutral condition. The letters in the pair were the same color (black) and therefore were capable of priming a "same" response. They did not result in as much competitive response priming as when they were both red or both green because the red and green colors were more salient in the experimental situation. Red and green may be inherently more salient than black or shades of grey in that they are given a greater weighting in the comparison process. Their greater salience may also have resulted from the fact that they were manipulated variables in the experimental context.

At best, the evidence is not sufficient to prove a facilitation process rather than a lesser degree of response competition. In a number of experiments using the response competition paradigm (e.g., Eriksen & Eriksen, 1974, 1979; Flowers & Wilcox, 1982; Grice, Boroughs, & Canham, 1984), little or no evidence has been obtained that RT is facilitated when the target is simultaneously flanked or accompanied by response-compatible noise stimuli. Again, this may result from the inability to find the appropriate neutral noise condition. The whole issue of response or processing facilitation arising from irrelevant stimuli or redundant stimuli in the visual field is controversial, with conflicting results (see Eriksen, Goettl, St. James, & Fournier, 1989; Mullin, Egeth, & Mordkoff, 1988, for discussion of some of these results). For the present, we prefer to interpret our results and those of Garner in terms of response competition because the mechanism underlying the effect is more clearly explicated and supported by a body of research evidence than is a facilitation process.

References

Bagnara, S., Simion, F., & Umiltà, C. (1984). Reference patterns and the process of normalization. *Perception & Psychophysics*, *35*, 186–192.
Bundesen, C., & Larsen, A. (1975). Visual transformation of size. *Journal of Experimental Psychology: Human Perception and Performance*, *1*, 214–220.

Bundesen, C., Larsen, A., & Farell, J. E. (1981). Mental transformation of size and orientation. In J. Long & A. Baddeley (Eds.), *Attention and performance IX* (pp. 279–294). Hillsdale, NJ: Erlbaum.

Coles, M. G. H., Gratton, G., Bashore, T. R., Eriksen, C. W., & Donchin, E. (1985). A psychophysiological investigation of the continuous flow model of human information processing. *Journal of Experimental Psychology: Human Perception and Performance, 11*, 529–553.

Derks, P. L. (1972). Visual recognition of similarity and identity. *Journal of Experimental Psychology, 103*, 978–984.

Eriksen, B. A., & Eriksen, C. W. (1974). Effects of noise letters upon the identification of a target letter in a nonsearch task. *Perception & Psychophysics, 16*, 143–149.

Eriksen, C. W., Coles, M. G. H., Morris, L. R., & O'Hara, W. P. (1985). An electromyographic examination of response competition. *Bulletin of the Psychonomic Society, 23*, 165–168.

Eriksen, C. W., & Eriksen, B. A. (1979). Target redundancy in visual search: Do repetitions of the target impair processing? *Perception & Psychophysics, 26*, 195–205.

Eriksen, C. W., Goettl, B., St. James, J. D., & Fournier, L. R. (1989). Processing redundant signals: Coactivation, divided attention or what? *Perception & Psychophysics, 45*, 356–370.

Eriksen, C. W., O'Hara, W. P., & Eriksen, B. A. (1982). Response competition effects in same–different judgments. *Perception & Psychophysics, 32*, 261–270.

Eriksen, C. W., & Schultz, D. W. (1979). Information processing in visual search: A continuous flow conception and experimental results. *Perception & Psychophysics, 25*, 249–263.

Farell, B. (1985). "Same"–"different" judgments: A review of current controversies in perceptual comparisons. *Psychological Bulletin, 98*, 419–456.

Flowers, J. H., & Wilcox, N. (1982). The effect of flanking context on visual classification: The joint contributions of interactions at different processing levels. *Perception & Psychophysics, 32*, 581–591.

Garner, W. R. (1988). Facilitation and interference with a separable redundant dimension in stimulus comparison. *Perception & Psychophysics, 44*, 321–330.

Gilmore, G. C., Hersh, H., Caramazza, A., & Griffin, J. (1979). Multidimensional letter similarity derived from recognition errors. *Perception & Psychophysics, 25*, 425–431.

Grice, G. R., Boroughs, J. M., & Canham, L. (1984). Temporal dynamics of associative interference and facilitation produced by visual context. *Perception & Psychophysics, 36*, 499–507.

Krueger, L. E. (1978). A theory of perceptual matching. *Psychological Review, 85*, 278–304.

Kubovy, M., & Podgorny, P. (1981). Does pattern matching require the normalization of size and orientation? *Perception & Psychophysics, 30*, 24–28.

Mullin, P. A., Egeth, H. E., & Mordkoff, J. T. (1988). Redundant-target detection and processing capacity: The problem of positional preferences. *Perception & Psychophysics, 43*, 607–610.

Nickerson, R. S. (1972). Binary-classification reaction time: A review of some studies of human information-processing capabilities. *Psychonomic Monograph Supplement, 4*(17, Whole No. 65).

Nickerson, R. S. (1975). Effects of correlated and uncorrelated noise on visual pattern matching. In P. M. A. Rabbitt & S. Dornic (Eds.), *Attention and performance V* (pp. 655–668). San Diego, CA: Academic Press.

Proctor, R. W. (1981). A unified theory for matching-task phenomena. *Psychological Review, 88*, 291–326.

Ratcliff, R. (1981). A theory of order relations in perceptual matching. *Psychological Review*, *88*, 552–572.

Santee, J. L., & Egeth, H. E. (1980). Selective attention in the speeded classification and comparison of multidimensional stimuli. *Perception & Psychophysics*, *28*, 191–204.

St. James, J. D. (1990). Observations on the microstructure of response competition. *Perception & Psychophysics*, *48*, 517–524.

Taylor, D. A. (1976). Effects of identity in the multiletter matching task. *Journal of Experimental Psychology: Human Perception and Performance*, *2*, 417–428.

CHAPTER 11

EARLY SELECTION, LATE SELECTION, AND THE PARTITIONING OF STRUCTURE

DONALD BROADBENT

A small set of features may create a larger array of possible events, each identified by the particular combination of features it possesses. A subset of this array can then be selected in a number of different ways. In a known set of words, for example, all those possessing a particular letter, or heard coming from one spatial location, may be selected. Alternatively, the subset may be chosen only on combinations of the underlying features, as when letters are selected from among irrelevant digits. Garner (1962) analyzed the structure of such selections and the way they partitioned the same total "constraint" in different ways. In this chapter, a parallel is drawn between Garner's analysis and the experimental paradigms used in studying attention. The results of a number of such experiments are reviewed and used to demonstrate that the structure is important in predicting human performance. Thus, the attentional mechanisms adapt to the form of constraint, and Garner's original analysis is reaffirmed.

One of the most intriguing contributions of Garner (1962) was the distinction among different forms of structure. Suppose that a person is choosing among four possible actions, such as ordering one of four possible breakfasts in a restaurant. Suppose also that there are three aspects of a breakfast that are noticeable to this person: Does the meal have juice or cereal, ham or sausage, rolls or toast? Those three features would have allowed a choice of eight menus, so the restaurant has clearly simplified the decision by producing only four. There is a "constraint" of one bit in the situation. Early calculations of information (see Garner, 1962, for a review) considered only the fact that the constrained choice might be easier than an unconstrained one, without considering the point that the eight choices could be cut down to four in a number of different ways. Garner, however, emphasized these various forms of constraint and that it matters psychologically which form has been used.

For example, suppose that the management has been ruthless about the orange juice and allows only cereal. Every other possible combination is available, but to reach a choice only two features of each menu have to be weighed in the balance. Alternatively, suppose that there is one of the breakfasts that would suit the customer perfectly, but each feature is absent from a different one of the other three alternatives. In such a choice, every feature has to be scrutinized for every breakfast. Mathematically, the total constraint in the system is equal for both of these situations, but it is distributed differently between internal and external constraints. Garner's point was that this difference matters psychologically.

A slightly different example illustrates the same principle and the way it is linked to problems of attention and selection. Suppose people are told to read aloud a page of three-letter strings, half of which are nonsense strings and half of which form common English words. From the earlier literature reviewed by Garner (1962), we can safely assume that their task will be easier if they are told to ignore the nonsense strings and say only the meaningful ones. That cuts down (constrains) the number of possible responses. Furthermore, suppose that each string is constructed using R or F as the first letter, E or I as the second letter, and D or T as the third letter. The possibilities are shown in Table 1; there are four English words and four others that are not usually known as such (although at least one does appear in the dictionary). This further constraint will again improve human performance.

There is, however, a residual problem for human processing of this imaginary task; each possible letter occurs in at least one of the possible words. Thus, the visual system must take into account every one of the three letters before it is safe to conclude that the string is a nonword.

The situation is different if the strings are made using B or P as the first letter, A or U as the second letter, and T or F as the third letter. There are still four possible words, but now all of the strings containing F are nonwords, and all of those without F are words. The total constraint is the same, but now one needs only to look at the final letter of each string, and if it is F, that settles the matter (see Table 1). If the last letter is not F, the other two letters need to be examined to decide which of the four responses has to be made.

LEVELS OF EXPLANATION

Of course, the everyday wording in the last sentence above must not be taken seriously, because it implies some sort of serial operation; that is not Garner's

Table 1.

TWO SETS OF LETTER STRINGS WITH DIFFERENT STRUCTURE

SET A: EIGHT STRINGS IN WHICH NO LETTER DISTINGUISHES WORDS AND NONWORDS

Words	Nonwords
RED	RET
FED	FET
RID	RIT
FIT	FID

SET B: EIGHT STRINGS IN WHICH ONE LETTER DISTINGUISHES NONWORDS

Words	Nonwords
BUT	BUF
BAT	BAF
PUT	PUF
PAT	PAF

Note. In Set A, every letter must be examined, even to decide to make no response (selective set). In Set B, the nonwords can be rejected on one letter alone (filtering).

point. The difference in the structure of the constraint is a mathematical fact that may or may not be psychologically important. If human search and/or attention are affected by this difference, that tells us something at the level of explanation that is functional, or, as Marr (1982) called it, "computational." It tells us what function the system achieves, not how it does it. Different algorithms might be used to achieve the same computation, and even when one knows the algorithm, it could be implemented in various kinds of neural systems.

For example, one situation that shows these differences in structure is the kind of visual search task used by Treisman (e.g., 1986), who showed that a target marked out from background events by a single unique feature is seen rapidly, almost regardless of the number of nontarget events in the field. A target defined as a combination of features, each of which is also possessed by some of the nontargets, takes much longer when the number of nontargets is large. This strongly suggests that the structure of the situation is psychologically important and therefore computationally relevant. Treisman's results are suggestively linked to contemporary knowledge about the physiology of the nervous system (Cowey, 1985). It is not essential to the value of Treisman's computational distinction, however, that one identify exactly how it is implemented in physiology. Similarly, Treisman argues that targets in the "combined-feature" situation are detected by serial scanning, but this is not necessarily so, because parallel mechanisms can undoubtedly be devised to give the same results (Broadbent, 1987; Townsend & Ashby, 1983). Furthermore, the behavioral data do not always favor perfect seriality, merely some kind of capacity limit (Pashler, 1987). This is not, however, an issue at the higher levels of explanation, only at lower ones that are algorithmic or even implementational.

EARLY AND LATE SELECTION

Treisman's studies are part of a continuing tradition, not of visual search, but of studies of attention. That tradition usually asks the subject for more than mere detection of a relevant signal. Rather, the task requires discriminative reaction to the identity of some events in the environment, whereas others are ignored. Identification may make an important difference as compared with detection (Broadbent & Broadbent, 1987; Duncan, 1980). That again would be expected from Garner's analysis because the structure of the situation is quite different.

Even in tasks requiring identification of some but not all events, however, there is an important difference of paradigms that has been called by Kahneman and Treisman (1984) the difference between *filtering* and *selective set*. *Filtering* is exemplified by studies of listening to multiple speech channels, (Broadbent, 1954) in which the subject is asked to identify the meaning of words coming from one location in space but to ignore those localized elsewhere. In that task, the array of features belonging to each word includes a localization feature if the word is relevant, but does not include it if the word is irrelevant. The "filtering" paradigm is thus analogous to that in the lower section of Table 1.

However, another "selective set" paradigm is possible that is more comparable to the upper part of Table 1. In this paradigm, the person is asked to identify, for example, any letters spoken (or, more usually in current research, shown) in a mixture of letters and digits (e.g., Broadbent, 1970; Broadbent & Gregory, 1964; Duncan, 1983). The key features controlling response are less easy to determine in this case, but certainly there is no single part of the visual field that distinguishes relevant from irrelevant. Broadbent (1971) claimed that the two paradigms are affected differently by variables such as giving selective instructions before rather than after presentation. He explained this difference by the fact that the two feature structures would impose different processing requirements. His view was that the filtering paradigm would allow greater economy of processing. There would thus be an advantage if people had been instructed in advance and could use the key feature to avoid processing irrelevant items.

This is the approach sometimes called "early selection," the notion that partial analyses of the input can be used to guide further analyses even before the identity of the external event is known. There is also the "late selection" approach, stemming from Deutsch and Deutsch (1963) through various sophisticated descendants. According to that view, the identity of the event is always computed and is thus available to guide selection or rejection of each event for further action.

Many researchers who use a selective set paradigm find data showing that much information has been gathered even from irrelevant events, and they therefore hold a late selection view, whereas those supporting an early selection view have often used a filtering paradigm (see Kahneman & Treisman, 1984). If filtering indeed reduces the amount of processing that is needed, it ought on average to give better performance than selective set does. Some reviewers, such as Broadbent (1971), Kahneman and Treisman (1984), and Johnston and Dark (1986), argue that filtering does give better performance. It is fair to say, however, that most studies with filtering paradigms use different physical features from those that are used in selective set. A difference in spatial location may be inherently faster or more accurate to detect than a difference in a vowel or consonant, quite apart from the structural difference. If one believes in late selection and that the identity of all events discriminable by the senses is computed unselectively, then a parsimonious line of argument is that the usual difference between filtering and selective set is due to some such sensory factor (e.g., Allport, Tipper, & Chmiel, 1985; Duncan, 1980).

In recent years, however, there have been a number of studies that use the same stimulus events in the two paradigms, altering the task by altering the instructions. The main thrust of this chapter is therefore to review some of these studies and to reaffirm the importance of Garner's distinction.

RSVP AND THE TWO PARADIGMS

Some Methodological Points

In experiments using filtering, the features that specify the target are usually quite separate from those that identify the appropriate response. The spatial location of a voice or the color of a visual stimulus are not the same physical dimensions that inform the person which word or number is being presented. Experiments on selective set, however, usually require the person to use the same stimulus features both for finding the target and for identifying it. The features that discriminate letters from digits are quite possibly the same ones that discriminate one digit from another. There is an imbalance of unknown extent in the comparison, and this is the key problem in comparing filtering and selective set.

An answer to this difficulty is to separate the task of detection from that of identification, to use quite different dimensions for defining targets and for identifying responses, as in Table 2. Suppose, for example, that one presents a set of colored letters one after another in rapid serial visual presentation (RSVP). The target may then be the item in a particular color, but the response is the identity of the letter. It is equally possible, of course, that the target could be a particular

Table 2.

PATTERNS IN WHICH SEPARATE FEATURES DEFINE TARGETS AND
IDENTIFY RESPONSES

Target		Response		
F1	F2	F3	F4	RESPONSE
X	X	O	O	R1
X	X	X	O	R2
X	X	O	X	R3
X	X	X	X	R4
O	X	O	O	Inaction
O	X	X	O	Inaction
O	O	O	X	Inaction
O	O	X	X	Inaction

Note. Feature 1 (F1) defines which events are to receive a response (R); Features 3 and 4 specify which response is to be made. Those features also occur in nontargets. Feature 2 is an unreliable way of detecting targets (e.g., reading black letters among red ones that are on average slightly smaller).

letter and the response the color in which it is presented. Both discriminations have to be carried out in either case, the same visual display can be used, and any differences must be due to the structure of the task.

One suggestive difference appears immediately. In either form of task, one finds certain "illusory conjunctions" in which the person names a letter or color that did appear but that objectively preceded or followed the target. If the target is defined by color, a following letter is more likely to be associated with that color. Similarly, if the target is defined as a certain letter, and the response is to name its color, any error is more likely to be a later rather than an earlier color. (Gathercole & Broadbent, 1984; McLean, Broadbent, & Broadbent, 1982). One way of explaining this might be to say that the processing of target-defining (detection) features is slower than that of response-defining (identifying) features. Why should this be true, however, when they are balanced physically? A more plausible explanation is that there is a delay in starting to identify the response until after the target has been detected. The response may then be controlled by the next event, not by the true target. This looks very much like partial analysis of each event determining whether or not it needs further analysis.

A second preliminary point is that the extent of this lag differs according to the target feature used; when first assessed (McLean et al., 1982), the lag was found to be greater for targets defined by color than for targets defined by identity. In later studies (Broadbent & Broadbent, 1986), it was found that this asymmetry could be balanced by making the colors more discriminable;

with clearly visible colors, the two kinds of task resulted in about the same lag. This is consistent with the idea that the identification of the response is held up until the target is at least partly detected; if the detection is easier, the delay is less.

The Effect of Structure

Constructing a Task

The RSVP task separates the features that detect the target from those that identify the response. As we have seen, one can equate the difficulty of discrimination of the color features and the difficulty of the features that pick one particular letter. In doing this, we are limited to using five letters in the task to match the five colors, which are as many as one can reasonably expect to be discriminated. With so few letters, each letter has some spatial region of the display that is stimulated by that letter and by none of the others in the set. When we designate one letter as marking the target, therefore, we are telling the subject to look at one spatial part of the display and that only the target will stimulate that part. Just as in the case of specifying the target by color, all responses must follow an event that is marked by a unique feature shared with none of the nontargets. In both cases, therefore, whether naming the color of a certain letter or naming the letter in a certain color, the task is essentially filtering. Whatever features are designated as target-specifying, on the one hand, or as response-specifying, on the other, one is carrying out a task of the type shown in Table 2.

How can we produce a task in which a large set of features must all be processed to detect the target and in which many of the features are in common with nontargets? We wish, in fact, to get something as near as possible to the configuration shown in Table 3, in which no one feature characterizes the targets. One way to do this is to tell the person that the target will be a digit among the series of letters; if they are told exactly which digit it will be, that task is essentially the same as looking for a specific letter. But suppose we say that the target is a digit without saying which digit it will be. Now it is no longer true that some single visual region will reliably identify whether each event represents a letter or a digit, and therefore the situation begins to approximate the configuration shown in Table 3. This structural difference matters psychologically, as we shall see.

Filtering Really Is Better than Selective Set

The selective set version (Table 3) makes performance considerably worse than the filtering version (Table 2; Broadbent & Broadbent, 1986). Yet the physical stimuli are still the same; it is only the task that has altered. The long-standing argument of reviewers such as Kahneman and Treisman (1984) or Johnston and

Table 3.

TARGET DEFINITION WITHOUT SINGLE UNIQUE FEATURE

Target		Response		
F1	F2	F3	F4	**RESPONSE**
X	X	O	O	R1
O	O	X	O	R2
X	X	O	X	R3
O	O	X	X	R4
O	X	O	O	Inaction
X	O	X	O	Inaction
O	X	O	X	Inaction
X	O	X	X	Inaction

Note. Features 3 and 4 (F1 and F2) identify the response, but do not distinguish events that need no response; neither do Features 1 and 2 in isolation, only in combination.

Dark (1986), that filtering is more effective than selective set, remains true even when the two tasks are compared using the same physical stimuli.

Overlap of Processes With Selective Set
Because the processing demands are clearly greater for people who do not know which digit is going to occur in a stream of letters, one might expect that simple target detection would take longer. That would be expected from a number of results found in similar situations (Dick, 1971; Posner, 1970; Taylor, 1978), and in unpublished work we confirmed that it is true for simple detection in our situation. One might therefore expect that the more difficult detection task would produce illusory conjunctions even later in time than those found with the easier detection task. That, after all, is what happened when a less discriminable color was used to define the target.

In fact, the result is the exact opposite. When one uses selective set to locate the target, it is less likely that one will identify a color coming after the true target than before it (Gathercole & Broadbent, 1984; McLean et al., 1982). This finding applies even if the experimental stimuli are completely new words on every trial, so that there is no chance of the subject learning some complicated trick applicable only to a familiar and restricted set of items.

With filtering, then, there seems to be a delay in starting to process the response features, compared with the few target-defining features. With selective set, the response starts to be computed without waiting as long for the target to be detected. The pattern of behavior is altered by the change of structure in the stimulus events.

Interference Between Two Targets

It has been clear since the work of Duncan (1980) that the alleged automatic processing of nontarget events, found by Schneider and Shiffrin (1977), depends on the absence of any necessary action in response to such events. Two simultaneous targets do interfere in such tasks. If one is a late selectionist, then this phenomenon can be ascribed to some overlap or interference in response processes. Early selectionists, on the other hand, who think that partial analysis of each event guides later and more complex computation, may rather think that the two targets would interfere even if there were no immediate demand for overt action.

The RSVP task does not demand any overt response to targets immediately; targets merely have to be remembered until the end of the sequence. Memory itself is limited, but remembering two words falls well below those limits. If one presents a long sequence of words, all but two in lower-case print, and includes within it two target words in upper case separated by a couple of seconds, those words can both be reported as well as either word alone. There seems to be no postperceptual problem about holding two targets in store.

As the two targets are brought closer together in time, however, performance begins to decline. If they are only 100–200 ms apart, then for all practical purposes the person reports one or the other, but not both (Broadbent & Broadbent, 1987). This again looks like the early selection view, the notion that partial analysis can take place for many events, that it later guides the system in more thorough computation using some of the incoming information, and that once this is happening for one event it is difficult to perform it also for another. That limitation on capacity provides a functional reason for use of early selection when the task allows.

The Filtering–Selective Set Distinction

When one is using words as events in an RSVP task, it is possible to define the target either by a single unique feature or by a combination of features, just as in the color–letter task. The version mentioned above, in which the task is to report a word presented in upper-case letters, is clearly filtering. But it is also possible to require the person to report every occurrence of some category of words, such as animal names, and this task becomes selective set. This kind of task also shows the two-target effect, so, if the interpretation given above is correct, animal names can also be detected by a partial analysis but then need a fuller one for identification of the response. That is not surprising with a fixed set of twelve names; if one receives the information that "?o?se" is present, one cannot identify the word as *horse* or *mouse*, but it clearly repays further processing. In the parallel case of finding letters among digits, it has been demonstrated that each symbol has characteristics that reveal its category without determining its identity, even in the character set deliberately designed by Duncan (1983) to maximize the difficulty of doing this (Broadbent, 1987). These situations are, in fact, of the kind shown in Table 3, where some features point toward the target when examined in combination but do not identify it perfectly. On the other hand, a partial analysis of this kind is already fairly complex, and even if the correct outcome never emerges, it might well interfere with detection of another target. The simple decision "capitals or not?" that is required in filtering would be less demanding.

Correspondingly, a close analysis of the two-target case shows that the filtering paradigm gives no impact of a first target that has not been detected. The selective set paradigm, on the other hand, does show an impact of the first target being present, even though the person failed to respond to it correctly. Once again, this looks like the processing of a structure like that shown in Table 3.

SELECTION USING LOCATION IN SPACE

The studies mentioned so far presented target and nontarget items at the same location in space, the difference being solely in their time of arrival. The virtue of this approach is that it adds some generality to the wide literature on spatial selection, and this is needed because position in space may well be more fundamental than other features. Treisman (e.g., 1986) points to the spatial coding of the visual projection areas as providing a means for linking different features of the same object, and there is behavioral evidence (e.g., Broadbent, 1977; Hoffman, Nelson, & Houck, 1983; Styles & Allport, 1986) that other target markers, such as color or flicker, have their effect through increasing processing in their spatial neighborhood. In the spatial domain, however, there is widespread evidence for early selection, provided that the paradigm is a filtering one and that information about the location of the target becomes available slightly before the target itself. Some recent findings and summaries are given by Hoffman (1986), Eriksen and St. James (1986), Eriksen and Yeh (1985), and Murphy and Eriksen (1987). Typically, a choice reaction to a target stimulus (such as A or B) is measured while nontarget events occur in other places. If the nontarget is B when the target is A, then this slows response, but only if B is close to the area where the person expects a target. To use Eriksen's happy analogy, it is as if a zoom lens is pointing at the display and irrelevant events have an effect only within the field that the zoom lens covers.

This analogy is not quite perfect because the results of Eriksen and St. James (1986) show that the edge of the field is not sharp but declines gradually. We also suspect that the distant nontargets are not shut out altogether, but rather delayed in their impact. If they are given a time lead over the target, they still have an effect, even though they are distant from the expected location of the latter (Gathercole & Broadbent, 1987). I therefore prefer an analogy with a spotlight, which has a vague edge; however, the zoom lens analogy brings out the point that the size of the field can be varied according to the task (Eriksen & Yeh,

1985). Eriksen and Yeh's method of showing this brings me back to the distinction between Tables 2 and 3.

In a filtering paradigm, the target-defining feature can be a bar marker rather than an unmarked spatial location. In that case, the spatial information can be given in advance, in which case nontargets have an effect only close to the target position. Alternatively, the bar marker may arrive only when the whole display does, in which case a wider array of locations needs to be processed to detect the marker. Nontargets may have an effect within this whole area, not merely close to the target.

Suppose one deliberately constructs a version of the filtering task of Eriksen and Eriksen (1974) and a comparison task using selective set; the reaction is always a choice of A or B, but in one case the location is known, whereas in the other the location is unknown and the target must be identified by being a letter rather than a digit (Broadbent, Broadbent, & Jones, 1989). Immediately, a number of differences appear between the tasks; structure has an effect on behavior.

Two minor differences confirm those found by Eriksen and his colleagues: The presence of a nontarget that is neither A nor B does not matter with filtering but impairs selective set, and the spatial separation of targets and nontargets is helpful for filtering but harmful to selective set. A third minor point, from an earlier study, is negative: All indices of the efficiency of selection in one task fail to correlate across individuals with any index of selective efficiency in the other task (Broadbent, Broadbent, & Jones, 1986).

A fourth point is more novel and positive: The difference between the two tasks does correlate, weakly but significantly, with an independent verbal questionnaire of the frequency of failures of attention in everyday life (Broadbent et al., 1986).

Finally, the two tasks show different effects of external variables. One of the least expected is time of day; the traditional spotlight phenomenon, the disappearance of nontarget effects outside of a certain radius, is heavily dependent on the time the experiment was performed, in a way that interacts with liability to cognitive failure (Broadbent et al., 1989). Yet the nearest equivalent score in the selective set task shows no consistent effects; if there is an impact of time of day on selective set, it must be of a different kind.

It is extremely difficult to see how one can explain results of this kind if one uses a theory that identity is always and universally computed.

CONCLUSIONS

The conclusion from both areas, selection in space as well as selection in time, is that processing depends on structure. At the algorithmic level of Marr (1982), this probably means early selection rather than late selection; the analysis of some features determines the analysis of others before full identity is available. Yet let us remember the distinction of levels; even if some ingenious late selection theory can be devised, it will not alter the importance of structure at the computational level. We are all in debt to Garner.

References

Allport, D. A., Tipper, S. P., & Chmiel, N. R. J. (1985). Perceptual integration and post-categorical filtering. In M. I. Posner & O. S. M. Marin (Eds.), *Attention & performance XI* (pp. 107–132). Hillsdale, NJ: Erlbaum.

Broadbent, D. E. (1954). The role of auditory localization in attention and memory span. *Journal of Experimental Psychology, 47,* 191–196.

Broadbent, D. E. (1970). Stimulus set and response set: Two kinds of selective attention. In D. Mostofsky (Ed.), *Attention: Contemporary theories and analysis* (pp. 51–60). New York: Appleton-Century-Crofts.

Broadbent, D. E. (1971). *Decision and stress.* San Diego, CA: Academic Press.

Broadbent, D. E. (1977). The hidden pre-attentive processes. *American Psychologist, 32,* 109–118.

Broadbent, D. E. (1987). Simple models for experimentable situations. In P. E. Morris (Ed.), *Modelling cognition* (pp. 169–185). New York: Wiley.

Broadbent, D. E., & Broadbent, M. H. P. (1986). Encoding speed of visual features and the occurrence of illusory conjunctions. *Perception, 15,* 515–524.

Broadbent, D. E., & Broadbent, M. H. P. (1987). From detection to identification: Response to multiple targets in rapid serial visual presentation. *Perception & Psychophysics, 42,* 105–113.

Broadbent, D. E., Broadbent, M. H. P., & Jones, J. L. (1986). Performance correlates of self-reported cognitive failure and of obsessionality. *British Journal of Clinical Psychology, 25,* 285–299.

Broadbent, D. E., Broadbent, M. H. P., & Jones, J. L. (1989). Time of day as an instrument for the analysis of attention. *European Journal of Cognitive Psychology, 1,* 69–94.

Broadbent, D. E., & Gregory, M. H. P. (1964). Stimulus set and response set: The alternation of attention. *Quarterly Journal of Experimental Psychology, 16,* 309–317.

Cowey, A. (1985). Aspects of cortical organization related to selective attention: A tutorial review. In M. I. Posner & O. S. M. Marin (Eds.), *Attention & performance XI* (pp. 41–62). Hillsdale, NJ: Erlbaum.

Deutsch, J. A., & Deutsch, D. (1963). Attention: Some theoretical considerations. *Psychological Review, 70,* 80–90.

Dick, A. O. (1971). Processing time for naming and categorization of letters and numbers. *Perception & Psychophysics, 9,* 350–352.

Duncan, J. (1980). The locus of interference in the perception of simultaneous stimuli. *Psychological Review, 87,* 272–300.

Duncan, J. (1983). Perceptual selection based on alphanumeric class: Evidence from partial reports. *Perception & Psychophysics, 33,* 533–547.

Eriksen, B. A., & Eriksen, C. W. (1974). Effects of noise letters upon identification of target in a non-search task. *Perception & Psychophysics, 16,* 143–149.

Eriksen, C. W., & St. James, J. D. (1986). Visual attention within and around the field of focal attention: A zoom lens model. *Perception & Psychophysics, 40,* 225–240.

Eriksen, C. W., & Yeh, Y.-Y. (1985). Allocation of attention in the visual field. *Journal of Experimental Psychology: Human Perception and Performance, 11,* 583–597.

Garner, W. R. (1962). *Uncertainty and structure as psychological concepts.* New York: Wiley.

Gathercole, S. E., & Broadbent, D. E. (1984). Combining attributes in specified and categorized target search: Further evidence for strategic differences. *Memory & Cognition, 12,* 329–337.

Gathercole, S. E., & Broadbent, D. E. (1987). Spatial factors in visual attention: Some compensatory effects of location and time of arrival of non-targets. *Perception, 16,* 433–443.

Hoffman, J. E. (1986). Spatial attention in vision: Evidence for early selection. *Psychological Research, 48,* 221–229.

Hoffman, J. E., Nelson, B., & Houck, M. R. (1983). The role of attentional resources in automatic detection. *Cognitive Psychology, 51,* 379–410.

Johnston, W. A., & Dark, V. J. (1986). Selective attention. *Annual Review of Psychology, 37,* 43–75.

Kahneman, D., & Treisman, A. (1984). Changing views of attention and automaticity. In R. Parasuraman & D. R. Davies (Eds.), *Varieties of attention* (pp. 29–61). San Diego, CA: Academic Press.

Marr, D. (1982). *Vision.* San Francisco: Freeman.

McLean, J. P., Broadbent, D. E., & Broadbent, M. H. P. (1982). Combining attributes in rapid sequential visual presentations. *Quarterly Journal of Experimental Psychology, 35A,* 171–186.

Murphy, T. D., & Eriksen, C. W. (1987). Temporal changes in the distribution of attention in the visual field in response to precues. *Perception & Psychophysics, 42,* 576–586.

Pashler, H. (1987). Detecting conjunctions of color and form: Reassessing the serial search hypothesis. *Perception & Psychophysics, 41,* 191–201.

Posner, M. I. (1970). On the relationship between letter names and superordinate categories. *Quarterly Journal of Experimental Psychology, 22,* 279–287.

Schneider, W., & Shiffrin, R. M. (1977). Controlled and automatic human information processing: I. Detection, search, and attention. *Psychological Review, 84,* 1–66.

Styles, E. A., & Allport, D. A. (1986). Perceptual integration of identity, location, and colour. *Psychological Research, 48,* 189–200.

Taylor, D. A. (1978). Identification and categorization of letters and digits. *Journal of Experimental Psychology: Human Perception and Performance, 4,* 423–439.

Townsend, J. T., & Ashby, F. G. (1983). *Stochastic modeling of elementary psychological processes.* Cambridge, England: Cambridge University Press.

Treisman, A. (1986, November). Features and objects in visual processing. *Scientific American,* pp. 106–115.

CHAPTER 12

PERCEPTION OF COLOR:
A COMPARISON OF ALTERNATIVE
STRUCTURAL ORGANIZATIONS

BRYAN E. SHEPP

The perception of color may be characterized according to either of two forms of organization: color categories or the subjective dimensions of hue, saturation, and brightness. The experiments reported test the hypothesis that categorical relations are primary and constrain the perception by dimensions, which are secondary. Subjects were given restricted classification tasks in which the classifications could be based on holistic or dimensional relations. They were instructed to classify by dimension and to name the dimension that provided the dimensional relation. Subjects failed to identify hue when members of the triad were chosen from the same category, but were successful when the triads provided a between-category comparison. The classifications by either saturation or brightness identities were modestly successful both within and between color categories. Naming responses, however, indicated that brightness identities were often confused with saturation identities, and vice versa. Taken together, the results indicate that color categories are organized holistically and that although the classification by either brightness or saturation dimensional relations is unaffected by within- or between-category contrasts, the classification according to hue identity relations is affected by such contrasts.

The integrality of color stimuli is well established; combinations of hue, saturation, and brightness yield phenomenal wholes, and the properties of these wholes, as distinct from separable features, are revealed in a variety of converging tasks, including direct distance scaling, restricted classification, and speeded sorting (see, e.g., Garner, 1974).

This holistic description of color contrasts sharply with the traditional view that color is organized along the subjective dimensions of hue, saturation, and brightness, which correspond, respectively, to variations in wavelength, purity, and intensity. Among the sources of evidence that support the dimensional view of color are the multidimensional scaling studies of the Munsell system, which show that sets of hue versus chroma (saturation) are described by a two-dimensional Euclidean space (Indow & Uchinzono, 1960) and that sets that vary in hue, chroma, and value (brightness) are described by a three-dimensional space (Indow & Kanazawa, 1960).

Garner (1974) has suggested a view of object perception that reconciles these contrasting views of color perception. According to Garner, objects may be characterized by either holistic or dimensional relations, and either type of relation may be the primary basis for organization by the perceiver. For integral stimuli, overall similarity or holistic relations are primary; they occur first and are automatic. Dimensional relations are secondary and are the result of more derived or cognitive operations. For separable stimuli, the situation is reversed. A similar view of the organization of integral and separable stimuli has been proposed by Lockhead (1972).

The view that integral stimuli are perceived first as wholes and then as dimensions suggests that attention may be directed to dimensional relations even though such relations are not primary. For some integral stimuli, this view of Garner's appears to hold quite well. The height and width of rectangles, for example, yield integral results in both speeded tasks (e.g., Felfoldy, 1974) and restricted classification (e.g., Shepp, 1984). However, subjects classify rectangles by the dimensions of height and width with perfect accuracy when instructed to do so (Burns & Shepp, 1988).

The analysis of color stimuli by dimensions, however, is not easily accomplished. Foard and Kemler Nelson (1984) gave subjects a variety of tasks in which the subject's attention was directed to the dimensional structure of saturation and brightness. Their subjects performed at better-than-chance levels, but accuracy levels were poor. Burns and Shepp (1988) also report that the subjects' accuracy in identifying stimuli that shared values of hue, saturation, or brightness in the restricted classification of color, although sometimes better than chance, was poor.

The difficulty in extracting dimensional relations from color stimuli may be related to the degree of integrality. The dimensions of hue, saturation, and brightness may interact very strongly in such a way that the appearance of a particular value on one dimension is so transformed by variations on the others that identity relations are difficult to perceive. It is possible, however, that our ability to perceive dimensional relations is related to the organization of color by category.

According to Rosch (1973), color categories are perceptual bins of equivalent stimuli that correspond to the eight basic color terms that Berlin and Kay (1969) have proposed as universal. The internal organization of a color category is based on the prototype and the relation of other members of the category to the prototype. The prototype is the best example of the category, and in a series of studies, Rosch (1973, 1974, 1975) has shown that prototypes are very prominent in the color perception of young children, are more easily learned and remembered than nonprototypes, and that nonprototypes are ordered according to their goodness relative to the prototype. Finally, priming by a category name facilitates the matching of prototypic stimuli but delays the matching of nonprototypic stimuli.

Prototypic stimuli are specified by a particular hue that is highly saturated and, with the exception of yellow, slightly dark. For that particular hue, variations in saturation and brightness from prototypic values generate a series of increasingly less good examples of the category. It is possible, of course, to develop models of categorical perception on the basis of the processing of features (e.g., Homa, 1984), but the concepts of prototypes and perceptual goodness are entirely compatible with the view that color stimuli are integral wholes. Furthermore, these concepts suggest a dimension, namely, perceptual goodness, on which such wholes might be located, and suggest as well some constraints on dimensional perception.

Consider the triads of stimuli illustrated in Figure 1, which show the relations among the members of triads that are often used in restricted classification tasks to assess the relative dominance of different perceived structures. Stimuli A and B share an identical value on dimension x, but are very dissimilar on dimension y; B and C share no identical values but are highly similar on both dimensions; and A and C share no identical values and are even more dissimilar on x and y than are B and C. When subjects are presented with such triads and are asked to classify the stimuli according to "which two go together best," the patterns of classifications differ for different types of stimuli. When the stimuli are separable, subjects classify A and B together, indicating that the shared value on x provides the most compelling perceptual relation. But when the stimuli are integral, B and C are classified together, indicating that the overall similarity of the holistic stimuli provides the most compelling perceptual relation (e.g., Handel & Imai, 1972).

Color stimuli are classified by overall similarity, and even when they are instructed to classify by dimension, subjects fail to do so with hue and are only minimally successful with saturation and brightness (Burns & Shepp, 1988). The results obtained by Burns and Shepp suggest that category membership may affect classification. Consider first the classification of hue. When the stimuli are members of the same category, the similarities and differences in particular hues are masked by the invariant property of the category. Suppose that the stimuli in Figure 1 vary in hue (on the x axis) and saturation (on the y axis) and that subjects have been instructed to classify by dimension. If the stimuli are all blue, the subject may be presented with two vivid blues (B and C) and one weak blue (A). The subject may classify the two best blues together or, alternatively, given some pretraining with Munsell colors, classify A with either B or C. In either case, the

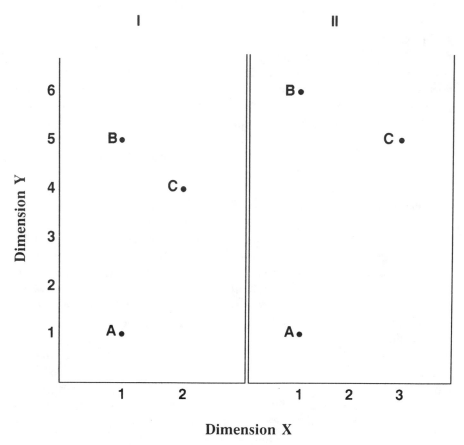

Figure 1.   An illustration of a triad for restricted classification.

subject has failed to detect consistently the stimuli with identical hues. But suppose that A and B are blue and C is purple. The classification of A and B together then becomes possible on the basis that A and B are members of one category and C is a member of another.

Now consider classifications based on shared values of either saturation or brightness, which Burns and Shepp found that subjects could perform successfully with instruction. It is possible, of course, that subjects can detect identical values in saturation or brightness in triads of color stimuli. But relative to the prototype of a category, changes in saturation and brightness produce changes in the goodness of the stimuli. Thus, subjects may classify A and B together in either saturation or brightness triads because they are perceptually better (or worse) than C, and not because they share identical values of saturation or brightness. If perceptual goodness provides the basis for classification, subjects may misperceive identities in saturation as identities in brightness, and vice versa.

EXPERIMENT 1

We first pursued the hypotheses about the dimensions of color in an experiment that used the stimuli and the general method of Burns and Shepp (1988). In this experiment, subjects were asked to classify the two stimuli in the triad that shared an identical value of hue, saturation, or brightness, and then to name the dimension that provided the identity relation. The triads were composed such that either hue and saturation (brightness constant) or hue and brightness (saturation constant) covaried in a triad, and were chosen from the set of commercially available levels of six hues (2.5YR, 10.R, 7.5R, 5R, 2.5R, and 10RP), six levels of chroma (2, 4, 6, 8, 10, and 12), and six levels of value (2, 3, 4, 5, 6, and 7). When hue and saturation covaried, hue provided the identity relation in half of the triads and saturation provided the identity relation in the other half of the triads. An analogous arrangement was presented when hue and brightness covaried. The dimension that provided the identity relation in any given triad was determined randomly. Two types of triads, illustrated in Figure 1, were presented in an attempt to vary the salience of the dimensional relation. The critical difference between the triads was the difference in the number of steps between stimulus C and stimuli A and B on dimension x. In Type I triads, the value of C on dimension x differed by one step from the shared value of A and B; in Type II triads, the value of C differed by two steps.

In this experiment, and in the others described in this chapter, there are several common procedural steps. The subjects were first given a color blindness test. The task was then described and the subjects were given a trial series with Type I triads, using stimuli that varied in size and brightness (or height and width of rectangles). The dimensions of hue, saturation, and brightness were then illustrated by Munsell charts from a section of the color space different from that used in the classification task, and subjects were practiced on the charts until they could identify the changes in the stimuli that were associated with changes in the specific dimensions. Finally, the subjects were presented with the triads of color stimuli.

The principal results are shown in Tables 1–3. Before discussing the results on color, it is important to note that subjects can readily perform the task with analyzable dimensions. With size versus brightness, the subjects classified by dimension and named the dimension that displayed the identity relation with perfect accuracy. These performances contrast sharply with performances on any of the color triads.

Consider first the hue triads. The proportion of each type of classification, shown in the first row of Table 1 for each type of triad, indicates that subjects do not classify hue triads by dimensional relations and that the instruction to do so produces an even distribution of classifications in both types of triads. Statistical tests showed that none of the classifications differed from chance or from each

Table 1.

PROPORTION OF DIMENSION SIMILARITY AND HAPHAZARD
CLASSIFICATIONS FOR SHARED VALUES OF HUE, SATURATION, AND
BRIGHTNESS

| | Type of triad classification | | | | | |
| | Type I | | | Type II | | |
Shared values	Dim.	Sat.	Hap.	Dim.	Sim.	Hap.
Hue	.28	.40	.32	.29	.39	.32
Saturation	.49	.32	.21	.72	.22	.06
Brightness	.48	.41	.11	.71	.27	.02

Note. Dim. = dimension similarity; Sat. = saturation; Hap. = haphazard classifications; Sim. = similarity.

other. An inspection of the naming data in Table 2 also indicates little success in hue identification. When the subjects classify by overall similarity, naming is evenly distributed among all three dimensions. When the subjects do classify by dimension, they name hue reliably more often than either saturation or brightness, but the same pattern of naming occurs when the subjects classify by the unsystematic haphazard relation. Although the subject may perceive the triad as a "hue" triad, they classify C with A as often as they classify B with A, and report that shared hue was the basis for the classification.

The classifications of saturation and brightness triads are shown in the last two rows of Table 1 for each type of triad. In Type I triads, the classifications of brightness were evenly divided between dimensional and overall similarity

Table 2.

PROPORTION OF NAMING RESPONSES FOR HUE TRIADS

Triad/Named dimension	Dim.	Sim.	Hap.
Type I			
Hue	.59	.36	.54
Saturation	.25	.31	.26
Brightness	.16	.33	.20
Type II			
Hue	.72	.33	.70
Saturation	.19	.38	.20
Brightness	.09	.29	.10

Note. Dim. = dimension; Sim. = similarity; Hap. = haphazard classifications.

Table 3.

PROPORTION OF NAMING RESPONSES FOR SATURATION AND BRIGHTNESS
TRIADS

Triad/Shared values	Named dimension					
	Dimension			Similarity		
	Hue	Sat.	Bri.	Hue	Sat.	Bri.
Type I						
Saturation	.04	.62	.34	.85	.05	.10
Brightness	.00	.38	.62	.90	.06	.04
Type II						
Saturation	.00	.60	.40	.89	.03	.08
Brightness	.00	.37	.63	.96	.01	.03

Note. Sat. = saturation; Bri. = brightness.

relations, whereas saturation was classified more often by dimensional than either of the other relations. In Type II triads, however, there was a reliable difference between dimension and overall similarity classifications when either saturation or brightness presented the identity relation.

The naming responses, presented in Table 3, indicate that the subjects can successfully name the dimension that provides the shared identity relation. The effect, although relatively small, is significant for saturation and brightness in both types of triads. But it is also important to note that saturation is frequently named following a dimensional classification of a brightness triad, and brightness is frequently named following a dimensional classification of a saturation triad. The latter finding suggests that perceptual goodness may provide the primary basis for classification, even though subjects can identify saturation and brightness identities with modest success. The importance of perceptual goodness is further supported by the observation that although subjects classify by dimensional relations more frequently in Type II than in Type I triads, the proportions of correct naming responses are equivalent in the two triads.

The results with saturation and brightness are consistent with the claim that subjects react primarily to perceptual goodness in the classification of such triads, and have difficulty in discriminating saturation identities from brightness identities when instructed to do so. It is possible, of course, that the task in which saturation is held constant when brightness provides the identity relation or in which brightness is held constant when saturation provides the identity relation is a perceptually difficult one. We have run several other experiments, however, in which saturation and brightness were covaried, and the general picture remains the same. With one exception, subjects classified only Type II triads by dimensional relations with

Table 4.

AN ILLUSTRATION OF WITHIN- AND BETWEEN-CATEGORY HUE TRIADS

Category status/ Step size	Stimuli		
	A	B	C
Within triads			
2	7.5B 8/4	7.5B 4/10	2.5PB 5/12
3	7.5B 8/4	7.5B 4/10	5PB 5/12
Between triads			
2	5PB 8/4	5PB 4/10	10PB 5/12
3	5PB 8/4	5PB 4/10	2.5P 5/12

Note. The notations of stimuli A, B, and C are Munsell conventions. The first notation (e.g., 7.5B) refers to hue. In the second notation (e.g., 8/4), the first number indicates the level of brightness, and the second number refers to the level of saturation.

modest success, and when they did so they often failed to identify the dimension that provided the shared values. The exception comes in triads in which shared values of saturation are arranged at very weak levels of chroma. At these levels, the shared values appear very gray, and subjects classify very accurately by dimension and name the dimension as saturation.

EXPERIMENT 2

The classifications of hue in Experiment 1 were not successful, and I would claim that the failure to classify by hue is the result of the stimuli's being exemplars of the same color category. When a triad is composed of within-category members, all three stimuli have the category hue (e.g., blue) even though variation in saturation or brightness may produce considerable variation in goodness. As the difference in hue is increasingly emphasized, however, some members of the triad begin to take on the appearance of a different category. When their appearance changes in this way, the basis for hue classification becomes categorical in nature.

Contrasts among different hue categories are often difficult because the difference in hue is so much greater than the difference in either saturation or brightness that the appropriate similarity relations cannot be created. Rosch (1974), however, reports two focal colors, blue (2.5PB) and purple (2.5P), that are relatively similar in hue and that do permit the appropriate similarity relations. In Table 4, triads that arrange hue variations within and between categories are presented. Stimuli A and B present identical hues; Stimulus C differs in hue by two steps or three steps from A and B. The values of saturation and brightness were chosen to preserve the customary similarity relations among A, B, and C. The systematic basis for the classification can be either the dimensional relation

(Stimuli A and B) or the overall similarity relation (Stimuli B and C). The difference in hue between stimuli B and C was varied at two and three steps because pilot work suggested that more spontaneous dimensional classifications occurred at a three-step between-category hue difference than at a two-step difference.

The subjects in Experiment 2 were first given the classification task with only the instructions to "put the two that look alike together." They were then instructed on the color dimensions and told that the color stimuli would vary in hue, saturation, and brightness but that two of the stimuli would have the same hue, and that their task was to report those two stimuli. By hypothesis, we anticipated that the classifications of the within-category stimuli would yield a pattern similar to that of Experiment 1. The stimuli were all blue, and the subjects would be unable to find hue identities consistently. For the between-category stimuli, on the other hand, we expected classification by hue, because A and B were members of one category (blue) and C was a member of another category (purple). Furthermore, we expected more dimensional classifications at three steps than at two steps.

It is important to note that subjects may perceive dimensional relations more often in between-category triads than in within-category triads, either because of the hypothesized category effect or because discriminability differences between the stimuli of the two types of triads are not comparable. If the discriminability of A–B or B–C relations in between-category triads is greater than such relations in within-category triads, more dimensional classifications of the former could be due to discriminability rather than category effects. To provide a basis for discriminating between the two interpretations, an experiment was run to assess discriminability. The subjects were asked to make dissimilarity judgments of pairs of A versus B and B versus C stimuli chosen from both between- and within-category triads. The results showed that A versus B pairs were consistently judged as more dissimilar than B versus C pairs. Moreover, the judgments of dissimilarity of two-step between-category pairs did not differ from the dissimilarity ratings of three-step within-category pairs.

The results of the classification experiment are summarized in Table 5. Note first the classifications before the instructions about the dimensions of color. The subjects classified the stimuli by overall similarity, although the level of responding was less for the three-step between-category stimuli than for the 2-step difference. This pattern of results indicates that the overall similarity relation is still the primary perceived structure for color stimuli.

The results following the dimensional instructions, however, indicate that different information is available in the two sets of stimuli. The proportions of responses for the within-category triads are distributed across the types of classifications fairly evenly, which means that the subjects could not find the dimensional relations consistently. In contrast, the pattern of responses to the between-category triads shows a strong tendency to classify by dimension. Moreover,

Table 5.

PROPORTION OF HUE CLASSIFICATIONS IN WITHIN- AND BETWEEN-
CATEGORY TRIADS PRECEDING AND FOLLOWING DIMENSIONAL
INSTRUCTIONS

Category status/ Step size	Predimensional training			Postdimensional training		
	Dim.	Sim.	Hap.	Dim.	Sim.	Hap.
Within categories						
2	.03	.94	.03	.36	.26	.38
3	.11	.88	.04	.44	.23	.33
Between categories						
2	.06	.92	.02	.73	.18	.09
3	.27	.70	.03	.85	.12	.03

Note. Dim. = dimension; Sim. = similarity; Hap. = haphazard classification.

subjects made reliably more dimensional responses to the three-step triads than the two-step triads.

SUMMARY

Garner (1974) has taken the view that although combinations of wavelength, purity, and intensity are perceived first as integral wholes, the dimensions of hue, saturation, and brightness may be accessed at a derived, more cognitive level. This chapter has considered the view that the analyzability of color stimuli into perceptual dimensions depends on the categorical relation among the stimuli to be analyzed.

In Experiment 1, subjects were asked to classify triads of stimuli within the same category according to the two stimuli that shared an identity relation in hue, saturation, or brightness, and to name the dimension that provided the relation. The analyzability of hue proved to be very different from that of either saturation or brightness. By hypothesis, the recognition that two stimuli in a category have the same hue should be masked by the invariant categorical property, and changes in the hue, saturation, or brightness of a particular stimulus should result in changes in the perceptual goodness of that stimulus relative to the prototype. Although the patterns of dimensional naming provided some evidence that subjects could perceive hue triads as such, subjects were unable to identify or name reliably the two stimuli that shared the identity relation.

In contrast, the subjects could classify reliably the triads that provided shared values of either saturation or brightness, and they could name the dimension that provided the identity relation at above-chance levels of accuracy. But accuracy was poor, and the subjects' frequent naming of saturation identities as brightness identities and vice versa strongly implicates perceptual goodness as the basis for classification. Perceptual goodness is further implicated by the finding that although the proportion of dimensional classifications is improved by increasing the salience of dimensional relations, the proportion of correct dimensional naming is unchanged. These findings suggest the possibility that when subjects are instructed to classify by dimension, they first classify by perceptual goodness and then attempt to assess whether the stimuli share saturation or brightness.

In Experiment 2, subjects were asked to classify triads of stimuli that presented shared values of hue. The triads were arranged such that either all stimuli were members of the same category or the two stimuli that presented shared values were in one category and the third stimulus was a member of an adjacent category. The subjects were first asked to classify the stimuli according to which two looked alike, and, subsequently, to classify the two stimuli that shared the same hue. By hypothesis, the within-category classification should be difficult because the invariant category property (e.g., blue) should mask the identity of a specific hue. In contrast, the between-category classification should be relatively easy because the classification can be accomplished by the categorical properties. The subjects first classified the within-categories or between-categories stimuli by overall similarity relations. Following instructions to classify by hue, however, subjects made classifications between categories on the basis of dimensional relations, whereas the classifications within a category were evenly distributed among the possible stimulus relations. Recalling the results of the dissimilarity judgment experiment, it is important to note that the perceptual differences in hue that occur between and within categories cannot be readily addressed by discriminability differences among the members of the two types of categorical triads.

Space limitations in this chapter have precluded the inclusion of experiments on the classification of saturation or brightness within and between categories. But no difference should occur in the classification of shared identities in saturation or brightness within and between categories, and our results show that none was observed. Generally, accuracy in recognizing shared values of either saturation or brightness was poor, and when all three dimensions varied in the triads, the proportions of dimensional classifications were not reliably greater than overall similarity classifications.

Taken together, our results indicate that color stimuli are first perceived as integral wholes and are classified by overall similarity relations. When subjects are instructed to classify by dimensional relations, they resort to classifications based on perceptual goodness and then, having done so, attempt to identify dimensional relations. This pattern of analysis is consistent for saturation or brightness triads whether the stimuli are chosen from within- or between-color categories.

The pattern of analysis also occurs for hue triads when the stimuli are chosen from the same color category, but the analysis of the stimuli arranged between categories permits the recognition of hue.

References

Berlin, B., & Kay, P. (1969). *Basic color terms: Their universality and evolution*. Berkeley: University of California Press.

Burns, B., & Shepp, B. E. (1988). Dimensional interactions and the structure of psychological space: The representation of hue, saturation and brightness. *Perception and Psychophysics, 43*, 494–507.

Felfoldy, G. L. (1974). Repetition effects in choice reaction time to multidimensional stimuli. *Perception and Psychophysics, 15*, 453–459.

Foard, C. F., & Kemler Nelson, D. G. (1984). Holistic and analytic modes of processing: The multiple determinants of perceptual analysis. *Journal of Experimental Psychology: General, 113*, 94–111.

Garner, W. R. (1974). *The processing of information and structure*. Potomac, MD: Erlbaum.

Handel, S., & Imai, S. (1972). The free classification of analyzable and unanalyzable stimuli. *Perception and Psychophysics, 12*, 108–116.

Homa, D. (1984). On the nature of categories. In G. H. Bower (Ed.), *The psychology of learning and motivation* (pp. 49–94). San Diego, CA: Academic Press.

Indow, T., & Kanazawa, K. (1960). Multidimensional mapping of Munsell colors varying in hue, chroma and value. *Journal of Experimental Psychology, 59*, 330–336.

Indow, T., & Uchinzono, T. (1960). Multidimensional mapping of Munsell colors varying in hue and chroma. *Journal of Experimental Psychology, 59*, 321–329.

Lockhead, G. R. (1972). Processing dimensional stimuli: A note. *Psychological Review, 79*, 410–419.

Rosch, E. (1973). The nature of mental codes for color categories. *Journal of Experimental Psychology: Human Perception and Performance, 1*, 303–322.

Rosch, E. (1974). Linguistic relativity. In A. Silverstein (Ed.), *Human communication: Theoretical explorations*. New York: Halsted Press.

Rosch, E. (1975). Universals and cultural specifics in human categorization. In R. Brislin, S. Bochner, & W. Lonner (Eds.), *Cross-cultural perspectives on learning*. New York: Halsted Press.

Shepp, B. E. (1984). The analyzability of multidimensional stimuli: Some constraints on perceived structure and attention. In T. J. Tighe & B. E. Shepp (Eds.), *Perception, cognition and development*. Hillsdale, NJ: Erlbaum.

CHAPTER 13

THE STRUCTURE OF VISUAL CONFIGURATIONS:
STIMULUS VERSUS SUBJECT CONTRIBUTIONS

JAMES R. POMERANTZ

Visual configurations offer perceivers a wealth of features to which they could attend. Garner's research has provided converging operations that help identify which features the perceiver actually does attend to. This chapter explores results of experiments inspired by Garner's work, with a particular emphasis on one question: To what extent is the set of features to which people attend dictated by the stimulus itself rather than chosen strategically by the perceiver? In other words, is the structure of visual configurations essentially in the stimulus or in the head? Results from previously reported speeded classification tasks show many instances in which perceivers apparently fail in tasks designed to demand selective attention to specified features, suggesting that subjects may be incapable of accessing these features individually. However, more recent experiments reviewed here provide instances in which subjects are free to choose the features to which they attend, suggesting that the earlier results should not be interpreted as failures of selective attention. In certain cases, simply instructing subjects to attend to specific features is sufficient to produce compliance. To be sure, the stimulus limits the ensemble of possible features, and early perceptual processes may bind or "glue" certain physical features together, thus preventing them from being attended to selectively. But within these constraints, perceivers may have more latitude than has previously been suspected. We need additional converging operations to help us discriminate between situations in which perceivers cannot attend to specific features and situations in which they simply choose not to attend to them.

DETERMINANTS OF STIMULUS STRUCTURE

When people examine a visual configuration, they can usually detect various forms of underlying structure (such as component parts), local features, and global attributes (such as size and symmetry). This chapter will focus on the role of the stimulus versus the role of the perceiver in determining the structure of visual configurations.

This topic might please Wendell Garner because it involves the intersection of at least two different problems on which he has written extensively. The problem of stimulus structure is, of course, the dominant theme of this volume, and the application of this concept to visual configurations is familiar turf to many researchers reading this book. Visual configurations, like most other stimuli, can be distinguished from one another by their dimensional and featural differences, and thus they possess alternatives from which the perceiver can select. Many authors in this volume have worked for years on the problem of identifying experimentally those features, dimensions, and alternatives that are used for the perception and recognition of forms.

My second tie to Garner's work concerns the role of the perceiver versus the role of the stimulus in determining stimulus structure. Stated most directly, the question is whether and when the dimensions and features by which we identify forms are determined by the organism—the active perceiver—as opposed to being determined by the stimulus itself interacting with fixed, perhaps physiologically determined, detector mechanisms.

STIMULUS DETERMINATION

The issue of mandatory allocation of attention to stimulus dimensions is one on which Garner has written often, perhaps most extensively in his chapter titled "Attention: The Processing of Multiple Sources of Information" (Garner, 1974a). Central to the concept of integral stimulus dimensions (Garner, 1970, 1974b; Garner & Felfoldy, 1970; Lockhead, 1966; Shepard, 1964) is the notion that such dimensions cannot be attended to selectively by the perceiver, at least not in a direct fashion. That is, although they could be accessed through a secondary or postperceptual process of scrutiny, individual integral dimensions cannot be accessed directly or immediately. This in turn implies that the stimulus, not the active perceiver, determines this stimulus structure; more colloquially, structure resides "in the stimulus," not "in the head."

However, the notion of integrality has only limited applications to the dimensions of form perception, because few if any dimensions of form show all of the defining characteristics of integrality (including redundancy gains), and many show additional characteristics not diagnostic of integrality (including performance on divided-attention tasks that is superior to that on selective-attention tasks).

Nevertheless, the question remains whether the dimensions or features of forms that perceivers do use are rigidly imposed on them or whether perceivers can exert cognitive control over which dimensions or features they use (cf. Cutting, 1986).

INITIAL EXPERIMENTS WITH GARNER ON DOTS AND PARENTHESES

My two published papers with Garner involved two types of stimuli. The first was his well-known dot patterns (Pomerantz & Garner, 1973a); the second was the parenthesis pairs we introduced together (Pomerantz & Garner, 1973b). Both of these studies were aimed at determining the effective stimulus dimensions used by our subjects in various perceptual and memory tasks. I will describe some of our methods below. However, in each case we concluded from our results that the *nominal* stimulus dimensions (i.e, the dimensions from which we generated the stimuli) were not the effective dimensions or features by which subjects perceived these forms. Dot patterns were not perceived as a collection of discrete dots at varying locations, nor were parenthesis pairs perceived as two individual line segments, differing in orientation of curvature, that happened to be placed in close proximity to each other.

It is important to note that our experiments did not reveal the dimensions to which subjects *were* attending; they showed only the ones to which subjects were *not* attending. That is, they showed that subjects were not attending selectively to an individual dot in the first experiment and to a single parenthesis in the second. The method works through hypothesizing a set of dimensions and then confirming (or, in these two cases, disconfirming) the use of these dimensions by the subject.

EVIDENCE FOR STIMULUS-DETERMINED STRUCTURE: DOT PATTERNS

In addition to showing that the nominal dimensions of stimulus configurations were not the effective dimensions used by perceivers, our experiments and those of others indicated that the perceptual structure of these stimuli was determined by the stimuli themselves and was not influenced significantly by the momentary intentions of the perceiver. To cite one early and compelling example, Clement and Varnadoe (1967) showed that when subjects discriminated between Garner dot patterns like those shown in Figure 1, their performance benefited from pattern goodness, such that patterns from small rotation and reflection subsets were classified more quickly than those from large subsets. Clement and Weiman (1970) then tested whether subjects were attending to whole configurations only because the strategy of discriminating between any two dot patterns simply by noting the presence or absence of a dot in a particular location had not occurred to them.

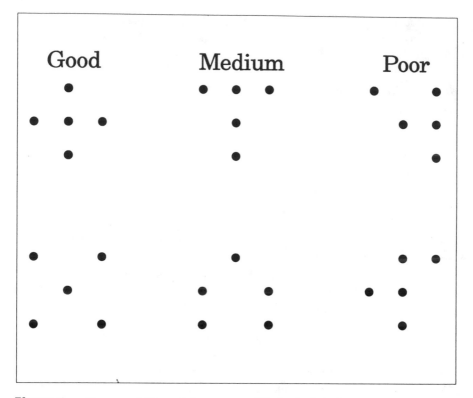

Figure 1.   Garner and Clement dot patterns, differing in their degrees of pattern goodness. The good patterns have small rotation and reflection subsets, whereas
the poor ones have large subsets.

This study led to experiments in which instructions were manipulated to induce
subjects to attend to a single dot location. Clement and Weiman's results, which
have been described in detail elsewhere, showed that subjects will not voluntarily
attend to individual dot locations; in fact, it takes virtual coercion to get them to
do so. Subjects' reluctance to attend to individual dots suggests that compliance
would entail secondary, attention-demanding processing.

EVIDENCE FOR STIMULUS-DETERMINED STRUCTURE: PARENTHESIS PATTERNS

These conclusions for dot patterns were echoed in the conclusions drawn from
experiments using parenthesis pairs, as shown in Figure 2A. Although the methods
used in the parenthesis studies were different, the evidence showed subjects to be
unable or at least unwilling to attend to the orientation (or direction of curvature)

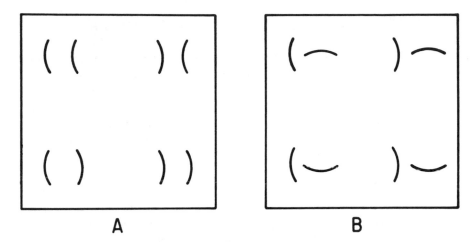

Figure 2.   A: The normally oriented parenthesis pairs of Pomerantz and Garner (1973b), whose nominal dimensions are the orientations of the left and the right parenthesis. B: The misoriented parenthesis pairs, whose right-hand member has been rotated 90°. (From Pomerantz, 1981. Reprinted by permission.)

of an individual parenthesis while ignoring the orientation of an irrelevant, neighboring parenthesis.

The parenthesis experiments used the speeded classification method used in the Garner and Felfoldy (1970) integrality paradigm, such that the subject's task was to judge the orientation of one parenthesis, for example, the one on the left. We examined whether variation of the orientation of the irrelevant parenthesis interfered with subjects' ability to determine the orientation of the relevant parenthesis, relative to a control condition in which the irrelevant parenthesis did not vary. Our main result (Pomerantz & Garner, 1973) was that irrelevant variation hurt performance. Substantial amounts of *Garner interference*, as this drop in speed or accuracy of performance is often called, have been observed many times in replications of this basic experiment. In experiments that I performed with Sager, Stoever, and others (Pomerantz, Sager, & Stoever, 1977), we showed that this result generalizes to other visual patterns, including motion configurations.

These results with dot and parenthesis patterns pointed, unequivocally it seemed, toward the stimulus rather than the perceiver as the source of structure. In both cases, subjects appeared to fail at their apparent aim of attending selectively to the nominal stimulus elements or parts, and such a failure would indicate processing not under voluntary control. In other words, with both dot patterns and parenthesis pairs, subjects seemed to perceive not parts but holistic properties of the stimulus on a mandatory, first-priority basis. From these results, it did not seem possible for perceivers to adjust their processing to allow the nominal features to be attended to first.

EVIDENCE FOR SUBJECT-DETERMINED STRUCTURE

Although the initial results with dot, parenthesis and other configurations seemed unequivocal, later experiments have produced evidence that perceivers are, in fact, able to attend to individual parts, at least for some of these configurations. In two series of experiments (Pomerantz, 1983; Pomerantz & Pristach, 1989) that used similar methods as in the experiments with the parentheses, subjects classified arrow–triangle stimuli like those shown in the left panel of Figure 3. The nominal dimensions here are the positions or the orientations of component line segments.

These arrows and triangles lead to the same, sizable levels of Garner interference as shown by the parentheses, suggesting again a failure of selective attention to the individual line segments from which they are constructed. From these experiments, however, we now believe that the apparent "failure" of selective attention revealed by Garner interference is not really a failure to attend selectively; rather, it is a voluntary decision to avoid selective attention (cf. Shepard's notion in this volume that stimulus generalization is not the result of a failure of sensory discrimination). For example, when the same speeded classification experiment is performed using the arrows and triangles in the right panel of Figure 3, which are constructed from a similar set of line segments, virtually no Garner interference is observed (Pomerantz & Pristach, 1989). To understand this result, consider the task in which subjects discriminate between the configurations shown in the upper left and lower left cells of the left panel of Figure 3. Although these forms differ nominally in the position or orientation of their horizontal and vertical line segments, we believe that subjects prefer to perceive

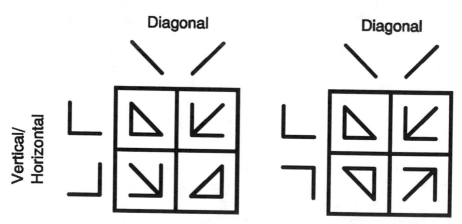

Figure 3.   A: The arrow and triangle stimuli of Pomerantz, Sager, and Stoever (1977), whose nominal dimensions are the positions or orientations of the three component line segments. B: A modified arrow and triangle set that yields no Garner interference. (From Pomerantz & Pristach, 1989. Copyright 1989 by the American Psychological Association. Adapted by permission.)

them simply as a triangle and an arrow. With the corresponding configurations in the right panel of Figure 3, which likewise differ only on their horizontal and vertical segments, subjects can no longer use the arrow-versus-triangle distinction because both forms are triangles. Thus, subjects are induced to attending to the horizontal and vertical segments. The absence of Garner interference with these stimuli shows that no cost is incurred in attending selectively to the component segments of these global configurations.

These experiments show that when subjects have a proper incentive, they can and indeed do selectively attend, and do so without experiencing noticeable Garner interference from the other line segments. These results imply that the stimulus itself is not the sole determinant of perceptual structure; rather, the subject has considerable latitude in selecting voluntarily from alternative structures.

On the basis of these results, we have concluded that there is no "perceptual glue" binding together the line segments of arrows and triangles. Subjects will attend to emergent, wholistic features of the arrow–triangle configurations (potentially including closure and others) when it is in their best interest to do so. However, spreading attention across the whole stimulus is neither mandatory nor dictated by the structure of the stimulus. This conclusion departs significantly from previous Gestalt statements on grouping, which emphasized the mandatory nature of autochthonous forces binding together visual configurations in a strictly bottom-up fashion. For example, Boring (1942) characterized one of the major Gestalt laws as stating, "A strong form coheres and resists disintegration by analysis into parts or by fusion with another form" (p. 253). In our view, strong forms offer alternative emergent features to which the subject has the option of attending, but they do not in any way actively resist attention to individual parts.

RESULTS FROM OTHER EXPERIMENTS

The experiments described above hardly exhaust the literature on mandatory grouping and perceptual glue. I will now mention three other results that bear on the matter and that also fail to point to a single conclusion. First, Treisman and Paterson (1984), in examining feature migration with arrow and triangle stimuli, found no evidence for perceptual glue, in that a component line segment belonging to these configurations was as likely to float freely and form an illusory conjunction with other segments as was an isolated, otherwise unattached line segment. In other words, participating in an arrow or a triangle does not bind a line segment to that configuration.

Second, and in potential contradiction to this result, is Prinzmetal's (1981) finding that line segments are more likely to float within perceptual groups than between them in forming illusory conjunctions. This result could indicate some type of perceptual glue, perhaps at the boundaries between perceptual groups.

Third and last, in an unpublished study, Pristach and I confirmed a result suggested by our previous data that when subjects must classify parenthesis pairs according to one parenthesis while the irrelevant parenthesis is varying orthogonally, performance is actually better with the weaker, "misoriented" parenthesis configurations shown in Figure 2B than with the normally oriented pairs we saw earlier. This result suggests that the two parentheses are glued together in the normally oriented pairs and so must be unglued to perform the task. With the poorer configurations of the misoriented pairs, no glue exists and so performance is faster because no ungluing is required.

To summarize, the evidence is at best mixed on the issue of whether stimulus structure in visual configurations is mandatory and dictated by the geometric layout of the stimulus itself, or whether the subject retains some or total control over effective perceptual structure. More work is needed and, as we shall see, more work has been done. I will discuss some new experiments that manipulate attentional strategies through instructions and that use as stimuli variants of the parentheses and arrow–triangle configurations.

INSTRUCTIONS TO ATTEND WITH PARENTHESIS CONFIGURATIONS

Some of these studies were motivated by a result involving the parenthesis stimuli produced by Nelson Toth, a former member of my laboratory (Toth, 1988). Toth departed from our customary procedure of avoiding specific instructions to subjects regarding what or where in the stimulus to attend. Our rationale has been that to determine subjects' natural strategies of attention, it is better to avoid encouraging particular strategies or describing stimulus dimensions to which they might attend. Toth, however, specifically told his subjects to attend to just one designated parenthesis and to ignore the other.

Toth's striking result was a reduction in Garner interference arising from the irrelevant parenthesis, down to levels not significantly different from zero. This outcome stands in contrast to the typical 200-ms level of Garner interference when no such instructions are given. Toth's finding would add to the evidence against perceptual glue and would suggest that subjects can and will determine for themselves the appropriate stimulus structure to which they will attend, given some incentive to do so.

Because Toth's result was so impressive, and because his procedure departed from our own in several other ways and used a small number of subjects, Edward Pristach, Cathy Carson and I replicated his instructional manipulation in an experiment that otherwise conformed to our standard procedure. In brief, subjects were presented with parenthesis pairs like those shown in Figure 2A, and they were explicitly instructed to classify the stimuli through button presses on the

Table 1.

REACTION TIMES (MS) FROM SPEEDED CLASSIFICATION TASKS WITH AND
WITHOUT INSTRUCTIONS TO ATTEND TO THE NOMINAL DIMENSIONS

Experiment	Control condition	Orthogonal condition	Garner interference
Parentheses–No instructions	566	754	188
Triangles and arrows–No instructions	441	585	144
Parentheses with instructions	508	569	61
Triangles and arrows with instructions	413	520	107

Note. The control condition consists of tasks in which the irrelevant stimulus dimension (e.g., the left parenthesis, when the right one is relevant) is held constant throughout the presentation sequence. In the orthogonal condition, the irrelevant dimension varies randomly. The decline in performance in the orthogonal condition relative to the control condition is expressed as Garner interference. Data within a row come from a single experiment and are directly comparable; data from different rows come from different experiments using different subjects, and so are less comparable.

basis of the orientation of one parenthesis while ignoring the orientation of the other, irrelevant parenthesis.

Our results were in the direction of those reported by Toth, but they were far less extreme in magnitude. Specifically, we found that variation on the irrelevant parenthesis yielded about 60 ms of Garner interference (see Table 1). Although this magnitude is sizable and is certainly significantly different from zero, it amounts to only one third the interference we typically find when no attentional instructions are given. Thus, telling subjects where to focus their attention with parentheses is indeed effective, but not completely effective, as would have been evidenced by zero Garner interference.

The fact that subjects comply with instructions partially but not completely indicates either that (a) the stimulus itself has a partial (neither a zero nor a dominant) role in determining the effective dimensions to which subjects attend or that (b) subjects themselves wholly determine the effective dimensions, but at least some subjects in some of the conditions in the experiment choose to ignore our directions. Although we cannot rule out the former hypothesis in this chapter, the following evidence supports the latter.

INSTRUCTIONS TO ATTEND WITH ARROW–TRIANGLE CONFIGURATIONS

If the focus of attention is so readily swayed by instructions on how and where to attend with the parenthesis stimuli, the same might be true with other configurations. To test this possibility, we repeated our basic arrow–triangle experiment using the familiar stimuli shown in Figure 3A but with instructions telling subjects to attend to a designated line segment while ignoring the other segments. To illustrate, subjects in one set of conditions were told to attend to the vertical line segment of each arrow or triangle (while ignoring the horizontal and diagonal segments) and to press one button if the vertical were on the left side of the figure and the other button if it were on the right.

Our results were different from those with the parentheses: Instructing subjects where to attend had little effect on attending to the arrows and triangles. Specifically, the instructions reduced Garner interference by only 26%, compared with 68% reduction for the parentheses (see Table 1).

Two interpretations for the result with arrows and triangles are possible: either (a) stimulus structure is dictated entirely by the stimulus itself, in which case instructions will never have an effect on performance, or (b) stimulus structure is decided on by subjects, who listened to our instructions but apparently chose to ignore them almost entirely, perhaps because the instructions asked them to follow a strategy they viewed to be far from optimal. In any case, we must explain why instructions that had such a large effect on the parentheses had so little an effect here with the arrows and triangles. Such an explanation will be offered below.

Regarding the two possible interpretations, we are confronting an asymmetry that limits any experiment attempting to manipulate strategies through instructions: If the instructions have their intended effect, we demonstrate that subjects can control their allocation of attention; if instructions have no effect, we cannot tell whether this is because subjects cannot follow instructions or merely because they choose not to follow them.

Nevertheless, the data are all consistent with the perceiver's determining perceptual structure. It is impossible from the present data to rule out partial or even total stimulus determination in some instances, but this notion is strained. For example, with arrows and triangles, the inefficacy of instructions to attend selectively could mean that the subject is forced to accept as structure such global emergent features as closure and that component line segments are bound by perceptual glue and thus not available individually. But this would be inconsistent with the results with the parentheses, where we would have to appeal to "weak" glue because instructions worked partially with these stimuli. More important, it would be inconsistent with data showing the absence of perceptual glue with other sets of arrows and triangles (i.e., results showing successful selective attention to an individual line segment). On those grounds, the present data argue that stimulus structure is under a considerable degree of subject control.

Motivated by our positive results with the parenthesis patterns, we are continuing with new experiments aimed at determining whether subjects can strategically control their allocation of attention to configural stimuli. Nevertheless, the parentheses may be the exceptions and, for most other configurations, instructions may make little or no difference on the dimensions that subjects process. For example, in his doctoral dissertation recently completed in my laboratory, Ed

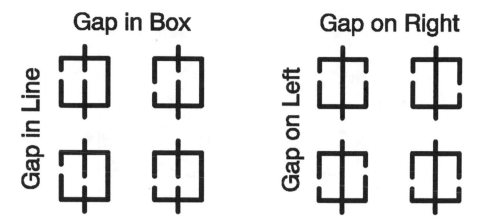

Figure 4. The box and line with gap stimuli used by Pristach (1989) and modeled after Duncan (1984). Adapted by permission.

Pristach (1989) found no effect of instructions on configurations modeled on those first used by Duncan (1984) and shown in Figure 4. Pristach found significant levels of Garner interference in judgments of the position of the relevant gap, both when the irrelevant gap fell within the same apparent object (i.e., within the outline rectangle in the figure) and when it fell within a different but overlapping object (i.e., within the vertical line segment bisecting the rectangle). Most important, this interference persisted even when subjects were instructed to attend to just the rectangle or just the vertical line segment.

EXPLAINING WHY INSTRUCTIONS AFFECT PARENTHESES BUT NOT ARROWS AND TRIANGLES: ROBUSTNESS OF EMERGENT FEATURES

The difference we have just seen between parenthesis pairs, in which instructions to attend selectively have a large effect, and arrows and triangles, in which such instructions have none, parallels another difference we have discovered between these two stimulus sets. The basic configural effect we find with parenthesis pairs—namely, the massive failure (or absence) of selective attention coupled with highly successful divided attention—is quite easy to destroy by altering physical characteristics of the parentheses. For example, separating the parentheses in space as in Figure 5 (Pomerantz & Schwaitzberg, 1975) or rotating one of the parentheses 90°, as we saw with the "misoriented" parentheses back in Figure 2B (Pomerantz & Garner, 1973b), is sufficient to destroy the configural effect entirely. Not as dramatically, introducing a diagonal line connecting the individual parentheses, as shown in Figure 6, reduces the configural effect significantly, although it does not destroy the effect entirely.

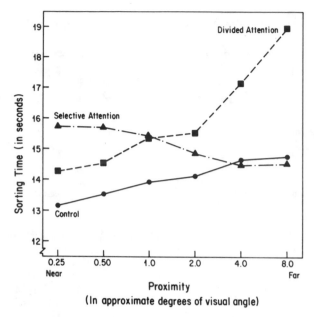

Figure 5.   Separating the parentheses in space weakens their configural effects, such as Garner interference (Pomerantz & Schwaitzberg, 1975). (From Pomerantz, 1981. Reprinted by permission.)

By contrast, the configural effect with arrows and triangles is surprisingly difficult to destroy by altering the stimulus physically (Pomerantz & Pristach, 1989). For example, lengthening or shortening the component line segments or adding or deleting line segments, as in Figure 7, has little if any influence on the configural effects these stimuli show. Even when the triangles are opened at the vertexes, as in the lower left stimulus set, which alters a number of seemingly critical emergent features, large levels of Garner interference remain, indicating a lack of selective attention, and we still see successful divided attention, another diagnostic of configural interactions. Other major alterations in the arrow–triangle configurations shown in Figure 7 also have little or no discernable effect on perceptual performance.

It is tempting to conclude that the emergent features of the parenthesis pairs are fragile, whereas those of arrows and triangles are robust and so are relatively impervious to physical manipulation. Evidence in favor of this conclusion is the differential effect of instructions on attention to these two sets of stimuli. Recall that instructions have a great effect on the parentheses, which would be expected if the emergent feature of parentheses were weak and fragile. Instructions have little effect on arrows and triangles, which likewise would be expected if the emergent feature of arrows and triangles were robust. Speaking against this conclusion, however, is the fact that robustness levels apparently cannot be measured

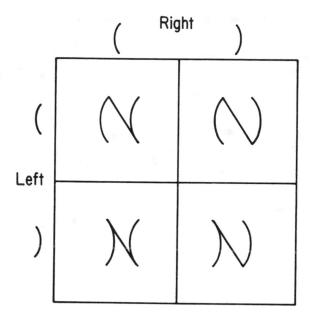

Figure 6. The "N" stimuli, constructed from the normally oriented parentheses of Figure 2A but with an identical diagonal line segment added to each stimulus. (From "Visual Form Perception: An Overview" by J. R. Pomerantz, 1986, in E. C. Schwab & H. C. Nusbaum, Eds., *Pattern Recognition by Humans and Machines: Vol. 2. Visual Perception*. Adapted by permission.)

through Garner interference levels because the parentheses generally produce the same, strong levels of Garner interference as do the arrows and triangles. This puzzle cannot be resolved at the present time.

We should not forget that, under some circumstances, subjects do selectively attend to an individual line segment of arrows and triangles without Garner interference from the remaining segments. But this outcome, when it occurs, is presumably the result of subjects' voluntarily directing attention to certain parts of a configuration. That is, under appropriately contrived conditions, subjects can be induced to ignore a robust emergent feature and attend to nominal parts of visual configurations. Instructions alone do not appear to be sufficient to induce subjects to do this, but nonetheless they can be induced through more compelling means that were noted previously (see Figure 3B).

GARNER VERSUS STROOP INTERFERENCE: EFFECTS OF INSTRUCTIONS

Before concluding this chapter, I wish to discuss one additional matter regarding the effect of instructions to attend to an individual parenthesis in a pair of normally

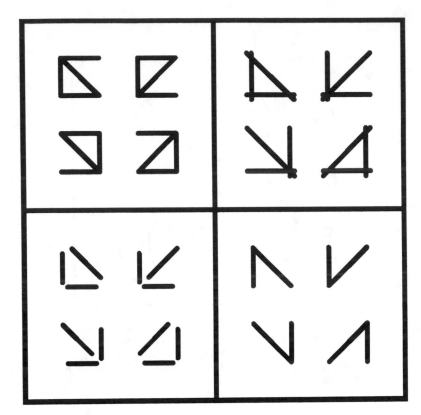

Figure 7.   Variations on the basic arrow and triangle configurations of Figure 3, in which component line segments have been shortened, lengthened, deleted, or added. (From Pomerantz & Pristach, 1989. Copyright 1989 by the American Psychological Association. Adapted by permission.)

oriented parentheses. As noted previously, such instructions reduce the level of Garner interference significantly, albeit to levels substantially greater than zero. This is consistent with the notion that when instructed to do so, subjects tend to focus their attention on a single parenthesis rather than the parenthesis pair.

For some time, we have been assessing selective attention in our experiments, not only by measuring Garner interference but also through Stroop interference. Whereas Garner interference assesses the deleterious effects on attending of *variation* on an irrelevant dimension and is computed between conditions, Stroop interference, considered generally as incongruity effects, assesses the deleterious effect of information presented on the irrelevant dimension that is *inconsistent* with that on the relevant and is computed between trials within a given condition. In our experiments, Stroop and Garner interference are computed from separate analyses of the same data, not from separate data collected in different tasks.

Across a variety of experiments summarized elsewhere (Pomerantz, Pristach, & Carson, 1989), we have found surprisingly little agreement between these two basic indexes of attentional selectivity. Regarding instructions to attend to individual parentheses, the effects on Stroop and Garner interference were, in fact, opposite: Whereas these instructions decreased Garner interference, as noted above, they actually increased Stroop interference. We believe that this apparently contradictory result reveals much about the difference in origins and sensitivity between the two measures.

When parenthesis pairs are perceived and responded to without special instructions, typically no Stroop interference is found. That is, pairs whose elements are oriented oppositely—)(and ()—are responded to neither more quickly nor more slowly than pairs whose elements agree in orientation—)) and ((. We interpret Garner interference as reflecting the fact that whole pairs are viewed as a single unit, and so the nominally irrelevant parenthesis is not ignored. Similarly, we view the absence of Stroop interference as indicating that the pairs are perceived as just one unit and thus are not capable of containing consistencies or inconsistencies between their constituent parts; that is, it takes at least two entities to produce a conflict. When subjects are instructed to focus on a single parenthesis, Garner interference drops because subjects comply with the instructions, whereas Stroop interference now arises because the pairs are seen as two individual parentheses that may now agree or disagree in orientation. Thus, the result with respect to Stroop interference leads to the same conclusion as with Garner interference, namely, that subjects have voluntary control over the dimensions by which they perceive configural stimuli.

CONCLUSION

To summarize, perceivers may have more latitude in determining stimulus structure than researchers have heretofore believed. An essential ingredient at this stage of research is new *converging operations* (Garner, Hake, & Eriksen, 1956) to help researchers distinguish cases where perceivers cannot direct their attention as instructed from cases where they simply elect not to do so. It is fitting indeed that this chapter, which has focused on concepts about configuration and attention that originated with Wendell Garner, should close on another concept that began with him and that promises to guide research for years to come.

References

Boring, E. G. (1942). *Sensation and perception in the history of experimental psychology.* New York: Appleton-Century-Crofts.

Clement, D. E., & Varnadoe, K. W. (1967). Pattern uncertainty and the discrimination of visual patterns. *Perception & Psychophysics, 2,* 427–431.

Clement, D. E., & Weiman, C. F. R. (1970). Instructions, strategies, and pattern uncertainty in a visual discrimination task. *Perception & Psychophysics, 7,* 333–336.

Cutting, J. E. (1986). *Perception with an eye toward motion.* Cambridge, MA: Bransford Press.

Duncan, J. (1984). Selective attention and the organization of visual information. *Journal of Experimental Psychology: General, 113,* 501–517.

Garner, W. R. (1970). The stimulus in information processing. *American Psychologist, 25,* 350–358.

Garner, W. R. (1974a). Attention: The processing of multiple sources of information. In Carterette and Friedman (Eds.), *Handbook of perception* (Vol. 2, pp. 23–59). San Diego, CA: Academic Press.

Garner, W. R. (1974b). *The processing of information and structure.* Hillsdale, NJ: Erlbaum.

Garner, W. R., & Felfoldy, G. (1970). Integrality of stimulus dimensions in various types of information processing. *Cognitive Psychology, 1,* 225–241.

Garner, W. R., Hake, H. W., & Eriksen, C. W. (1956). Operationism and the concept of perception. *Psychological Review, 63,* 149–159.

Lockhead, G. R. (1966). Effects of dimensional redundancy on visual discrimination. *Journal of Experimental Psychology, 72,* 95–104.

Pomerantz, J.R. (1981). Perceptual organization in information processing. In M. Kubovy & J. R. Pomerantz (Eds.), *Perceptual organization.* Hillsdale, NJ: Erlbaum.

Pomerantz, J. R. (1983). Global and local precedence: Selective attention in form and motion perception. *Journal of Experimental Psychology: General, 112,* 516–540.

Pomerantz, J. R., & Garner, W. R. (1973a). The role of configuration and target discriminability in a visual search task. *Memory & Cognition, 1,* 64–68.

Pomerantz, J. R., & Garner, W. R. (1973b). Stimulus configuration in selective attention tasks. *Perception & Psychophysics, 14,* 565–569.

Pomerantz, J. R., & Pristach, E. A. (1989). Emergent features, attention and perceptual glue in visual form perception. *Journal of Experimental Psychology: Human Perception and Performance, 15,* 635–649.

Pomerantz, J. R., Pristach, E. A., & Carson, C. E. (1989). Attention and object perception. In B. Shepp & S. Ballesteros (Eds.), *Object perception: Structure and process* (pp. 53–89). Hillsdale, NJ: Erlbaum.

Pomerantz, J. R., Sager, L. C., & Stoever, R. J. (1977). Perception of wholes and of their component parts: Some configural superiority effects. *Journal of Experimental Psychology: Human Perception and Performance, 3,* 422–435.

Pomerantz, J. R., & Schwaitzberg, S. D. (1975). Grouping by proximity: Selective attention measures. *Perception & Psychophysics, 18,* 355–361.

Prinzmetal, W. (1981). Principles of feature integration in visual perception. *Perception & Psychophysics, 30,* 330–340.

Pristach, E. A. (1989). *Locations versus objects as bases for attentional allotment.* Unpublished doctoral dissertation, State University of New York at Buffalo.

Shepard, R. N. (1964). Attention and the metric structure of the stimulus space. *Journal of Mathematical Psychology, 1,* 54–87.

Toth, N. (1988). Unpublished doctoral dissertation, Rutgers University.

Treisman, A., & Paterson, R. (1984). Emergent features, attention, and object perception. *Journal of Experimental Psychology: Human Perception and Performance, 10,* 12–31.

PART THREE

ANIMAL BEHAVIOR

CHAPTER 14

PERCEPTUAL ANALYSIS IN PIGEON VISUAL SEARCH

DONALD S. BLOUGH

Four lines of research are summarized in which data from visual search tasks are brought to bear on the question of perceptual analysis in pigeons. Birds received food for pecking at small black target forms that appeared among distractors on a white computer screen. The primary independent variable was the speed with which the target was found, and there were four major findings: (a) Search speed and accuracy were used to scale similarity among letters of the alphabet. Clusters of similar letters shared putative features such as loops or open centers; these data corresponded well to results from humans. (b) Search reaction times (RTs) based on forms differing in one dimension were largely independent of the level of an irrelevant dimension, suggesting separability or analytic perception. (c) Search asymmetries indicated that the aspects of simple forms that function as features for pigeons may be different from those that function as features for human subjects. (d) Covariation of search RTs across trial blocks suggested that pigeons shift their attention among features and that functional features can be identified by these shifts. Taken together, the studies illustrate a comparative approach to perceptual problems that heretofore have been studied primarily in humans.

Visual perception is not unique to humans. Among vertebrate classes, birds are certainly our rivals, if not our betters, in visual competence. What can we learn from them? Are there fundamental principles of visual perception that evolution has decreed shall rule all advanced visual systems? How may one characterize the analytic and selective processes that one presumes underlie birds' perception

This research was supported in part by National Science Foundation Grant BNS-8025515.

213

of objects and events? My purpose in this chapter is to exemplify the beginnings of answers to such questions with data that suggest analytic processing of forms by pigeons, of the sort for which there is evidence in humans (e.g., Treisman, 1986).

This brief overview is restricted to methods based on visual search tasks. As perceptual tasks, these differ little between pigeon and human subjects. Small forms are displayed on a computer-driven monitor; pigeons must find and peck at a target form that is more or less concealed among a number of distractors. Success leads occasionally to a food reward. Pigeons readily learn to hunt for targets in this way, perhaps because foraging for small food items is one of their common natural activities.

In some of our experiments, birds learned to look for a specific target, for example, a particular triangle (e.g., D.S. Blough, 1979; P.M. Blough, 1984), but the data reported here come largely from another procedure, which I have called *odd-item search* (D.S. Blough, 1986). In this task, a number of identical distractor forms appear on the screen, among which the pigeon must find the single different form, the "odd item." In odd-item search, both the distractors and the target vary from trial to trial; a form that is the target on some trials becomes the distractor on others. The forms are drawn from a pool of items, all of which appear equally often as both target or distractor. Thus, the pigeon cannot solve the odd-item search task by looking for any specific item, but only by looking for the item that is unique within a given display.

Accuracy is high in most of these search experiments. The birds find the target on almost every trial, so reaction time (RT) is the dependent variable in most of our work. RT has proven exceptionally informative, as in research with humans (Luce, 1986), and we strongly recommend that others consider its uses in animal experimentation. (For a discussion of the uses of RT in the study of animal perception, see D.S. Blough & P.M. Blough, 1990.)

DIMENSIONS AND CLUSTERS EXTRACTED FROM SEARCH DATA

My first example of data that suggest perceptual analysis comes from a study of similarities among letters of the alphabet. Odd-item search was used: The letters appeared in pairs, and the odd-item target was a cluster composed of one of the paired letters (for example, 9 As) displayed on a background composed of the other letter (for example, 144 Bs). The accuracy with which the target cluster was found measured the similarity of the two letters; low accuracy meant great similarity (D.S. Blough & Franklin, 1985). (This is the only experiment reported here that used accuracy rather than RT as the dependent variable.) Each letter was displayed with every other letter in all possible combinations, resulting in a large matrix of accuracy values.

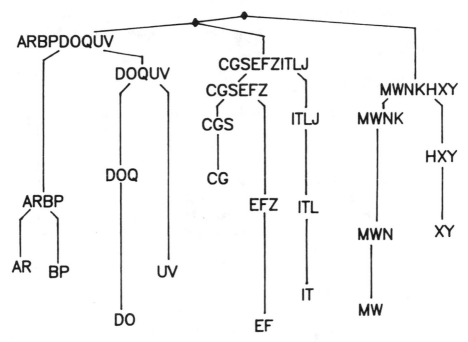

Figure 1. Hierarchical clusters based on pigeon search accuracy data. The letters were presented in pairs during search, one letter as target, the other as distractor. The abscissa is arbitrary; distance up the ordinate is proportional to the logarithm of the greatest interletter distance computed for a cluster at that level. (The exact fonts of the letters are given in D. Blough, 1985. Based on data obtained by D. S. Blough & Franklin, 1985.)

When the pigeon-data matrices were reduced through multidimensional scaling and cluster analysis, the resulting structure matched remarkably well the results from human judgments of letter similarity (Podgorny & Garner, 1979). Even more than for human data, the pigeon results could be accounted for by clusters of letters that shared apparent features, such as "small loop" (A,B,P,R), "open center" (D,O,Q), "vertical line" (F,I,J,L,T), and so on. This outcome may be illustrated by a hierarchical diagram, with clusters arranged according to interletter similarity (Figure 1). Clusters containing letters most similar to each other are toward the bottom of this diagram; as interletter dissimilarity rises, so does the level of the cluster.

The presence of apparent features common to the clusters suggests that the perception of the letters might have involved an analysis of such features. However, this categorization of course fails to demonstrate that such analysis actually occurred. For example, letters sharing a feature such as a loop may match quite well by superposition, and indeed a simple template model, blind to parts or features as such, can yield at least some aspects of the data structure exemplified here (D. Blough, 1985). Thus, such categorization remains only suggestive evidence for perceptual analysis, and we turn to other examples that may be more convincing.

COMBINATION RULES

My second example concerns the exploration of stimuli that are explicitly dimensionalized. A basic hypothesis about the processing of such stimuli is familiar: If dimensions are processed independently, the dissimilarity between two stimuli is the sum of the dissimilarities between them on each dimension alone, that is, the "city-block" combination rule (Shepard, 1964). In contrast, holistically processed "integral" stimuli are expected to yield the Euclidean combination rule. Although these alternatives by no means exhaust the possible combinatory structures, they still provide a convenient analytic framework.

I have previously reported (D.S. Blough, 1986, 1988) scaling results for a set of forms composed of apparently separable components, derived from the odd-item search method described above. This set of stimuli comprised 16 items, each of which was a black block and an elongated U. The block varied in height and the U varied in length (Figure 2). Each item in the set was paired in a search display with every other item, providing a matrix of search RTs that could be taken to reflect the pairwise similarities of the items. Figure 2 shows this set of forms, arranged in a two-dimensional representation of the similarities generated by the search task. It is evident that the two nominal dimensions of this form set were reflected in the data.

Although these data clearly reflect an orderly dimensional structure, multidimensional scaling typically does not provide a strong test of combination rules. Here, the fits generated by the city-block and by the Euclidean metrics were about equally good (D.S. Blough, 1988, p. 71), suggesting that there is at least some interaction in the processing of the two dimensions. Another test provided a more direct look at such possible interaction. If the dimensions were processed independently, forms differing by a certain amount on one dimension, but not differing at all on the other dimension, should be equally similar, regardless of the level at which the constant dimension was fixed. If this rule applied to the data just described, it would mean that the search RT for the four pairs of corresponding forms in any two rows or in any two columns of Figure 2 should be constant. Figure 3 compares RTs for form pairs in which the U shape was the same for each member of the pair (upper panel) and for form pairs in which the black block was the same for each member of the pair (lower panel). Results are shown for each of the four levels on the constant dimension (abscissa) and for differences on the varying dimension of one-, two-, or three-size steps. Independent processing of the two dimensions should yield straight horizontal lines in Figure 3. There is a small but systematic departure from this prediction for the difficult one-step

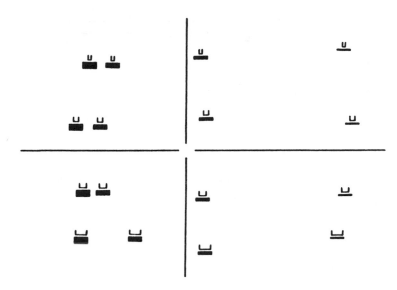

Figure 2.   Two-dimensional configuration produced by the nonmetric ALSCAL procedure from speeds of odd-item search. The configuration reflects two independently variable aspects of the stimulus forms: line length and block height. (From D. S. Blough, 1986, p. 417. Reprinted with permission.)

searches; these took a bit longer when the constant dimension was at its extreme values. Otherwise, the data support the notion that the two aspects of these forms acted independently to determine search speed.

SEARCH ASYMMETRY

My third example of perceptual analysis in pigeons is, I think, more instructive than either of the first two. It is based on a phenomenon that caught my attention some years ago in an article by Julesz and Schumer (1981). This phenomenon, now called "search asymmetry," struck me as a promising way to find out in animal subjects which parts of simple forms might function as separable features. For human subjects, this notion has since been confirmed in a number of experiments by Treisman and her colleagues (e.g., Treisman & Gormican, 1988).

To identify a search asymmetry, an experimenter has subjects look for a single target item amid a number of identical distractors. The target and distractor forms differ only by the presence of a putative feature in one and its absence in the other. For example, the target might be a circle and the distractors might be a set of circles each containing an intersecting line, or vice versa. If the target contains the feature (for example, if the line is a feature and it is in the target), the target "pops out" from the background. That is, the target is

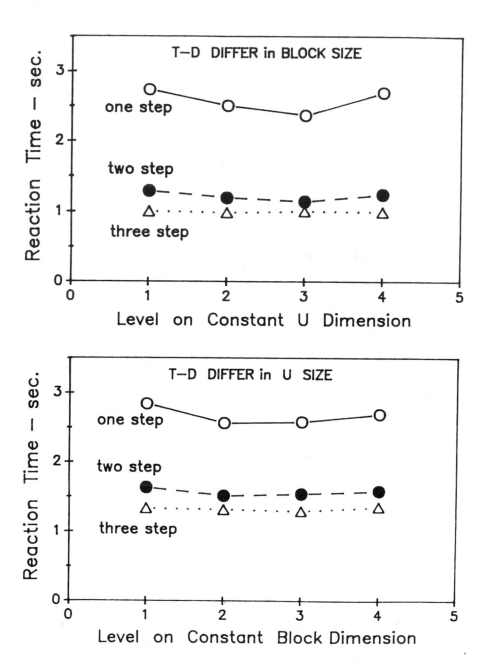

Figure 3.   Results of tests for independent constancy of the dimensional influences depicted in Figure 2. Data in the top panel came from form pairs differing only in the size of the black block, and in the bottom panel from form pairs differing only in the width of the U. The parameter is the size of this difference. (T–D Differ = target–distractor difference.)

quickly detected and search speed is relatively unaffected by the number of distractor items in the display. However, if the distractors contain the feature and the target does not, the target is detected more slowly, and search reaction time rises with the number of distractors. Of course, as with other tests, we cannot state that a part (such as a particular line or curve) is in any absolute sense a feature, but only that it functions as such in the context of some contrasting form.

Search asymmetry provides an objective definition of a feature that can be applied to pigeons as well as to humans. Using this method, Allan and I have compared some simple potential features in the two species (Allan & Blough, 1989). We had pigeons search for specific targets (for example, a circle with a line) in the types of displays described above. Our human subjects "pecked" the target with a light pen on larger versions of the same displays. In contrast with the other results I have presented, our data on search asymmetry suggest differences in feature analysis in the two species. For example, we found no evidence that either the presence or absence of a line intersecting a circle functions as a feature in the pigeon, whereas such a line clearly functioned as a feature for our human subjects, as previously reported (Triesman & Gormican, 1988). Even more intriguingly, where humans clearly see a gap in a triangle as a feature, "closure" or the absence of a gap seems more feature-like for pigeons. When this matter was tested, one display consisted of a complete triangle as target and triangles with gaps as distractors; the status of the forms was reversed in the alternative display.

The pigeon and human results are contrasted in Figure 4. The results at the right are from 6 human subjects, and they replicate the asymmetry that has previously been reported for these forms (e.g., Treisman & Gormican, 1988). The target was found most quickly and reaction time varied least with display size when the target, not the distractors, contained the gap; we conclude that the gap functions as a feature for human subjects. The results at the left are from 3 pigeons. Here, the asymmetry is reversed. The fastest search occurred when the complete triangle was the target. The target/display-size interaction that defines "gap absence" as a feature occurred in all three pigeons and was statistically significant, although it was not as large as the reverse result in humans.

It is far too soon to draw general conclusions from this initial contrast between the pigeon and human results. The differences shown in our studies could be the result of some uninteresting methodological quirk. We doubt this, although we think that practice effects on asymmetry should be explored more thoroughly than has been done so far (our birds had a lot of practice). It has been suggested that the asymmetry phenomenon reflects early visual processing that is essentially "wired in." If so, a difference such as that for the "gap feature" suggests a difference in avian and human visual processing that ought to show up in other places.

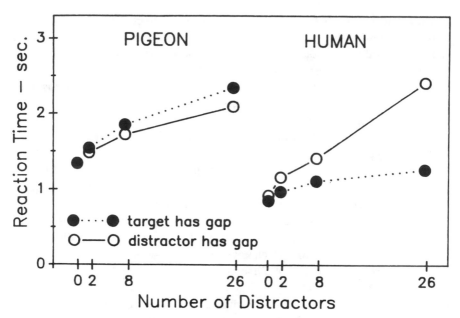

Figure 4. Search asymmetries based on displays of repeated small triangles. Either the target triangle had a gap in it or the distractor forms had the gap. Humans respond to the gap as a feature; the reverse is true for pigeons. (Based on data obtained by Allan & Blough, 1989.)

COVARIATION ACROSS TRIAL BLOCKS

My final look at potential analytic processing by pigeons is based on the covariation of search RTs across trial blocks. This method may provide the best evidence yet that aspects of forms are, to some extent, independently processed in pigeon visual search. To my knowledge, the method has not been used before with humans or animals, so I will supply somewhat more detail than in the above examples.

My example is an odd-item search experiment that used four square forms; these were distinguished from each other by the presence or absence of a vertical line at the bottom or a gap at the top (see Figure 5). I used the eight pairs of these forms in which the target differed from the distractor only with respect to the line or with respect to the gap. The target form on a given trial was concealed among 31 identical distractors in a rectangular array. Each form appeared with equal frequency as target or distractor, so the subjects had no reason to expect any particular form to appear in either role. Sessions consisted of 90 blocks of 16 trials each, for a total of 1,440 trials. Trials lasted approximately 2 hr.

The experiment sought evidence for the separate processing of parts of these forms. The analysis assumes, first, that separable features are definable in part

Figure 5.   Four forms that were paired in eight ways in an odd-item search experiment. The experiment measured correlations, across sessions, of reaction times to the different form pairs.

by the possibility that attention may be paid to them separately. Second, it assumes that attentional fluctuations may occur across blocks of trials. For example, in attempting to distinguish a target from distractors, a bird might sometimes be more attuned to "line" differences than to "gap" differences. At other times, attention might be directed to the gap. The key idea is that RTs for searches that depend on the same part or combination of parts will all speed up when attention shifts to that part and will slow down when attention shifts to another part. Thus, the method detects only attentional dispositions that are long enough for covariation to occur across a number of trials; it neither measures nor precludes rapid attentional switches within or between trials.

To appreciate the nature of the analysis, consider the data from a single bird. Through 16 sessions, the eight pairs of stimuli were presented with equal frequency. To rid the data of overall trends that might, for example, result from improvement with practice, I subtracted the mean RT over all pairs for each session from the mean RT for each pair for that session. Furthermore, to simplify graphical presentation, RTs from each target–distractor (T–D) pair were combined with those from the other T–D pair that displayed the same two forms with their roles as target and distractor reversed. This yielded four combinations. In two of these combinations, the target and distractor differed by the presence or absence of the gap at the top of the form; in the other two, the line was the crucial feature. Plots of the resulting mean RTs appear in Figure 6.

From Figure 6, it is clear, first, that this bird took longer to find the target when the forms differed by the gap than when they differed by the line. This was much less true of the other birds and is of little interest here. Secondly, there appears to be some general trend over the sessions in that performance with the gap-distinctive forms improves somewhat relative to that with the line-distinctive forms. Finally, we see some indication that RTs for these two sets of pairs tend to vary inversely over shorter intervals; several possible instances are indicated by arrows in the figure.

These and similar observations suggest that search RTs for form pairs distinguished by the same feature tend to vary together. This, in turn, suggests that attentional fluctuations act in common on these pairs. However, we need a more objective analysis to confirm such impressions and to explore alternative possibilities that may be concealed by this particular combination of data. For such analysis, the RTs from each of the three birds were combined within sessions for

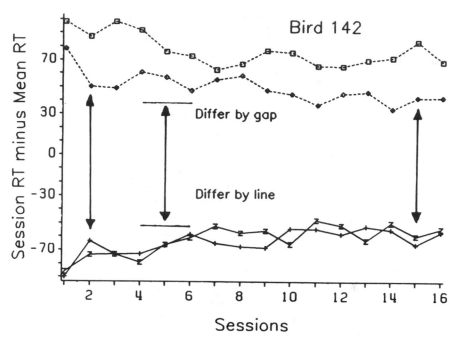

Figure 6. Changes in search reaction times to target–distractor pairs composed of the forms shown in Figure 5, for a single pigeon. For this illustration, RTs were combined for pairs composed of the same two forms, which differed only in that target–distractor roles were reversed. (RT = reaction time.)

individual form pairs and adjusted for the mean across pairs as described above. Then the adjusted RT scores of all possible combinations of form pairs were correlated across sessions, yielding a matrix of 28 intercorrelations for each bird.

The correlations among RTs for different form pairs were analyzed by several methods, including multidimensional scaling, cluster analysis, and regression analysis. The purpose of these analyses was to identify factors common to form pairs that contributed to the variation in search RT across days. All three methods identified two factors, which were also confirmed by principle component analysis of the RT matrix. These factors appeared as the two principal dimensions of a multidimensional scaling solution provided by INDSCAL (run under the SAS system, SAS Institute, 1985). By analyzing patterns across subjects, INDSCAL derived nonarbitrary dimensional axes, and the two-dimensional scaling solution on these axes is shown in Figure 7. Because the data here were correlations of RTs for target–distractor pairs, *form pairs*, not individual forms, are the objects placed in similarity space. Thus, if RTs for two stimulus pairs rose and fell together, those two pairs are near each other in Figure 7. If the RTs for two pairs were inversely related, those pairs are far apart.

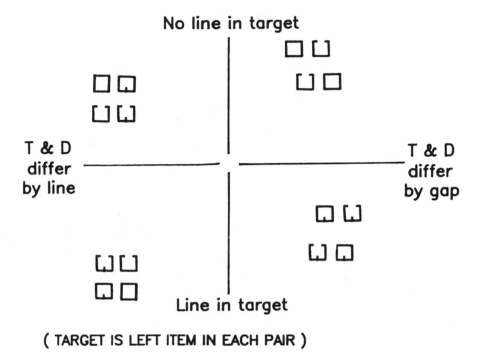

(TARGET IS LEFT ITEM IN EACH PAIR)

Figure 7.   The input for this two-dimensional INDSCAL plot was the table of cross-correlations between the search reaction times for the pairs of forms shown. Thus, form pairs, not individual forms, are placed in similarity space. (T & D = target and distractor.)

The two dimensions are identifiable, as the labels in Figure 7 indicate. They suggest control by (or attention to) several aspects of the display. The most specific of these is defined by the vertical dimension. The pattern here indicates attentional fluctuations limited to "line in the target." More variance was accounted for by the second dimension, which suggests somewhat more abstract analysis of the forms; the bird was being controlled by form *differences*, either with respect to a line or with respect to a gap. The covariation analysis here suggests comparative processing rather than absolute matching, as suggested by the vertical dimension.

These results illustrate the variety of different outcomes that could have been obtained even for this very simple set of forms. Note that "line in target" was not accompanied by search for "gap in the target" or "line in the distractor." Other patterns of covariation could have suggested attention to broader configural aspects of the forms. If RTs had varied in no systematic way over time, the result would have been consistent with the holistic perception of individual forms.

These results are interesting, but fragmentary as yet. As with search asymmetry, exploration of a much wider range of forms and experimental conditions is necessary before any sort of general picture of the pigeon's analytic processing can emerge.

SUMMARY AND CONCLUSION

Four examples of pigeon visual search have produced some tentative suggestions, among them the following: (a) Humans readily identify features in letters of the alphabet that correspond to pigeon classifications of letters; this suggests that humans and pigeons may process these forms in similar ways, but it does not necessarily mean that feature extraction occurs during processing. (b) Data from one instance of visual search was consistent with the hypothesis that pigeons analyze spatially distinct dimensions independently. (c) Sample data on search asymmetry suggested that functional features in pigeons and humans differ with respect to this test, which theoretically implicates early visual processing. (d) Covariation of search RTs across trial blocks suggested that pigeon attention can shift among features and that functional features can be identified by these shifts; the features found in the sample experiment were defined at two somewhat different levels of abstraction.

These conclusions are very tentative, of course. The examples presented here have mainly served to illustrate several ways to study perceptual processes in an animal subject. Other interesting approaches and other human–animal comparisons have appeared in recent research on animal perception, but it may be unwise to concentrate too much on specific species comparisons at this stage in our understanding. It is always difficult to accept any particular account of a species difference, because there are so many potential alternatives, including differences in methods, peripheral structures, motivation, and so on. Rather, species comparisons can be considered a sometimes helpful tool in progress toward a deeper purpose, which is to achieve a general understanding of the processes underlying perception and how these contribute to adaptive behavior.

References

Allan, S. E., & Blough, D. S. (1989). Feature-based search asymmetries in pigeons and humans. *Perception & Psychophysics*, *46*, 456–464.

Blough, D. S. (1979). Effects of the number and form of stimuli on visual search in the pigeon. *Journal of Experimental Psychology: Animal Behavior Processes*, *5*, 211–223.

Blough, D. S. (1985). Discrimination of letters and random dot patterns by pigeons and humans. *Journal of Experimental Psychology: Animal Behavior Processes*, *11*, 261–280.

Blough, D. S. (1986). Odd-item search by pigeons: Method, instrumentation, and uses. *Behavior Research Methods, Instruments, & Computers*, *18*, 413–419.

Blough, D. S. (1988). Quantitative relations between visual search speed and target–distractor similarity. *Perception & Psychophysics*, *43*, 57–71.

Blough, D. S., & Blough, P. M. (1990). Reaction time assessments of visual perception in pigeons. In M. Berkley & W. Stebbins (Eds.), *Comparative perception: Vol. II. Complex signals* (pp. 245–276). New York: Wiley.

Blough, D. S., & Franklin, J. J. (1985). Pigeon discrimination of letters and other forms in texture displays. *Perception & Psychophysics, 38,* 523–532.

Blough, P. M. (1984). Visual search in pigeons: Effects of memory set size and display variables. *Perception & Psychophysics, 35,* 344–352.

Julesz, B., & Schumer, R. A. (1981). Early visual perception. In *Annual review of psychology* (Vol. 32, pp. 575–627). Palo Alto, CA: Annual Reviews.

Luce, R. D. (1986). *Response times: Their role in inferring elementary mental organization.* New York: Oxford University Press.

Podgorny, P., & Garner, W. R. (1979). Reaction time as a measure of inter- and intra-object visual similarity: Letters of the alphabet. *Perception & Psychophysics, 26,* 37–52.

SAS Institute. (1985). *SAS System* [Computer program]. Cary, NC: Author.

Shepard, R. N. (1964). Attention and the metric structure of the stimulus space. *Journal of Mathematical Psychology, 1,* 54–87.

Treisman, A. (1986). Properties, parts, and objects. In K. R. Boff, L. Kaufman, & J. P. Thomas (Eds.), *Handbook of perception and human performance* (Vol. 2, pp. 35-1–35-70). New York: Wiley.

Treisman, A., & Gormican, S. (1988). Feature analysis in early vision: Evidence from search asymmetries. *Psychological Review, 95,* 15–48.

CHAPTER 15

REPRESENTATION OF MULTIDIMENSIONAL STIMULI IN PIGEONS

DONALD A. RILEY AND MICHAEL F. BROWN

Most researchers of animal learning have assumed that elements of stimulus compounds are processed independently and summed linearly. Research with pigeons in element and compound matching-to-sample tasks suggests that this assumption generally provides a good description of the data. Two exceptions are, however, of interest: (a) Precuing of one element of a compound is more efficient when the elements (i.e., a color and a line orientation) are separated than when they are unified (as in a colored line); and (b) although prior experience with elements only results in transfer to compounds, the reverse is not true—pigeons trained to process compounds with no experience with elements show no transfer to element matching-to-sample tasks. The results suggest that independent processing of elements of a compound results from a history of processing the elements outside of the compound.

Garner (1962) contrasts two varieties of structure that are present in sets of events, such as those that make up a stimulus: structure that is produced externally by the number and nature of relations between the stimulus and alternative stimuli, and structure that is inherent in the stimulus itself, resulting from relations among the attributes of which the stimulus is composed. A theoretical framework within which intrinsic stimulus structure can be studied (Garner, 1974) stimulated much

We thank Cynthia Langley and Spencer Morrison for their assistance in the conduct of the unpublished experiments reported here and in the preparation of this chapter, which was supported by National Institute of Mental Health Grant MH42646 to Michael F. Brown and Grant MH44741 to Donald A. Riley.

of the research and theory that will be described in this chapter. Our discussion will center on the issue of *multidimensional stimulus representation* as it has been studied by investigators using animal subjects. We, like Garner (e.g., 1974, 1976, 1978; Garner & Felfoldy, 1970), are particularly interested in the manner in which dimensional components of such stimuli interact as the stimulus is processed by the perceptual and memorial systems of the subject.

Most investigators in the tradition of associative learning have assumed that the elements of multidimensional stimuli are related in a simple fashion: Simultaneous presentation of two elements, according to this view, results in a linear summation of their independent effects (see Kehoe & Gormezano, 1980, for a review). With some exceptions, most notably the work of Donald Blough (1984) and Patricia Blough (1984), the properties of multidimensional stimuli have not been a matter of intense concern to students of animal learning. Instead, analyses of compound stimulus learning have typically assumed separability of the elements of a compound stimulus. This point of view has been implicit even in the context of experiments using compound flavor stimuli made up of arbitrary elements such as banana extract and almond extract (e.g., Durlach & Rescorla, 1980). Clear-cut evidence that two-dimensional stimuli had emergent properties that could not be interpreted in terms of their elements has been attributed to a third stimulus element, the "unique cue," the associative strength of which summates in a linear fashion with that of the two nominal elements (Rescorla, 1972, 1973). Clearly, researchers in the tradition of animal learning have tended not to look to stimulus structure for explanations of their results.

In the present chapter, we will first summarize some of the evidence that the elements of visual compound stimuli are processed and represented independently by pigeons under at least some conditions. We will then focus on investigations of the factors influencing the intrinsic structure of such stimuli as they have been studied using the matching-to-sample procedure. Although Garner and others have emphasized aspects of intrinsic stimulus structure that are determined by the nature of the stimulus dimensions used, we have not, in most cases, explicitly manipulated the nature of stimulus dimensions. Instead, we have been concerned with the way in which the spatial configuration of stimulus elements and the experience of the subject with the stimulus elements affect the animal's structure of the representation of the stimulus.

EVIDENCE THAT COLOR–LINE ORIENTATION COMPOUNDS MAY BE REPRESENTED ANALYTICALLY BY PIGEONS

Given the assumption among many learning theorists that stimulus elements are functionally independent, it may seem quite surprising that explicit evidence that the elements of multidimensional stimuli are *ever* processed and represented separately in animal subjects has been extremely slow in coming and remains controversial. The experimental analysis of compound stimulus representation in the pigeon grew out of a concern over the issue of selective stimulus control. Learning theorists such as Mackintosh (1965) and Kamin (1969), influenced by early proponents of the information processing approach, had suggested that the fundamental processes of learning include an attentional component to account for failures of association in overshadowing and blocking experiments.

An attempt to demonstrate independent processing and representation of two-dimensional visual stimuli in the pigeon began at the University of California, Berkeley over 15 years ago (Maki & Leith, 1973; Maki & Leuin, 1972). These experiments involved a matching-to-sample (MTS) procedure. On each trial of this procedure, the subject is first presented with a sample stimulus on the middle key of a three-key operant chamber, and the sample is then immediately replaced by two test stimuli presented on the two side keys. A peck to the correct test stimulus results in food reinforcement. In the "true matching" procedure used by Maki, Leuin, and Leith, the correct test stimulus was physically identical to the sample or to one of its elements. *Element* samples were one of two colored disks (red or blue) or one of two sets of line orientations (vertical or horizontal). They were elements in that only one nominal attribute of each sample stimulus was predictive of the correct test stimulus. *Compound* samples were combinations of one element from each of the two dimensions. Test stimuli following a compound sample were either the two colors or the two line orientation values (see Figure 1). In Maki and Leuin's study, the dependent variable was the sample duration required to match at an 80% correct level, whereas in Maki and Leith's work, sample duration was systematically varied and percent correct was the dependent variable. The results from these two studies are summarized in Figure 2.

The basic finding of Maki, Leuin, and Leith's work was that performance on element samples was superior to compound samples, especially at intermediate levels of accuracy. Furthermore, the sample duration required to maintain criterion accuracy (80% correct) with element samples was about half that required with compound samples. This *element superiority* effect has been replicated in numerous subsequent investigations (e.g., Cook, 1980; Maki, Riley, & Leith, 1976; Roberts & Grant, 1978; Santi, Grossi, & Gibson, 1982). It was originally interpreted as indicating that color–line orientation compounds are represented and processed separately by the pigeon's perceptual or memory systems and that as a result of capacity limitations in the processing system (Broadbent, 1958), only one element can be processed within any brief interval (see Riley & Leith, 1976). This *information overload* (or *shared attention*) hypothesis requires that the elements of compound samples be represented and processed analytically (i.e., separately) by at least some of the cognitive apparatus involved in the MTS task. This hypothesis was supported by two facts: (a) the apparent convergence of element and compound performance at longer presentation durations, which would

Examples of Old Stimuli

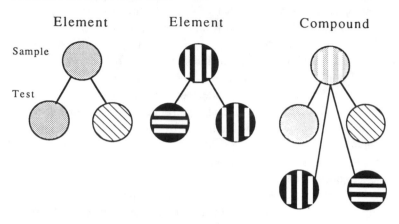

Examples of more recent stimuli

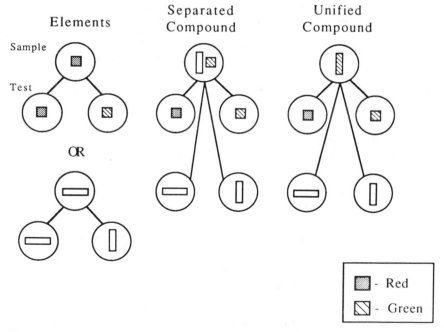

Figure 1.   An illustration of the matching-to-sample procedure and some of the stimuli used. The top panel shows two typical element trials and a typical compound trial, using the "in-line" stimuli of the earlier experiments. Following a compound sample, either the two color-test stimuli or the two line-orientation tests are presented. The bottom panel illustrates the stimuli used in some of our more recent experiments.

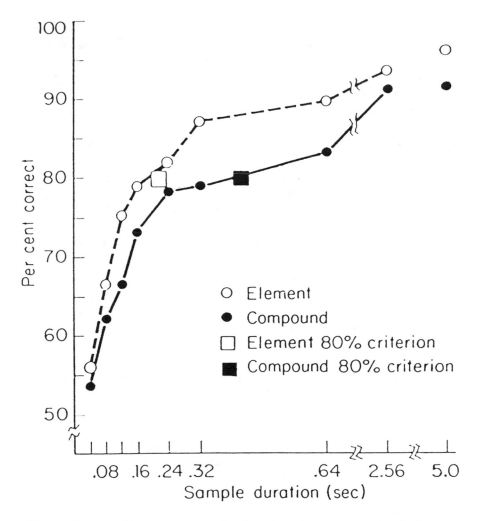

Figure 2. Matching accuracy as a function of sample presentation time in the experiments of Maki and Leith (1973; circles) and Maki and Leuin (1972; squares). The latter experiments used a titration procedure to determine the sample presentation time necessary to maintain a performance criterion of 80% correct. (From Riley & Leith, 1976. Copyright 1976 by the American Psychological Association. Reprinted by permission.)

allow time for the pigeon to process both elements of the compound about as well as in the element condition (Maki & Leith, 1973); and (b) the finding that prolonged repeated testing of only one of the two elements of the compound reduces the element–compound difference, presumably by focusing attention on the relevant dimension (Brown, Cook, Lamb, & Riley, 1984; Leith & Maki, 1975). Although subsequent studies have failed to replicate the convergence of element and compound matching accuracy (Grant & MacDonald, 1986; Lamb & Riley, 1981; Santi et al., 1982), this fact is not necessarily evidence against the independent processing assumptions adduced to account for the superiority of element performance. That is, some other factor or factors, such as a failure by the pigeon to continue inspection of the key, might be responsible for the lack of convergence.

Three alternative explanations for the element superiority effect have been proposed (Cox & D'Amato, 1982; Grant & MacDonald, 1986; Maki et al., 1976; Roberts & Grant, 1978), two of which reject the notion that the color and line orientation components are represented independently (Cox & D'Amato, 1982; Grant & MacDonald, 1986). The *generalization decrement* hypothesis attributes matching to generalization from the representation of the sample stimulus to the test stimulus. Superior levels of element matching are assumed to occur because the usual test stimuli, like element samples, are themselves element stimuli, thus providing an identical match. Compound samples, on the other hand, are only similar to the correct test stimulus, resulting in generalization decrement from the compound sample to the correct test stimulus (Cox & D'Amato, 1982; Maki et al., 1976; Roberts & Grant, 1978). A second alternative account attributes the element superiority effect to a *training artifact* (Grant & MacDonald, 1986). Typically, pigeons are trained to match element samples prior to being exposed to compound samples. Grant and MacDonald found that pigeons showed the typical element superiority effect when initially trained with element samples, but matched compound samples more accurately than element samples when they had been initially trained using compound samples. Third, Kraemer, Mazmanian, and Roberts (1987) argued that there are circumstances in which the element–compound difference is attributable to the effects of peripheral *gaze direction* rather than more central mechanisms. Specifically, under some conditions, the pigeon must look in different locations to acquire compound information, but only one place to acquire element information. In Kraemer et al.'s preparation, when the pigeon can extract two kinds of information from the same place, the superiority of element matching over compound matching disappears.

Maki et al. (1976) tested the generalization decrement hypothesis by comparing the use of compound tests with the use of element tests. For example, when compound tests were used, a Red Vertical sample would be followed by Red Vertical (+) versus Green Horizontal (−) tests. Maki et al. found that the use of compound test stimuli did not reduce element superiority, and they concluded that generalization decrement could not account for the compound sample inferiority. But Roberts and Grant (1978) subsequently showed that compound sample matching could exceed element sample matching if the positive test compound provided a perfect match and the negative consisted of a single negative element. This finding, although not providing a disproof of the shared attention interpretation, at least rendered the situation ambiguous. We have considered several procedures that appear to solve this problem, and are presently engaged in two different lines of research that we believe allow an evaluation of all four of the competing hypotheses. The two lines of research are (a) the use of symbolic matching-to-sample tasks in which *all* sample stimulus–test stimulus relations are arbitrary and learned, and (b) stimulus search experiments in which target recognition is measured directly. In this chapter, we will consider only the former.

SYMBOLIC MATCHING TESTS OF ELEMENT–COMPOUND DIFFERENCE EXPLANATIONS

A recently completed set of experiments by Brown and Morrison (1990) examined element–compound differences under conditions that ruled out both generalization decrement and training artifacts. One group of pigeons was first trained to match element samples and another was first trained to match compound samples in a *symbolic MTS* procedure shown in Figure 3. In symbolic MTS, the correct test stimulus is not physically related to the sample; instead, these pairings are arbitrary. For different birds, the pairings of sample and test stimuli varied. No effects of these different pairings were observed. After this initial training, these birds then matched both element and compound samples for many sessions, after which matching accuracy to both element and compound samples was measured under four different sample presentation durations, resulting in the accuracy levels shown in Figure 4. The important result is that for all birds, element matching was superior to compound matching regardless of whether the birds were first trained using compound samples or using element samples. This provides strong evidence that the superiority of element matching over compound matching does not depend on similarity relations between samples and tests (the generalization decrement hypothesis), because all sample–test relations are arbitrary. Nor can this superiority derive from prior training with element matching, because the difference occurs regardless of training condition. Therefore, superiority of element over compound matching cannot depend on this previous training artifact.

A second symbolic matching task recently completed by Langley and Riley (1991) provided additional evidence for element superiority under conditions that cannot be explained by generalization decrement or training history. The task is somewhat different from Brown's in that the pigeons are trained on both elements and compounds from the beginning. More important, however, the birds are trained with a different set of stimuli. Brown's stimuli, the type designated as ''old'' in Figure 1, allow the pigeon to visually orient toward different spatial locations for the colors and lines. In Langley's preparation, the color and line in the compound are *unified*. That is, the colored line carries both kinds of information. All of Langley's birds performed significantly better on the tests following element samples than following compound samples. Again, there is evidence that the differences between elements and compounds reflect processes related to initial perception or memory of the sample rather than to relations between the sample

The Symbolic Code:

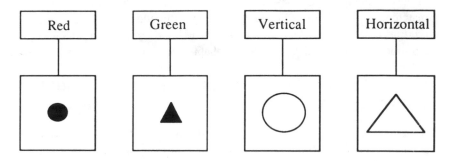

Examples of Stimuli:

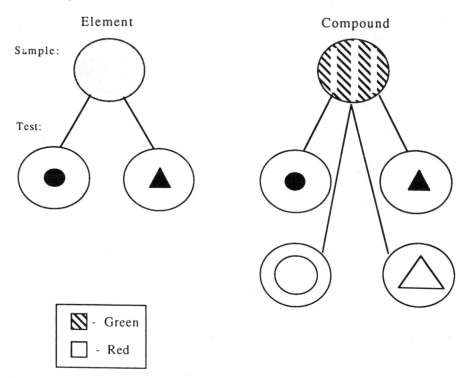

Figure 3.   An illustration of the symbolic matching-to-sample procedure used by Brown and Morrison (1990). The top panel shows the matching rules relating each sample element to an arbitrary-form test stimulus. The bottom panel shows a typical element trial and the two possible test configurations that followed compound samples. The test stimulus associated with each sample element varied among subjects.

Element–Trained Group

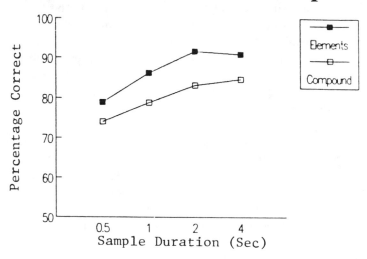

Compound–Trained Group

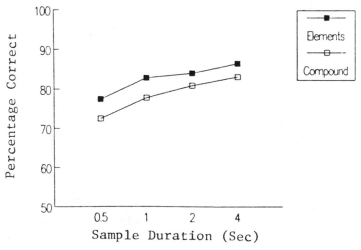

Figure 4. The results of Brown and Morrison's (1990) symbolic matching-to-sample experiment. Percentage correct is shown as a function of sample presentation time and sample type (element vs. compound) for the group trained on the element task (top panel) and the group trained on the compound task (bottom panel). (Copyright 1990 by the American Psychological Association. Reprinted by permission.)

and test or to training artifacts. Furthermore, in Langley's experiment, the difference occurred under stimulus conditions that appear to force the pigeon to extract information on both elements from the same location. This finding is of interest because of Kraemer et al.'s (1987) argument that element superiority depends on the pigeon's looking in only one place for element information but looking in two places for compound information. Kraemer et al. did find that when color and spatial location were used as the two elements in a symbolic matching-to-sample task, color and location in the same place were processed as efficiently as either alone. But as a number of writers (e.g., Kubovy, 1981) have argued, space and time have special properties not shared by other dimensions, and the use of either in a way that suggests they are psychologically equivalent to other dimensions should be viewed with caution. In particular, we do not know whether the cost of perceiving and remembering a nonspatial feature and its location is the same as the cost of perceiving and remembering two nonspatial features that occur in the same space at the same time.

We have seen that the use of symbolic matching-to-sample tests, in which the relation between sample and test is arbitrary, rules out interpretations of element–compound differences that rely on similarity relations between samples and tests. Furthermore, the use of procedures that ensure that element and compound samples are treated the same with respect to training procedures argues against differences in training history as a sole cause of the observed element superiority. Finally, we see in Langley and Riley's (1991) data evidence that the processing of two elements unified into a single object increases information load over the load for a single element.

EVIDENCE FOR DIFFERENCES IN COMPOUND STIMULUS REPRESENTATION AS A FUNCTION OF SPATIAL CONFIGURATION

Although the evidence that compound visual stimuli are processed analytically is accumulating, there is also evidence that increasing spatial separation of the elements affects representation of the compound. In contrast with the recent data of Langley and Riley (1991) described above, Lamb and Riley (1981) reported that unified compound samples were matched more efficiently than compounds consisting of barely separated elements. They inferred that the dimensional information contained in such unified stimuli might be processed in a qualitatively different manner than the information in spatially separated compound samples. Unfortunately, the location of the elements of the separated compounds changed from trial to trial, whereas those of the unified compounds were always together in the same place. A recent experiment by Cook, Riley, and Brown (in press) designed to replicate the Lamb and Riley study with an improved stimulus set and an experimental design that eliminated this confound, indicates that, in contrast with the findings of Lamb and Riley, unified samples are matched less accurately than elements and no more accurately than spatially separated, but contiguous, compound samples.

From this finding, as well as from Langley and Riley's (1991) data, one might conclude that separated and unified stimuli are processed and represented in the same way; this conclusion would, it seems, be false. Lamb (1988) compared the effect of selective attention cuing on unified and separated stimuli and found clear evidence of a difference. Lamb used a cuing procedure in which compound sample stimuli were either preceded or followed by an element stimulus. The correct test stimulus matched this element pre- (or post-) sample cue. When the element stimulus preceded the compound sample, it was logically possible for the pigeon to selectively process only the appropriate element of the compound sample and thus, in effect, receive two presentations of the element. This did not occur in the control condition when the element cue was presented after the compound, a condition that eliminated selective attention to the relevant element of the compound. On infrequent probe trials, the test pitted the two values from the dimension not represented by the element cue. If compound stimuli are represented in an analytic fashion, thereby allowing the possibility of selective processing, then presample cues should elevate matching accuracy levels relative to postsample cues. On the other hand, tests of the neglected (i.e., noncued) dimension should produce a decrease in accuracy levels relative to cues presented after the compound. If compound samples are processed in a unitary fashion, the temporal location of the cue stimulus should not matter. Figure 5 shows the mean results for the four pigeons tested under these conditions. For separated compounds, cuing had a significant effect on matching accuracy. There was no effect of cuing on unified compounds, however. These means are representative of all but one subject, which showed the cuing effect with both unified and separated compounds.

It appears that the spatial configuration of compound visual stimuli is critical in allowing selective attention to operate in the separated condition and in making it difficult in the unified condition. The data from the probe trials on which discrimination of the noncued dimension was tested are also of considerable interest for the light they shed on the mechanism of selective attention. These data show that the noncued element presented in compound with a cued element is actually processed less than the same element when neither member of the compound is cued. This outcome shows that the attention effect involves both facilitation of the cued element and a drop in processing of the noncued element, as would be expected from a limited-capacity hypothesis.

Lamb's (1988) experiment is of particular interest with regard to issues both of method and theory when contrasted with Cook, Riley, and Brown (in press). The introduction of the cuing procedure may be critical in revealing a processing difference between the unified and separated compounds that was not observed

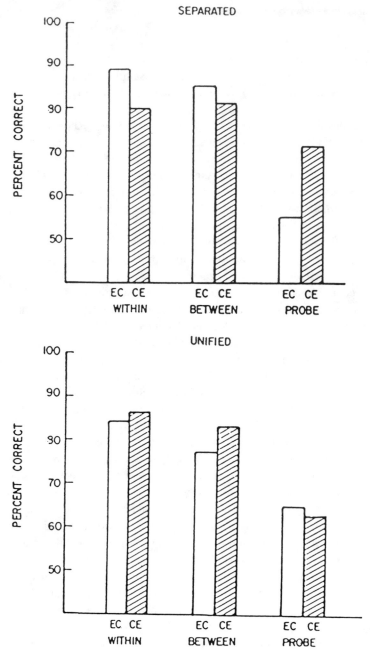

Figure 5. The results of Lamb's (1988) cuing experiment. Mean percentage correct is shown as a function of trial type for trials involving spatially separated compounds (top panel) and unified compounds (bottom panel). Trial type is defined by whether the compound sample or the element cue was presented first (CE vs. EC, respectively) and by whether the cue served as a valid k2 predictor of the to-be-tested dimension ("WITHIN") or was a probe trial on which the subject was miscued. (The "between" trials are not discussed in this chapter.) Copyright 1988 by the American Psychological Association. Reprinted by permission.

in the noncued conditions of Cook et al. This difference in susceptibility to the effect of cuing in the unified and separated conditions raises the possibility that differential selective attention between two features may be easier when the two features are perceived as parts of two different objects, as opposed to being different parts of the same object. Thus, these results may share some features with Garner's (1974) work on stimulus integrality and attention.

EVIDENCE FOR DIFFERENCES IN COMPOUND STIMULUS REPRESENTATION AS A FUNCTION OF EXPERIENCE

A study recently reported by Brown (1987) indicates that compound stimulus representation may also depend on the experimental history of the pigeon. Using a symbolic MTS procedure, Brown trained three pigeons to match element stimuli and three others to match compound stimuli as shown in the bottom panel of Figure 1. Immediately following training, birds in both groups were tested using element samples, separated compound samples with varying degrees of spatial separation between the elements, and unified compound samples. If MTS is thought of as involving the application of sample-specific "matching rules" (Carter & Werner, 1978; e.g., "If the sample was red, then peck triangle"), then the birds trained with element samples learned four rules, as shown in Figure 6: If red (R), then filled circle; if green (G), then filled triangle; if vertical (V), then open circle; if horizontal (H), then open triangle. The birds trained with compound samples could acquire the ability to match correctly in either of two ways. First, if they processed the compound in a unitary fashion, they could learn eight separate matching rules (if RV, then filled circle; if RV, then open circle; if RH, then filled circle, etc.). The second way stems from the observation that for each element of the compound sample there is one and only one test stimulus that, when it is used, is consistently correct following compounds containing that element. Thus, in the example shown, the solid circle is always correct on those trials when color is tested following compounds containing red. A parallel rule holds for each of the three other test stimuli relative to its appropriate element. Therefore, if compound stimuli are processed analytically, one would expect that element matching rules would be acquired as a result of this compound training and that element samples tests following compound training would show an appropriate level of transfer.

Immediately after these two sets of pigeons were trained in their respective tasks, they were exposed to sessions in which both element and compound samples were presented. The data for each bird are shown in Figure 7. The matching ability of the birds trained with element samples transferred readily to compound samples. However, no pigeon trained with compound samples was able to match element samples at above-chance levels. This finding was interpreted as indicating that these pigeons processed compound samples in a unitary fashion during training

Examples of matching rules that might be used by a bird
independently processing color and line both during element
sample presentation and during compound sample presentation.

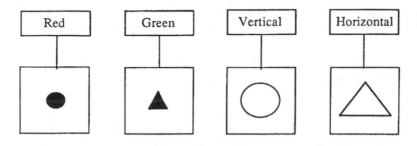

Examples of matching rules that might be used by a bird
which combines the elements of a compound stimulus
and learns a rule for each combination.

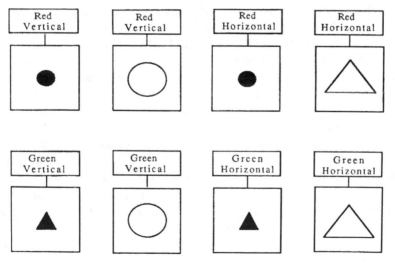

Figure 6.   An illustration of two types of matching rules that might be acquired in the
symbolic matching-to-sample experiment of Brown (1987). The top panel
shows element-matching rules that would be acquired by subjects trained
to match element samples (these same matching rules would be acquired
by subjects trained to match compound samples if the compounds were
processed analytically). The bottom panel shows matching rules that would
be acquired by subjects trained to match compound samples if the compounds
were processed in a unitary fashion.

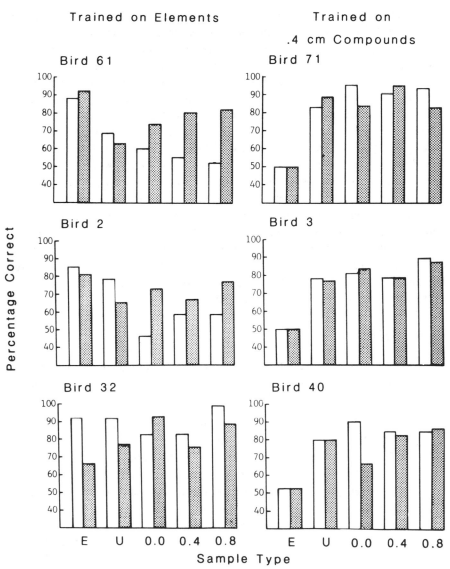

Figure 7. The asymmetrical transfer effect of Brown (1987). The matching ability of pigeons trained with element samples in a symbolic matching-to-sample task (left column) transferred readily to a variety of compound samples differing in spatial configuration. The matching ability of pigeons trained with spatially separated compounds (separated by 0.4 cm) transferred to other compound stimuli but did not transfer to element stimuli. Solid bars depict color-matching accuracy; stippled bars depict line-orientation-matching accuracy. (E and U denote element and unified compound samples, respectively.) Copyright 1987 by the American Psychological Association. Reprinted by permission.

and therefore did not acquire the element matching rules. Instead, they acquired two matching rules for each of the four unitary compound samples.

This asymmetrical transfer effect suggests that prior exposure to the elements that make up compound stimuli is necessary for analytic processing. The birds trained with compound samples had never been exposed to the elements of the compounds outside of the context of the compounds. That this lack of prior exposure to the element alone was critical is supported by the results of a second experiment that used the same experimental design except that *true* matching, rather than symbolic matching, was used. Thus, pigeons trained to match compound samples in this experiment were exposed to the elements of the compounds as test stimuli. In this experiment, both the element-trained subjects and the compound-trained subjects readily transferred to the alternate stimulus set.

Taken together, the results of the two experiments suggest that these compound stimuli are represented in a unitary fashion unless the pigeons have been exposed to the elements in isolation from the compound. The process that produces this change in representational structure may be similar to the idea of dissociative learning first proposed by William James (1890/1950) or to the concept of perceptual learning discussed by Gibson (1969).

CONCLUSIONS

In this chapter, we have asked three questions and have provided what we believe, given our present information, are the answers to them. Those conclusions are as follows:

1. There are conditions under which pigeons independently process the two elements of a visual compound stimulus.
2. The spatial configuration of the stimuli affects the extent to which the elements of compound stimuli are processed independently, in that separated stimulus compounds are more susceptible to selective attention instructions than are unified compounds.
3. The past experience of the pigeon in the matching-to-sample task may affect the way in which it organizes the stimuli. At least under some conditions, pigeons with only element experience transfer effectively to compound tests. Pigeons trained only on compounds, however, show no comparable transfer to elements. Apparently, these latter animals perceive the compounds as unified wholes.

We conclude that independent processing of elements in a compound does occur, just as Maki, Leith, and Leuin suggested. Furthermore, this independence can be modified both by stimulus arrangements and by experience.

It should be obvious that the kind of research we have described is arduous and time-consuming. Progress is slow. Given that many of these questions can and have been investigated with humans more efficiently, the question of why we should bother observing pigeons might have occurred to some, considering that old arguments about nonhuman animals (rats) allowing a better preparation and better control no longer seem valid. Three answers that make sense to us are the following:

1. The first reason is related to the current concern with the evolution of cognitive processes (e.g., MacPhail, 1982). By asking about the generality of processes observed in humans, one can ask, for example, about the occurrence of rather complex flexible control processes in small-brained nonverbal animals. Their occurrence in such animals may suggest their basic importance, their simplicity, or possibly both. Concern for the similarities and differences of the outcomes observed in humans and in other species should enrich both endeavors. For example, the failure to find such processes in other species may lead to a consideration of how animals occupying different niches and equipped with different abilities solve similar problems.

2. Although we do not see the matching-to-sample paradigm as directly bearing on the functional value of stimulus segregation and selective attention, closely related research that inquires into prey search and discovery does have the ingredients for helping to understand the function of such processes and perhaps their evolution (see Bond, 1983).

3. Some researchers (e.g., Spitzer, Desimone, & Moran, 1988) are beginning to understand the neurophysiology of selective attention in monkeys. Neurophysiological comparisons across species should aid in understanding similarities and differences in their behavior.

References

Blough, D. S. (1984). Form recognition in pigeons. In H. L. Roitblat, T. G. Bever, & H. S. Terrace (Eds.), *Animal cognition* (pp. 333–350). Hillsdale, NJ: Erlbaum.

Blough, P. M. (1984). Visual search in pigeons: Effects of memory set size and display variables. *Perception & Psychophysics, 35*, 344–352.

Bond, A. B. (1983). Visual search and selection of natural stimuli in the pigeon: The attention threshold hypothesis. *Journal of Experimental Psychology: Animal Behavior Processes, 9*, 292–306.

Broadbent, D. E. (1958). *Perception and communication.* New York: Pergamon Press.

Brown, M. F. (1987). Dissociation of stimulus compounds by pigeons. *Journal of Experimental Psychology: Animal Behavior Processes, 13*, 80–91.

Brown, M. F., Cook, R. G., Lamb, M. R., & Riley, D. A. (1984). The relation between response and attentional shifts in pigeon compound matching-to-sample performance. *Animal Learning and Behavior, 12*, 41–49.

Brown, M. F., & Morrison, S. K. (1990). Element and compound matching-to-sample performance in pigeons: The roles of information load and training history. *Journal of Experimental Psychology: Animal Behavior Processes, 16*, 185–192.

Carter, D. E., & Werner, T. J. (1978). Complex learning and information processing by pigeons: A critical analysis. *Journal of the Experimental Analysis of Behavior, 29*, 565–601.

Cook, R. G. (1980). Retroactive interference in pigeon short-term memory by a reduction in ambient illumination. *Journal of Experimental Psychology: Animal Behavior Processes, 6*, 326–338.

Cook, R. G., Riley, D. A., & Brown, M. F. (in press). Spatial and configural factors in compound stimulus processing by pigeons. *Animal Learning and Behavior.*

Cox, J. K., & D'Amato, M. R. (1982). Matching to compound samples by monkeys (*Cebus apella*): Shared attention or generalization decrement? *Journal of Experimental Psychology: Animal Behavior Processes, 8*, 209–225.

Durlach, P. J., & Rescorla, R. A. (1980). Potentiation rather than overshadowing in flavor-aversion learning: An analysis in terms of within-compound associations. *Journal of Experimental Psychology: Animal Behavior Processes, 6*, 175–187.

Garner, W. R. (1962). *Uncertainty and structure as psychological concepts.* New York: Wiley.

Garner, W. R. (1974). *The processing of information and structure.* Potomac, MD: Erlbaum.

Garner, W. R. (1976). Interaction of stimulus dimensions in concept and choice processes. *Cognitive Psychology, 8*, 98–123.

Garner, W. R. (1978). Selective attention to attributes and to stimuli. *Journal of Experimental Psychology: General, 107*, 287–308.

Garner, W. R., & Felfoldy, G. L. (1970). Integrality of stimulus dimensions in various types of information processing. *Cognitive Psychology, 1*, 225–241.

Gibson, E. J. (1969). *Principles of perceptual learning and development.* New York: Appleton-Century-Crofts.

Grant, D. S., & MacDonald, S. E. (1986). Matching to element and compound samples in pigeons: The role of sampling coding. *Journal of Experimental Psychology: Animal Behavior Processes, 12*, 160–171.

James, W. (1950). *The principles of psychology.* New York: Dover. (Original work published 1890)

Kamin, L. J. (1969). Predictability, surprise, attention, and conditioning. In B. A. Campbell & R. M. Church (Eds.), *Punishment and aversive behavior* (pp. 279–296). New York: Appleton-Century-Crofts.

Kehoe, E. J., & Gormezano, I. (1980). Configuration and combination laws in conditioning with compound stimuli. *Psychological Bulletin, 87*, 351–378.

Kraemer, P. J., Mazmanian, D. S., & Roberts, W. A. (1987). Simultaneous processing of visual and spatial stimuli in pigeons. *Animal Learning and Behavior, 15*, 417–422.

Kubovy, M. (1981). Concurrent-pitch degradation and the theory of indispensable attributes. In M. Kubovy & J. R. Pomerantz (Eds.), *Perceptual organization* (pp. 55–98). Hillsdale, NJ: Erlbaum.

Lamb, M. R. (1988). Selective attention: Effects of cuing on the processing of different types of compound stimuli. *Journal of Experimental Psychology: Animal Behavior Processes, 14*, 96–104.

Lamb, M. R., & Riley, D. A. (1981). Effects of element arrangement on the processing of compound stimuli in pigeons (*Columba livia*). *Journal of Experimental Psychology: Animal Behavior Processes, 7*, 45–58.

Langley, C. M., & Riley, D. A. (1991). *Processing of unified shape and color compound stimuli in pigeon matching to sample.* Unpublished manuscript.

Leith, C. R., & Maki, W. S., Jr. (1975). Attention shifts during matching-to-sample in pigeons. *Animal Learning and Behavior*, *3*, 85–89.

Mackintosh, N. J. (1965). A theory of attention. *Psychological Review*, *82*, 276–298.

MacPhail, E. M. (1982). *Brain and intelligence in vertebrates*. Oxford, England: Oxford University Press.

Maki, W. S., & Leith, C. R. (1973). Shared attention in pigeons. *Journal of the Experimental Analysis of Behavior*, *19*, 345–349.

Maki, W. S., & Leuin, T. C. (1972). Information processing by pigeons. *Science*, *176*, 535–536.

Maki, W. S., Riley, D. A., & Leith, C. R. (1976). The role of test stimuli in matching to compound samples by pigeons. *Animal Learning and Behavior*, *4*, 13–21.

Rescorla, R. A. (1972). "Configural" conditioning in discrete-trial bar pressing. *Journal of Comparative and Physiological Psychology*, *79*, 307–317.

Rescorla, R. A. (1973). Evidence for "unique stimulus" account of configural conditioning. *Journal of Comparative and Physiological Psychology*, *85*, 331–338.

Riley, D. A., & Leith, C. R. (1976). Multidimensional psychophysics and selective attention in animals. *Psychological Bulletin*, *83*, 138–160.

Roberts, W. A., & Grant, D. S. (1978). Interaction of sample and comparison stimuli in delayed matching-to-sample with the pigeon. *Journal of Experimental Psychology: Animal Behavior Processes*, *4*, 68–82.

Santi, A., Grossi, V., & Gibson, M. (1982). Differences in matching-to-sample performance with element and compound sample stimuli in pigeons. *Learning and Motivation*, *13*, 240–256.

Spitzer, H., Desimone, R., & Moran, J. (1988). Increased attention enhances both behavioral and neuronal performance. *Science*, *240*, 338–340.

PART FOUR

LANGUAGE

CHAPTER 16

LEXICAL ECHOES OF PERCEPTUAL STRUCTURE

GEORGE A. MILLER

Many concepts found in scientific theories of perception originated in common sense and were later refined or redefined for more precise use. One place to begin an exploration of these ideas is with words that are used to refer to concrete objects, because object identification presupposes features that everyone can recognize or discriminate. The folk psychology of perception, as seen from the perspective of lexical analysis, presupposes three major kinds of distinguishing features: attributes, parts, and functions. Attributes were the first features to be extracted from common sense and studied extensively. Gestalt psychologists opened the systematic study of parts and their relations to one another. The perception of function, however, has been relatively neglected, although affordance theory recognizes its importance. Most scientific theories of perception have much to say about attributes and parts, but the recognition of function is only beginning to receive the attention it deserves.

The usefulness of language derives in no small measure from the fact that it permits reference to a nonlinguistic world—to objects and events, to properties and relations, to all of the distinct phenomena of which perception informs us. This observation is not new: recognition that words can acquire meaning by

Preparation of this paper was supported in part by Contract MDA 903-86-K-0242 with the Army Research Institute (ARI) and Contract N00014-86-K-0492 with the Office of Naval Research (ONR), and in part by a grant from the James S. McDonnell Foundation. The views and conclusions are those of the author and should not be represented as official policies of the ARI, the ONR, the McDonnell Foundation, or Princeton University. The author is indebted to Susan Chipman for helpful comments on an earlier draft.

association with perceptual objects must have been one of the earliest semantic insights. At this stage in language's history, it is unlikely that anything new or surprising could be said either for or against this basic empiricist assumption.

But not all words have perceptible referents. Common sense says that although some words have immediate perceptual referents, others float free in an abstract world of pure thought where a learner has nothing to grab on to but other words. Children can learn what a *nose* or a *tooth* is through a simple ostensive gesture to a salient perceptual feature, but when they ask what a *policy* or an *insult* is, simple pointing will not serve. Because children learn words like *dog* and *tree* long before they learn words like *quality* and *cognition*, common sense suggests that vocabulary is built on a perceptual foundation.

Psychological discussion of the relation between words and their referents has also begun with ostension—with the perception and naming of concrete objects—and with the familiar hierarchical semantic structure that is characteristic of those nominal concepts. Object naming is obviously fundamental: If perception did not organize the world into objects and arrangements of objects, there would be little for language to assign names to. The assignment of a word to a category of objects does two things: It indicates that a certain perceptual generalization is possible, and it endows the word with meaning.

Because the perception and the naming of concrete objects are so intimately related, the study of either one might be expected to enrich the study of the other. But traffic across this boundary seems to have been heavily one-way. The perceptual implications of object naming have been of little value to students of perception. Successful use of the word *tree*, for example, proves that people can do whatever information processing is required to recognize trees, but it sheds little light on the nature of those perceptual processes. The conceptual implications of object naming, on the other hand, have been critically important for psycholinguists because it is a word's meaning that makes it useful.

The claim I advance here is that an analysis of the lexicon can tell us something about the nature of perception. Words represent concepts that people have found sufficiently useful to merit lexicalization, and useful concepts almost always play a role in some larger system of beliefs that people share. Consequently, lexical analysis can reveal conceptual systems shared by speakers of a given language (D'Andrade, 1987). In particular, analysis of the words used to discuss perception can provide insight into folk theories of perception.

REFERENCE, NOUNS, AND HYPONYMY

Two meanings of *meaning* are usually distinguished. One is a term's extension, or the class of objects that the term can be used to refer to. The extension of *chair* is the set of all chairs. The second is a term's intension: the knowledge required to determine its extension. The intension of *chair* is whatever one must know in order to recognize a chair. Psychologists are principally concerned with intensional meaning; the intension of a term is said to be the concept that the term can express. In the case of concrete objects, of course, intensional meaning is heavily perceptual.

This approach is sometimes interpreted to mean that one does not know the meaning of a term unless one can resolve all questions concerning membership in its extension. That is to say, one does not know the meaning of a term unless one knows all the individually necessary and jointly sufficient conditions defining category membership. But that view is clearly too narrow. (By that interpretation, only oncologists know the meaning of *cancer*, only metallurgists know the meaning of *gold*, and so on). In the everyday use of language it is seldom necessary to make absolute determinations. Relative distinctions usually suffice; an expression can refer successfully if it is informative enough to distinguish an intended referent from other things that are also relevant to the purposes of the communication.

Garner (1962) once wrote, "It is never possible to define words precisely enough, even in science, to avoid ambiguities and misunderstandings" (p. 14). But he went on at considerable length to demonstrate that particular situations impose their own characteristic redundancies, and to explain how redundancy, or structure, can make discrimination easier and more accurate. In short, the potential ambiguities and misunderstandings of imprecisely defined terms can be avoided with the help of situational redundancy. The important thing for successful communication about concrete objects is not an ability to identify referents correctly by name in any conceivable situation, but rather an ability to distinguish one object from any others with which it is likely to be confused at the time.

For speakers to draw such pragmatic distinctions, however, a language must not only provide names for objects, but also names for features by which they can be distinguished. In one situation, for example, it might suffice to ask for "the book," but in another it might be necessary to specify "the little book with the tan binding at the end of the second shelf," where a description including size, color, and location supplements the head noun. These terms for features of objects are also a part of the lexicon.

Words denoting distinguishing features play an important role in referring expressions, but they are most clearly displayed in definitional expressions. An example that has received some attention from psychologists (Collins & Quillian, 1969) is the following: "*canary*: a bird that is small, yellow, and sings." The superordinate noun phrase "a bird" identifies a category of objects, and the relative clause "that is small, yellow, and sings" is intended to distinguish the canary from other members of the same category. *Bird*, in turn, may be defined as an animal that is warm-blooded, has feathers, wings, and a beak, and characteristically (but not necessarily) eats worms and can fly. The resulting hierarchy of terms—canary, bird, animal—is part of a folk taxonomy of the animal kingdom.

Canaries, being birds, have all of the features of birds plus the additional features that distinguish them from other birds. This semantic relation is called *hyponymy* (subname): *Canary* is a hyponym of *bird*. If you are told, "He named his canary Spike," you do not need to ask whether Spike is a bird, or is small, or has a beak—the naming convention ensures that Spike will inherit all the features of canaries. Much psychological discussion of hyponymy has focused on whether features are also inherited by common nouns—whether, say, canaries simply inherit the features of birds or whether the features of canaries and the features of birds should be viewed as two independent lists (Smith, Shoben, & Rips, 1974).

The concern here, however, is less with the folk taxonomy per se than with the features it requires to distinguish species from genera. The canary–bird example illustrates three important types: *attributes*, such as size, color, temperature—"is small," "is yellow," and "is warm-blooded"; *parts*, such as "has feathers," "has wings," and "has a beak"; and *functions*, such as "sings," "eats worms," and "can fly." The perceptual nature of such features is obvious, of course. Taken together, they should enable a person to distinguish canaries from other animals. The validity of that claim is not at issue here. It is the features themselves, and their perceptual bases, that are central to what follows.

The point is that the importance of perception for the organization of lexical knowledge goes well beyond its role in the recognition of concrete objects that are denoted by nouns. Attributes, parts, and functions could not enter into definitions at all if they were not also expressible in words: Attributes are most conveniently expressed by adjectives, parts by nouns, and functions by verbs and adverbs. Exploring the meanings of these terms leads deeper into the folk psychology of perception.

ATTRIBUTES, ADJECTIVES, AND ANTONYMY

Historians of science could debate precisely when the transformation from folk theories to scientific theories of perception began, but surely one important step in that transformation was taken by the empiricist philosopher John Locke. In 1690, Locke opened his discussion of ideas in the second book of his *Essay* with a famous passage that included the following: "First, our Senses, conversant about particular sensible objects, do convey into the mind several distinct perceptions of things, according to those various ways wherein those objects do affect them. And thus we come by those *ideas* we have of *yellow, white, heat, cold, soft, hard, bitter, sweet*, and all those which we call sensible qualities" (Locke, 1690/1959, pp. 122–123). The excerpt is of interest here because the kind of ideas that Locke took as a starting point are not objects but values of attributes of objects. And most of the words that he used to refer to those ideas are not nouns but predicative adjectives.[1] Locke's goal was to explain the origin of ideas of concrete objects, but he began by introducing their "sensible qualities."

It must be noted, however, that changing from nouns to adjectives is accompanied by a major shift in cognitive organization. Whereas words that refer to objects are organized hierarchically, words that denote values of attributes are not. The basic relation organizing predicative adjectives has generally been assumed to be antonymy (Deese, 1964, 1965). It is amusing that when Locke wanted to list examples of sensible qualities, he fell naturally into giving antonyms: *heat–cold, soft–hard, bitter–sweet*. There is even a sense in which *yellow–white* can be considered antonyms.

Perhaps one reason nouns have been studied more than adjectives is that antonymy is a difficult relation to define. It involves a commonsense notion of contrast or opposition, but words can contrast or stand in opposition to one another in many ways. For example, the antonyms *perfect–imperfect* are mutually exclusive; logicians call them contradictories because both cannot be true, but both cannot be false (*not perfect* means *imperfect*). The antonyms *hot–cold*, on the other hand, are not mutually exclusive; they are called contraries because they cannot both be true, but both can be false (*not hot* does not mean *cold*). Because many antonyms are contraries, antonymy cannot be defined logically in terms of simple negation.

The important psychological generalizations that emerge from this suburb of the folk theory of perception are that adjectives presuppose attributes and that attributes tend to be bipolar. Exceptions exist, of course, color adjectives being the most obvious, but bipolarity is the general rule. Moreover, predicative adjectives express values of attributes: *x is Adj* means that there is an attribute A such that $A(x) = Adj$. In short, *Adj* is the value of the function $A(x)$. For example, height is an attribute that ranges over a continuum of values, from values labeled *short* to values labeled *tall*: *Ted is tall* means that $Height(Ted) = tall$.

When the semantics of antonymy is phrased in terms of attributes rather than negation, the logicians' distinction between contradictory and contrary antonyms can be seen to follow from the fact that attributes can be gradable (continuous) or ungradable (dichotomous). To continue the preceding example, because height varies continuously, *tall–short* are contraries. Contradictory antonyms express values of attributes, like gender, that are dichotomous.

In other words, the semantics of predicative adjectives, and the fact that semantic memory for adjectives is organized in terms of antonymy, follow directly from commonsense assumptions about the bipolar attributes whose values such adjectives are used to express.

---

[1] A predicative adjective is one that, unlike *rather* or *former*, can be used in such sentences frames as "The *Noun* is *Adjective*" (e.g., "The canary is yellow").

A possible objection to this psychological formulation might be that antonymy is too limited a relation to serve as an organizing principle for all adjectives. Many predicative adjectives do not have antonyms. What is the antonym of *cute*, for example, or *indolent*? If antonymy is the basic evidence for bipolar attributes, then the existence of many adjectives having no antonyms should invalidate—or at least limit—claims that predicative adjectives express values of bipolar attributes.

The answer to this objection is that there are two kinds of antonyms. Gross, Fischer, and Miller (1989) have drawn a distinction between direct and indirect antonyms: indirect antonyms express conceptual contrasts, whereas direct antonyms express both conceptual and lexical contrasts. Not all adjectives have direct antonyms, but they all have indirect antonyms.

According to Gross et al. (1989), adjectives are organized into clusters having similar meanings; two clusters that are conceptually opposed will include one or more pairs of adjectives that are lexically opposed. For example, *wet*, *moist*, *damp*, and *soggy* belong to one cluster, and *dry*, *arid*, *parched*, and *desiccated* are a conceptually contrasting cluster; *wet–dry* are direct antonyms, whereas *wet–arid* or *moist–dry* are indirect antonyms. Although *arid* does not have a direct antonym, it is in a cluster with *dry*, which does have a direct antonym—so *arid* inherits an indirect antonym.

Why some pairs of adjectives that express contrasting values are selected to serve as direct antonyms is an interesting question in its own right. Charles and Miller (1989) noted that direct antonyms co-occur in sentences far more frequently than do indirect antonyms, and Gazzaniga and Miller (1989) speculated that it might be useful to overlearn some antonym pairs in order to use them as names of attributes. But the important point for the present discussion is that predicative adjectives express values of bipolar attributes. Moreover, this use of adjectives sets a pattern that is then extended and adapted to express values of more abstract, nonperceptual attributes. Once that formulation is accepted, the influence of perceptual structure on this large lexical domain becomes apparent.

A word of warning, however. Defining predicative adjectives by values of perceptual attributes may be necessary, but it is not a sufficient theory of adjectival meaning. In particular, this account ignores the influence of the head noun on the interpretation of adjectives that modify it: A canary is a small bird and a pony is a small horse, but the size conveyed by *small* is different in the two cases. Apparently, the nouns *bird* and *horse* carry with them, as part of their meaning, some information about expected size; *small* means small relative to those expectations. To be generally useful to scientists, of course, folk notions of size must be transformed into absolute scales of measurement. But it is relative size that is important perceptually, and relative size is what the lexical folk wisdom expresses.

One conclusion to draw from this interaction between the adjective and the noun it modifies is that the interpretation of many adjectives draws more heavily on perceptual knowledge than can be made explicit by defining them simply in terms of the attribute values they express. This shortcoming is part of a more general problem with feature theories of meaning, a problem that becomes even more apparent with parts and functions.

SHAPE, NOUNS, AND MERONYMY

Shape is surely the most informative perceptual feature for distinguishing among concrete objects. Although it is frequently referred to as an attribute, on a par with such bipolar attributes as size, value, frequency, animacy, or familiarity, shape is clearly not bipolar.[2] A relatively simple vocabulary of antonymous adjectives suffices for communication about bipolar attributes, but communication about the shapes of objects requires a much more elaborate lexicon for the description of part–whole relations.

The importance of shape is recognized in the definition of *basic objects* by Rosch, Mervis, Gray, Johnson, and Boyes-Braem (1976), who claim that there is a particular level in the folk taxonomy of object terms that is more informative than are terms above or below it. In the canary–bird–animal example, *bird* is the basic object term. One of the criteria used by Rosch et al. (1976) is that basic-level terms are the most generic terms that denote objects with similar and recognizable shapes. But Rosch et al. (1976) also use a variety of other criteria to establish that basic-level terms convey more information than do more general terms and that more specific terms convey little information that is not also conveyed by basic-level terms. Many different criteria converge at the same level; basic-level terms are preferred for labeling objects, are most rapidly verified, are learned earliest, denote objects used in similar ways, and so on.

Tversky and Hemenway (1984) offer an explanation for this convergence. When people are asked to list features of objects, terms denoting parts are frequent at the basic level but rare at more generic levels: "Basic level objects are distinguished from one another by parts, but members of subordinate categories share parts and differ from one another on other attributes" (p. 169). Tversky and Hemenway propose that part configurations underlie all of the various criteria that converge at the basic level.

---

[2]Garner (1974) has referred to perceptual features like shape and color as nominal dimensions, but terminology is not standardized. Garner (1978) attempts to bring order to the diverse uses that psychologists have made of such terms as *property, attribute, dimension, feature, component, variable, aspect,* and *configuration.* Roughly, he uses *property* or *aspect* to mean what is here called *feature; dimension* or *variable* for what is here called *attribute; level of a variable* for what is here called *value of an attribute*; and *wholistic property* for what is here called *shape* or *part.*

Although the importance of parts for the perception of shape has long been recognized (Biederman, 1987), psycholinguists have paid less attention to the role of part names than to the role of hyponymy in the organization of lexical knowledge. Miller and Johnson-Laird (1976) compared the ''part of'' relation to the ''kind of'' relation: Both are asymmetric and transitive and both can relate terms hierarchically. That is to say, parts can have parts: A finger is a part of a hand, a hand is a part of an arm, and an arm is a part of a body. In linguistic terminology (Cruse, 1986), this semantic relation is called *meronymy*.[3] The term *finger* is a meronym of the term *hand, hand* is a meronym of *arm*, and *arm* is a meronym of *body*. But the ''part of'' construction is not always a reliable test of meronymy.

In many instances, transitivity seems to be limited. Lyons (1977), for example, notes that *handle* is a meronym of *door* and *door* is a meronym of *house*, yet it sounds odd to say ''The house has a handle'' or ''The handle is a part of the house.'' Winston, Chaffin, and Hermann (1987) take such failures of transitivity to indicate that different part–whole relations are involved in the two cases. For example, ''The branch is a part of the tree'' and ''The tree is a part of a forest'' do not imply that ''The branch is a part of the forest'' because the *branch–tree* relation is not the same as the *tree–forest* relation. For Lyons's example, Winston et al. suggest, following Cruse (1986), that ''part of'' is sometimes used where ''attached to'' would be more appropriate: ''Part of'' should be transitive, whereas ''attached to'' is clearly not. ''The house has a door handle'' is acceptable because it negates the implicit inference in ''The house has a handle'' that the handle is attached to the house.

Such observations raise questions about how many different ''part of'' relations there are. Winston et al. (1987) differentiated six types of meronyms: component–object (*branch–tree*), member–collection (*tree–forest*), portion–mass (*slice–cake*), stuff–object (*aluminum–airplane*), feature–activity (*paying–shopping*), and place–area (*New Haven–Connecticut*). Chaffin, Hermann, and Winston (1988) added a seventh: phase–process (*adolescence–growing up*). Meronymy is obviously a complex semantic relation—or set of relations.

The stuff–object relation demonstrates the limits of folk theories of object composition. With the help of modern science, it is now possible to analyze ''stuff'' into smaller and smaller components. At some point, this analysis loses all connection with the object being analyzed. For example, because all concrete objects are composed of atoms, having atoms cannot serve to distinguish one category of objects from any other. *Atom* would be a meronym of every term denoting a concrete object. Something has gone wrong here. For commonsense purposes, the dissection of an object terminates at the point where the parts no longer serve to distinguish this object from others with which it might be confused.

---

[3]Miller and Johnson-Laird (1976) call it *partonymy*.

Knowing where to stop requires commonsense knowledge of the contrasts that need to be drawn.

This problem arises for many parts other than atoms, of course. Some components can serve as parts of many different things: Think of all of the different objects that have gears. It is sometimes the case that an object can be two kinds of thing at the same time—a piano is both a kind of musical instrument and a kind of furniture, for example—but that situation is rare in the hyponymic hierarchy. In the meronymic hierarchy, on the other hand, it is common; *point*, for example, is a meronym of *arrow, awl, dagger, fishhook, harpoon, icepick, knife, needle, pencil, pin, sword*, and *tine*. Because the points involved are so very different, it is remarkable that this situation causes so little confusion.

Confusion and uncertainty result only when we begin with a part and try to think of all the different things that it is a part of. It is much easier to start with the object and recall what parts it has. In thinking about meronymy, we move most easily down the hierarchy from whole to part (in contrast to hyponymy, where it is usually easier to move up the hierarchy). This preferred direction for meronymy may provide an argument that information about parts is organized by perceptual imagery (Kosslyn, 1975). It is easier to form an image of one object and then scan it for its parts than it is to form images of many objects whose only common feature is a shared part.

The role of imagery is so important that Lakoff (1987; Brugman & Lakoff, 1988) has used it in a general argument that meanings cannot be defined by specifying categories of objects that are characterized by lists of individually necessary and jointly sufficient conditions. A more conservative formulation might be that lists of features are useful, perhaps even necessary, for characterizing contrasts between categories of objects, but that the importance of configurational or topological features in the understanding of meronymic relations indicates that mere lists of features are certainly not sufficient. The interpretation of common-sense part–whole relations draws more heavily on perceptual knowledge than can be made explicit by simply listing names of the parts.

FUNCTIONS, VERBS, AND PREDICATION

The term *function* has been used in many ways and is easy prey to misinterpretation. I use the term here to refer to something like the functional utilities and action possibilities that Gibson (1979) called *affordances*. Whereas attributes have been studied extensively for many years, and part–whole relations are a familiar problem, the third type of distinguishing feature that plays a role in folk theories of perception—the perception of function—has only recently received attention from perceptual psychologists. Recognizing the function of an object—what it does or what can be done with it—depends so heavily on general knowledge that some psychologists would deny that it is a perceptual feature at all. Where to draw a line between perception and inference has always been a difficult question.

If it is granted that part–whole relations are important for perception, it is difficult to exclude functional judgments. Tversky and Hemenway (1984) comment that parts frequently enjoy a kind of duality that is not apparent in simple attributes. Part names refer both to a perceptual entity and to a functional role: The *leg* of a table or the *handle* of a door have particular shapes, but they also have particular functions. Tversky and Hemenway note that "part configuration is especially important because of its role as a bridge between appearance and activity, between perception and behavior, between structure and function. Because structure is related to function via part configuration, part configuration underlies the informativeness of basic level hierarchies" (p. 188).

Knowledge of its function can influence where the boundaries of a part are perceived. Although good design dictates that function determine form, the correlation between shape and function, even for artifacts, is not always as close as Tversky and Hemenway (1984) seem to assume. Even table legs and door handles come in a variety of shapes and are recognizable as much by their place in the total configuration of a table or a door as by their shapes in isolation. The shape of a concrete object is ordinarily a static feature of the object; its function is revealed over time. Miller and Johnson-Laird (1976) went so far as to deny that function is a perceptual feature, but their rejection may be excessive; if a concrete object has any function, the function can usually be determined by watching the thing long enough to determine what it does or what is done with it.

The blurring of the distinction between structure and function is best illustrated by cases in which an object serves a familiar function but does not have a familiar shape. Miller (1978) considers the case of two people using a tree stump for a picnic. One of them says, "This stump is a good table." A stump, of course, is not a table—calling a stump a table does not make it one. But calling it a good table seems perfectly acceptable. How can something that is not a table be a good table?

A plausible answer has been suggested by Katz (1964), who proposes that functional information is stored with most head nouns. His suggestion resembles an assumption we have already adopted: From the fact that a large table is larger than a large bench, we assume that part of the meaning of *table* is the expected size of tables. Katz's suggestion for *good* is similar: From the fact that a good table need not be a table at all, we conclude that part of the meaning of *table* is the expected function of tables. The functional information determines the interpretation of the adjectives *good* and *bad*; these adjectives select the functional component of the noun's meaning and assign it a positive or negative value. Something is a good table, for example, if it serves well the function that tables are supposed to serve; a bad table serves that function poorly. Thus, a good knife is a knife that cuts well, a good violinist is a violinist who plays well, a good chair is a chair that supports well, and so on. If Katz (1964) is right—if *good* selects functional information—then the function that an object is expected to serve is a separable component of the meaning of the noun used to refer to that object. (Indeed, for words like *ornament*, the functional component seems to be all there is to the meaning.)

From such arguments, it seems plausible to conclude that words like *table* have a functional component and, following the precedent set by attributes and parts, such meaning components should signal a folk concept awaiting scientific clarification and development.

There is an unfortunate vagueness to the concept of function, however. Tversky and Hemenway (1984) suggest that function and action might be equated, but they seem to me to be independent features. It is true that for many man-made artifacts known directly through manipulation (spoon, ball, comb, hammer, foods) the function is an intrinsic part of the relevant action system. But for other artifacts (wall, bridge, mine, buildings) the function is obvious, although a distinctive action system is not. Similarly, some natural objects have been given familiar functions (apples are eaten, horses are ridden, and trees provide shade) but others (atoms, clouds, mountains) have not. The functional component of meaning involves general knowledge to a far greater extent than do attributes or shapes.

From a lexical point of view, to characterize the function of some category of objects is to indicate the class of verbs (or verb phrases) that can be predicated of that object. For example, because foods are eaten, *eat* can be predicated of *food* and all of its hyponyms; because blades are for cutting, *cut* can be predicated of every noun having *blade* as a meronym, and so on. As in the case of meronymy, there seems to be an asymmetry in retrievability: Most people find it easier to begin with a verb and list all of the nouns that can serve as its arguments than to begin with a noun and list all of the predicates that can take it as an argument. And here again, a plausible speculation would be that the asymmetry reflects the role of imagery, and of the transformability of imagery, deriving ultimately from perception of goal-directed episodes.

Some of this functional information appears in dictionary definitions. Conceivably, more complete lists of the predication relations between verbs and nouns could be added to the lists of attributes and parts already discussed. Even more than for attributes and parts, however, the interpretation of lists of predicates would depend on perceptual and world knowledge that could not be made explicit by merely listing the predicates.

CONCLUSION

The analysis of terms denoting object features—*attributes, parts,* and *functions*— leads deeper into the folk psychology of perception than would an analysis of terms denoting the objects themselves, and shows more clearly the general pattern of lexical organization that is generalized to linguistic communication in more abstract semantic domains. At this level of analysis, lexical organization parallels perceptual organization, and an adequate characterization of the meaning of terms denoting objects can provide valuable clues concerning the kinds of information provided by perception. Much remains to be learned about the perception of attributes and shapes, of course, but the most challenging question for students of perception concerns the role of information about function. It is not clear how knowledge of function contributes to the perceptual recognition and naming of objects, but it is clear that the role of function in folk theories of perception is as important as are the roles of attributes or part–whole relations.

But perhaps a more important lesson to be learned from listening to these lexical echoes of perceptual structure is how complex the relation between word and object really is, and how little of it can be captured by simply enumerating necessary and sufficient conditions (when there are any). The development of a satisfactory theory of object identification still awaits our understanding of some extremely complex cognitive processes.

References

Biederman, I. (1987). Recognition-by-components: A theory of human image understanding. *Psychological Review, 94*, 115–147.

Brugman, C., & Lakoff, G. (1988). Cognitive topology and lexical networks. In S. L. Small, G. W. Cottrell, & M. K. Tanenhaus (Eds.), *Lexical ambiguity resolution: Perspectives from psycholinguistics, neuropsychology, and artificial intelligence* (pp. 477–508). San Mateo, CA: Kaufmann.

Chaffin, R., Hermann, D. J., & Winston, M. (1988). An empirical taxonomy of part–whole relations: Effects of part–whole relation type on relation identification. *Language and Cognitive Processes, 3*, 17–48.

Charles, W. G., & Miller, G. A. (1989). Contexts of antonymous adjectives. *Applied Psycholinguistics, 9*, 357–375.

Collins, A. M., & Quillian, M. R. (1969). Retrieval time from semantic memory. *Journal of Verbal Learning and Verbal Behavior, 8*, 240–247.

Cruse, D. A. (1986). *Lexical Semantics*. New York: Cambridge University Press.

D'Andrade, R. (1987). A folk model of the mind. In D. Holland & N. Quinn (Eds.), *Cultural models in language and thought* (pp. 112–148). New York: Cambridge University Press.

Deese, J. (1964). The associative structure of some English adjectives. *Journal of Verbal Learning and Verbal Behavior, 3*, 347–357.

Deese, J. (1965). *The structure of associations in language and thought*. Baltimore: Johns Hopkins Press.

Garner, W. R. (1962). *Uncertainty and structure as psychological concepts*. New York: Wiley.

Garner, W. R. (1974). *The processing of information and structure*. New York: Wiley.

Garner, W. R. (1978). Aspects of a stimulus: Features, dimensions, and configurations. In E. Rosch & B. B. Lloyd (Eds.), *Cognition and categorization* (pp. 99–133). Hillsdale, NJ: Erlbaum.

Gazzaniga, M. S., & Miller, G. A. (1989). The recognition of antonymy by a language-enriched right hemisphere. *Cognitive Neuroscience, 1,* 185–191.

Gibson, J. J. (1979). *The ecological approach to visual perception.* Boston, MA: Houghton Mifflin.

Gross, D., Fischer, U., & Miller, G. A. (1989). The organization of adjective meanings. *Journal of Memory and Language, 28,* 92–106.

Katz, J. J. (1964). Semantic theory and the meaning of "good." *Journal of Philosophy, 61,* 739–766.

Kosslyn, S. M. (1975). Information representation in visual images. *Cognitive Psychology, 7,* 341–370.

Lakoff, G. (1987). *Women, fire, and dangerous things: What categories reveal about the mind.* Chicago: University of Chicago Press.

Locke, J. (1959). *An essay concerning human understanding* (Vols. 1–2; A. C. Fraser, Ed.). New York: Dover. (Original work published 1690)

Lyons, J. (1977). *Semantics.* New York: Cambridge University Press.

Miller, G. A. (1978). Practical and lexical knowledge. In E. Rosch & B. B. Lloyd (Eds.), *Cognition and categorization* (pp. 305–319). Hillsdale, NJ: Erlbaum.

Miller, G. A., & Johnson-Laird, P. N. (1976). *Language and perception.* Cambridge, MA: Harvard University Press.

Rosch, E., Mervis, C. B., Gray, W. D., Johnson, D. M., & Boyes-Braem, P. (1976). Basic objects in natural categories. *Cognitive Psychology, 8,* 382–439.

Smith, E. E., Shoben, E. J., & Rips, L. J. (1974). Structure and process in semantic memory: A featural model for semantic decisions. *Psychological Review, 81,* 214–241.

Tversky, B., & Hemenway, K. (1984). Objects, parts, and categories. *Journal of Experimental Psychology: General, 113,* 169–193.

Winston, M. E., Chaffin, R., & Hermann, D. J. (1987). A taxonomy of part–whole relations. *Cognitive Science, 11,* 417–444.

CHAPTER 17

WORDS, THE WORLD, AND THEIR POSSIBILITIES

HERBERT H. CLARK

By the principle of possibilities, we understand what an entity is with reference to what it could have been. The word red, *for example, belongs to both a domain of lexical possibilities (all English words) and a domain of conceptual possibilities (all conceivable denotations). But on any occasion, the word is intended to be understood against much narrower domains. Speakers and addressees restrict the domains on the basis of their momentary common ground—the information that they believe they share and that is readily accessible at the moment. For an utterance of* red potato, *the two domains might be the primary color words and the possible colors of potatoes. The color denoted by* red, *therefore, changes with the occasion of use; compare* red cabbages and red hair, *or a face that is red from sunburn, embarrassment, or clown makeup. Word meanings, I argue, are not static dictionary entries but products of a lexical process.*

In communication, we use words to signify things in the world around us. I might use *scholar* for a type of object, *eminent* for a type of state, *think* for a type of process, and *Garner* or *he* for a particular man. On the one side we have words—*scholar, eminent, think, Garner*—and on the other side, the world—its objects, states, events, and processes, both as types and as particulars. We use the words to talk about the world. But how? What is the relation between the two? This is one of the fundamental questions of language use.

I thank Susan B. Brennan and Eve V. Clark for discussions of these issues and for suggestions on the manuscript. The research was supported in part by Grant BNS 83-20284 from the National Science Foundation.

One of the basic insights into this issue was brought home to me by Wendell R. Garner in 1962 in his book *Uncertainty and Structure as Psychological Concepts*, and this insight has permeated my work ever since.[1] What Garner argued was this: We can never make sense of an entity—a word, object, process, state, or event—on its own. Whatever meaning it has for us, whatever structure we see in it, comes from our understanding of the system it belongs to. If we "see a single stimulus as structured," Garner argued, it is only because we "generate an implied set of stimuli against which the particular stimulus can be contrasted, or within which the particular stimulus can be subsumed." Let me call this the *principle of possibilities*: We understand what an entity is with reference to what it could have been—the set of possibilities we infer it came from.

For Garner, this principle was crucial in understanding how two systems are linked. English words, he noted, bear relations to one another, and this set of relations he called *internal structure*. They also bear relations to French words; for example, *house* corresponds to *maison*. This he called *external structure*. The crucial point for Garner was that we cannot account for external structure without considering internal structure, the possibilities in each separate system. To translate from English to French, we need to know the inner workings of both English and French. Garner's arguments were drawn mostly from perception, but they are clearly more general than that. They apply to language use as well.

So how do words relate to the world? Most accounts have at their core a theory of word meaning based on the analogy of the dictionary. These *dictionary theories*, as I will call them, go as follows: Every word has a lexical entry in memory that pairs a phonological shape, like /dog/, with a conventional meaning, like "canine animal." The conventional meaning is really a brief, partial description of some aspect of the world. All words taken together form a list called the *mental lexicon*. When we need a word, we search this list for a word with the right conventional meaning. And when we hear the phonological sequence /dog/, we search the list for that shape and retrieve its conventional meaning. Although this may be somewhat of a caricature of the dictionary theories, it is not far from the truth.

Dictionary theories of word meaning, I will argue, are inadequate, largely because they ignore the principle of possibilities. Let me call the domain of all possible words the *lexical domain*, and the domain of all possible objects, processes, states, and events in the world, as people conceive of them, the *conceptual domain*. Dictionary theories tend to disregard the internal structure of the two domains. They try to specify what words signify independently of the lexical and

---

[1] I participated in a seminar with Garner on his book my very first semester in graduate school. (On the inside cover of my copy of the book is written "August 1962.") So, as a mere foundling in the field, I was raised thinking that uncertainty and structure were important psychological concepts, and I continue to believe that. If that is a mistake, it is Garner who must be held responsible.

conceptual possibilities. The right account of signification, I will suggest, must assess both sets of possibilities. It will not be a static dictionary, but a lexical process. One of my goals in this chapter is to suggest what that process might be like. As groundwork, I must begin by describing how words are used for coordinating in communication.

WORDS AND COORDINATION

Communication is a collective activity, and collective activities take coordination. When Kate says to Jess, "Hand me that book," the two of them have to coordinate. For one thing, they must synchronize Jess's listening with Kate's speaking. If he isn't listening and trying to understand precisely as Kate speaks, Jess is likely to miss what she says. They must also coordinate on content. Kate must be sure, among other things, that Jess knows English, that he sees she is the person speaking (to get *me* right), and that he notices what she is pointing at (to get *that book* right).

To coordinate, in turn, Kate and Jess must act on the basis of their current common ground—the knowledge, beliefs, and assumptions that they believe they share at the moment. Their current common ground is itself based on three main sources of information (H. H. Clark & Marshall, 1981). The first source is their joint membership in various communities or cultural groups. If Kate and Jess know they are both English speakers, Californians, university graduates, clinical psychologists, and Giants fans, they can take everything that is universally known, believed, or assumed within these communities to be part of their common ground. The second source is their prior conversation. All of the information they have exchanged up to that moment, once they allow for memory loss, can also be assumed to be in common ground. The third source is their joint perceptual experiences. If they are both looking at a book on a table and see each other doing so, they can assume the book and its appearance are also in common ground. Two people's common ground is constantly changing. For the hypothetical Kate and Jess, it would accumulate with every new bit of conversation and every new joint experience (H. H. Clark & Schaefer, 1989; Lewis, 1979; Stalnaker, 1978).

Common ground is needed for coordinating on both the processes and the content of language use. Kate and Jess cannot synchronize her speaking with his listening without assessing who is doing what at each moment. For this, they work from the joint perceptual evidence of eye gaze, gestures, facial expressions, and speech timing (Goodwin, 1981; Jefferson, 1973; Schegloff, 1984). Nor can they coordinate on content without appealing to common ground. Kate cannot use French with Jess unless she takes it as common ground that both know French. Nor can she mention RBIs, ERAs, or the infield fly rule without assuming that baseball is common ground (Nunberg, 1978).

What does all of this have to do with signification? Signification obviously requires coordination too. When Kate uses a word, she must coordinate with Jess on what it signifies on that occasion. To do this, by the argument just presented, the two of them must rely on elements in their current common ground. But what elements?

The simplest assumption is that all they need is the mental lexicon. This is, in effect, what dictionary theories assume. For Kate to use *book*, she must assume that she and Jess have the same lexical entry for *book*. Most dictionary theories go no further. Indeed, they generally take for granted that everyone who speaks English has the same mental lexicon. That, of course, isn't true. Kate may know the whole field of baseball terms—*RBI*, *ERA*, *infield*, *shortstop*, *fly out*—whereas Jess doesn't. How can she discover what he knows? Here, joint membership in a community or cultural group comes in handy. If it is common ground that they are both baseball fans, it is also probably common ground that they both know baseball jargon. Ultimately, every convention, such as a word meaning, is in common ground for a particular community or cultural group (Lewis, 1969). *Maison* is conventional for French speakers, *RBI* for baseball aficionados, and *quark* for students of physics.

Yet, on the face of it, certain conceptual possibilities must be common ground as well. How can Kate really expect Jess to understand *RBI* if he doesn't know a lot about baseball, or *quark* if he doesn't know a lot about subatomic physics? Intuitively, it isn't enough for them to have *RBI* or *quark* in the lexical domain. They need to know the corresponding sets of possibilities in the conceptual domain as well. To see this, let us begin with a simple case and see what is required for successful signification.

CONCEPTUAL POSSIBILITIES

Consider the word *red*. In dictionary theories, its lexical entry would pair the phonological shape /red/ with a conventional meaning something like this:[2] *Red* denotes the color of blood when predicated of most objects, except that *red* denotes (a) tawny when predicated of a skin type; (b) pinkish red when predicated of potatoes; (c) orange when predicated of hair; (d) purply red when predicated of wine; (e) pinkish red when predicated of wood; and so on. The precise color that *red* denotes depends on what it is predicated of, and the mental lexicon would have to list each of these exceptions. But there is something very wrong here. I

---

[2] The *American Heritage Dictionary of the English Language* defines *red* as follows: "Any of a group of colors that may vary in lightness and saturation, whose hue resembles that of blood; the hue of the long-wave end of the spectrum; one of the additive or light primaries; one of the psychological primary hues, evoked in the normal observer by the long-wave end of the spectrum." I am concerned with the first part of this definition.

submit that it comes from flouting the principle of possibilities and its role in coordination.

Suppose that Kate is talking to Jess and uses the word *red*. In doing this, she takes as common ground two sets of possibilities. The first is the lexical field from which *red* is drawn. It might be represented as follows:

primary brightness terms: <black, white>
primary hue terms: <red, yellow, green, blue>
secondary color terms: <grey, pink, orange, brown, purple>
exotic color terms: <maroon, ecru, chartreuse, etc.>
modifiers: <light, dark>, etc.

Red belongs to the set of primary hue terms <red, yellow, green, blue>, which contrast with the primary brightness terms on one side and with the secondary and the exotic color terms on the other. It also contrasts with *light red*, *dark red*, and other modified terms.

The second set of possibilities is the conceptual field Kate is talking about. Suppose that the field is skin color. What Kate and Jess know about that might include information like the following: (a) Skin color in humans comes in a limited number of types; (b) skin color is genetically determined; (c) skin color is highly correlated with race; (d) skin color can change with emotion and illness; (e) skin color can change with exposure to the sun; and (f) the skin colors determined by these factors have such and such appearances. Even if we never talked about skin colors, we would have tacit knowledge about their types, range, and origins.

But Kate and Jess also know that only part of the general color vocabulary gets applied to skin. The lexical field for skin color looks something like the following:

primary skin color terms: <black, white, red, yellow, brown>
skin color from sun exposure: <tan, brown, red>
skin color from emotions: <red, white, pale, green, purple>
exotic skin color terms: <sallow, ashen, livid, olive, etc.>

Ultimately, any color term could be applied to skin in the right circumstances.

When Kate speaks of ''red skin,'' just what color is she denoting? Well, it certainly isn't fire-engine red. If she is talking about the skin type, it is tawny. If she is talking about white skin with too much sun, it is the sort of dark pink that is caused by burning. If she is speaking of a red face from embarrassment, it is another sort of pink, the one caused by blood invading the capillaries. Let us focus first on the five common skin types. As English evolved, these skin types were assigned color terms from the general vocabulary. Indeed, the commonest skin colors got covered by the commonest general color terms—*black*, *brown*, *red*, *yellow*, and *white*—even though they lay far from the focal colors usually denoted by these terms. (*Blue* and *green* didn't come up because there are no skin types in those regions.) The puzzle is why so-called white skin was called *white* instead of *pink*. The answer is that *white* is the commoner term, a basic brightness term, and so it is preferred over *pink*. That is, as English evolved, there was a preference for assigning the commonest possibilities in the lexical field to the commonest possibilities in the conceptual field, even when this tendency led to distortions outside that field.

There are three broad constraints for taking the nomenclature for a general conceptual field (color in general) and applying it to a specialized conceptual field (skin color):

1. *Similarity constraint*: For each salient possibility in the specialized conceptual field, apply the term for the most similar possibility in the general conceptual field.
2. *Preference constraint*: For terms in the specialized lexical field, prefer common over uncommon terms from the general lexical field.
3. *Exhaustiveness constraint*: Partition the possibilities in the specialized conceptual field in such a way that, for most practical purposes, they are exhaustively covered by the chosen terms with the maximum amount of information value.[3]

These three constraints account not only for the color terms for skin types, but also for the color terms for sun exposure and emotions.

The same three constraints make sense of other conventional transfers of the color vocabulary. In the local market, we find the following: red, brown, white, and russet potatoes; red and green cabbages; red, yellow, and green bell peppers; red, yellow, and white onions; red and white grapes; white and pink grapefruit; red, white, black, green, and yellow beans; and, of course, red, white, rosé, and green wine (green as in "green Hungarian"). Among hair colors, we find black, brown, red, blond (instead of yellow), gray, and white. None of these nomenclatures makes sense if we go strictly by the standard Munsell color chips. The reds in red hair, red potatoes, red cabbage, red bell peppers, red onions, red grapes, red beans, red wine, and red skin are very different from the blood red of the focal red Munsell chip. They are also very different from each other. They only make sense with the similarity, preference, and exhaustiveness constraints. And these constraints couldn't work if it weren't for the principle of possibilities.

To summarize, what we take someone to mean by a color term depends on two sets of possibilities in current common ground—those in the lexical field and those in the conceptual field. This example might tempt us into treating the mapping from one to the other as entirely conventional—as when *red* is applied

---

[3] This notion was also introduced to me in Garner's (1962) book *Uncertainty and Structure as Psychological Concepts*.

to hair color—but we must not succumb to that temptation. To see why, we must look at other examples.

SITUATIONAL POSSIBILITIES

What a word signifies depends not only on generic properties of the conceptual domain, but on the situation being described at the moment. Consider a study by Hörmann (1983) on the quantifiers *some*, *several*, and *a few*—or rather, their German translations *einege*, *mehrere*, and *ein paar*.

In English, there are many terms for quantifying number, and they form a rich lexical field with contrast sets such as the following:

  exact number: <zero, one, two, three, four, . . .>
  existence: <some, none>
  universality: <all, some>
  contrastive number: <many, a few>
  estimates: <a lot, numerous, several, a couple, . . .>

When Kate says she has "six" or "some" or "a few" paperclips, Jess takes her as saying something about the number of paperclips she has. With "six," he may infer the number to be exactly six, but what about the other quantifiers? They are useful precisely because they suggest a range of numbers rather than an exact count. Still, that range is usually centered around a middle value. How do we compute that value?

Hörmann's (1983) study suggests an answer. He gave people expressions like "several crumbs" and asked them to judge how many objects were being denoted. For each judgment, they were to provide a range of values. Indeed, their judgments varied with what was being described. The median estimate was 9.69 for "several crumbs," 8.15 for "several paperclips," 7.27 for "several pills," but only 5.75 for "several children," 5.50 for "several cars," and 5.27 for "several mountains." The numbers got smaller as people went from "several small cars" to "several cars" to "several large cars." As Hörmann observed, the larger the object, generally the fewer objects inferred. Why should this be so?

The answer I will suggest depends crucially on the principle of possibilities. When we hear "several crumbs" or "several mountains," we imagine a scene typical of crumbs or mountains. To decide how many crumbs or mountains we should put in that scene, we consider how many of them could possibly inhabit the scene. Let me call this the maximum number possible. That number should be larger for crumbs than for mountains because in a scene typical of crumbs or mountains, we will imagine more crumbs than mountains.

On the other side, within the lexical field, *several* contrasts with the other quantifiers. It cannot denote an exact number like one, two, three, or four because otherwise the speaker would have used *one*, *two*, *three*, or *four*. Also, it must contrast with *none* on the low side and with *all, many,* and *a lot* on the high side. That is, *several* will be more than *none,* different from *one, two,* and so on, different from *a few,* and less than *many, numerous, a lot,* and so on. So when the maximum number possible is large, as with crumbs, its median number should be high, and when the maximum number possible is small, as with mountains, the median number should be low. This is what Hörmann found.

Other evidence Hörmann collected fits this view. Consider the following sentences (translated from German) and people's median estimates for "a few":

In front of the hut are standing a few people: 4.55
In front of the house are standing a few people: 5.33
In front of the city hall are standing a few people: 6.34
In front of the building are standing a few people: 6.69

The larger the space, the more possible people there can be, and the higher the median estimates. The same is true for the following examples:

Out of the window, one can see a few people: 5.86
Out of the window, one can see a few cars: 5.45
Through the peephole, one can see a few people: 4.76
Through the peephole, one can see a few cars: 3.95

So people appear to assess the possibilities afforded by the physical situation and to estimate the numbers accordingly.

People make surprisingly subtle judgments of the situation in assessing the possibilities, as shown in the following three pairs:

In front of the city hall, there are a few people standing: 6.34
In front of the city hall, there are a few people working: 5.14

Out of the window, one can see a few people: 5.86
Out of the window, one can see a few people arguing: 3.60

In the morning, he read a few poems: 4.59
In the morning, he wrote a few poems: 3.44

In the scheme I am proposing, people can imagine more possible gawkers than workers, more possible silent people than arguing people, and more possible poems read than poems written in an average morning. That is the source of their differing judgments.

As Hörmann argued, it is impossible to provide a dictionary account for these findings. Suppose the entry for *a few* read as follows: "denotes from 2 to 20, with a median of about 10 when applied to crumbs, from 2 to 18 with a median of about 7 when applied to paperclips," and so on. Already the definition is problematic because it contains a long, perhaps infinite, list of items. But it has a more fundamental flaw. The number for *a few* isn't really fixed for each item on the list. For poems, it changes with whether they are written or read. For people, it changes with whether they are in front of a hut or a city hall, standing or working, arguing or not arguing, or seen through a window or through a peephole.

Suppose, instead, the entry for *a few* read "denotes the 25th percentile (range: 10th to 40th percentile) on the distribution of items inferred possible in that situation." This comes close to the picture just presented. But, as I will argue, it still doesn't take account of the particular quantifiers that *a few* contrasts with in each situation, and these change with the situation. So a dictionary theory is problematic for quantifiers. What they signify is tightly constrained by the possibilities both in their lexical neighborhoods and in the situations being described (see also Morrow & Clark, 1988).

LEXICAL POSSIBILITIES

But why should lexical neighborhoods matter? For an answer, let me start with the view of language use taken by the philosopher Paul Grice (1975). Conversations, he argued, "are characteristically, to some degree at least cooperative efforts; and each participant recognizes in them, to some extent, a common purpose or set of purposes, or at least a mutually accepted direction" (p. 45). In Grice's view, the participants expect each other to follow what he called the *cooperative principle*: "Make your conversational contribution such as is required, at the stage at which it occurs, by the accepted purpose or direction of the talk exchange in which you are engaged" (p. 45).

For people to contribute to the accepted purpose or direction of the talk exchange, they must get their addressees to recognize their own purposes. So at the core of Grice's program is a principle I characterize as the *choice principle*: Speakers choose each expression they use from a set of possible expressions for a purpose that they m-intend[4] their addressees to recognize. When Kate uses the word *dog*, as in "I have a dog," she does so for a purpose that she expects Jess to recognize. One may argue that this is obvious: Kate wants to denote a dog, and the way to do this in English is with the word *dog*. But she had options. She could have used *hound*, *German shepherd*, *animal*, *canine*, or many other terms. Why *dog*? Jess can assume she had a reason, and one she intended him to recognize. Once again, the principle of possibilities comes to the fore. Each expression is chosen from a set of possible expressions, and each choice means something.

The choice principle has many consequences, and one of the most fundamental is the so-called *principle of contrast* (E. V. Clark, 1983, 1987). According to this principle, every two forms differ in meaning. As linguists have long noted, there are no true synonyms in the conventional lexicon. Consider these three pairs:

---

[4] For the notion of *m-intention*, which is essential here, see Grice (1957, 1968).

try and *attempt*, *often* and *frequently*, and *cop* and *policeman*. Although the two terms in each pair can be used to denote the same thing, the first term is of a lower register than the second. *Try*, *often*, and *cop* are appropriate for informal settings, and *attempt*, *frequently*, and *policeman* for more formal ones. What would Kate mean, then, by saying "I was approached by that cop" in a courtroom? In line with the choice principle, she would expect us to reason, "If Kate wanted to refer neutrally in a courtroom to a policeman, she would have chosen *policeman*, or even *police officer*. Instead, she chose *cop*, a term from a less formal register. To do so is to express a less formal and, therefore, less respectful attitude toward the policeman than expected, and that becomes part of what she meant." Reasoning by the choice principle, indeed, leads to meaning contrasts for all choices of words.

Effort counts as part of this reasoning. At any moment, some words take less effort to retrieve, utter, or understand than others, and the choice of one over the other means something relative to that effort. (I am temporarily assuming that a word that is easy to retrieve and utter is also easy to understand, even though this assumption isn't always true.) Take *pink* and *light red* (McCawley, 1978). Although they could conceivably denote the same color, the choice principle dictates otherwise. *Pink* is a common expression that is one word long, and *light red* is a less common expression that is two words long. When Kate tells Jess "I just bought a light red dress," he should reason, "If Kate's dress were true pink, she would have used the less effortful term *pink*. But since she went to the extra effort of using *light red*, she must have a special purpose that she intends me to recognize. She is distinguishing light red from true pink—and from true red—so the dress is between true red and true pink."

Reasoning about effort in word choice is everywhere in language use. It is needed for explaining the meaning differences we invariably find between a common word and its paraphrase. Compare "Jack killed the fly" with "Jack caused the fly to die" (McCawley, 1978). With *kill*, the causation is taken to be the normal, standard, or prototypical type (direct causation), whereas with the more effortful *cause to die*, it is ordinarily taken to be abnormal, nonstandard, or nonprototypical (indirect causation). Or compare "Jack is a New Yorker" with "Jack is a person who lives in New York." With *New Yorker*, we take Jack to be a standard resident of New York, a native, but with the more effortful *person who lives in New York*, we take him to be nonstandard in some respect—perhaps he is there only temporarily.

Reasoning about effort also leads to a phenomenon called *preemption* (E. V. Clark & Clark, 1979). If Kate wanted to refer to today, yesterday, and tomorrow, she would use *today*, *yesterday*, and *tomorrow*. She couldn't use *this day*, *the day before today*, and *the day after today*, even though they are well formed English constructions. Why not? Because *this day* requires more effort than *today*, so to choose it, Kate would have to mean something more specialized. Because she doesn't mean something special, she cannot use that term and mean the same thing. An entrenched term, like *today*, preempts a more effortful expression, like *this day*, that technically means the same thing.

Preemption is a central force in the use and interpretation of novel expressions. It has two main consequences: blocking and refinement. In English, we can turn nouns into verbs almost to our heart's content, as we "sty" pigs, "corral" horses, "barn" cows, "warehouse" goods, and so on. Yet we cannot hospital patients or prison felons. Why not? Because the two novel, hence effortful, verbs *hospital* and *prison* are preempted by the well-entrenched verbs *hospitalize* and *imprison*, which would mean the same thing. The usage of the novel terms is therefore blocked. We can also hip or shoulder people out of the way, and we can knee, elbow, or toe them. But to palm, foot, or fist people would have to be different from slapping, kicking, or slugging them, because otherwise we would have used *slap*, *kick*, or *slug*. The novel verb *to palm* gets refined by its contrasts with other words in the same lexical neighborhood.

Novel uses of language are a problem for dictionary theories (H. H. Clark, 1983; H. H. Clark & Gerrig, 1983). A newspaper agent once asked a friend of mine, "Is the delivery boy porching your newspaper now?" using *porch* with a meaning that couldn't be in the mental lexicon. It was a meaning the agent and my friend had to create on the spot. How did they manage this? One thing they considered, clearly, was the possible relations that newspapers could have to porches as brought about by delivery boys, and which of these relations was the most salient in their current common ground. But they also tacitly considered the lexical neighborhood; *to porch* had to contrast in meaning with every other expression in that neighborhood. Dictionary theories take neither of these possibilities into account.

MOMENTARY POSSIBILITIES

We know that lexical and conceptual possibilities matter. But if language use is a collective process, what should matter is not the lexical and conceptual possibilities in general, but those that are readily accessible in the participants' common ground at the moment the speaker issues an utterance. I will call these the *momentary possibilities*. The momentary possibilities change from instant to instant in any discourse—in any conversation, narrative, or news story—as the participants accumulate common ground. More than that, the participants can engineer these momentary possibilities and then exploit them in designing what they say next. Let us see how.

Many momentary possibilities are determined by the situation currently in the participants' focus of attention. Suppose Kate points at a group of ten men jogging and says, "That man's my neighbor." Which man should Jess infer that she is referring to? That depends on what is salient among the momentary possibilities afforded by their view. If one of the men is naked, or is wearing a business suit, or is only four feet tall, or is running backwards, or is yelling obscenities, or is the only person Jess doesn't know, he would be seen to be the most salient possibility in their current common ground and, because of that uniqueness, the referent of *that man*. What a speaker is taken to mean is, ultimately, the most salient of the momentary possibilities in the speaker and addressees' current common ground (H. H. Clark, Schreuder, Buttrick, 1983).

Word meaning is often determined by such momentary salience. Once, at a supermarket checkout counter, the clerk pointed at some radishes I was buying and asked, "Do you have one or two radishes there?" If I had taken *radish* in the conventional sense of "plant of the genus *Raphanus*," I would have answered, "No, about thirty." But given the momentary possibilities in our current common ground—largely determined by the scene in front of us—I created the novel sense "bunch of plants of the genus *Raphanus*" and answered, "Two." Sense creation like this is common, and it is especially dependent on the momentary possibilities (H. H. Clark & Gerrig, 1983).

The momentary possibilities are often engineered by the participants themselves. Take Kate's use of *red*. She may be selecting it from the first six color terms <black, white, red, yellow, green, blue>, or from these plus <orange, brown, pink, grey, purple>, or from these plus the exotic color terms. Let us call these Set A, Set B, and Set C. She can specify the set she is entertaining at the moment by her choice of contrast. If she says, "Julia just bought a pink dress, and Margaret a red one," Jess will assume Set B and infer that Margaret's dress is not pink or orange but closer to blood red. For "Julia just bought a maroon dress, and Margaret a red one," he will assume Set C and infer a color even closer to blood red. But for "Margaret's the woman over there in the red dress," Jess may assume Set A and infer that Margaret is the woman in the orange dress because the other woman is in black. So whether *red* is taken narrowly as "blood red as opposed to maroon," less narrowly as "red as opposed to orange or pink," or more broadly as "red as opposed to green, blue, and so on," depends on the momentary lexical possibilities Kate has engineered.

The momentary possibilities can also be determined by the partner. Recall that *some* belongs to two contrast sets: <none, some> and <some, all>. To choose *some* from the first set is to reject *none*, but to chose it from the second is to reject *all*. Which set is in focus at the moment can be set up by a question. If Jess asks "Did some of the students leave?" and Kate answers "Yes, in fact, all of them did," then *some* is taken to mean "some and possibly all." But if Jess asks "Did all of the students leave?" and Kate answers "No, but some of them did," then *some* is taken to mean "some but not all." Or take *two* in Kate's utterance "I have two dollars." If Jess has just asked "How much money do you have in your hand?" then her *two* means "exactly two." But if he has just said

"I need two more dollars to buy these tickets," now her *two* means "at least two."

The momentary lexical possibilities can also be determined by precedent. Suppose Jess and Kate are in front of a video terminal screen full of squares with passageways between them arranged in rows and columns. They are talking about these objects as part of a computer game (this was a setup investigated by Garrod & Anderson, 1987). Now Jess and Kate could use the terms *rows*, *lines*, or *columns* for either the horizontal or vertical paths. So when Jess calls a vertical path "the fifth row," he sets a temporary precedent. Rows are now vertical. By the choice principle, if Kate wants to refer to a vertical path, she has to use *row* too, and not *line* or *column*. If she wants to refer to a horizontal path, she has to use a term other than *row*, say *line* or *column*. If she were to use *row* unmodified, Jess would be justified in thinking she meant "vertical path." Garrod and Anderson called this type of phenomenon *entrainment*, and it was pervasive in the talk of their players. It has also been observed in other types of conversation (H. H. Clark & Schaefer, 1987; H. H. Clark & Wilkes-Gibbs, 1986; Isaacs & Clark, 1987; Jefferson, 1982).

The choice principle, in short, works ultimately from the possibilities in joint focus of attention at each moment in a conversation. These may arise from Jess and Kate's general knowledge of the language and of the objects being talked about. They can also arise from the lexical and conceptual possibilities that become salient to Jess and Kate only for the moment.

CONCLUSION

Words and the world, I have argued, have the meaning they do in part because of the possibilities from which we see them as being drawn. This is the principle of possibilities: We understand what a thing is in part by reference to what we infer it could have been. Garner applied his version of the principle mainly to perception. When it is applied to language use, it takes on a special character. In perception, the possibilities Jess infers for a stimulus are determined largely by the *physical* constraints on the situation as Jess perceives them. In language use, the possibilities Jess infers about what Kate means are determined ultimately by *social* constraints. These constraints arise from Jess and Kate trying to coordinate on some mutually accepted purpose. But how?

When two people talk to each other, I have argued, they are engaged in a collective activity. To succeed in any collective activity, they have to coordinate on what they are doing, and to coordinate successfully, they have to work on the basis of their common ground at that precise moment. It is ultimately this momentary common ground that determines the possibilities against which they try to interpret both words and the world.

Throughout this chapter, I have argued against the traditional view of word meanings as fixed entries in a mental lexicon. I have suggested instead that word meanings are the result of a process. This process assesses the lexical and conceptual possibilities readily accessible in common ground at the moment and selects the most salient one. The challenge is to discover how this process works.

References

Clark, E. V. (1983). Meanings and concepts. In J. H. Flavell & E. M. Markman (Eds.), *Handbook of child psychology: Vol 3. Cognitive development* (pp. 787–840). New York: Wiley.

Clark, E. V. (1987). The priniciple of contrast: A constraint on language acquisition. In B. MacWhinney (Ed.), *Mechanisms of language acquisition* (pp. 1–33). Hillsdale, NJ: Erlbaum.

Clark, E. V., & Clark, H. H. (1979). When nouns surface as verbs. *Language, 55*, 430–477.

Clark, H. H. (1983). Making sense of nonce sense. In. F. B. Flores d'Arcais & R. Jarvella (Eds.), *The process of language understanding*. New York: Wiley.

Clark, H. H., & Gerrig, R. J. (1983). Understanding old words with new meanings. *Journal of Verbal Learning and Verbal Behavior, 22,* 591–608.

Clark, H. H., & Marshall, C. R. (1981). Definite reference and mutual knowledge. In A. K. Joshi, B. L. Webber, & I. A. Sag (Eds.), *Elements of discourse understanding* (pp. 10–63). Cambridge, England: Cambridge University Press.

Clark, H. H., & Schaefer, E. F. (1987). Concealing one's meaning from overhearers. *Journal of Memory and Language, 26,* 209–225.

Clark, H. H., & Schaefer, E. F. (1989). Contributing to discourse. *Cognitive Science, 13,* 259–294.

Clark, H. H., Schreuder, R., & Buttrick, S. (1983). Common ground and the understanding of demonstrative reference. *Journal of Verbal Learning and Verbal Behavior, 22,* 1–39.

Clark, H. H., & Wilkes-Gibbs, D. (1986). Referring as a collaborative process. *Cognition, 22,* 1–39.

Garner, W. R. (1962). *Uncertainty and structure as psychological concepts.* New York: Wiley.

Garrod, S., & Anderson, A. (1987). Saying what you mean in dialogue: A study in conceptual and semantic co-ordination. *Cognition, 27,* 181–218.

Goodwin, C. (1981). *Conversational organization: Interaction between speakers and hearers.* San Diego, CA: Academic Press.

Grice, H. P. (1957). Meaning. *Philosophical Review, 66,* 377–388.

Grice, H. P. (1968). Utterer's meaning, sentence-meaning, and word-meaning. *Foundations of Language, 4,* 225–242.

Grice, H. P. (1975). Logic and conversation. In P. Cole & J. L. Morgan (Eds.), *Syntax and semantics: Vol 3. Speech acts* (pp. 113–128). New York: Seminar Press.

Hörmann, H. (1983). *Was tun die wörter miteinander im Satz? Oder Wieviele sind einige, mehrere und ein paar?* [What do words do to each other in a sentence? or How many are some, several, and a few?]. Göttingen, Germany: Verlag Für Psychologie.

Isaacs, E. A., & Clark, H. H. (1987). References in conversation between experts and novices. *Journal of Experimental Psychology: General, 116,* 26–37.

Jefferson, G. (1973). A case of precision timing in ordinary conversation: Overlapped tag-positioned address terms in closing sequences. *Semiotica*, *9*, 47–96.

Jefferson, G. (1982). On exposed and embedded correction in conversation. *Studium Linguistik*, *14*, 58–68.

Lewis, D. K. (1969). *Convention: A philosophical study*. Cambridge, MA: Harvard University Press.

Lewis, D. K. (1979). Scorekeeping in a language game. *Journal of Philosophical Logic*, *8*, 339–359.

McCawley, J. D. (1978). Conversational implicature and the lexicon. In P. Cole (Ed.), *Syntax and semantics: Vol 9. Pragmatics* (pp. 245–259). San Diego, CA: Academic Press.

Morrow, D. G., & Clark, H. H. (1988). Interpreting words in spatial descriptions. *Language and Cognitive Processes*, *3*, 275–291.

Nunberg, G. (1978). Slang, usage condition, and l'arbitraire du signe. In D. Farkas, W. M. Jacobsen, & K. W. Todrys (Eds.), *Papers from the parasession on the lexicon* (pp. 301–311). Chicago: Chicago Linguistic Society.

Schegloff, E. A. (1984). On some gestures' relation to talk. In J. M. Atkinson & J. Heritage (Eds.), *Structures of social action: Studies in conversation analysis* (pp. 266–296). Cambridge, England: Cambridge University Press.

Stalnaker, R. C. (1978). Assertion. In P. Cole (Ed.), *Syntax and semantics 9: Pragmatics* (pp. 315–332). San Diego, CA: Academic Press.

CHAPTER 18

ON THE INFLUENCE OF RESPONSE UNCERTAINTY AND TASK STRUCTURE ON RETRIEVAL FROM LEXICAL MEMORY

JAMES H. NEELY

Garner's research has provided three general principles of task analysis: (a) The theoretical inferences one draws from data must take into account the stimulus-to-response mappings required by the task in which those data were collected. (b) The "meaning" that a subject extracts from a particular stimulus on a particular trial depends on the nature of other stimuli that appear on other trials in the experiment. (c) Subjects are clever and will use whatever information is available to them for optimizing their performance. An application of these three principles to lexical decision and pronunciation tasks yields an explanation of the dissociative semantic priming effects that occur in these two tasks and at the same time causes us to challenge conventional wisdom that word-frequency effects in these two tasks are localized only in lexical access. The successful application of these three general principles to domains as diverse as word identification and the perception of the dimensional structure of "simple" geometric patterns encourages their continued use.

In this chapter, I apply to the domain of word recognition some general principles that come from Garner's innovative research on perception (e.g., Garner, 1974). Although his research has for the most part focused on analyses of how people perceive structure in relatively simple nonverbal stimuli, such as dot patterns, tonal sequences, and simple geometric forms, Garner's approach yields more general insights into the pitfalls one can encounter in devising and structuring an experimental paradigm so that it will permit strong theoretical inferences about general properties of the human information-processing system. In this chapter, I focus on three of these insights.

Perhaps the most important Garnerian principle is that a proper interpretation of psychological data demands detailed task analyses. Because our experimental tasks typically involve verbal instructions to subjects as to how they are to respond to stimuli, our knowledge about psychological processes must necessarily be filtered through these and other task constraints. Thus, in considering various theoretical interpretations of our data, we must examine how the particular task we chose might have constrained the outcomes of our experiment to only a subset of all logically possible outcomes, and devise alternative tasks with different constraints so as to provide a set of converging operations and data that can provide additional evidence relevant to these interpretations (e.g., Garner, Hake, & Eriksen, 1956).

A second principle also provided by Garner is that the "meaning" of a stimulus to which a subject must respond on a particular trial depends on what the subject infers as being the set of all other possible stimuli that might have occurred on that trial (e.g., Garner, 1962, 1974). For example, in an experiment consisting of only red or blue lights having equivalently perceived high intensities, the "meaning" extracted from the red light would likely be "red light." However, in an experiment consisting of red or blue lights of widely varying intensities, the "meaning" extracted from that very same red light might very well be "bright red light." Clearly, then, to interpret properly what mediates a subject's response to a particular stimulus, one must consider the context in which that particular stimulus was embedded.

A third theme implicit in Garner's approach is that subjects will likely use all sources of information that might potentially help them optimize their performance in responding to the task requirements we impose on them. Thus, in designing our experimental paradigms, we need to be as clever as our subjects so that we do not unwittingly provide information that is not germane to the particular mental operations we wish to study, but which subjects nevertheless use because it aids their performance in that particular paradigm.

In the remainder of this chapter, I discuss how these three Garnerian principles can be applied to research on how skilled readers identify a string of visually presented letters as being a particular one of the several thousand words they know. Although this research is seemingly far removed from Garner's research on how people analyze perceptual dimensions and process the perceptual structure of "simple" geometric forms and tonal patterns, when the three Garnerian principles just outlined are applied to experiments on lexical memory retrieval, one begins to perceive a simpler and more orderly structure in some seemingly chaotic semantic priming phenomena and at the same time begins to perceive a richer, more complex structure in word-frequency effects.

RETRIEVAL FROM LEXICAL MEMORY: LEXICAL DECISION AND PRONUNCIATION TASKS

Many researchers who study retrieval from lexical memory seek to specify the mental operations that people perform when, for example, they recognize that the visual pattern "lion" is an English word associated with a particular pronunciation and meaning. Most researchers who work in this area have assumed that each word a person knows is represented as a separate entity in his or her lexical memory.[1] These individual word representations, called *logogens* by some (Morton, 1969) and *word nodes* by others (e.g., McClelland & Rumelhart, 1981), are assumed to be activated by the visual features of the individual letters that compose the word that they represent. For simplicity, I use the term "lexical access" to refer to that point in time at which a word's lexical node is activated above the threshold value necessary for that word's identification.

Semantic Priming and Lexical Access

An issue of interest is how the processes involved in the identification of a target word such as *pink* are influenced by the prior presentation of a priming word that is either semantically related (e.g., *blue*) or unrelated (e.g., *bench*) to the target word. The two tasks most often used to examine this issue are the lexical decision task (LDT) and the pronunciation task. In a commonly used version of both of these tasks, the prime is briefly presented, with no overt response being required to it, and is then followed by the presentation of the target. In the LDT, the subject presses one of two keys to indicate whether the target is a word or a nonword (which is typically pronounceable). In the pronunciation task, the subject is instructed to pronounce the target aloud as quickly as possible. In both tasks, the dependent variable of primary interest is the subject's reaction time (RT) to respond to the target. Not surprisingly, in both tasks, RTs to a target are faster when it follows a semantically related prime than when it follows an unrelated prime (e.g., Lorch, Balota, & Stamm, 1986; Seidenberg, Waters, Sanders, & Langer, 1984). This finding is called *semantic priming*.

That semantic priming occurs in both the LDT and the pronunciation task can be construed as providing converging operations (Garner et al., 1956) for the claim that a related semantic context speeds lexical access. This conclusion is proper under the plausible assumption that the only difference in the mental

---

[1]Recently, Seidenberg and McClelland (1989) have developed a connectionistic parallel distributed processing model of word identification in which individual word nodes do not exist. In their model, different words activate different, but partially overlapping, sets of features rather than activating a separate word node. Although space limitations preclude a discussion of such models, I have argued elsewhere (Neely, 1991) that presently there is no compelling reason for abandoning the concept of individual word nodes (see also Besner, Twilley, McCann, & Seergobin, 1990).

processes used to perform these two tasks resides in response selection and response execution, both of which follow the identical set of processes that lead to lexical access in both tasks. By this analysis, once lexical access has occurred in the LDT, subjects select and execute the response associated with pressing the "word" key. (Exactly how "nonword" responses are selected need not concern us here. One idea is that a "nonword" response is executed if lexical access has not occurred before some deadline time has expired, e.g., Coltheart, Davelaar, Jonasson, & Besner, 1977.) Once lexical access has occurred in pronunciation (and exactly as it would have in the LDT), subjects select and execute the articulatory motor commands necessary to say the target word aloud. Because semantic priming occurs in both tasks, the parsimonious conclusion is that semantic priming affects the identical lexical access processes that presumably occur in both tasks. This conclusion is also supported by the finding that semantic priming and visual degradation of the target have similar interactive effects in both tasks (e.g., Meyer, Schvaneveldt, & Ruddy, 1975). Because visual degradation of the target most likely affects processes that occur prior to lexical access, the similar Visual Degradation × Semantic Priming interactions that occur in the LDT and the pronunciation task imply that semantic priming is also affecting a single process or a set of "temporally overlapping" processes that occurs prior to lexical access in both tasks (see McClelland, 1979; Schweickert, 1978; Sternberg, 1969).

Automatic Spreading Activation and Expectancy Accounts of Priming

According to Posner and Snyder (1975), semantic priming affects lexical access through the operation of an automatic spreading activation process and a limited-capacity expectancy mechanism. Automatic spreading activation produces priming by virtue of activation in the prime's node spreading and partially pre-activating "nearby" semantically related nodes that correspond to target words related to that prime. This spreading activation process is fast-acting, does not inhibit activation in unrelated nodes, and is automatic in the sense that it is not under a person's strategic control. Expectancy, on the other hand, produces priming by virtue of the subject's strategically using the prime to generate an expectancy for related targets. Priming occurs because the processing of expected (related) targets is facilitated, whereas the processing of unexpected (unrelated) targets is inhibited. Unlike spreading activation, the slow-acting expectancy mechanism operates only if a person strategically invokes its operation.

One source of evidence favoring Posner and Snyder's (1975) two-process theory comes from the relatedness proportion effect, which is the finding that semantic priming increases in magnitude as the proportion of trials in which a prime is related to its word target increases (e.g., Tweedy, Lapinski, & Schvaneveldt, 1977). Because the amount of priming that occurs for a particular related prime–target pair (e.g., *doctor–nurse*) depends on the proportion of other trials in the experiment in which the word prime and word target are related, this relatedness proportion effect exemplifies the Garnerian principle that responses to a particular stimulus will depend on the complete stimulus context provided by the other experimental trials in which that stimulus is embedded (see Becker, 1980, for another example of this principle).

According to Posner and Snyder's (1975) theory, the relatedness proportion effect is due to the operation of the expectancy mechanism. The greater the number of related prime–target pairs, the more likely subjects are to use the prime to generate an expectancy for a related target. This results in more facilitation in the processing of a target that is related to its prime and more inhibition in the processing of a target that is unrelated to its prime, both of which serve to increase priming. However, this relatedness proportion effect occurs only if the stimulus onset asynchrony (SOA) between the prime and the target is long enough (i.e., 400 ms or more) to give the subject enough time to generate an expectancy from the prime before the target appears (e.g., den Heyer, Briand, & Dannenbring, 1983; Favreau & Segalowitz, 1983; Neely, 1977). The priming that occurs at shorter SOAs and that is insensitive to variations in the relatedness proportion is presumably being produced by the fast-acting spreading activation process that is not under the subject's strategic control.

Dissociative Priming Effects in the LDT and Pronunciation

As is often true in an intensively researched area, as more data come in, conventional theoretical wisdom is challenged. Such was the case for the view that semantic priming affects lexical access in both the LDT and pronunciation task through the operation of the spreading activation and expectancy mechanisms. These challenges took the form of there being dissociations in the priming effects that were observed in the LDT and the pronunciation task. Here, I consider only two such dissociations (see Neely, 1991, and Neely & Keefe, 1989, for others).

One dissociative priming effect is the backward priming effect, which occurs in the LDT but not in pronunciation.[2] In the LDT, subjects are faster to respond that *bell* is a word when it is primed by *hop* rather than by *fly* (e.g., Seidenberg et al., 1984; see also Koriat, 1981). At first glance, this seems bizarre in that there seems to be no associative or semantic relation between *hop* and *bell*. However, imagine that you have just identified the target *bell* and you decide to check back to determine if it is related to the prime *hop*. (Why subjects might do this will be made clear shortly.) You should now appreciate that there is a backward

---

[2]Peterson and Simpson (1989) have recently obtained backwards priming in a pronunciation task, but only with a short SOA and an auditory single-word prime that did not occur in a sentence. However, these conditions differ from those that produce the dissociative priming effects discussed here (i.e., a visual prime presented at longer SOAs).

association between the prime and the target. Clearly, an expectancy account cannot handle this effect because it would be impossible to use the prime *hop* to generate an expectancy for the target *bell* within less than a second, even if you knew to search for a backward associate. That backward priming does not occur in pronunciation (e.g., Seidenberg et al., 1984) also rules out a spreading activation account, because spreading activation is a strategy-free process that should operate independently of task demands.

The second dissociative priming effect is the mediated priming effect. When considered together, mediated and backward priming effects represent what is known as a *double dissociation*. That is, unlike backward priming, which occurs in the LDT but not in pronunciation, mediated priming occurs in pronunciation (Balota & Lorch, 1986) but not in the standard LDT (Balota & Lorch, 1986; de Groot, 1983). In mediated priming, subjects are faster to pronounce *stripes* following the prime *lion* than following a prime such as *soap*. This is called mediated priming because priming is presumably being mediated by activation in the "tiger" node. That is, *lion* produces activation in the "tiger" node and this activation spreads to the "stripes" node. (That this effect does not occur in the LDT rules out an explanation of the dissociative backward priming effect that says that the LDT is in general more sensitive to priming effects than is pronunciation.) But if a strategy-free automatic spreading activation process that operates independently of task requirements is producing the mediated priming effect and is doing so by affecting the speed of lexical access for the target, then why does it not occur in the LDT? Clearly, then, the double dissociation that backward priming and mediated priming produce in the LDT and pronunciation task provides a strong challenge to the idea that semantic priming produces its effects on RTs only by influencing the lexical access processes that are shared in common in these two tasks. In the next section, I attempt to become a good Garnerian and turn to a detailed task analysis in an attempt to resolve these issues.

Dissociative Priming Effects and a Response Uncertainty Analysis

One approach to solving the problem posed by the double dissociated backward priming and mediated priming effects is to deny that the LDT and the pronunciation task share the same lexical access process. But this approach requires that one devise an alternative explanation of why these two tasks often yield similar priming effects (see Neely, 1991, and Neely & Keefe, 1989). A second, and I believe preferred, approach is to retain the shared lexical-access assumption and account for dissociative priming effects in terms of the different stimulus-to-response mappings required by the two tasks. Specifically, in the binary LDT, there is a many-to-one mapping from the many different word (or nonword) stimuli to the

Table 1.

RELATIVE NUMBERS OF RELATED (R) AND UNRELATED (U) WORD-PRIME/
HIGH-DOMINANCE AND LOW-DOMINANCE EXEMPLAR WORD-TARGET
TRIALS AND WORD-PRIME/NONWORD TARGET (WP/NW) TRIALS AND
PRIMING EFFECTS

Group	Type of trial			Priming effects		
	R	U	WP/NW	HD	LD	NWF
RP(.88)/NR(.89)	7	1	8	67	52	36
RP(.33)/NR(.60)	1	2	3	37	23	23
RP(.89)/NR(.75)	8	1	3	66	50	51
RP(.33)/NR(.78)	1	2	7	33	51	35
RP(.33)/NR(.50)	1	2	2	37	21	22

Note. RP = relatedness proportion; NR = nonword ratio; HD = priming for high-dominance word targets (e.g., *BIRD* priming *sparrow*); LD = priming for low-dominance word targets (e.g., *BIRD* priming *vulture*); NWF = nonword facilitation effect. (From Neely, Keefe, & Ross, 1989, pp. 1006–1007. Copyright 1989 by the American Psychological Association. Adapted by permission.)

single word (or nonword) key-press response. In the pronunciation task, on the other hand, there is a many-to-many mapping from the several different word stimuli to their several different individually unique responses (ignoring rarely occurring homophones such as *here* and *hear*).

How might the binary decision–response requirement imposed by the LDT induce subjects to use a strategy that they do not use in pronunciation? An answer to this question is available in the entries in the first two rows of Table 1, which represent the relative numbers of the different kinds of trials that Neely, Keefe, and Ross (1989) used to manipulate relatedness proportion in the standard way in their LDT. In their experiment, category names (e.g., *BIRD*) served as primes, and high- and low-dominance category exemplars (e.g., *robin* and *vulture*) served as targets. For the group in which the relatedness proportion (RP) was .88, as indicated by the RP(.88) designation, seven of every eight word targets were preceded by a related prime and only one of every eight word targets was preceded by an unrelated prime (the meaning of the NR designation will be given shortly). For the group in which the relatedness proportion was .33, only one of every three word targets was preceded by a related prime and two of every three word targets were preceded by an unrelated prime. As shown in Table 1, priming increased by around 30 ms for both high- and low-dominance exemplars as relatedness proportion increased from .33 to .88.

The foregoing, standard analysis of the relatedness proportion effect ignores the nonword target trials. Because nonword targets that follow a word prime typically never look like a word related to that prime, one can consider the nonword targets as always being unrelated to their word primes. This results in a subtle confounding between variations in the relatedness proportion and variations in another probability, which I call the nonword ratio, which is the probability that a target is a nonword given that it is unrelated to its prime. As shown in the first row of Table 1, in Neely et al.'s (1989) RP(.88) group, for every nine trials in which the prime and target were unrelated, eight contained nonword targets and only one contained a word target, yielding a nonword ratio (NR) of .89, as indicated by the designation NR(.89). In the RP(.33) group, for every five trials in which the prime and target were unrelated, three contained nonword targets and two contained word targets, yielding a nonword ratio of .60. Thus, as the relatedness proportion increased from .33 to .88, there was a concomitant increase in the nonword ratio from .60 to .89. This raises the logical possibility that the increase in priming that was associated with the increase in relatedness proportion was in actuality caused by the increase in the nonword ratio.

But why should priming in the LDT be modulated by the nonword ratio? The reason is that in the binary-response LDT, the higher the nonword ratio is, the more response uncertainty is reduced by information that the target is unrelated to its prime. (If the target is related to its prime, the correct response to the target must be "word," regardless of the value of the nonword ratio.) To understand this, consider the RP(.88)/NR(.89) group. If information that the target is unrelated to its prime became available after lexical access but before the subject had enough time to make a word–nonword decision or to execute the proper response, the odds would be 8:1 that the target was a nonword. This information could be used to bias a "nonword" decision or response. If it takes time to overcome this "nonword" bias when other information indicates that the target is actually a word, then RTs would be slowed in the unrelated priming condition, thereby enhancing overall priming. In my early work (Neely, 1977), I called this strategy of checking back to determine if the target is related or unrelated to its prime the semantic-matching strategy.[3]

On the basis of this semantic-matching strategy, one can also predict that RTs to nonword targets that follow a neutral prime (usually a string of Xs) should be faster than RTs to nonword targets that follow an (unrelated) word prime. This prediction is made because word and nonword targets are equally likely following the neutral prime, whereas nonword targets are much more likely than word targets (in this case in the ratio of 8:1) once it has been determined that the target is unrelated to the word prime that precedes it. Although this predicted *nonword facilitation effect* has been observed in several experiments (e.g., Balota, 1983; de Groot, 1984; den Heyer, 1985; Neely, 1976, 1977; Neely et al., 1989), it has

---

[3]Because the present volume shows the intellectual debt that the field owes to Wendell Garner for the many innovative methodologies and ideas he introduced, I think it appropriate to note that I was able to conduct my original research on semantic priming (Neely, 1977) because of Garner's generosity in letting me use his lab facilities and equipment.

often been ignored as a nuisance or an artifact. However, it is interesting that nonword facilitation numerically increased from 23 ms to 36 ms as the nonword ratio increased from .60 to .89 and the confounded relatedness proportion increased from .33 to .88. (De Groot, 1984, obtained a similar effect, whereas den Heyer, 1985, did not.) Increases in nonword facilitation with increases in the nonword ratio is exactly what one would expect if indeed the nonword facilitation effect is being produced by a semantic-matching strategy that is more likely to be invoked as the nonword ratio increases.

To find out if subjects do indeed adopt a semantic-matching strategy in the LDT, Neely et al. (1989) tested 12 different groups of subjects so as to orthogonally manipulate relatedness proportion (from .20 to .89) and the nonword ratio (from .08 to .91). Because relatedness proportion and nonword ratio effects will always be perfectly confounded as long as the ratio of word to nonword targets is held constant across the various relatedness proportion groups (as had always been the case in previous experiments), the overall probability of a nonword had to be manipulated in order to unconfound the two effects. The bottom three rows of Table 1 present information for three other groups from Neely et al. to illustrate how this was achieved.

Consider first the RP(.89)/NR(.75) and RP(.33)/NR(.78) groups, which have similar nonword ratios but dissimilar relatedness proportions. The ratios of words to nonwords were 9:3 and 3:7, respectively, in these two groups. As shown in Table 1, with the nonword ratio held constant, priming for high-dominance exemplars increased by 33 ms (from 33 ms to 66 ms) and nonword facilitation increased by 16 ms (from 35 ms to 51 ms), whereas priming for low-dominance exemplars remained constant at around 50 ms. More relevant to the semantic-matching hypothesis are the RP(.33)/NR(.78) and RP(.33)/NR(.50) groups, which have dissimilar nonword ratios and similar relatedness proportions. (This was accomplished by having the ratios of words to nonwords be 3:7 and 3:2, respectively, for these two groups.) As the nonword ratio increased, priming for high-dominance exemplars remained constant at around 35 ms, whereas priming for low-dominance exemplars increased dramatically from 21 ms to 51 ms and nonword facilitation increased from 22 ms to 35 ms.

On the basis of the data from only these three groups, one might conclude that high-dominance priming is modulated by the relatedness proportion, low-dominance priming by the nonword ratio, and nonword facilitation by both. However, when a multiple linear-regression analysis was performed on the data from all 12 groups to measure the effects of one variable (relatedness proportion or the nonword ratio) with the effects of the other partialled out, the results showed that relatedness proportion by itself affected priming for high-dominance exemplars but did not influence priming for low-dominance exemplars or the nonword facilitation effect, whereas the nonword ratio by itself had a significant effect on all three. Additional regression analyses were performed, with the nonword ratio and the overall probability of a nonword both being included as predictor variables. Although overall "word" RTs and "nonword" RTs were strongly directly and inversely related, respectively, to the overall probability of a nonword, priming effects for high- and low-dominance exemplars and the nonword facilitation effect were better predicted by the nonword ratio than by the overall probability of a nonword.

Neely et al.'s (1989) findings suggest that expectancy and semantic matching both play a role in producing priming effects. Because high-dominance exemplars are much easier to generate from a category name than low-dominance exemplars (indeed, this defines category dominance), the greater use of an expectancy with increasing relatedness proportions will lead to an increase in priming for high-dominance exemplars but not for low-dominance exemplars (nor will it have any effect on nonword facilitation). On the other hand, if subjects become more likely to use a semantic-matching strategy as the nonword ratio increases, nonword facilitation and overall priming for both high- and low-dominance exemplars will increase with increases in the nonword ratio. The latter is predicted because the semantic match for prime–target relatedness will be affected little, if at all, by category dominance. That is, after the target and prime have both been presented, it is probably little or no more difficult to determine that a *vulture* is a BIRD or not a SPORT than to determine that a *robin* is a BIRD or not a SPORT. Thus, priming effects for low- and high-dominance exemplars are both influenced by increases in the nonword ratio, which is modulating the subject's use of a semantic-matching strategy that is equivalently effective for the low- and high-dominance exemplars.

The foregoing analysis can also be extended to explain the dissociative priming effects that occur in the LDT and pronunciation. Imagine that you are ready to pronounce a target in a pronunciation task and that information has just become available that the target is related to its prime, SPORT. What response do you make? (If you were in the LDT, you could press the "word" key with complete confidence.) Or what response do you make if information becomes available that the target is not related to the prime? (If you were in the LDT and the nonword ratio were high, you could press the "nonword" key with considerable, though not complete, confidence.) The degree of uncertainty you had in answering these questions should make it clear that whereas a semantic-matching strategy can be very useful in the LDT, it is much less useful in pronunciation. Thus, our adaptive subjects will not waste their time using a semantic-matching strategy in a pronunciation task, but will use it in the LDT (at least if the nonword ratio is relatively high, as it typically is).

The idea that a semantic-matching strategy is used in the LDT but not in pronunciation can be used to explain the dissociative priming effects obtained in these two tasks. Consider first backward priming. If you are given the target *bell* in the LDT and check back and discover that it is related to the prime *hop*, this biases a "word" response, which produces priming relative to the unrelated condition in which you are biased to respond "nonword" because you failed to find a target-prime relationship. Because this semantic-matching process is not used in pronunciation, backward priming does not occur. Why, then, does mediated priming occur in pronunciation but not in the LDT? As noted earlier, mediated priming from *lion* to *stripes* occurs in pronunciation because of the spread of activation from the "lion" to "tiger" to "stripes" node. However, in the LDT, the subject would be biased to respond "nonword" upon failing to find a relation between *stripes* and *lion*. This "nonword" bias could override any facilitation produced by spreading activation, thereby eliminating mediated priming. Although it is ad hoc, this analysis also correctly predicts that mediated priming will occur in the LDT if one reduces the utility of the semantic-matching strategy by either reducing the nonword ratio or using a go/no-go LDT in which there are no overt "nonword" responses to facilitate the speed of using the semantic-matching strategy (see McNamara & Altarriba, 1988; den Heyer, Sullivan, & McPherson, 1987, respectively).

Finally, the semantic-matching analysis can also account for why increases in the relatedness proportion (confounded with nonword ratio increases) result in an increase in priming for both high- and low-dominance exemplars in the LDT (see the Neely et al. results in the first two rows of Table 1), but result in an increase in priming for only high-dominance exemplars in pronunciation (Keefe & Neely, 1990). Priming for low-dominance exemplars increases with relatedness proportion in the LDT because the confounded increase in the nonword ratio is leading to a greater reliance on the semantic-matching strategy that produces priming for low-dominance exemplars. Because this semantic-matching strategy is not used in pronunciation, it will not produce a relatedness proportion effect (which is actually being mediated by the confounded nonword ratio effect) on priming for low-dominance exemplars.

In pronunciation, relatedness proportion has its effect on priming by modulating an expectancy that, for reasons outlined earlier, produces priming primarily for high-dominance exemplars. Because expectancy operates in the LDT and is presumably modulated by the relatedness proportion only, the slope of the "pure" relatedness proportion effect derived from the regression equation found for high-dominance priming in Neely et al.'s (1989) LDT should yield accurate predictions of the magnitude of the relatedness proportion effect obtained using the same high-dominance targets in a pronunciation task (a result that Keefe & Neely, 1990, observed). As relatedness proportion increases from .33 to .88, this equation predicts a "pure," expectancy-based 22-ms increase in priming for high-dominance exemplars, which is remarkably close to the 19-ms increase that Keefe and Neely (1990) actually observed in their pronunciation task. (As a point of reference, low-dominance priming in pronunciation increased by only 1 ms in these same groups.) These data provide converging evidence for the idea that expectancy produces priming in both the LDT and the pronunciation task, whereas semantic matching contributes to priming in only the LDT.

Word-Frequency and Other Effects

There are other examples in the literature in which a detailed analysis of the LDT and the pronunciation task has revealed that certain variables exert their influence on RTs by influencing decisional and/or response processes rather than by the speed of lexical access. However, because of space limitations, I can only briefly mention two of these examples. One comes from Balota and Chumbley (1984, 1985), who showed that word-frequency effects on lexical access time may be overestimated in the LDT and the pronunciation task because of decisional and/ or response factors. Specifically, in the LDT, because word targets are more familiar than nonword targets, subjects are biased to respond "word" to a familiar letter string and "nonword" to an unfamiliar letter string. This bias would speed "word" responses to highly familiar high-frequency words and slow "word" responses to unfamiliar low-frequency words (for which there would be a bias to respond "nonword"). This would contribute to the word-frequency effect, which is the finding that lexical decision times are faster for high- than for low-frequency words (Balota & Chumbley, 1984). Clearly, these familiarity-induced response biases on binary "word"–"nonword" decisions cannot be contributing to the word-frequency effect in the pronunciation task.

To examine the effects of word frequency on response processes in pronunciation, Balota and Chumbley (1985) used a delayed pronunciation task in which plenty of time (i.e., from 400 to 2,900 ms) was permitted for lexical access for a target word to occur before the presentation of a delayed signal informed the subject to now say that target word aloud. Because the word-frequency effect was nearly as large in this delayed pronunciation task, in which it would affect only the time to retrieve and organize the motor code for pronunciation, as in the standard pronunciation task, in which it could affect lexical access as well, Balota and Chumbley (1985) conservatively concluded that at least part of the word-frequency effect in the standard pronunciation task was localized in motor code retrieval and organization, rather than occurring only in lexical access.[4]

A second demonstration of the role that response factors can play in the LDT was reported in Chumbley and Balota (1984). They failed to find effects of

---

[4]McRae, Jared, and Seidenberg (1990) have recently shown that delayed pronunciation times are equivalent for low- and high-frequency homophones such as *daze* and *days*. However, this does not undermine Balota and Chumbley's (1985) conclusion that the typical word-frequency effect in pronunciation is due in part to output processes, because in the standard pronunciation paradigm the low- and high-frequency words are not phonologically identical. The question of the degree to which word frequency affects lexical access versus decisional/response processes in the LDT and pronunciation has also been addressed by Monsell, Doyle, and Haggard (1989) and Balota and Chumbley (1990).

target "meaningfulness" on RTs in an LDT when they inadvertently chose their word and nonword targets such that the words were on average .99 letters longer than their nonwords. However, in a replication experiment, meaningfulness effects were found with these very same word targets when they were equated in length with the nonword targets. Internal analyses revealed that when the lengths of the word and nonword targets had not been equated, subjects had used the target's length to bias their "word"–"nonword" decisions and/or responses. Thus, because Chumbley and Balota's (1984) long words turned out to be less meaningful than their short words, the effect of meaningfulness on RTs was cancelled out by the bias to respond "word" having sped up responses to the long, less meaningful words and by the bias to respond "nonword" to the short words having slowed up responses to the short, more meaningful words. This effect once again demonstrates that subjects will use whatever subtle information they can to optimize their performance in the tasks experimenters devise for them.

CONCLUDING COMMENTS

In this chapter, I have discussed detailed analyses of the special demands of two tasks that have been used to study lexical access, the LDT and the pronunciation task. These task analyses, which exemplify the spirit of the three Garnerian principles outlined at the beginning of this chapter, were successful in providing an integrated explanation for the diverse and heretofore theoretically intractable dissociative effects that some variables have on performance in these two tasks. They also raise interesting questions about the theoretical inferences that have been drawn concerning the mechanism(s) by which word-frequency exerts its similar influence on performance in these two tasks. The success of such task analyses encourages the view that by following the path laid by the general principles that Garner derived from his research on how people analyze stimulus dimensions and process structure in the perception of dot patterns, tonal sequences, and "simple" geometric forms, one can make general progress in delineating the mental processes involved in many other tasks, including those as seemingly far removed from Garner's research domain as the LDT and the pronunciation task.

References

Balota, D. A. (1983). Automatic semantic activation and episodic memory encoding. *Journal of Verbal Learning and Verbal Behavior, 22*, 88–104.

Balota, D. A., & Chumbley, J. I. (1984). Are lexical decisions a good measure of lexical access? The role of word frequency in the neglected decision stage. *Journal of Experimental Psychology: Human Perception and Performance, 10*, 340–357.

Balota, D. A., & Chumbley, J. I. (1985). The locus of word-frequency effects in the pronunciation task: Lexical access and/or production? *Journal of Memory and Language, 24*, 89–106.

Balota, D. A., & Chumbley, J. I. (1990). Where are the effects of frequency in visual word recognition tasks? Right where we said they were! Comment on Monsell, Doyle, and Haggard (1989). *Journal of Experimental Psychology: General, 119*, 231–237.

Balota, D. A., & Lorch, R. (1986). Depth of automatic spreading activation: Mediated priming effects in pronunciation but not in lexical decision. *Journal of Experimental Psychology: Learning, Memory, and Cognition, 12*, 336–345.

Becker, C. A. (1980). Semantic context effects in visual word recognition: An analysis of semantic strategies. *Memory & Cognition, 8*, 493–512.

Besner, D., Twilley, L., McCann, R. S., & Seergobin, K. (1990). On the association between connectionism and data: Are a few words necessary? *Psychological Review, 97*, 432–446.

Chumbley, J. I., & Balota, D. (1984). A word's meaning affects the decision in lexical decision. *Memory & Cognition, 12*, 590–606.

Coltheart, M., Davelaar, E., Jonasson, J., & Besner, D. (1977). Access to the internal lexicon. In S. Dornic (Ed.), *Attention and performance VI* (pp. 535–556). Hillsdale, NJ: Erlbaum.

de Groot, A. M. B. (1983). The range of automatic spreading activation in word priming. *Journal of Verbal Learning and Verbal Behavior, 22*, 417–436.

de Groot, A. M. B. (1984). Primed lexical decision: Combined effects of the proportion of related prime–target pairs and the stimulus-onset asynchrony of prime and target. *Quarterly Journal of Experimental Psychology, 36A*, 253–280.

den Heyer, K. (1985). On the nature of the proportion effect in semantic priming. *Acta Psychologica, 60*, 25–38.

den Heyer, K., Briand, K., & Dannenbring, G. (1983). Strategic factors in a lexical decision task: Evidence for automatic and attention-driven processes. *Memory & Cognition, 11*, 374–381.

den Heyer, K., Sullivan, A., & McPherson, C. (1987). *Mediated priming in a single-response lexical decision task.* Unpublished manuscript.

Favreau, M., & Segalowitz, N. (1983). Automatic and controlled processes in the first- and second-language reading of fluent bilinguals. *Memory & Cognition, 11*, 565–574.

Garner, W. R. (1962). *Uncertainty and structure as psychological concepts.* New York: Wiley.

Garner, W. R. (1974). *The processing of information and structure.* New York: Wiley.

Garner. W. R., Hake, H. W., & Eriksen, C. W. (1956). Operationism and the concept of perception. *Psychological Review, 63*, 149–159.

Keefe, D. E., & Neely, J. H. (1990). Semantic priming in the pronunciation task: The role of prospective prime-generated expectancies. *Memory & Cognition, 18*, 289–298.

Koriat, A. (1981). Semantic facilitation in lexical decision as a function of prime–target association. *Memory & Cognition, 9*, 587–598.

Lorch, R. F., Balota, D., & Stamm, E. (1986). Locus of inhibition effects in the priming of lexical decisions: Pre- or post-lexical access? *Memory & Cognition, 14*, 95–103.

McClelland, J. L. (1979). On the time relations of mental processes: An examination of systems of processes in cascade. *Psychological Review, 86*, 287–330.

McClelland, J. L., & Rumelhart, D. E. (1981). An interactive model of context effects in letter perception: Part 1. An account of basic findings. *Psychological Review, 88*, 375–405.

McCrae, K., Jared, D., & Seidenberg, M. S. (1990). On the roles of frequency and lexical access in word naming. *Journal of Memory and Language, 29*, 43–65.

McNamara, T. P., & Altarriba, J. (1988). Depth of spreading activation revisited: Semantic mediated priming occurs in lexical decisions. *Journal of Memory and Language, 27*, 545–559.

Meyer, D. E., Schvaneveldt, R. W., & Ruddy, M. G. (1975). Loci of contextual effects on visual word recognition. In P. M. A. Rabbitt & S. Dornic (Eds.), *Attention and performance V* (pp. 98–118). San Diego, CA: Academic Press.

Monsell, S., Doyle, M. C., & Haggard, P. N. (1989). Effects of frequency on visual word recognition tasks: Where are they? *Journal of Experimental Psychology: General, 118*, 43–71.

Morton, J. (1969). Interaction of information in word recognition. *Psychological Review, 76*, 165–178.

Neely, J. H. (1976). Semantic priming and retrieval from lexical memory: Evidence for facilitatory and inhibitory processes. *Memory & Cognition, 4*, 648–654.

Neely, J. H. (1977). Semantic priming and retrieval from lexical memory: Roles of inhibitionless spreading activation and limited-capacity attention. *Journal of Experimental Psychology: General, 106*, 226–254.

Neely, J. H. (1991). Semantic priming effects in visual word recognition: A selective review of current findings and theories. In D. Besner & G. W. Humphreys (Eds.), *Basic processes in reading: Visual word recognition* (pp. 264–336). Hillsdale, NJ: Erlbaum.

Neely, J. H., & Keefe, D. E. (1989). Semantic context effects on visual word processing: A hybrid prospective/retrospective processing theory. In G. H. Bower (Ed.), *The psychology of learning and motivation: Advances in research and theory* (Vol. 24, pp. 207–248). San Diego, CA: Academic Press.

Neely, J. H., Keefe, D. E., & Ross, K. (1989). Semantic priming in the lexical decision task: Roles of prospective prime-generated expectancies and retrospective semantic matching. *Journal of Experimental Psychology: Learning, Memory, & Cognition, 15*, 1003–1019.

Peterson, R. R., & Simpson, G. B. (1989). Effect of backward priming on word recognition in single-word and sentence contexts. *Journal of Experimental Psychology: Learning, Memory, & Cognition, 15*, 1020–1032.

Posner, M. I., & Snyder, C. (1975). Attention and cognitive control. In R. L. Solso (Ed.), *Information processing and cognition: The Loyola symposium*. Hillsdale, NJ: Erlbaum.

Schweickert, R. (1978). A critical path generalization of the additive factor method: Analysis of a Stroop task. *Journal of Mathematical Psychology, 18*, 105–139.

Seidenberg, M. S., & McClelland, J. L. (1989). A distributed, developmental model of word recognition and naming. *Psychological Review, 96*, 523–568.

Seidenberg, M. S., Waters, G., Sanders, M., & Langer, P. (1984). Pre- and post-lexical loci of contextual effects on word recognition. *Memory & Cognition, 12*, 315–328.

Sternberg, S. (1969). The discovery of processing stages: Extensions of Donder's method. *Acta Psychologica, 30*, 276–315.

Tweedy, J. R., Lapinski, R., & Schvaneveldt, R. (1977). Semantic-context effects on word recognition: Influence of varying the proportion of items presented in an appropriate context. *Memory & Cognition, 5*, 84–89.

PART FIVE

DEVELOPMENT

CHAPTER 19

PERCEPTUAL STRUCTURE AND DEVELOPMENTAL PROCESS

LINDA B. SMITH

Garner argued that we do not perceive individual stimuli but instead perceive structured sets of stimuli. Individual stimuli are understood in context by their relation to alternative stimuli. Moreover, according to Garner, the relations that structure perception are given in the world; structure is in the stimulus and exists independently of the perceiver. This chapter considers evidence of developmental changes in perceived structure and argues for a view in which structure is not in the stimulus but is created and emergent in interacting psychological processes. Evidence on developmental changes in the polar structure of dimensions is presented. The evidence indicates that between the ages of 2 and 5 years, a cross-dimension relation between big *and* loud *emerges and a cross-dimension relation between* big *and* dark *dissolves. It is argued that these developmental changes stem from multiple interacting processes that include perception and language. The results indicate that basic perceptual relations can change radically with development. They also show that structure is not a stimulus concept, but a psychological one. A metaphor for thinking about perceptual structure as a stable and emergent process is offered.*

In all of his work, Garner emphasized the importance of structure and relations in perception. He convincingly argued that we do not so much perceive an individual stimulus as we perceive the relations between that single stimulus and some alternatives. Moreover, according to Garner, the structures we perceive are

This research was supported by Grants K04 HD00589 and R01 HD19499 from the National Institute of Child Health and Human Development.

in the stimulus; structure is a stimulus property and not a creation of the perceiver. Thus, Garner (1974) wrote,

> The world is real and this reality includes such things as structure. But the organism also interacts with reality to seek and select structure. Rarely, however, does the organism create structure. There is no need. Structure is everywhere to be found and the information processing organism need only look, find, and select. (p. 186)

The picture suggested by this critical–realist approach to perception is one of the perceiver as a shopper selecting suitable percepts—good fits and bargains—from the structures readily available in the world. The overriding metaphor is of structures as things, entities that exist in the world independently of the organisms that perceive them. In many ways, the critical realists' view of perception is apt. For example, studies of the perception of biological motion and natural categories suggest that there is considerable structure in the world just waiting to be used (see, for example, Bertenthal, Profitt, & Kramer, 1987; Johansson, von Hofsten, & Jansson, 1980; Rosch, 1973).

The structure-as-things metaphor also suggests a particular hypothesis about development. Differences in younger and older perceivers' performances may be "explained" by differences in their selection of the perceptual goods available in the world. This view that the principal source of developmental change in perception is in the "pick-up" of relevant available information is one that has been a powerful force in developmental psychology (see Gibson, 1969; Gibson & Spelke, 1983). This approach to development emphasizes the *what* of development—the different structures that younger and older children perceive—and downplays process and change. In the structures-as-things metaphor, the only process is selection of available information, and the metaphor itself offers no insights as to why or how there are changes in the structures selected by perceptual systems at different points in time.

The structure-as-things metaphor is, of course, just a metaphor, and it is not the only one. In this chapter, I argue for a new metaphor. Garner and those who have followed his lead have used the structure-as-things metaphor much to all our advantage. However, the best way to build on Garner's contribution may be to consider a new metaphor—one that provides the "flip-side" view to the critical realist approach. This new metaphor concentrates on the dynamics of developmental change. The emphasis is not on the structure of perception or the information. Instead, the emphasis is on developmental movement between structures—on the speed, direction, and nature of developmental change. When we look at the nature of the movement from one perceived structure to another, when we look at the *dynamics* of development, we get a new view of structure. In this view, perceptual structure is created and is emergent in developmental process.

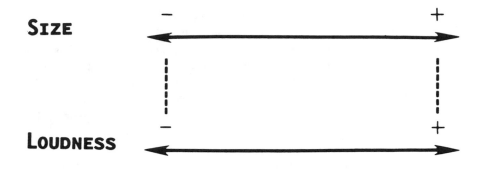

Figure 1.   A candidate representation of the perceived magnitude marking of the dimensions of loudness, size, and darkness.

In arguing for this new metaphor, I will consider evidence about developmental changes in the polar structure of dimensions. This evidence concerns changes in both perception and language. I will suggest that it is the interaction among perception, language, and other processes that causes the observed changes in the perceived structure of dimensions. This analysis highlights the critical importance of studying development for an understanding of perceptual structure. Finally, I will present a metaphor for thinking about structure as an emergent stable process.

THE POLAR STRUCTURE OF DIMENSIONS

Big is more than little; loud is more than quiet. In this way, big and loud are alike; they are both the "more" end of their respective dimensions. Not all dimensions have "more" ends (see Boring, 1933; Stevens, 1957); for example, dark grey is not unambiguously more or less than light grey (see Marks, 1974, 1978). We can ask two questions about these facts. First, *what* do size and loudness have that achromatic color does not? Second, *where* do cross-dimension similarities like that between size and loudness come from?

The *what* question—the question of what size and loudness have that achromatic color does not—can be answered in terms of candidate structural representations. One such candidate description is illustrated in Figure 1. Dimensions are represented as lines. The dimensions of size and loudness are both marked for magnitude and the similarity between the "more" and "less" ends of the two dimensions is indicated by an associative connection. Achromatic color, however, is not marked for magnitude and is not related to either size or loudness. The *where* question—the question of where such structures as those represented in Figure 1 come from—is answered by the critical realist by pointing to the structure of the world. But the facts of developmental change in perceived structure require a richer answer than that. A central tenet of the research presented here is that neither the *what* nor the *where* question can be answered without an understanding of developmental process.

The critical importance of developmental process in perceptual structure is revealed by considering children's and adults' cross-dimension matches across three dimensions: size, loudness, and achromatic color (see Smith, 1989; Smith & Sera, 1990). These three dimensions present an interesting case because for adults, size and loudness are clear quantitative dimensions and achromatic color is not. In one experiment (Smith & Sera, 1990), we specifically asked (a) whether big objects are perceived to be like loud sounds and little objects are perceived to be like quiet sounds, and (b) whether big objects are perceived to be like dark grey and little objects are perceived to be like light grey (or vice versa). In the first case, then, we asked whether there was a cross-dimension correspondence between two quantitative dimensions. In the second case, we asked whether there was a cross-dimension correspondence between a clear quantitative dimension and one of less clear character.

Before turning to the data, the ambiguous nature of achromatic color—and particularly its relation to brightness—merits discussion. The evidence indicates that brightness (or amount of light) and achromatic color (or surface darkness) are perceptually distinct dimensions with distinct psychophysical properties (Stevens, 1957). For example, in cross-modal matching experiments analogous to the task we used, adults consistently map bright lights to loud sounds and dim lights to quiet sounds, but they do not consistently map dark greys to loud sounds and light greys to quiet sounds (or vice versa). Indeed, Marks (1974) found that about half of adults link darker greys to louder sounds and that the other half link lighter greys to louder sounds. However, and despite the fact that achromatic color and brightness are distinct perceptual dimensions, discussions of achromatic color are complicated because of linguistic and conceptual confusions between achromatic color and brightness. Our language confuses the two perceptual dimensions in that *dark* sometimes refers to achromatic colors close to black and sometimes refers to a lack of light, and *light* is the name we give illumination as well as certain surface colors. People also often conceptually confuse darkness (or achromatic color) and brightness in their naive theories that hold that white looks light because of the amount of light reflected; introductory psychology students need to be instructed as to the meaning of their many experiences of darkness constancy—of black objects remaining black and white objects remaining white as the dimmer switch increases and decreases overall illumination.

The following experiment examined only achromatic color (not brightness) and size and loudness. To avoid confusion, I will use the term *darkness* only to refer to achromatic color and not to lack of light.

Method

Twenty-four subjects at each of five age levels participated: 2-year-olds (M = 29 months, SD = 2.4), 3-year-olds (M = 42 months, SD = 3.0), 4-year-olds (M = 55 months, SD = 2.9), 5-year-olds (M = 66 months, SD = 4.1), and college undergraduates. Half of the subjects at each age level were randomly assigned to the size–darkness condition, and half were assigned to the size–loudness condition.

The stimuli were cardboard mice covered in uniform grey papers that varied in size (base length = 4.5, 7.5, or 11.5 cm), surface darkness (in Coloraid notation, the values were 2 [light grey], 5 [medium grey], and 8 [almost black]), and the loudness of a tone (610-Hz tone, 700 ms, repeated twice with 100 ms of silence in between at 53 dB SPL or 82 dB SPL) that emanated from the same location as the mouse.

Each subject participated in two tasks—the percept-to-percept task and the word-to-percept task. Figure 2 illustrates the structure of the trials for the size–darkness (left) and size–loudness (right) conditions. On each of these trials, three mice were placed on the table. The subject was shown the demonstration mouse and was told that this mouse was looking for his friend and that this friend was very much like the demonstration mouse. The subject was asked to indicate which of the two choice mice was the friend. There were four unique trials, as illustrated in Figure 2, in each condition of dimensional combination.

The demonstration mouse possessed either the positive or negative extreme value on one dimension and the middle value on the other dimension. So, for example, on the first trial shown in Figure 2, the demonstration mouse was the extreme darkness and the middle size values. The two choice mice differed extremely on one dimension, but both possessed the middle value on the other dimension. In this way, the trials were structured to determine what extreme value on one dimension was like which pole on the other dimension. The structure of the four unique trials allows for the diagnosis of a correspondence between the polar ends of the dimensions. For example, if big and dark (and little and light) are perceived as corresponding poles, then on the first size and darkness trial shown in Figure 2, the child should choose the big mouse as like the dark demonstration mouse. On the second trial in Figure 2, the child should choose the little mouse as like the light demonstration mouse. Analogously, on the third and

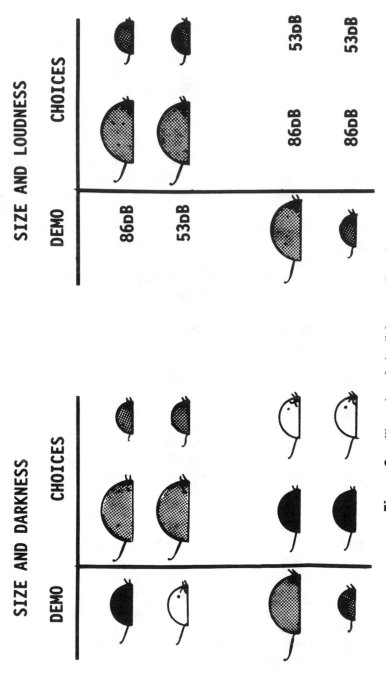

Figure 2.   Illustration of stimuli for cross-dimension matching study.

fourth illustrated trials, the child should choose a dark friend for the big demonstration mouse and a light friend for the little demonstration mouse. Each of the four unique trial types was repeated four times. The order of the 16 trials was randomly determined.

The percept-to-percept task for size and loudness was comparable, except that all mice were a uniform mid-grey. The mice indicated in Figure 2 by the loudness of the sound were also the middle size value. Each mouse sat on its own box, which hid a small audiocassette player that could be activated by the experimenter. The mice making sounds were the demonstration mice on the first two trials illustrated for this condition in Figure 2 and the choice mice on the last two illustrated trials. On each trial, the sounds were played twice before the subject was asked to choose the friend, and were replayed as often as necessary.

The word-to-percept tasks were identical to the corresponding percept-to-percept tasks except that the demonstration mouse was not perceptually present. Instead, a toy house was set on the table and the child was told that the (demonstration) mouse was in the house. The mouse in the house was then verbally described as *big, little, dark, light, loud,* or *quiet,* depending on condition, and the subject from the two perceptually present choices. Again, the task is a cross-dimension matching task; for example, when the mouse in the house was described as big, the potential friends differed only in darkness (or only in loudness). Order of the two tasks was counterbalanced within subjects.

Results

Figure 3 shows the results. Statistical analyses indicated no reliable differences among the four unique trial types in each task and condition. Thus, the figure shows the mean proportion of cross-dimension matches consistent with one cross-dimension mapping across all 16 trials in the percept-to-percept condition and separately across all 16 trials in the word-to-percept condition. For size and loudness, the y axis includes the two trial types involving positive pole matches (big to loud and loud to big) and the two trial types involving negative pole matches (little to quiet and quiet to little). The mean proportions of opposing matches (big–quiet and little–loud) are given by one minus the proportion in the figure. For size and darkness, the y axis indicates the mean proportion of big–dark/little–light matches. The mean proportions of opposing matches, big–light/little–dark, are given by one minus the proportion in the figure.

As is obvious from the figure, the developmental trends for size–loudness and size–darkness are different. For size–loudness, there is a dramatic increase with age in the matching of the "more" ends and "less" ends of the two dimensions. This increase is seen in both the percept-to-percept and word-to-percept tasks. This description of the data was confirmed by the results of an analysis of variance (ANOVA) for a 5 (age) × 2 (condition: word/percept) × 4 (trial type)

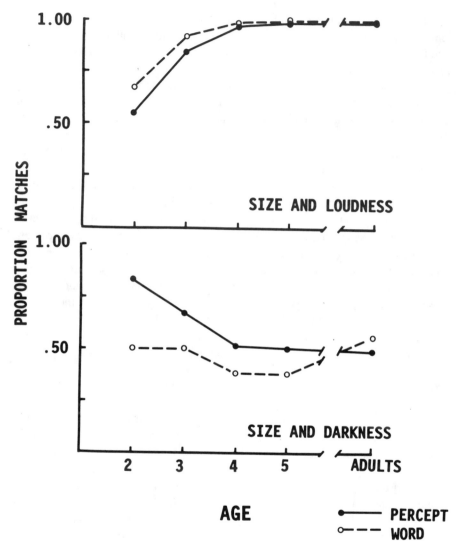

Figure 3. Mean proportion of cross-dimension matches in the two conditions of dimensional combination for 2-, 3-, 4-, and 5-year-olds and adults. Performance in the percept-to-percept conditions is indicated by the solid line. Performance in the word-to-percept conditions is indicated by the dashed line.

mixed design, which yielded a reliable main effect only for age, $F(4, 55) = 24.84, p < .001$. Post hoc analyses (Tukey's honestly significant difference $\alpha = .05$) confirmed a reliable age difference only between the 2- and 3-year-olds.

These results have been replicated in other similar tasks (see Smith & Sera, 1990, for a full report).

Figure 3 shows that for size and darkness, in marked contrast with size and loudness, there is a decrease in cross-dimension matches with age. There is an early strong mapping of big to dark and little to light in the youngest age group, but no consistent cross-dimension correspondence for older children. Moreover, this developmentally early similarity between big and dark (and little and light) appears to have no analogue in the word-to-percept task. Indeed, there is a hint of a correspondence in the word task between big and light for the older children. These conclusions are supported by the results of an ANOVA for a 5 (age) × 2 (condition: word/percept) × 4 (trial) mixed design. This analysis yielded a main effect only for condition, $F(1, 45) = 22.95$, $p < .001$ and a reliable interaction between age and condition, $F(4, 55) = 3.37$, $p < .02$. Post hoc analyses (Tukey's honestly significant difference) indicated reliably more big–dark and little–light matches by 2-year-olds in the percept-to-percept condition than by any other group in either condition. Again, these results of a changing perceptual correspondence between size and darkness have been replicated (see Smith & Sera, 1990).

How shall we explain these results? How shall we explain one cross-dimension relation that increases with development and is seen in both a perceptual task and a language task? At the same time, how shall we explain a second cross-dimension relation that is found only in the perceptual task and that decreases with development? Concentrating on the *what* question—on representations of perceived structures at different points in development—is not helpful. Representations of developmental changes in perceived structure would show size and darkness connected early in development and disconnected later in development. They would show size and loudness not well-connected early, but strongly connected later. But what are these connections? How do dimensions become connected and disconnected with development? Insights into these questions can be gained from a reexamination of the data.

THE DYNAMICS OF THE DEVELOPMENTAL TREND

Figure 4 presents the data in Figure 3 in a way that emphasizes the dynamics: the perception–language interactions and the speed and direction of developmental change. Each numeral or letter in Figure 3 indicates the performance of one subject. Each subject's performance in the word-to-percept task is plotted as a function of that individual's performance in the percept-to-percept task. In the size–loudness condition, the y axis indicates the proportion of combined big–loud and little–quiet matches across all 16 trials in the word-to-percept condition, and the x axis indicates the proportion of big–loud/little–quiet matches across all 16 trials in the

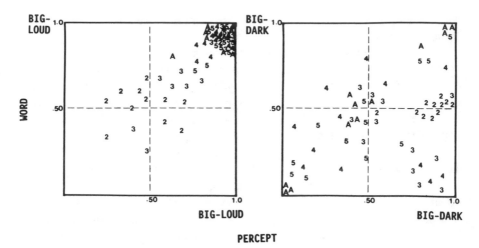

Figure 4.   Each individual's performance in the word-to-percept task is plotted as a
function of that individual's performance in the percept-to-percept task.
Individual 2-year-olds' performances are indicated by the numeral 2, 3-
year-olds' by the numeral 3, 4-year-olds' by the numeral 4, and 5-year-
olds' by the numeral 5. The performances of individual adults are indicated
by the letter A.

percept-to-percept condition. The figure for the size–darkness condition is constructed analogously.

Each enclosed figure is a state space within which all possible patterns of
individual performance may fall. An individual who fell in the center of the size–
loudness space would be one who made big–loud/little–quiet matches half of the
time and big–quiet/little–loud matches the other half of the time in both the percept
condition and the word condition. As individual performances fall at increasing
distances from the center in any direction, there is increased indication of a
directional correspondence between the two dimensions. Individual judgments that
fall in the upper right quadrant of the size–loudness space indicate a correspondence between big–loud and little–quiet in both the percept and word conditions.
Individuals whose judgments deviate from the center toward the lower left quadrant
indicate a correspondence between big and quiet and between little and loud in
both conditions. Deviations from the center toward the remaining two quadrants
indicate noncorresponding judgments in the percept and word conditions. For
example, an individual who fell in the upper left size–loudness quadrant would
be one who judged big to be like loud and little to be like quiet in the word-to-
percept condition, but judged big to be like quiet and little to be like loud in the
percept-to-percept condition.

Consider, first, performances with the dimensions of size and loudness. The
2-year-olds' performances are scattered widely around the center of the state space.

As a group, they show no consistent relation between the size and loudness poles in either the perception or language task. But there is swift, constrained, developmental change. Performance is propelled in one direction to one narrow location in the state space—to the area in which big is like loud (and little is like quiet) in both the percept and word conditions. The correspondence between size and loudness starts out disorganized; individuals are scattered widely around the center. But from this disorganized beginning, performance moves rapidly to one place. With development, everyone comes to do the same thing—to judge big to be like loud and little to be like quiet.

Now consider the developmental dynamics of size and darkness; they contrast greatly with those of size and loudness. The 2-year-olds' performances are localized in one region. The region corresponds to a cross-dimension map between big and dark in the percept-to-percept task and to chance-level judgments in the word-to-percept task. Early in development, everyone does the same thing. But from this initial localized starting point, we see a scattering of individual performances throughout the state space. Finally, there is a reorganization of individuals into a small number of localized regions in the state space. More specifically, adult performances tend to settle into one of three regions: (a) a mapping between big and dark (and little and light) in both the percept and word task, (b) a mapping between big and light (and little and dark) in both the percept and word task, and (c) no correspondence between big and dark (or little and light) in either task. The developmental trend for size and darkness thus seems to be from a tight organization of performances in one region to disorganization and then to the organization of performances into three disparate areas in the state space.

Figure 5 offers a theoretical generalization and summary of the developmental data. Each panel represents the state space, as in Figure 4, and the shaded area indicates the region in the state spaces where performances tend to fall at a given level of development. With increasing age, there is a change both in the location of individuals in the state space and in the spread (or variability) of individuals. Moreover, the developmental trajectories through these state spaces for size–loudness and size–darkness are very different. For size and loudness, there is a rapid and regular shift from diverse individual performances to a tightly constrained performance of one kind. For size and darkness, there is initially a narrow range of performances, then dispersion, and then a settling into three distinct patterns of cross-dimension correspondence.

FORCES AFFECTING DEVELOPMENT

Representations of the speed and direction of developmental change, as in Figure 5, make clear how much we do not know about the origins of perceptual structure. What sort of process could make everyone come to the same point in the state space so rapidly—as in the case of size and loudness? What sort of process could

SIZE
LOUDNESS

SIZE
DARKNESS

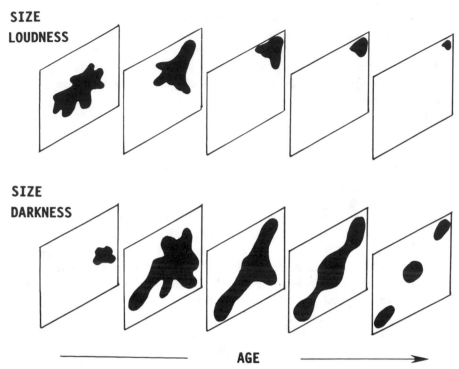

AGE ────────►

Figure 5.   Theoretical state spaces, as in Figure 4. Enclosed area represents the region
in which subjects' performances fall.

cause the scattering of individuals throughout the state space and the setting up
of individual differences—as in the case of size and darkness? The data and these
questions emphasize the fact that perceptual structure is the product of development. But what makes development go forward?

Size and Loudness

In the case of size and loudness, development may move rapidly to one point—
to a perceived correspondence between big and loud and between little and quiet—
because of multiple converging forces that organize size and loudness in the same
way. One potentially relevant force is the physical correlation between size and
loudness. The correlation is far from perfect, but it is positive; big objects tend
to make more noise than little ones. The acquisition of this knowledge may make
big and loud (and little and quiet) more alike.

Size and loudness are also interconnected through their correlations with
other dimensions, for example, number and weight. When we have many objects,
they tend to be louder, take up more space, and weigh more as a group than when

we have few. As these patterns of associations between dimensions are acquired, they will make big and loud seem more similar and little and quiet seem more similar.

A second force affecting the development of a correspondence between size and loudness is language. The words by which we label the "more" ends of size and loudness share a number of linguistic properties (e.g., Bierswisch, 1970; Clark, 1973). For example, the terms that label the positive pole are also used in the language as neutral terms to refer to the dimension as a whole. *Big* and *loud* can be used as neutral terms; *little* and *quiet* cannot. If we ask how *little* or *quiet* some object is, we imply that it is little or quiet. If we ask how *big* or *loud* some object is, there is no such strong implication that the object is big or loud. *Big* and *loud* are therefore linguistically alike. *Big* and *loud* are also correlated in their use in language; we talk about the fact that objects that are big are often loud and that objects that are little are often also quiet. Moreover, the words *big* and *loud* are interconnected in language to many other dimensions— for example, to the words *heavy*, *many*, and *bright*. As children acquire the multiple patterns of associations among dimensional terms, *big* and *loud* and also *little* and *quiet* will become increasingly interconnected. This suggested role of language fits well with the data; there is a close proximity in developmental time between size–loudness matches in the percept-to-percept and word-to-percept tasks.

My suggestion that there are patterns of correlations in the world and in language that are responsible for the perceived similarity of size and loudness is a point of clear agreement between Garner's critical realism and the present developmental perspective. But notice what Figures 4 and 5 tell us: The perceived similarity of size and loudness develops. The similarity is not "out there" waiting to be perceived. Instead, the similarity—the patterns of covariation that exist between size and loudness—is a force on development and on the dynamics of development, and it leads development in one way. Big and loud are interconnected through a sprawling network of associations, all of which push development in one direction.

Size and Darkness

In the case of size and darkness, there is a perceptual correspondence that is evident in all young perceivers but that weakens and becomes variable with development. The forces that make size and darkness cohere for very young perceivers are unknown. There could be some underlying sensory basis or perhaps some specific correlation between size and darkness that is particularly potent early in development (see Smith, 1987). Whatever the cause of the early connection between size and darkness, the connection diminishes. Apparently, the early similarity of size and darkness is not supported by other forces that accrue as development progresses.

No support for a correspondence between size and darkness is to be found in patterns of covariation in the world. Big objects are neither darker nor lighter than little objects. Moreover, achromatic color is not correlated with other dimensions (loudness, number, weight) that covary with size. The patterns of correlations in language and in language use also do not support a relation between size and darkness. Neither the words *dark* nor *light*—nor *black* nor *white*—clearly possess the properties of positive terms in the language.

This lack of correlation between darkness and size that characterizes the structure of the world and of language may be enough to undo the earlier similarity (whatever its cause). However, the most damaging force on the developmentally early similarity of size and darkness may be one that operates to organize darkness in the direction opposite to that of its early relation to size. The critical countering force may be the complex relation between darkness and brightness in the world, in language, and in conceptual structure.

Although they are distinct perceptual dimensions, surface darkness and brightness are nonetheless physically related. Darkness constancy is a demonstration of the perceptual independence or lack of correlation between brightness and achromatic color. However, the independence is far from complete. When illumination is increased (or decreased), dark objects still look darker than light ones over the middle ranges of illumination. When we turn off all of the lights, everything is dark. Moreover, the words we use to talk about darkness and brightness are indistinct. The words *dark* and *light* are used to talk about the dimness and brightness of illuminating sources, as well as the surface color of objects. Perhaps with age, children know more and more about the dependencies between dark and dim and between light and bright in perception and in language. These dependencies work directly against the initial similarity of big and dark and of little and light.

A third factor in the irregular trajectory that characterizes the perceptual relations between size and darkness may be people's concepts, or "naive psychophysics," of light and color. In a preliminary study, we found that adults who maintain that light is like big and that dark is like little justify their choices by the claim that more light energy hits the eye from big objects and from light grey ones than from little ones and dark grey ones. Interestingly, adults who maintain that dark is like big (and that light is like little) do not justify their choices in terms of light energy but instead characterize big and dark as both being "powerful" or "potent."

My point here is that the forces that push development forward do not converge in the case of size and darkness. There is some initial force that makes big like dark (and little like light); there is a lack of correlation between darkness and size in the world and in language; there is the countering force of the relation between darkness and brightness; and for some individuals there are beliefs about the relation among amount of light energy, size, and color. Presumably, the developmental trajectory is irregular and the outcome of development is nonuniversal because these antagonistic forces can have slightly different strengths at different points in development for different individuals. Given the antagonism between the forces, slight differences in the action of any one may be sufficient to cause divergent developmental paths.

PERCEPTUAL STRUCTURE AND PERCEPTUAL DEVELOPMENT

The results and my explanation of them suggest that cross-dimension correspondences emerge in development as the outcome of a network of associations between dimensions. These associations arise from the structure of the world, language, and probably also knowledge. We could stop at this point, having learned something new about dimensional structures. But it is of value to think a little harder about what these developmental results mean—about what *development* means. The consequence of thinking harder is a radical restructuring of our ideas about perceptual structure and about what is knowable from a psychology that concentrates only on the endstate.

Most theorists do concentrate on the facts of adult perception; many classic distinctions depend on just these facts. In the present case, if we had studied just the endstate—just what adults do—it would be easy to conclude that size and loudness are special. For adults, size and loudness are distinct kinds of dimensions with special, quantitative properties that set them apart from achromatic color. For adults, the similarity between big and loud is a universal fact, whereas the similarity between big and dark is variable. However, we may get ourselves in trouble if we make too much of these "endstate" facts. I illustrate this point through a consideration of the present developmental results and S. S. Stevens's distinction between prothetic and metathetic dimensions. My purpose is not to argue against Stevens's distinction or its larger value. Rather, my purpose is to illustrate the difficulty of reconciling endstate theories with the fact of development.

S. S. Stevens (1957, 1975) studied just the endstate of perception and based his distinction between prothetic and metathetic dimensions solely on adult psychophysics. According to Stevens (1957), prothetic dimensions are quantitative, or *how much*, dimensions. In terms of their psychophysics, prothetic dimensions constitute a unitary and well-behaved class of dimensions. Metathetic dimensions, in contrast, are qualitative and have to do with *what kind*. The class of metathetic dimensions includes disparate kinds of orderable and nonorderable scales. Stevens classified size and loudness as prothetic, and color, including surface darkness, as metathetic. Stevens further assumed that the differences between prothetic and metathetic dimensions in psychophysical tasks were due to basic differences in underlying physiological processes. There is no unambiguous evidence to support or refute this conjecture.

If we accept Stevens's assumption (and the circularity it entails), then we might conclude that size and loudness are alike for adults because both are *how much* dimensions with a similar sensory physiology. Size is unlike darkness because size is prothetic and darkness is not, and the two have distinct sensory physiologies. By this seductive account, the developmental trajectory for size and loudness goes rapidly and universally to one point precisely because size and loudness are both prothetic dimensions; their common sensory structure constrains development. In contrast, the irregular developmental trajectory for size and darkness could stem from the fact that the two dimensions are of two different kinds with no underlying relationship.

This kind of argument—using well-studied adult phenomena to develop theory and interpret developmental data—is not atypical in psychology, but it is logically troublesome. There are two problems with this approach. First, it reifies data from one developmental time (adulthood) and dismisses data from another developmental time (early childhood). There is no a priori reason why the judged similarity of size and loudness by adults should have greater scientific status than the judged similarity of size and darkness by 2-year-olds. Granted, we do not yet know the source of the perceived similarity between size and darkness for young children. But we also have no firm evidence on the source of the perceived similarity between size and loudness for adults. Moreover, on the face of it, very young children's data are more likely to reflect basic sensory processes than are adults' data; the neural bases of perception are fully developed at quite a young age (see Aslin & Smith, 1988), and young children's performances are less likely than adults' to be contaminated by learning, cognition, and task strategies.

Second, using facts about adults to explain the course of development is causally backward. Data about the metathetic–prothetic distinction collected at time $t + n$ (adulthood) is used to "explain" data collected at time t (childhood). But causality works forward in time. Processes of perceptual development will ultimately explain where the *adult* metathetic–prothetic distinction comes from; the metathetic–prothetic distinction as defined in adults cannot explain where development comes from.

The point is that perceptual dimensions have a developmental history. We ought not to reify the endstate and study only it. A complete and correct account of perceptual structure requires a consideration of all of the data, including data about development. Developmental data may not even be predictable from studies of the endstate, because the endstate may be related to developmental precursors only through the (perhaps nonlinear) interactions of multiple processes. Size and darkness offer a clear example: There is nothing in the adult data to suggest that big and dark are alike early in development. The prothetic–metathetic distinction in adults does not predict the observed developmental trend. But the developmental history of perceptual dimensions may well predict and explain the psychophysically

Figure 6.   The emergence of convection rolls when a gas is heated from below.

well-behaved class of adult prothetic dimensions described by Stevens and the vagaries of individual members of the adult metathetic class.

A METAPHOR FOR STRUCTURE

Garner wrote about structure as a thing that exists in the world. Structure does exist in the world. The metaphor that Garner used to talk about perceptual structure is one of a perceiver selecting structures from the structure that exists in the world. This metaphor does not work well for thinking about development. The structure of the world is not *selected* by the perceiver; it is a force that interacts with psychological processes in development to yield perceptual structures. The fact of perceptual development requires a new metaphor—a metaphor in which perceptual structures are created in psychological processes.

A new metaphor for perceptual structure is suggested by thinking about convection rolls. Figure 6 illustrates the movement of a gas in four chambers. The chambers differ only in the amount of heat added from below the chamber. When gas is in an unheated chamber (the left-most chamber in the figure), it has a particular structure, which is no structure at all. Individual molecules move about independently. If we add heat from below, the gas organizes itself into cylindrical rolls as in the second chamber. Hot gas rises on one side, is cooled, and descends on the other side. We have the process of convection. We also have a structure: the cylindrical rolls. However, this structure is not a thing; it is, instead, a dynamically stable process. Processes are inherently changeable. If we increase the heat below the chamber, nothing happens at first, but with a sufficient increase in heat, a new structure emerges: rolls with wobbles as in the third illustration in Figure 6. Finally, if we further increase the heat a sufficient amount, another structure emerges: the very complex structure of turbulence. It is important to note that the structure in the chamber depends on more than just the amount of heat; for example, it also depends on the shape of the chamber and the particular gas used.

Convection rolls offer a suitable metaphor for thinking about perceived structure and development. Human perceivers do not peruse structures in the environment, selecting some and rejecting others—just as neither the oven nor the heat *selects* convection rolls. Structure is a dynamically stable process that emerges in the interaction of multiple forces. There are changes in structure because there are changes in the contributing forces. The structure of gas in a chamber changes as we change the heat from below; the structure of cross-dimension relations changes as children acquire a particular language and association among dimensions in their world. The value of the convection-roll metaphor is that it makes clear that we cannot just study structure at one point in time. If we were to study the structure of convection rolls in only one shape of chamber and with only one amount of heat, we would lack a full understanding of the system and might even come to some wrong conclusions. If we study perceptual structure only in adults (and only in adults of one culture), we may similarly come to some wrong conclusions. We have to study changes in perceptual structure as they arise in interacting processes. We have to study the dynamics of the system. We have to study development.

CONCLUSION

Garner cogently argued for the importance of structure in perception. This chapter has argued for the importance of developmental process for perceptual structure. As Robert Cairns[1] so clearly put it, "Development is to psychology what evolution is to biology—the process that creates the structure."

References

Aslin, R. N., & Smith, L. B. (1988). Perceptual development. *Annual Review of Psychology, 39,* 435–474.

Bertenthal, B., Proffitt, D. R., & Kramer, S. J. (1987). Perception of biomechanical motions by infants: Implementation of various processing constraints. *Journal of Experimental Psychology: Human Perception and Performance, 13,* 577–585.

Bierswisch, M. (1970). On semantics. In J. Lyons (Ed.), *New horizons in linguistics* (pp. 164–184). London: Penguin Books.

Boring, E. G. (1933). *The physical dimensions of consciousness.* New York: Century.

Clark, H. H. (1973). Space, time, semantics, and the child. In T. Moore (Ed.), *Cognitive development and the acquisition of language* (pp. 43–62). San Diego, CA: Academic Press.

Garner, W. R. (1974). *The processing of information and structure.* Potomac, MD: Erlbaum.

Gibson, E. J. (1969). *Principles of perceptual learning and development.* New York: Appleton-Century-Crofts.

Gibson, E. J., & Spelke, E. S. (1983). Development of perception. In P. H. Mussen (Ed.), *Handbook of child psychology* (Vol. 3, p. 942). New York: Wiley.

Johansson, G., von Hofsten, C., & Jansson, G. (1980). Event perception. *Annual Review of Psychology, 31,* 27–64.

---

[1]Spoken comments at the Centennial Celebration of the Department of Psychology, Indiana University, Bloomington, Indiana, March 1988.

Marks, L. E. (1974). On associations of light and sound: The mediation of brightness, pitch, and loudness. *American Journal of Psychology, 87,* 173–188.

Marks, L. E. (1978). *The unity of the senses: Interrelations among the modalities.* San Diego, CA: Academic Press.

Rosch, E. H. (1973). Natural categories. *Cognitive Psychology, 4,* 328–350.

Smith, L. B. (1987). Perceptual relations and perceptual language: Commentary on Mark et al. *Monographs of the Society for Research in Child Development, 52*(1, Serial No. 215).

Smith, L. B. (1989). From global similarities to kinds of similarities: The construction of dimensions in development. In S. Vosniadou & A. Ortony (Eds.), *Similarity and analogy* (pp. 146–178). New York: Cambridge University Press.

Smith, L. B., & Sera, M. (1990). *A developmental analysis of the polar structure of dimensions.* Manuscript submitted for publication.

Stevens, S. S. (1957). On the psychophysical law. *Psychological Review, 64,* 153–181.

Stevens, S. S. (1975). *Psychophysics: Introduction to its perceptual neural and social prospects.* New York: Wiley.

CHAPTER 20

THE PERCEPTION OF FACIAL STRUCTURE IN INFANCY

JOHN MORTON AND MARK JOHNSON

It has recently been claimed that the reaction of newborn infants to face-like stimuli is mediated by stimulus energy. We examine and reject this proposal and describe an alternative view whereby it is the structure of the face that attracts the infant's gaze through the operation of a detection device that we call CONSPEC. *We show, in addition, that the infant is still learning the structural description of the face between 3 and 5 months of age, at which age dynamics are integrated into face perception.*

How do young infants extract the invariant structure of a face from their total perceptual input? Empirically, this general question has focused on two issues. First, does the newborn infant preferentially attend to faces because faces merely happen to be optimal stimuli for the infant's sensory system, or is there some reason to suppose that facial patterns are special in some way? Second, what types of invariance related to the face are extracted by the infant over the first few months of life? We shall begin by considering the first of the two issues.

STRUCTURE OR ENERGY?

Young infants seem to be interested in stimulus energy. The techniques used to establish this fact simply involve measuring the amount of time an infant will

The influence of Wendell Garner on me has been profound. He gave me an extra way of looking at the world. He also set me standards of behavior as a scientist that I have not always been able to live up to but which form a good basis for the advice I give others. He has my admiration and affection.—*John Morton* look at a pattern, either when it is presented by itself or when two patterns are presented at the same time. With a variety of patterns, the best account of the amount of interest an infant will have in a pattern is given by the linear systems model (LSM; Banks & Salapatek, 1981; Banks & Stephens, 1982).

To make predictions on the basis of the LSM, the amplitude spectrum of any stimulus pattern, collapsed over orientation, is filtered through a function representing the sensitivity of the infant's visual system to different spatial frequencies. For a newborn, this filtering effectively removes all information at frequencies greater than about 2 cycles per degree. Newborns are most sensitive to frequencies between 0.2 and 0.5 cycles per degree (Atkinson, Braddick, & French, 1979), so energy in that range, according to the model, will be most effective in attracting and holding the infant's attention. How that energy is arranged—its phase spectrum—does not contribute to determining newborn preferences in this model.

Can an energy model of this kind account for infants' responses to faces or face-like stimuli? A number of studies have shown that newborn infants will track a schematic face further than certain control stimuli (Goren, Sarty, & Wu, 1975; Johnson, Dziurawiec, Ellis, & Morton, 1991, Experiments 1 and 2; Maurer & Young, 1983). Our own studies used infants with a mean age of 37 min, and the data and stimuli for one of these experiments can be seen in Figure 1. However, these studies do not allow a direct evaluation of the LSM because the appropriate control stimuli were not used. Instead, control stimuli were constructed by scrambling the features of a schematic face. Such stimuli test the importance of the way in which the elements of the face are configured, and control for a number of variables that have been thought to be important, such as the number of elements, the average illumination, the amount of contour, and so on. However, when the features are rearranged, the amplitude spectrum changes, however slightly. It remains possible that the scrambled faces that newborns tracked less far than a schematic face had amplitude spectra containing less energy in the optimal range.

The experiment involving faces that has manipulated amplitude and phase spectra most appropriately is one performed by Kleiner (1987). Kleiner's primary stimuli were a schematic face and a lattice pattern, labeled A and B in Figure 2. These stimuli underwent a Fourier analysis to determine an amplitude spectrum and a phase spectrum for each. The spectra were crossed to provide two further stimuli. Stimulus C, with the phase spectrum of the face, looks face-like to an adult viewer, although its resemblance to a face is somewhat concealed by the lattice pattern. Stimulus D, with the amplitude spectrum of the face, does not look face-like at all to the adult viewer. The prediction of the LSM is that newborns' preferences would depend entirely on amplitude spectrum and not at all on the phase spectrum of the pattern.

Kleiner (1987) used a two-choice preference paradigm with infants of an average age of 1.7 days. When presented with the basic face (A) and lattice pattern

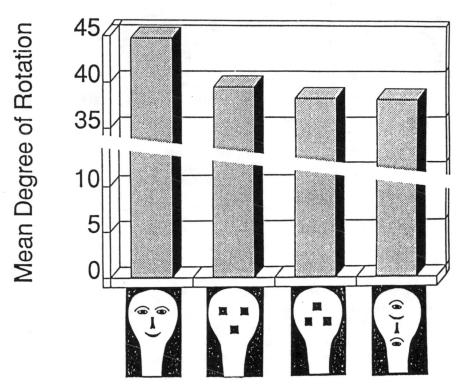

Figure 1.   Data from Johnson, Dziurawiec, Ellis, and Morton's (1991) Experiment 2. The experiment involves testing the extent to which newborn infants (mean age 37 min) will track stimuli. The response to the "face" stimulus was significantly greater than to the "scrambled" or the "inverse" stimuli.

(B) together, the infants looked at the face 67% of the time. When Stimuli C and D were compared, the infants looked 63% of the time at stimulus D, which had the amplitude spectrum of the face, in accordance with the LSM.[1]

However, Kleiner's (1987) data produced one result that is not predicted by the LSM. As we have already stated, this model explicitly claims that the phase relationships will be irrelevant for newborns, and thus predicts that the original schematic face, A, will be no more attractive to the infant than Stimulus D, because they possess the same amplitude spectrum. But in the condition using these two stimuli, the newborns overwhelmingly preferred the face pattern, looking at it 69% of the time. This cannot be because the phase spectrum of the face is preferred to that of the lattice, because the infants showed no preference for Stimulus C over B.

---

[1] Because a face is preferred to a lattice, the advantage of C over D cannot be due to C having the lattice phase spectrum.

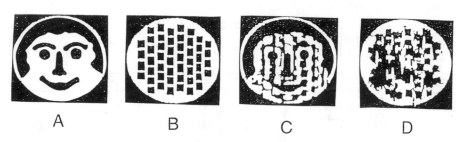

A   B   C   D

Figure 2.   The stimuli used by Kleiner (1987). Stimulus A has the amplitude spectrum
of the face and the phase spectrum of the face. Stimulus B has the amplitude
spectrum of the lattice and the phase spectrum of the lattice. Stimulus C
has the amplitude spectrum of the lattice and the phase spectrum of the face.
Stimulus D has the amplitude spectrum of the face and the phase spectrum
of the lattice. Kleiner showed that infants (mean age 1.7 days) preferred D
to C and preferred A to D. In addition, they preferred A to B, preferred A
to C, preferred D to B, and showed equal preference for B and C. Reprinted
with the permission of Abelex Publishing Corporation.

Kleiner (1987) acknowledged this result as a problem for the LSM and
erected a three-stage model including phase to rescue the position. Subsequent
interpretations of Kleiner's results have not been as careful. As an example, Kleiner
and Banks (1987) write that "the results showed rather clearly that neonates'
preferences were predicted from the amplitude spectrum and not from the phase
spectrum" and that, therefore, "neonates' preferences were based on stimulus
energy" (p. 595). Furthermore, Dannemiller and Stephens (1988), Aslin and Smith
(1988), and Nelson and Ludemann (1989) all reported that neonates' preferences
conform to predictions based on the LSM. A myth is in danger of being created.
(Further discussion of this issue can be found in Morton, Johnson, & Maurer,
1990.)

The alternative is that the newborn infant possesses a mechanism that has
structural information about the human face. This information could be something
as simple as three high-contrast blobs in a formation corresponding to the eyes
and mouth; elsewhere, we have termed this mechanism CONSPEC (Johnson &
Morton, 1991; Morton & Johnson, 1991). Stimuli in peripheral vision that satisfy
the specification would attract the infant's interest.[2] In postulating CONSPEC, we
acknowledge the possible influence of evolutionary pressures in a way parallel to
that believed to be the case with the domestic chick (Johnson, 1990).

We suggest that some mechanism whose function is predicted by the LSM
effectively operates in parallel with a mechanism sensitive to face structure. The
face in Stimulus C, masked as it is by elements of the lattice pattern, fails to

---

[2] Note that the similarity metric for such detection devices cannot be understood in terms of
amplitude and phase spectra. Stimulus C in Figure 1 has the same phase spectrum as A, but would
not be recognized by CONSPEC because it does not fit the structural description.

match the information in CONSPEC. Stimulus C does not, then, qualify as a face and is evaluated solely on the basis of its energy. Stimuli with the amplitude spectrum of the face will then be preferred over stimuli with the amplitude spectrum of the lattice, in accordance with the predictions of the LSM. For this reason, Stimulus D is preferred to Stimulus C. Stimulus A is preferred to Stimulus D, on the other hand, by virtue of its structural characteristics, through the operation of CONSPEC. Kleiner's (1987) data is thus accounted for by the two mechanisms acting in parallel.

THE EXTRACTION OF APPROPRIATE INVARIANTS

A face-like stimulus does not have a meaning for a newborn infant in the same sense that it does for an older infant. We do not wish to argue that it is a "social" stimulus to the newborn, to use the term used by Kleiner and Banks (1987). Rather, we propose that CONSPEC is a mechanism that merely causes newborn infants to orientate toward faces, thereby providing a separate, more general learning mechanism with ample experience in this important class of stimulus (Johnson, 1988; Johnson & Morton, 1991; Morton & Johnson, 1988, 1991). We have been exploring how this learning mechanism develops the perceptual specification of "faceness" with respect to one dimension.

Johnson, Dziurawiec, Bartrip, and Morton (in press) carried out a set of experiments designed to confirm earlier work using the "infant control procedure." This technique involves simply presenting the stimulus to the infants until they look away. With this method, Maurer and Barrera (1981) found that 2-month-olds looked longer at a schematic face than at control stimuli. Infants 1 month old, however, did not show any difference in preference among the stimuli. We have replicated this finding (Johnson et al., in press, Experiment 1).[3]

Johnson et al. (in press) also found that 5-month-olds actually looked less at the face than at any of the control stimuli. We surmised that this might be because these infants found the schematic face relatively impoverished. Once infants reach a certain level of perceptual sophistication, they may no longer find the schematic face stimuli interesting. If this is the case, then adding some of the appropriate cues of real faces ought to result in the return of the preference for the face. Among the most prominent characteristics of real faces is movement of the internal features.

---

[3] The alert reader may be puzzled as to why 1-month-old infants are reported here as not preferring faces when in the previous section it was claimed that newborn infants were already doing so. The answer lies in the difference between the two preference testing techniques that have been used, which we suppose to tap two different mechanisms. Briefly, the tracking task taps a subcortical mechanism that operates from birth but declines at about 30 days, whereas the other preference tests tap a cortically mediated system. See Johnson (1988), Johnson and Morton (1991), and Morton and Johnson (1991) for further details.

Johnson et al. (in press) used three different computer-generated configurations of facial features: normal, scrambled, and linear (see Figure 3). The linear stimulus was chosen because it preserved the features of the face stimulus without the configuration. In the scrambled stimulus, the eyes were broken up into their component parts. For each of the three stimuli, there were two conditions, moving and static. In the moving condition, the internal features of the face were made to move slightly (a maximum of 3 mm) by making transitions from one static presentation to another. The effect was one of animation of an otherwise constant stimulus, with a slight change in the smile accompanied by partial hooding of the eyes and slight movements of the eyebrows and nose. In the other condition, a static frame was used. Each 5-month-old child was exposed to six stimuli, three static and three moving.

In the top panel of Figure 3 we show the geometrical mean values of looking time for the three configurations and two conditions. For the static presentations, there were no significant differences between the times spent looking at the three different configurations on the Friedman test ($\chi^2 = 1.00$, $df = 2$, ns). In contrast, for the moving stimuli there was an effect of configuration on looking time ($\chi^2 = 7.44$, $df = 2$, $p = .024$). The face stimulus was significantly preferred over the other two ($p < .05$ in both cases, Wilcoxon test, planned comparisons). There was no difference in the overall length of time the infants spent looking at moving versus static stimuli ($p = 0.48$, sign test). This surprising result could be because these small movements were meaningless except in the context of the face, and because the static stimuli were interesting enough to hold the infants' attention. We may conclude that movement alone is not important for the 5-month-old infants' preference. However, the movement of the internal features restores preference for a face-like configuration.

By the time a child is 5 months of age, it seems that such schematic faces are treated the way adults would treat them: as face-like but not real. Scrambled faces may sometimes, then, be more interesting to these children than schematic faces (as we found in the Johnson et al., in press, experiment mentioned above) by virtue of being novel patterns. However, if face-like internal movement is added to the schematic face, it becomes much more interesting, perhaps as interesting as a real face in motion.

Of particular interest is the fact that movement affected the looking time only in the context of a normal, schematic face. With the other two patterns, movement made no difference at all. Before interpreting this result, we can contrast it with the results of another experiment in which the same procedure was carried out on 3-month-old and 1-month-old infants (Johnson et al., in press). These data can be seen in the middle and bottom panels, respectively, of Figure 3. The geometrical mean looking times are plotted in both cases. Because we had no prior expectations as to outcome, we simply performed a two-way analysis of variance on the log-transformed looking times. For the 3-month-old infants, this

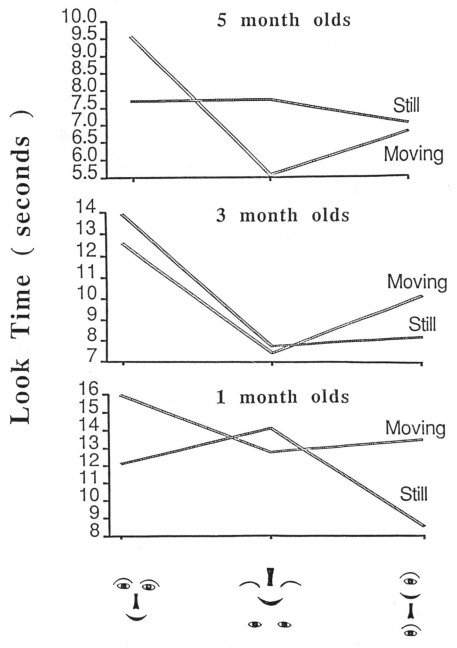

Figure 3. Mean length of time for which 5-, 3-, and 1-month-old infants look at stimuli with static versus moving internal features. The stimuli are called *normal*, *scrambled*, and *linear*, respectively. Data from Johnson, Dziurawiec, Bartrip, and Morton (in press).

showed a highly significant effect of stimulus ($F = 3.46$, $df = 2$, $p = .041$) and an insignificant effect of movement ($F = 0.17$). The interaction term was virtually zero, indicating that inasmuch as movement affected how interesting the stimuli were for these infants, it did so independently of the nature of the stimulus. For the 1-month-old infants, the effect of movement was significant ($F = 4.55$, $df = 1$, $p = .043$). There was no significant effect of the nature of the stimulus.

The first thing about these data is that the results with static faces replicate the findings previously mentioned in that, in contrast with the 3-month-olds, 1-month-old and 5-month-old infants do not look longer at schematic faces (Johnson et al., in press). Second, it seems that the way in which movement has its effects changes with age. With the youngest group of infants, internal feature movement was the only factor to have an effect. With the 3-month-old infants, internal feature movement had no effect on preference, although the arrangement of the pattern did have an effect. By 5 months, however, movement becomes integrated into the infant's characterization of a face.

CONCLUSIONS

Our work has confirmed that newborn infants have a special interest in face-like patterns. Our analysis of Kleiner (1987) leads us to conclude that this interest is not simply attributable to the spatial frequency components of the stimuli used. Rather, we have shown that there exists some innate specification of certain structural characteristics of faces. This results in newborn infants' preferentially orienting toward faces around them. Subsequently, developing cortical circuits configure themselves according to the faces' input. That this process is gradual can be seen from the fact that between 3 and 5 months of age there is a change in the way movement is integrated into the structural description of the face.

References

Aslin, R. N., & Smith, L. B. (1988). Perceptual development. *Annual Review of Psychology, 39*, 435–473.

Atkinson, J., Braddick, O., & French, J. (1979). Contrast sensitivity of the human neonate measured by the visually evoked potential. *Investigative Ophthalmology and Visual Science, 18*, 210–213.

Banks, M. S., & Salapatek, P. (1981). Infant pattern vision: A new approach based on the contrast sensitivity function. *Journal of Experimental Child Psychology, 31*, 1–45.

Banks, M. S., & Stephens, B. R. (1982). The contrast sensitivity of human infants to gratings differing in duty cycle. *Vision Research, 22*, 739–744.

Dannemiller, J. L., & Stephens, B. R. (1988). A critical test of infant pattern preference models. *Child Development, 59*, 210–216.

Goren, C. C., Sarty, M., & Wu, P. Y. K. (1975). Visual following and pattern discrimination of face-like stimuli by newborn infants. *Pediatrics, 56*, 544–549.

Johnson, M. H. (1988). Memories of mother. *New Scientist, 1600*, 60–62.

Johnson, M. H. (1990). Information processing and storage during filial imprinting. In P. G. Hepper (Ed.), *Kin recognition*. Cambridge: Cambridge University Press.

Johnson, M. H., Dziurawiec, S., Bartrip, J., & Morton, J. (in press). Infants' preferences for face-like stimuli: Effects of the movement of internal features. *Infant Behaviour and Development*.

Johnson, M. H., Dziurawiec, S., Ellis, H. D., & Morton, J. (1991). Tracking and orienting to face-like stimuli during infancy. *Cognition, 40*, 1–21.

Johnson, M. H., & Morton, J. (1991). *Biology and cognitive development: The case of face recognition*. Oxford, England: Basil Blackwell.

Kleiner, K. A. (1987). Amplitude and phase spectra as indices of infant's pattern preferences. *Infant Behavior and Development, 10*, 49–59.

Kleiner, K. A., & Banks, M. S. (1987). Stimulus energy does not account for 2-month-old preferences. *Journal of Experimental Psychology: Human Perception and Performance, 13*, 594–600.

Maurer, D., & Barrera, M. (1981). Infants perception of natural and distorted arrangements of a schematic face. *Child Development, 52*, 196–202.

Maurer, D., & Young, R. (1983). Newborns' following of natural and distorted arrangements of facial features. *Infant Behavior and Development, 6*, 127–131.

Morton, J., & Johnson, M. H. (1988). Four ways for faces to be 'special'. In A. W. Young & M. D. Ellis (Eds.), *Handbook of research on face processing*. Amsterdam: North Holland.

Morton, J., & Johnson, M. H. (1991). CONSPEC, CONLERN and the development of face recognition in the infant. *Psychological Review, 98*, 164–181.

Morton, J., Johnson, M. H., & Maurer, D. (1990). On the reasons for newborns' responses to faces. *Infant Behavior and Development, 13*, 99–103.

Nelson, C. A., & Ludemann, P. M. (1989). Past, current and future trends in infant face perception research. *Canadian Journal of Psychology, 43*, 183–198.

AFTERWORD:
A FINAL COMMENTARY

WENDELL R. GARNER

COMMENTARY

This is a final commentary and thank you. My commentary will be a light review of some of the topics I have researched, but with a special emphasis on methodological issues and problems that I have encountered along the way and that I think have a great deal to do with our understanding or failure of understanding of the perception of structure.

Temporal Pattern Perception

My first interest in the perception of structure began as early as 1951 or 1952. I had been doing auditory sensory work for several years and wanted to shift to more perceptual work. I felt that the future of such perceptual work lay in trying to understand pattern perception, and for audition, temporal patterns were natural to consider.

I started my life of perceiving structure by using four tones of different pitches. I had some equipment made so that by simply pushing a button I could have any of the 24 possible sequences of the four tones played, at a speed of my choosing. Thus I could play a b c d, or c a d b, and so on. When these patterns are allowed to play continuously, of course, they reduce to just six different patterns, because, for example, b c d a is the same as a b c d in the continuous pattern. I had a lot of fun sitting in my lab and listening to these different sequential patterns, and it was obvious that there were some interesting perceptual differenc between them. But I simply could not figure out how to do an experiment with them. I could hear interesting things, but I could not perform things with them. I was too brainwashed by behavioristic and psychophysical methodologies, and these were not appropriate to what I was hearing.

Some years later, I took another try, with Fred Royer, who was working at a Veterans Administration hospital near Baltimore. I went there for one day every two weeks, so the joint work was not all that intensive. This time we used binary sequences that were eight elements long at a rate of two per second. The two sounds were cheap doorbell buzzers, but otherwise the equipment was quite elegant, so we could introduce any of the 256 possible sequences at will. These too reduce to many fewer patterns when played continuously. As before, we first just listened to the patterns. There were obvious differences in the patterns, their simplicity and Gestalt goodness, but once again we could not figure out how to do any experiments with them. Subjects could not tap in synchrony with them, to allow us to measure errors, because at that rate the tapping interfered with the perception of a pattern. And we were still trying for a performance measure.

Finally, we hit on the payoff technique of letting the subjects do what we ourselves were doing—just listening. After a while they heard a pattern, and they were then able to tap it out on two telegraph keys very easily. But they had to hear the pattern first. We then noted at what point in the pattern the subjects began to tap when describing it. We learned that some patterns were started at very few points, and others at many, and these numbers of starting points were related to perceived simplicity and goodness. We had hit on a procedure that might be called a finger phenomenological report. As a by-product, we actually got a performance measure of how long it took before a pattern could be described (Royer & Garner, 1966).

One further example of the methodological problem involved the learning of visual temporal patterns of length five produced by two lights, presented at a rate of one every four seconds, at different starting points. At this slow rate, and with reasonably simple patterns, subjects could learn by anticipating the next light, and in fact did so. This work was done with Richard Gottwald, then a student at Johns Hopkins, in the mid-1960s. We planned to analyze the errors to learn something about how the patterns were perceived by the subjects. Shortly after data collection began, Gottwald came to my office and suggested that we simply ask the subjects to describe the patterns after they had learned them. After feeling foolish for not having thought of that myself, I agreed. That verbal description gave us more information about how the patterns were perceived than any other measure (Garner & Gottwald, 1967). I am a slow learner on these things, but since then we have used some form of description by the subject in every experiment on temporal patterns.

Actually, with time we got better at figuring out how to do experiments using standard behavioral methodologies but without their disadvantages. More sophisticated equipment is what made it possible. As an example, David Preusser in his dissertation (Preusser, 1972) used binary patterns at a rate of two per second. He started the patterns as random, then gradually changed them into a fixed pattern, thus avoiding the problem of where to start a pattern. He was concerned with verbal and manual phenomenological descriptions. A major conclusion was that pattern phenomena are better reported through our mouths than through our fingers.

Redundancy and Inferred Subsets

The focal concept of this conference was described as the concept of inferred subsets, an idea I developed in my 1962 book. Many psychologists had felt that the information theory idea of redundancy had something to do with the psychological idea of goodness of structure or pattern. The information theory concept of redundancy says that for any given total set of possible events, the smaller a subset from this total set, the greater the redundancy. Eleanor Rosch, in reviewing my 1974 book, used the review title of "The World is a Subset." I could not have said it better: Structure, goodness, and redundancy are all related to the size and existence of subsets.

In its formal sense, however, redundancy is a property of subsets of stimuli, not of single stimuli. Yet single stimulus patterns can differ in perceived goodness. Consider two sequences: XOXOXOXOXO and OXXXOOXOXO. Each pattern has five Xs and five Os, and each is unique and equally likely to occur from the 1,024 possible patterns. Yet all but the most perverse of subjects would say that the first pattern is better in the Gestalt sense than the second. So how do we deal with the redundancy and goodness of the single stimulus? The idea is that of an inferred subset: The first pattern has fewer inferred alternatives than the second because it is perceived as more regular and predictable than the second. So these two patterns differ in their perceived goodness and redundancy by differing in the sizes of the psychologically inferred subsets.

In my work with Royer on auditory temporal patterns, as well as my other work on such patterns, I used this basic idea. By measuring the number of points in a sequence at which subjects were describing the patterns, we were measuring the number of psychologically perceived alternatives. This concept has been widely used by me and by others, even by Daniel Kahneman (Kahneman & Miller, 1986) in a *Psychological Review* article on social judgment just about five years ago.

Visual Pattern Goodness

To continue on the methodological theme, and to relate it to inferred subsets, I now want to mention the first work I did on the goodness of dot patterns. This work was done with David Clement, and the first article was published in 1963 (Garner & Clement, 1963). We used 90 patterns, each having five dots in an imaginary 3 × 3 matrix. Actually, 120 such patterns are possible, but we, unnecessarily as it turned out, did not use any in which a row or column was vacant. We had two groups of subjects perform two different tasks. One group did a free classification of the patterns, in which they could sort all 90 patterns into as many classes of any size as they wanted. The average size of the class for each pattern was the measure for these subjects. The second group rated the goodness of each pattern. The mean rated goodness was the measure for these subjects. By the hypothesis that goodness is inversely related to subset size, these two measures should be correlated, and they were, with a .84 linear correlation. So the concept of inferred subsets as related to goodness was validated for these patterns.

Our main hypothesis was that two psychological measures, size of class and goodness, would be correlated. The article was published in the *Journal of Verbal Learning and Verbal Behavior* because I did not think it would get through David Grant, then editor of the *Journal of Experimental Psychology*; it used ratings and classification and, horror of horrors, was a correlational study. But Leo Postman was editor of the new *Journal of Verbal Learning and Verbal Behavior*, and he was tolerant enough to publish it. However, methodological problems were still around and did influence how I and others did our research and published it.

Free Classification

I did some later work with Shiro Imai, using the free classification procedure, in which the subject is simply asked to classify a stimulus set in any way that seems reasonable. But we also used constrained speeded classification. The stimuli were visual, differing in position, size, and orientation of a pair of dots. Free classification was to determine whether one dimension was preferred as the basis of classification; speeded classification was to determine discriminability of the dimensions. What we learned was that there were indeed dimensional preferences, but these were not related to discriminability. So phenomenological report was a necessary procedure (and free classification is phenomenological report in that the actual classification is the outcome of interest rather than speed or accuracy). This article was published in the *Journal of Experimental Psychology* when Grant was still editor (Imai & Garner, 1965). Speeded classification was clearly a received methodology, and phenomenological free classification was all right if used as a converging operation.

Imai and I did a couple of other experiments in which free classification was used, and this work was difficult to publish, not just because of reluctant editors, but because it is inherently difficult to communicate efficiently when the actual outcome or description is the result rather than a measure of performance.

Imai, as a Japanese student, was good for me, because it was only American psychologists who were caught up in the required behavioristic methodology, in which some measure of performance is used. The Japanese and the American presented a good combination of the phenomenological and behavioristic approaches.

Dimensional Interaction

In my more recent work on dimensional interaction, I have primarily used speeded classification or reaction time to single stimuli in a tachistoscope. In other words, I (and most of the students who have worked with me) have used some measure of performance, like a good behaviorist should. My reason for doing so was primarily because the particular questions to which I wanted answers seemed to require the constrained methodologies. But there was also the feeling that if my students were not trained in these methodologies, they would have trouble doing dissertations that would get published, and maybe even have trouble getting jobs. The phenomenological techniques are still not highly regarded in this country.

However, not all of the work on dimensional interactions has involved measuring speed or accuracy. The early work of Fred Attneave, Warren Torgerson, and Roger Shepard measured similarity (although sometimes indirectly), and Gregory Lockhead has used similarity a great deal in more recent years. The use of similarity comes closer to what I mean by phenomenological than time and errors, because the goal of such research is actual description of sets of stimuli rather than a performance consequence (see Garner, 1974).

Fortunately, other students of mine have used free classification techniques on the dimensional interaction problems. In particular, Stephen Handel and Shiro Imai (Handel & Imai, 1972) developed a free classification technique in which dimensions are pitted against similarity; these techniques have been widely used in the developmental work. So it would appear that my use of the constrained techniques did not constrain my students too much, and for that I am grateful.

There is just one last comment I want to make on this methodological issue. One day I was lamenting to Michael Kubovy about the lack of use of the freer methods. Although he agreed in general with my lament, he also commented that psychology has come pretty far for many years with the behavioristic methods, so maybe they were not so bad after all. Perhaps so, and if so, then my final comment on this methodological issue ought to be that we should use all of the methods available to us, with no one type having special or received status. I think I can be comfortable with such an attitude. Certainly it fits with my liking of converging operations.

Thank You

The final commentary is over, and now comes the more important part: A thank you to many different people. First, I thank all of my friends who have participated in this conference; also, former students of mine (all of whom are also friends)

And then there are the former colleagues, those of you who have shared one or the other of the two universities in which I have split my career; still further, there are people who have simply shared research interests with me. And last but not least, there is George Miller, with whom I shared graduate training and even living quarters for about a year, and who, as a consequence, has known me longer than any other participant in this conference.

Now, thanks for the conference itself. It has been a truly great conference, and the book that will result from it will be equally great. It has been especially fun for me to see how broad is the topic of the conference: The Perception of Structure. It has been broad in my own research, but much, much broader in the research of those who have participated in this conference.

Finally, I extend very personal thanks to the two former students who have organized this conference: Gregory Lockhead, representing my Johns Hopkins years, and James Pomerantz, representing my Yale years. I thank both of you with affection. But every conference has to have somebody on location to take care of the myriad details that come with an enterprise of this sort. Robert Crowder was the local faculty contact, and I thank you. Carolyn Paul, who has worked with me for 12 years, put a great deal of effort into making this conference come off as planned, and, Carolyn, I thank you with fondness. And after 12 years, I will miss you greatly.

References

Garner, W. R. (1962). *Uncertainty and structure as psychological concepts.* New York: Wiley.

Garner, W. R. (1974). *The processing of information and structure.* Potomac, MD: Erlbaum.

Garner, W. R., & Clement, D. E. (1963). Goodness of pattern and pattern uncertainty. *Journal of Verbal Learning and Verbal Behavior, 2,* 446–452.

Garner, W. R., & Gottwald, R. L. (1967). Some perceptual factors in the learning of sequential patterns of binary events. *Journal of Verbal Learning and Verbal Behavior, 6,* 582–589.

Handel, S., & Imai, S. (1972). The free classification of analyzable and unanalyzable stimuli. *Perception & Psychophysics, 12,* 108–116.

Imai, S., & Garner, W. R. (1965). Discriminability and preference for attributes in free and constrained classification. *Journal of Experimental Psychology, 69,* 596–608.

Kahneman, D., & Miller, D. T. (1986). Norm theory: Comparing reality to its alternatives. *Psychological Review, 93,* 136–153.

Preusser, D. (1972). The effect of structure and rate on the recognition and description of auditory temporal patterns. *Perception & Psychophysics, 11,* 233–240.

Royer, F., & Garner, W. R. (1966). Response uncertainty and perceptual difficulty of auditory temporal patterns. *Perception & Psychophysics, 1,* 41–47.

INDEX